Logging and Log Management

Logging and Log Management

The Authoritative Guide to Understanding the Concepts Surrounding Logging and Log Management

Dr. Anton A. Chuvakin

Kevin J. Schmidt

Christopher Phillips

Partricia Moulder, Technical Editor

AMSTERDAM • BOSTON • HEIDELBERG • LONDON
NEW YORK • OXFORD • PARIS • SAN DIEGO
SAN FRANCISCO • SINGAPORE • SYDNEY • TOKYO

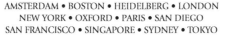

Syngress is an Imprint of Elsevier

Acquiring Editor: *Chris Katsaropoulos*
Editorial Project Manager: *Heather Scherer*
Project Manager: *Priya Kumaraguruparan*
Designer: *Alan Studholme*

Syngress is an imprint of Elsevier
225 Wyman Street, Waltham, MA 02451, USA

Library of Congress Cataloging-in-Publication Data
Application submitted.

British Library Cataloguing-in-Publication Data
A catalogue record for this book is available from the British Library.

ISBN: 978-1-59749-635-3

For information on all Syngress publications, visit our website at *www.syngress.com*

Contents

v

Acknowledgments

Dr. Anton A. Chuvakin

First, the most important part: I'd like to thank my wife Olga for being my eternal inspiration for all my writing, for providing invaluable project management advice, and for tolerating (well, almost always tolerating…) my work on the book during those evening hours that we could have spent together.

Next, I'd like to specially thank Marcus Ranum for writing a foreword for our book.

Finally, I wanted to thank the Syngress/Elsevier crew for their tolerance of our delays and broken promises to deliver the content by a specific date.

Kevin J. Schmidt

First off I would like to thank my beautiful wife, Michelle. She gave me the encouragement and support to get this book over the finish line. Of course my employer, Dell, deserves an acknowledgment. They provided me with support to do this project. I next need to thank my co-workers who provided me with valuable input: Rob Scudiere, Wayne Haber, Raj Bandyopadhyay, Emily Friese, Rafael Guerrero-Platero, and Maro Arguedas. Robert Fekete from BalaBit IT Security provided great input on the syslog-ng chapter. Ernest Friedman-Hill provided valuable suggestions for the section on Jess in Chapter 9. Jimmy Alderson, a past colleague of mine, graciously provided code samples for Chapter 13. Finally, I would like to thank my co-authors, Anton and Chris, for providing great content for a great book.

Christopher Phillips

I would like to thank my beautiful wife, Inna, and my lovely children, Jacqueline and Josephine. Their kindness, humor, and love gave me inspiration and support while writing this book and through all of life's many endeavors and adventures. I would also like to thank my father for always supporting and encouraging me to pursue a life in engineering and science. Rob Scudiere, Wayne Haber, and my employer Dell deserve acknowledgment for the valuable input they provided for this book. I would especially like to thank my co-author Kevin Schmidt for giving me the opportunity to be part of this great book. Kevin has provided tremendous guidance and encouragement to me over our many years together at Dell Secureworks and has helped me grow professionally in my career. His leadership and security knowledge have been inspiration to me, our customers, and to the many people he works with everyday.

About the Authors

Dr. Anton A. Chuvakin is a recognized security expert in the field of log management, SIEM, and PCI DSS compliance. Anton is the co-author of *Security Warrior* (ISBN: 978-0-596-00545-0) and a contributing author to *Know Your Enemy: Learning About Security Threats*, Second Edition (ISBN: 978-0-321-16646-3); *Information Security Management Handbook*, Sixth Edition (ISBN: 978-0-8493-7495-1); *Hacker's Challenge 3: 20 Brand-New Forensic Scenarios & Solutions* (ISBN: 978-0-072-26304-6); *OSSEC Host-Based Intrusion Detection Guide* (Syngress , ISBN: 978-1-59749-240-9); and others.

He has published dozens of papers on log management, correlation, data analysis, PCI DSS, security management, and other security subjects. His blog, www.securitywarrior.org, is one of the most popular in the industry. In addition, Anton has taught classes and presented at many security conferences around the world; he recently addressed audiences in the United States, United Kingdom, Singapore, Spain, Russia, and other countries. He has worked on emerging security standards and served on the advisory boards of several security start-ups.

Until recently, he ran his own consulting firm, Security Warrior. Prior to that, he was a Director of PCI Compliance Solutions at Qualys and a Chief Logging Evangelist at LogLogic, tasked with educating the world about the importance of logging for security, compliance, and operations. Before LogLogic, he was employed by a security vendor in a strategic product management role. Anton earned his Ph.D. from Stony Brook University.

Kevin J. Schmidt is a senior manager at Dell SecureWorks, Inc., an industry leading MSSP, which is part of Dell. He is responsible for the design and development of a major part of the company's SIEM platform. This includes data acquisition, correlation, and analysis of log data. Prior to SecureWorks, Kevin worked for Reflex Security, where he worked on an IPS engine and anti-virus software. And prior to this, he was a lead developer and architect at GuardedNet, Inc., which built one of the industry's first SIEM platforms. He is also a commissioned officer in the United States Navy Reserve (USNR). He has over 19 years of experience in software development and design, 11 of which have been in the network security space. He holds a Bachelor of Science in Computer Science.

Christopher Phillips is a manager and senior software developer at Dell SecureWorks, Inc. He is responsible for the design and development of the company's Threat Intelligence service platform. He also has responsibility for a team involved in integrating log and event information from many third-party providers so that customers can have their information analyzed by the Dell SecureWorks systems and security professionals. Prior to Dell SecureWorks, Chris worked for McKesson and Allscripts, where he worked with clients on HIPAA compliance, security, and healthcare systems integration. He has over 18 years of experience in software development and design. He holds a Bachelor of Science in Computer Science and an MBA.

About the Technical Editor

Patricia Moulder, CISSP, CISM, NSA-IAM, is a Senior Security Subject Matter Expert and consultant. She holds a Master of Science in Technology from East Carolina University. She has over 19 years' experience in assessing network security, auditing web applications, and wireless networks for commercial and US government clients. Patricia served for five years as an adjunct professor in network security for Sinclair Community College. She also has extensive cross platform experience in SDLC application security auditing and data privacy compliance standards.

Foreword

It's been 25 years since I first encountered syslog. I was a newly minted system administrator with a little cluster of Sun-2s surrounding a Sun-3, trying to debug a UUCP connection over the phone with a friend, who told me "check the log" and talked me through it. There was something that practically hypnotized me about watching the syslog; I saw in retrospect that it was the best way to see that my computer was actually *doing* something. Windowing systems first showed me their value when they allowed me to have a window open in the upper corner of my screen, with 'tail –f /usr/spool/messages' running; I could watch the emails work, the USENET news flow, processes start and stop—I could see that my computer was actually doing something! It wasn't until years later when I experienced my first security incident, that I discovered that logs were useful for looking at the past as well as function in the present. By then it was already far past the time where a system administrator could watch their logs in the corner of the screen. Nowadays it'd just be a blur.

Why are some of us fascinated with logs, while others could not care less about them? I think it's the association that system administrators make in their minds between "the log is doing something" therefore "the computer is doing something" and "it's working so I am therefore happy." My first log analysis algorithm was simply:

```
If the syslog stops, the Pyramid's I/O processor is wedged again
```

Any tool that saves you headaches time and time again becomes one that you turn to time and time again. In the 25 years since I started working with syslogs I have used them to:

- Ferret out traces of a "shopping cart exhaustion attack" against a major E-tailer
- Extract where a piece of malware was dropped automatically in 1,000+ systems

- Spend some of my summer vacation analyzing 10 years of a supercomputer center's logs and accidentally discovering I could detect major Linux releases through log-volume alone
- Build a data-replication system for a website, using syslogs as atomic transaction records
- Identify who had sent a threatening email to President Clinton @whitehouse.gov
- Calculate how much time one of my software engineers was spending playing Diablo II
- Reconstruct a mangled database by parsing and replaying transactions from 6 months of logs

And that's in addition to the "usual stuff" like making sure things are working, looking for unusual activity, and trying to figure out what failed and why. Unlike virtually everything else about our computers, system logs allow us a limited look back into the past—limited by what we collected, and how long we kept it—but it's a view, it's something useful. This is why I've always said that if you see a system with the logs turned off, it's the system administrator's way of showing they don't care to do their job. I don't want to think about how many times I've heard of an incident response in which critical systems had their logs turned off "for performance reasons." To someone like me, who is fascinated with logs, that simply doesn't compute: performance is easy to fix with a faster processor or a flash disk. Without your logs, you're flying blind.

Strangely, there aren't a lot of good books about system logs. You would expect there to be lots of them, given how generally useful logging can be, but there aren't. Perhaps it's because the topic can be a little bit dry and utilitarian, and it's so—huge—you have to cover everything from the nuts and bolts of getting the data back and forth to what to do with it once you've got it. And therein lies one of the big problems: there's no simple prescription for what to do with your logs. There's no useful "top 10 things to do with your syslog on Sunday" because everyone's logs are different and so are their needs. It's hard to write a book that basically says, "engage your brain, then go look at your logs and think about what you see." A security guy is going to see intrusion attempts. A system administrator will see signatures indicating a correctly functioning system. A CIO will see usage metrics and business justification. An auditor will see a check-box that can be filled in. And so it goes. The trick is to explain to all of those people that system logs are a general-purpose floor wax, dessert topping, and foot-massager all rolled up in one—oh, and, by the way: do-it-yourselfers only.

Perhaps it's the do-it-yourself requirement of logging that makes it hard for people to get excited about. This book that you're holding is as close to a cookbook for logging as you're going to find, but there are no simple turn-key recipes. Every idea is one that you have to think about, then adapt and apply to your specfic situation. When I used to teach classes in system log analysis (embarrassingly long ago!) I always knew that a certain number of people in my class were going to go away unhappy: they had come with the expectation that they'd leave with the *One True Pie-chart That Reveals Everything* or perhaps the *Mystical +5 Log Analysis Perl-script of Great Finding of Stuff*. Instead, you get frameworks for how to think about analyzing and sorting through data. I used to put on the class prerequisites "must know how to program, in something" and I fondly remember one guy whose preferred log analysis programming language was MATLAB. Whatever gets you the data you're looking for is the best tool for the job.

It's probably not appropriate to try to add my own advice in a foreword but I will, anyway. The best way you can do something useful with your logs is to get three or four smart people into a meeting room with some pizza and beer and spend a couple hours just looking at your logs. Project them on a big screen so everyone can see them, and just scroll back and forth and see what you've got. Then, when you get bored, start asking yourself what you've got in there that you want to know about, what you'd like to generate summaries about, what might make a useful metric for system work accomplished, and what might indicate a critical error. This book has more of the useful details for exactly how to do that; but trust me, I'm right about the pizza and the beer.

I've probably already said too many things that you already know, and it's time for me to stop. Now, turn the page and read this book!

Marcus J. Ranum, CSO, Tenable Network Security, Inc.

Preface

Welcome to *Logging and Log Management: The Authoritative Guide to Understanding the Concepts Surrounding Logging and Log Management.* The goal of this book is to provide you, the Information Technology (IT) Professional, with an introduction to understanding and dealing with log data. Log data comes in many forms and is generated by many types of systems. A long-running problem is what one should do with all this log data and how to analyze it. This book presents techniques and tools that can help you analyze your log data and find malicious activity.

It used to be that system administrators perused log files to look for disk errors or kernel panics. Today system administrators often do double duty as security administrators. The need to better understand what to do with security log data has never been more important. Security analysts are among the group of IT professionals who must also keep up with log analysis techniques. Many seasoned veterans have learned under "trial by fire" mode. This book aims to distill what many people have taken years to learn by presenting material in a manner that will allow you to understand the concepts quickly.

Let's talk about an issue that has recently come to the forefront: regulatory compliance. With the corporate oversight debacle that was Enron and others, regulatory compliance is now a central theme for many corporate entities. The focus is now on policy and procedure. Can you, as an IT engineer, show that Bob was unable to access his corporate email account after he was let go? These are the sorts of things that companies are being asked to prove. The system and network logging landscape is changing in these and many other ways.

INTENDED AUDIENCE

The audience for this book is anyone who is interested in learning more about logging and log management. Here are some profiles of individuals who should read this book.

System Administrator: You may be a system administrator who just inherited the task of monitoring log data for your enterprise.

Junior Security Engineer: Maybe you're a newcomer to network security and want to learn about log analysis techniques.

Application Developer: Maybe you are interested in building a log analysis system from the ground up. This book provides example code for doing just that. The entire book, however, provides excellent background for why log analysis is important. These areas should not be skipped.

Manager: Managers can gain great insights into topics such as log data collection, storage, analysis, and regulatory compliance. As previously mentioned, these issues are ever more present in the corporate landscape and will continue to be where IT professionals focus much of their time.

PREREQUISITES

It is assumed that you have a basic understanding of concepts like networking, operating systems, and network security. However, you don't need to be a computer scientist or networking guru to understand the material in this book. Topics that require background information are presented with necessary detail. The Perl and Java programming languages are used to present most code examples. You don't have to be a Java guru to understand or follow the code samples, so I encourage everyone to at least look over the examples when they come up.

ORGANIZATION OF THE BOOK

The format of this book is one that builds upon each previous chapter. Having said this, many of the chapters can be read as one-offs. There are 22 chapters in this book.

Chapter 1: Logs, Trees, Forest: The Big Picture

Chapter 1 provides background information on logging systems. If you are familiar with concepts like Syslog, SNMP, secure logging, log data collection, storage, etc., then you can safely skip this chapter.

Chapter 2: What is a Log?

Chapter 2 takes time to describe what a log message is. Discussions include why logs are important.

Chapter 3: Log Data Sources

Chapter 3 describes the Syslog protocol, SNMP, and the Windows Event Log. Additionally, classes of log data sources are presented.

Chapter 4: Log Storage Technologies

This is a great chapter if you want to learn more about log retention, storage formats, and storing logs in a relational database management system (RDBM). We even present examples of how Hadoop can be used for this endeavor.

Chapter 5: Case Study: syslog-ng

This chapter provides insight into how syslog-ng is deployed in a real environment for log collection. We also discuss some of the more advanced features of syslog-ng.

Chapter 6: Covert Logging

If you have the need to use collection logs in a covert manner, this chapter provides lots of details on how to accomplish this task.

Chapter 7: Analysis Goals, Planning, and Preparation: What Are We Looking for?

Before you begin analyzing log data, you first need to set goal, plan, and prepare for the task at hand. Topics covered in this chapter include looking for past bad things, future bad things, and never before seen things.

Chapter 8: Simple Analysis Techniques

Before discussing advanced analysis techniques, the basics need to be covered. This includes manual log analysis and the tools that enable this. In addition to this, we discuss an advanced tool that can make reading Windows Event Logs much easier. And of course we discuss the process of responding to the results of log analysis.

Chapter 9: Filtering, Normalization, and Correlation

This is an action-packed chapter. Chapter 9 presents techniques and tools that can help you perform correlation in order to help find issues that simple manual log analysis may overlook. Topics covered include filtering, normalization, taxonomy, correlation, and some common patterns to look for. Two valuable sections in this chapter are for developers who are interested in building their own correlation engine. Jess and Esper are covered to show how to build a rules-based and stream-based engine.

Chapter 10: Statistical Analysis

Chapter 10 discusses how statistics can be used to perform analysis. Frequency counting, baselines, thresholds, and anomaly detection are covered. We even present the ways in which machine learning can be used for analysis.

Chapter 11: Log Data Mining

This chapter is devoted to log mining or log knowledge discovery—a different type of log analysis, which does not rely on knowing what to look for. This takes the "high art" of log analysis to the next level by breaking the dependence on the lists of strings or patterns to look for in the logs.

Chapter 12: Reporting and Summarization

Chapter 12 looks at reporting as a way of log analysis. We specifically focus on trying to define what the best reports are for log data.

Chapter 13: Visualizing Log Data

It is often useful to visualize log data. By visualize we don't mean viewing alerts, emails, or whatever your particular log analysis system may emit. What we are more interested in discussing is viewing log data in the context of directed graphs and other visual tools.

Chapter 14: Logging Laws and Logging Mistakes

This chapter covers common mistakes organizations have made (and, in fact, *are making*) with logs. It also covers some of the general rules and dependencies—perhaps too ambitiously labeled "laws"—that govern how organizations deal with logs.

Chapter 15: Tools for Log Analysis and Collection

This chapter provides a review of open source and commercial toolsets available for the analysis and collection of log data. The review will provide the reader many options to choose from when choosing a toolset to manage log data on a daily basis. Examples of using the tools for log analysis are interspersed within the contents of the chapter with real-world examples of using the tools to review common logging tasks and scenarios. The chapter will help the reader review the set of tools available and find the right tool for analyzing logs in their organization today.

Chapter 16: Log Management Procedures: Log Review, Response, and Escalation

This chapter provides an introduction to log review, response, and escalation for log management. Examples using Payment Card Industry (PCI) Data Security Standard (DSS) will be a running theme throughout this chapter. The idea is to illustrate how to apply the concepts in the real world. This means examples are geared toward PCI standards, but they can easily be adapted and extended to fit any environment. In essence, this chapter develops a set of steps and procedures you can begin using today. An added side benefit of this chapter is insight into interpreting and applying standards to log management.

Chapter 17: Attacks Against Logging Systems

This chapter covers attacks against logging, log analysis systems, and even log analysts that can disrupt the use of logs for security, operation, and compliance.

Chapter 18: Logging for Programmers

This chapter will be useful for programmers of all kinds. This includes system administrators, Perl programmers, C/C++ programmers, Java programmers, and others. Basically, anyone who writes scripts, programs, or software systems will benefit from the content in this chapter. It has often been said that bad log messages are the result of bad programmers. While this is not entirely true, this chapter aims to change this notion by providing concepts and guidance to programmers and others on how better log messages can be produced. More ultimately, this will help with debugging, information gathering, parse-ability, and increase overall usefulness of the log messages their software generates.

Chapter 19: Logs and Compliance

This chapter is about logging and compliance with regulations and policies. Chapter 19 will be a value to anyone who has to contend with regulatory compliance.

Chapter 20: Planning Your Own Log Analysis System

This chapter will provide practical guidance on how to plan for the deployment of a log analysis system. The chapter is not meant to provide a detailed blueprint of how to install any particular log analysis system. Instead, material is presented so that you can apply the concepts to any log analysis deployment situation in which you find yourself. This chapter will arm you with questions to ask and items to consider during any such undertaking.

Chapter 21: Cloud Logging

Cloud computing is a hot topic right now. And it's only getting hotter. As we see traditional shrink-wrapped software migrate from company-owned data centers to the cloud (it's already happening), the opportunity for IT managers to spend less capital expenditure (CAPEX) on hardware, switches, racks, software, etc., to cover things like log data collection, centralization, and storage, and even Security Information and Event Management (SIEM) will be greatly reduced. This chapter introduces cloud computing and logging and also touches on regulatory and security issues related to cloud environments, big data in the cloud, SIEM in the cloud, pros and cons, and an inventory of a few key cloud logging providers.

Chapter 22: Log Standards and Future Trends

This chapter provides an expert opinion on the future of log standards and future developments in logging and log analysis.

Logs, Trees, Forest: The Big Picture

INFORMATION IN THIS CHAPTER:

- Log Data Basics
- A Look at Things to Come
- Logs Are Underrated
- Logs Can Be Useful
- People, Process, Technology
- Security Information and Event Management (SIEM)
- Case Studies

INTRODUCTION

This book is about how to get a handle on systems logs. More precisely, it is about how to get useful information out of your logs of all kinds. Logs, while often under-appreciated, are a very useful source of information for computer system resource management (printers, disk systems, battery backup systems, operating systems, etc.), user and application management (login and logout, application access, etc.), and security. It should be noted that sometimes the type of information can be categorized into more than one bucket. User login and logout messages are both relevant for both user management and security. A few examples are now presented to show how useful log data can be.

Various disk storage products will log messages when hardware errors occur. Having access to this information can often times mean small problems are resolved before they become really big nightmares.

As a second example, let's briefly consider how user management and security logs can be used together to shed light on a user activity. When a user logs onto a Windows environment, this action is logged in some place as a logon record. We will call this a user management log data. Anytime this user accesses

1

various parts of the network, a firewall is more than likely in use. This firewall also records network access in the form of whether or not it allowed network packets to flow from the source, a user's workstation, to a particular part of the network. We will call this as security log data. Now, let's say your company is developing some new product and you want to know who attempts to access your R&D server. Of course, you can use firewall access control lists (ACLs) to control this, but you want to take it a step further. The logon data for a user can be matched up with the firewall record showing that the user attempted to access the server. And if this occurred outside of normal business hours, you might have reason to speak with the employee to better understand their intent. While this example is a little bit out there, it does drive home an important point. If you have access to the right information, you are able to do some sophisticated things.

But getting that information takes some time and some work. At first glance (and maybe the second one too) it can seem an overwhelming task—the sheer volume of data can alone be daunting. But we think we can help "de-whelm" you. We'll present an overall strategy for handling your logs. We'll show you some different log types and formats. The point of using different log types and formats is twofold. First, it will get you accustomed to looking at log messages and data so you become more familiar with them. But, second it will help you establish a mindset of understanding basic logging formats so you can more easily identify and deal with new or previously unseen log data in your environment. It's a fact of life that different vendors will implement log messages in different formats, but at the end of the day it's all about how you deal with and manage log data. The faster you can understand and integrate new log data into your overall logging system, the faster you will begin to gain value from it.

The remainder of this chapter is geared toward providing a foundation for the concepts that will be presented throughout the rest of this book. The ideas around log data, people, process, and technology will be explored, with some real-world examples sprinkled in to ensure you see the real value in log data.

LOG DATA BASICS

So far we have been making reference to logging and log data without providing a real concrete description of what these things are. Let's define these now in no uncertain terms the basics around logging and log data.

What Is Log Data?

At the heart of log data are, simply, log messages, or logs. A log message is what a computer system, device, software, etc. generates in response to some sort of stimuli.

What exactly the stimuli are greatly depends on the source of the log message. For example, Unix systems will have user login and logout messages, firewalls will have ACL accept and deny messages, disk storage systems will generate log messages when failures occur or, in some cases, when the system perceives an impending failure.

Log data is the intrinsic meaning that a log message has. Or put another way, log data is the information pulled out of a log message to tell you why the log message generated. For example, a Web server will often log whenever someone accesses a resource (image, file, etc.) on a Web page. If the user accessing the page had to authenticate herself, the log message would contain the user's name. This is an example of log data: you can use the username to determine who accessed a resource.

The term *logs* is really used to indicate a collection of log messages that will be used collectively to paint a picture of some occurrence.

Log messages can be classified into the following general categories:

- *Informational:* Messages of this type are designed to let users and administrators know that something benign has occurred. For example, Cisco IOS will generate messages when the system is rebooted. Care must be taken, however. If a reboot, for example, occurs out of normal maintenance or business hours, you might have reason to be alarmed. Subsequent chapters in this book will provide you with the skills and techniques to be able to detect when something like this occurs.
- *Debug:* Debug messages are generally generated from software systems in order to aid software developers troubleshoot and identify problems with running application code.
- *Warning:* Warning messages are concerned with situations where things may be missing or needed for a system, but the absence of which will not impact system operation. For example, if a program isn't given the proper number of command line arguments, but yet it can run without them, is something the program might log just as a warning to the user or operator.
- *Error:* Error log messages are used to relay errors that occur at various levels in a computer system. For example, an operating system might generate an error log when it cannot synchronize buffers to disk. Unfortunately, many error messages only give you a starting point as to why they occurred. Further investigation is often required in order to get at the root cause of the error. Chapters 7, 8, 9, 10, 11, 12, 13, 15, and 16 in this book will provide you with ways to deal with this.
- *Alert:* An alert is meant to indicate that something interesting has happened. Alerts, in general, are the domain of security devices and security-related systems, but this is not a hard and fast rule. An Intrusion Prevention System

(IPS) may sit in-line on a computer network, examining all inbound traffic. It will make a determination on whether or not a given network connection is allowed through based on the contents of the packet data. If the IPS encounters a connection that might be malicious it can take any number of pre-configured actions. The determination, along with the action taken, will be logged.

We will now turn to a brief discussion of how log data is transmitted and collected. Then we will discuss what constitutes a log message.

How is Log Data Transmitted and Collected?

Log data transmission and collection is conceptually simple. A computer or device implements a logging subsystem whereby it can generate a message anytime it determines it needs to. The exact way the determination is made depends on the device. For example, you may have the option to configure the device or the device may be hard coded to generate a pre-set list of messages. On the flip side, you have to have a place where the log message is sent and collected. This place is generally referred to as a loghost. A loghost is a computer system, generally a Unix system or Windows server, where log messages are collected in a central location. The advantages to using a central log collector are as follows:

- It's a centralized place to store log messages from multiple locations.
- It's a place to store backup copies of your logs.
- It's a place where analysis can be performed on you log data.

While this is all well and good, how are log messages transmitted in the first place? The most common way is via the Syslog protocol. The Syslog protocol is a standard for log message interchange. It is commonly found on Unix systems, but it exists for Windows and other non-Unix based platforms. But basically there is a client and server component implemented over the User Datagram Protocol (UDP), although many open source and commercial Syslog implementations also support the Transmission Control Protocol (TCP) for guaranteed delivery. The client portion is the actual device or computer system that generates and sends log messages. The server side would typically be found on a log collection server. Its main job is to take receipt of Syslog-based log messages and store them to local disk storage where they can be analyzed, backed up and stored for long-term use.

Syslog is not the only mechanism for log data transmission and collection. For example, Microsoft implements their own logging system for Windows. It is called the Windows Event Log. Things like user login and logoffs, application messages, and so on are stored in a proprietary storage format. There are open source and commercial applications that run on top of the Event Log which will convert event log entries to Syslog, where they are forwarded to a Syslog server. We will discuss the Windows Event Log in a little more detail in Chapters 3 and 16.

The Simple Network Management Protocol (SNMP) is a standards based protocol for managing networked devices. The protocol is based on two concepts: traps and polling. A trap is merely a form of log message that a device or computer system emits whenever something has happened. A trap is sent to a management station, which is analogous to a loghost. A management station is used to manage SNMP-based systems. Polling is where the management station is able use SNMP to query a device for pre-defined variables such as interface statistics, bytes transferred in and out on an interface, etc. A key differentiator between SNMP and Syslog is that SNMP is supposed to be structured with respect to data format. But this not always found in practice. If you would like to learn more about SNMP, **see Essential SNMP** (Mauro & Schmidt, 2005).

Databases have become a convenient way for applications to store log messages. Instead of generating a Syslog message, an application can write its log messages to a database schema. Or in some cases, the Syslog server itself can write directly a relational database. This has great advantages, especially around providing a structured way to store, analyze and report on log messages.

Finally, there are proprietary logging formats. These are third-party devices and applications which implement their own proprietary mechanisms for generating and retrieving log messages. In this realm the vendor either provides you with an Application Programming Interface (API) in the form of C or Java libraries, or you are left to implement the protocol on your own. The Windows Event Log can be seen as a proprietary format, but it is often times viewed as an unofficial logging standard, similar to Syslog, because it is so prevalent.

Some of the more common protocols we have discussed in this section:

- *Syslog:* UDP-based client/server protocol. This is the most common and prevalent mechanism for logging.
- *SNMP:* SNMP was originally created for use in managing networked devices. However, over the years, many non-networked systems have adopted SNMP as a way to emit log message and other status type data.
- *Windows Event Log:* Microsoft's proprietary logging format.
- *Database:* Structured way to store and retrieve log messages.
- *Common Proprietary Protocols:*
  - *LEA:* The Log Extraction API (LEA) is Checkpoint's API for gathering logs from its line of firewall and security products.
  - *SDEE:* The Security Device Event Exchange (SDEE) is Cisco's eXtensible Markup Language (XML)-based protocol for gathering log messages from its line of IPS products.
  - *E-Streamer:* E-Streamer is Sourcefire's proprietary protocol for its IPS.

> **TIP**
>
> **Beware of Supported Logging Methods**
> Some devices will support multiple logging methods. For example, an IPS device might support logging to a Syslog server and to a database system. The problem is that the Sylog version of the log message may only be a summary of the real alert generated by the IPS and is missing vital information. You might need to actually go to the database to get the full set of data. For example, packet captures (PCAPs). A PCAP contains the parts of the network connection that trigged the IPS to generate an alert or log message. This can be a critical piece of information for analysis, reporting, etc.

What is a Log Message?

As we have already discussed, a log message is something generated by some device or system to denote that something has happened. But what does a log message look like? Let's take a brief look at the answer to this question. This will be covered in great detail throughout the book.

Understanding the answer to this question will set the stage for the remainder of the book.

First off, the typical basic contents for a log message are the following:

- Timestamp.
- Source.
- Data.

It doesn't matter if the message is sent via Syslog, written to Microsoft's Event Log or stored in a database. These basic items are always part of the message. The timestamp denotes the time at which the log message was generated. The source is the system that generated the log message. This is typically represented in IP address or hostname format. Finally, the data is the meat of a log message. There is unfortunately no standard format for how data is represented in a log message. Some of the more common data items you will find in a log message include source and destination IP addresses, source and destination ports, user names, program names, resource object (like file, directory, etc.), bytes transferred in or out, etc.

The exact way a log message is represented depends on how the source of the log message has implemented its log data system. As we mentioned previously, Syslog is the most common format used by devices and computer systems. As such, let's look at a sample Syslog message. Figure 1.1 provides a sample for us to consider.

```
   1                  2                          3
Jul 13 19:17:23 10.240.46.16 15: *Mar  1 00:16:17: %LINEPROTO-5-UPDOWN: Line
protocol on Interface FastEthernet0/0, changed state to up
```

FIGURE 1.1 Example Syslog Message

The sample from Figure 1.1 is a Syslog message generated from a Cisco router and received on a loghost running a Syslog server. Note that the numbers 1, 2, and 3 above the log message are not part of the log message, but are used as reference points for this discussion. Reference point 1 is the timestamp of when the loghost received the log message. The timestamp includes the month, day, hour, minute, and second of receipt. Reference point 2 is the IP address of the Cisco router. Note that there is a colon after the IP address, which leads us to reference point 3. Everything after the IP address and colon is the log message data. It is a free form and contains a wealth of information. For example, one of the primary pieces of information that can be relayed in a log message is the priority of the log message. This is the vendor's interpretation of what the priority (sometimes called severity) of the log message is. In the case of Figure 1.1, the priority is embedded in this string: %LINEPROTO-5-UPDOWN. The number 5 denotes the severity. But what does a 5 mean? In cases like this you will need to consult the vendor's documentation in order to understand the log message format and any associated meaning the data in the message can relay. It should also be noted that the Syslog protocol has an inherit priority scheme as well. This concept will be discussed in Chapter 2.

Now notice that the router message data contains a timestamp, which differs from that of the one at reference point 1. This timestamp is from the router and it indicates a possible date and time issue. Either the Syslog server's system clock is not correct or the router's clock is wrong. At any rate, time synchronization is something to take seriously, and you should be aware of system clocks that are off, skewed, etc. At a minimum, clock skew can cause issues with log data consistency and call into questioning any sort of analysis you may wish to do.

You may be wondering how in the world do we deal with the fact that log messages can have free-form text? Well, the next section discusses the notion of a logging system and briefly discusses this and other topics.

The Logging Ecosystem

Now that we have discussed what a log data and log messages are at a high level, let's now look at how logs are used in an overall logging ecosystem. The logging ecosystem, sometimes referred to as a logging infrastructure, are all the components and piece parts that come together to allow for the generation, filtering, normalization, analysis, and long-term storage of log data. Ultimately our goal with such a system is to be able to use logs in ways that allow you to solve problems. The exact problems you may need to solve depend on your environment. For example, if you are a retail organization which processes credit card transactions, there are various regulatory and compliance requirements you must adhere to. The remaining chapters in this book will expand on the material presented in the rest of this section.

Let's begin our discussion with some of the things you might have to think about when you begin planning your logging infrastructure.

First Things First: Ask Questions, Have a Plan

Most organizations have a reason or set of reasons why logging must be employed. It is rarely the case that it is done for fun. The following questions are examples:

- What regulatory and compliance requirements might we have to adhere to? Certain regulations may require you to actually prove that you are in compliance. This can be in the form of reports which show you are logging things like access to critical assets like accounting systems, credit card processing systems, etc. Other proof comes in the form of auditors crawling through various parts of your environment like device configuration repositories, bug tracking systems, source code control systems, and so on. Chapters 12 and 16 will provide some detail on regulatory requirements and how it's applied to logging.
- What long-term storage requirements might we need, i.e. how long might we need to keep around log data? This can greatly affect the amount of disk storage you will need to store your log data.
- Will we be gathering log data from devices on a local area network (LAN) or wide area network (WAN)? This might impact network connectivity or throughput from log clients to the log server.
- What exactly are we interested in collecting? If you are only interested in gathering CPU performance information, then the exact way you go about this is different from monitoring your firewall. Although monitoring CPU consumption on your firewall might also be a something you care about, too.

Log Message Generation

We have discussed this before. Logs come from many sources such as:

- Unix and Windows Systems.
- Routers.
- Switches.

- Firewalls.
- Wireless Access Points.
- Virtual Private Network (VPN) Server.
- AntiVirus (AV) Systems
- Printers.

The list goes on and on. The take-away here is that just about every device, computer system, and application in your network is capable of logging. You just need to know where to look. But beyond looking, you will need to configure your source system to actually log. The following three steps outline the basic steps for enabling logging on most devices and systems:

1. Enable logging for your device. You will often find that you can turn on and off logging.
2. Configure it to send log messages. Some systems are either on or off with respect to what they log. In this case this step doesn't apply. Other systems allow you to tweak exactly what is logged in an effort not to impact resources on the source system, for example.
3. Configure it to send a loghost for further collection and analysis. This is pretty self explanatory.

Log Message Filtering and Normalization

Once a device or computer system is configured to generate log messages, the next step is to filter and normalize the messages. Filtering deals with including or excluding (exclusion is sometimes referred to as "dropping on the floor" or drop) log messages based on the content in the log message. Some sources support this natively, or, in some cases, you might have to employ the use of an agent, which effectively intercepts log messages and filters them based on user defined rules. Deciding what to filter greatly depends on your organization's needs. For example, it might be perfectly legitimate to drop Cisco router reboot messages during normal maintenance windows.

Normalization is the act of taking disparately formatted log messages and converting them to a common format. The term event is typically used to denote a normalized log message. Events are typically an intermediate state for a log message. Think of an event as the currency of exchange in a logging system. Typically, though, an event's final resting place is a relational database, where analysis and reporting can be performed. When your log data is in a common format it makes it much easier to manipulate the data so that meaning can be derived from it. It should be noted that normalization typically takes place regardless of the source and protocol used (i.e. Syslog, SNMP, database, etc.).

Before we look at some simple examples, let's discuss priorities. As we mentioned before, some log messages have a priority in the data itself, while other log messages may have the priority missing. The notion of a priority is something that you will need to normalize as well. A basic scheme is to take a log message's explicit and implicit priority and map it to some common scheme. An example is low, medium, and high scale. Descriptions of each follow, but these are just meant as examples and to provide you with a starting point:

- *Low:* Low events are ones that are informational and do not need to be addressed as they happen.
- *Medium:* Medium events tend to be things that may need to be looked at in a timely manner, but not necessarily immediately. For example, IPSs tend to have the ability to block network traffic when the engine detects malicious intent. This blocking of traffic is referred to as an action. If your IPS emits a log message to this affect, then you know that the traffic was blocked and you can investigate it at your leisure.
- *High:* High priority events are ones that require immediate intervention. Examples of high priority events include router reboots outside of sanctioned maintenance windows, IPS engine alerting of possible information leakage, a network device dropping off the network for an extended period of time, and so on.

But how is normalization accomplished? Normalization is covered in Chapter 9 in detail, but let's look at a simple example. The following is a Sourcefire IPS Syslog message:

```
Jul 16 10:54:39 SourceFire SFIMS: [1:469:1] ICMP PING NMAP
    [Classification: Attempted Information Leak] [Priority: 2] {ICMP}
    210.22.215.77 -> 67.126.151.137
```

There is a wealth of information in this message. In order to normalize it, we use a technique called parsing. Parsing entails scanning the log message from start to finish to pull out information we are interested in and place them into normalized fields in the event. The following is an example set of more common fields used for normalization:

Type: Attempted Information Leak
Timestamp: July 16 2010, 10:54:39
Priority: High
Protocol: ICMP
Source IP Address: 210.22.215.77
Destination IP address: 67.126.151.137
Source Port: NULL

Destination Port: NULL
Raw log: Jul 16 10:54:39 SourceFire SFIMS: [1:469:1] ICMP PING NMAP [Classification: Attempted Information Leak] [Priority: 2] {ICMP} 210.22.215.77 -> 67.126.151.137

A few notes are in order:

- Source and Destination IP addresses were easy to identify, since an arrow (->) is used to denote directionality of the possible leakage.
- We decided to make the priority of the event High since it is unlikely that that traffic was blocked, so we will need to look at this attempt immediately.
- Source and Destination ports are not part of the log message, so they are both set to NULL.
- Raw log contains the actual raw log message. This has the advantage of preserving the raw log message.

Let's look at another message from Snort:

```
Mar 12 18:02:22 snort: [ID 702911 local4.alert] [119:2:1]
   (http_inspect) DOUBLE DECODING ATTACK {TCP} 10.1.1.21:60312 ->
   10.1.1.69:80
```

We are fortunate in that the format is similar to the Sourcefire one. And, with good reason. Snort is the open source version of Sourcefire. Now, note that the source and destination IP address have a colon at the end of each as well as a number. These numbers represent the source port and destination port respectively. Also, this log message has no priority field, unlike the Sourcefire message. This makes mapping to our priority scale a little harder. We have to have intimate knowledge of this message, which means we will need to consult the documentation for this alert.

Now let's move on to look at what it means to collect log messages.

Log Message Collection

Figure 1.2 shows the basic concept behind log collection.

We have several different types of devices and systems all forwarding their log messages to a log server. This log server might reside at a particular location and serve as the only server for the organization. This is fine if the organization is small or isn't geographically spread out. But in the case of multiple sites that can span states or event countries, you might have the need to have a distributed set of servers. Figure 1.3 shows this particular configuration.

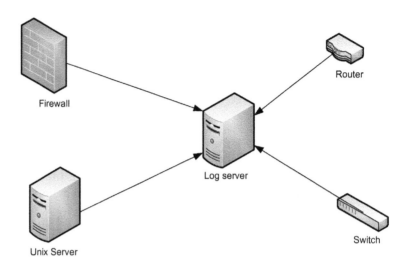

FIGURE 1.2 Logical Layout of Device Logging to a Log Server for Collection

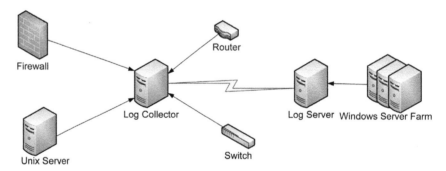

FIGURE 1.3 Logical Layout of a Distributed Logging Setup

Here we have our site specific log collector forwarding to a central log server. Since the log collector resides in a different location from the log server, the communication between the two is typically encrypted to prevent eavesdropping. While the log server is a central collection point, it too can take feeds of log messages, as depicted by the Windows Server Farm in Figure 1.3.

This sort of setup has several advantages:

- Redundancy: Your log data is stored in multiple places.
- Store and forward: The log collector, if it ever loses connection to the log server, can store up the logs and transmit them when the link comes back up. This mitigates possible data loss.
- Authentication: It is critical not only that the log collector can verify the sender as a trusted source, the sender also needs to be able to trust the system when it is sending logs.

- Privacy: It is often the case that devices and systems that log do so without the ability to encrypt their log messages. Since the log collector is on the local network, the unencrypted data is sent to the local collector where it is capable of sending the data upstream in a secure manner.

Now that we have presented the basics surrounding log data collection, let's now briefly discuss logging in the cloud.

Logging in the Cloud

Cloud computing has received a lot of press lately. Google lets you edit and share documents in their cloud. Microsoft has similar initiatives as well. But what about logging in the cloud? There are organizations such as Managed Security Service Providers (MSSP) and cloud logging companies that effectively allow you to point your log at them and they do the rest. Figure 1.4 shows the conceptual view of logging in the cloud.

What exactly happens in the logging cloud? Things like filtering, normalization, analysis, and long-term storage. Cloud logging vendors offer their services for varying price points. They manage the complexity associated with a traditional log collection system. Cloud logging is covered in more detail in Chapter 21.

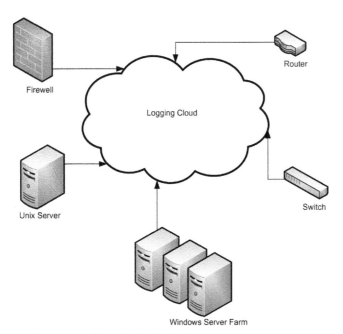

Firewell

Router

Logging Cloud

Unix Server

Switch

Windows Server Farm

FIGURE 1.4 Logical Layout of Logging in the Cloud

Log Analysis

Log message analysis, or simply log analysis, deals with analyzing log data to derive meaning from it. Recall Figure 1.3 and its centralized collection server. This is a central collection point and is crucial to analysis. Having your data in a single place allows you to pull together or correlate log message together in order to derive meaning. This is especially crucial in a highly distributed environment where you may have multiple remote log collectors and you need to correlate log message received at one collector with those received at another. Chapter 9 goes into more detail surround correlation and analysis.

Log Message Long-Term Storage

The final topic of discussion is long-term storage. Figure 1.5 shows the addition of a database to the log server.

The long-term data store is typically accomplished by using a relational database. It is also not uncommon to find small databases in use at remote log collectors, too:

- Reporting: Creation of reports which summarize log data for manager or for compliance audits.
- Forensic analysis: You might have the need to find out what a particular user was doing a month ago on your network.
- Backup: This is self-explanatory, but if keeping your log data, due to regulatory compliance, etc. you can never have too few copies of your data.

You are now up to speed on the components of a logging ecosystem. This information will be revisited in Chapters 7, 15, and 20 as we tackle in more detail the concepts presented in this section.

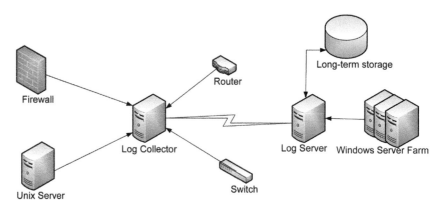

FIGURE 1.5 Addition of a Database for Long-Term Storage

A LOOK AT THINGS TO COME

Now let's briefly look at what sort of things you will encounter in the rest of this book. Since you can only extract good information from your logs if it's there to begin with, we'll look at the things that generate log information, and how to make them give you what you need. We'll show you how to build an infrastructure to collect, archive, and analyze log data. And along the way we'll try to present real-world examples and case studies.

We're going to talk in detail about Unix and Syslog data, because a lot of applications use Syslog automatically, and many others have the capability to use it (for example, most Cisco and Juniper devices speak Syslog). And, Syslog is the only cross-platform logging utility with a built-in mechanism for forwarding log messages to a central collection system. But we will talk about other types of logs that you can find on your systems. And we'll definitely talk about Windows logging, mostly in the context of getting your windows log data into your centralized infrastructure.

If you are a programmer, we have a whole chapter just for you. One of the biggest problems in analyzing log messages is that many of them are, frankly, poorly written, and don't have the information necessary to do anything useful with them. Logs would be much easier to work with if they were better written to begin with. For example, take a look at this log message:

```
Jun 21 14:38:25 10.2.2.1 rlogin: connection refused
```

What's wrong with that message? It's nice and explanatory, right? It informs us that a connection to the rlogin service was refused. Aside from some annoying things like the fact that there's no year or time zone, wouldn't it be nice to know where the connection was coming from that was refused? Wouldn't it be nice to know why it was refused? Maybe if you are diagnosing a problem, and testing as you watch the log messages it isn't so bad. But if you are looking at the logs because someone is attacking your system, it really helps to know where they're coming from.

Now consider this log message:

```
Jun 21 14:38:25 somehost rlogin: connection refused from 1.2.3.4
  because the address matches deny rule in hosts.allow: rlogind: all:
  deny
```

Isn't that a lot better?

And here's a virtually useless message (and no, we did not make it up):

```
May 21 00:00:07 baz.example.com kernel: "00 00 00 00 00 00 00 00 00 00
  00 00"
```

Maybe it means something to the kernel developers for that system, but not much help otherwise. It might as well say this:

```
May 21 00:00:07 baz.example.com kernel: something happened
```

Rather than just complain about lousy log messages, in our chapter for programmers we offer helpful suggestions on how to improve the quality of the logs that your applications generate.

LOGS ARE UNDERRATED

Logs are under-appreciated in many enterprise environments. Often logs are completely ignored, and only noticed when disk space runs low. At that point they are usually deleted without review. And in some cases, some of the messages in the logs might have indicated why the disk was full. We have certainly had the experience of being asked to look at a compromised machine, and upon inquiring as to where the logs were, we're told "oh, they were just taking up space so we deleted them." In most of those cases, there wasn't much we could do for them.

Why are logs under-appreciated? Well, for a number of reasons. Vendors don't want you to use them. Vendors of intrusion detection systems are going to tell you that you need the latest piece of technology (theirs being the best) otherwise you're toast. Vendors of IT management tools are going to tell you that you need their expensive products, with little agents on every host that go about reporting much of the same information that you find in your logs. But of course, if you can get the information from your logs, you don't need their products.

Logs aren't "sexy" even to system administrators. It's much cooler to get the Gigawombat-3000 Network Intrusion Detection System (NIDS) which includes Extra Sensory Perception that tells you about attacks before they happen. Especially when your favorite mailing list is going on nonstop about how that is the latest thing in intrusion detection/prevention/anticipation/whatever. By the way, that Gigawombat you just bought also requires somebody to analyze its logs…

Log analysis isn't easy, and can be messy. As opposed to the "plug-and-pray" approach, effective log analysis takes some work. Logs come in a variety of shapes and sizes, and at times it can be difficult to extract information from them. Syslog data can be especially bad, as much of the data is free-form text (as we discussed earlier). As we'll show you throughout this book, it takes some energy just to get the good bits of data out of Syslog. Plus there can be a lot of data to work with. For instance, some sites collect several gigabytes per week of log data, others that much in a day. Such volume can seem quite overwhelming to begin with—and the administrator often ends up cobbling together some scripts that look for a random set of things based on what they saw in the logs at a particular time.

Effective log analysis also requires knowledge of your environment; you have to know what's good and bad for your network, what's suspicious and what's normal. What's bad or strange for you may be perfectly normal for someone else. For instance, a user logging from foreign countries may be suspicious to you, especially if all of your users are local. However, another site may have users all over the place, so it's difficult for them to determine what would be considered unusual.

That's part of the reason there are no true plug-in log analysis tools, because it's your environment and policies that dictate what you want to get out of your logs.

And finally, there's not a lot of good information available on how to do log analysis. Gee, maybe someone should write a book about it...

LOGS CAN BE USEFUL

Beyond the many examples presented so far in this chapter, logs can tell you a lot of things about what is happening on your network, from performance information to fault detection to intrusion detection. Logs can be a good source of "forensic" information for determining "what happened" after an incident. And logs can make an audit trail for (what else?) auditing purposes. The following sections are a list of use-cases that logs enable.

Resource Management

Logs contain a wealth of hidden riches. For example, a typical way to monitor if a host is up or down is to use the Internet Control Message Protocol (ICMP) to "ping" a host. But this is not foolproof. Successfully pinging a host tells you that its network interface is configured. But sometimes a host can be crashed, yet the interface still responds as long as it's configured and has power. But seeing a message like:

```
May 24 02:00:36 somehost -- MARK --
May 24 02:20:36 somehost -- MARK --
May 24 02:40:36 somehost -- MARK --
May 24 03:00:36 somehost -- MARK --
```

tells you that the system is operating enough so that Syslog can write messages. (MARK messages are a special status message generated by the UNIX Syslog daemon at regular intervals).

Logs can not only tell you that a host is up, but also what the applications running on the host are doing. Failures, both hardware and software, often show up in logs before the system actually fails. And when recovering from a failure, logs often provide clues as to the cause.

Here's a classic example of a failure that you can find in your logs:

```
May 21 08:33:00 foo.example.com kernel: pid 1427 (dd), uid 2 inumber
    8329 on /var: filesystem full
```

Pretty informative! It shows that the *var* filesystem on the host has filled up. The other information in the message shows the name and process-id of the process that caused the error to occur. It even shows the i-node of the file being written to. Now in this case, the process shown may not be the one that filled up the disk, it may just be trying to write data after the partition had already filled up. But it's a starting point.

Intrusion Detection

Host logs (as opposed to NIDS logs) of course are very useful for intrusion detection. For example:

```
Sep 17 07:00:02 host.example.com: sshd[721038]: Failed password for
    illegal user erin from 192.168.2.4 port 44670 ssh2
```

This log message shows a failed login attempt, using the username *erin*. The words *illegal user* appear because there is no such account on the system. This message was the result of an attacker using an *ssh-scanner* which attempts to log into a host via ssh, using a set of well-known commonly used usernames and passwords. This example was selected from a set of several thousand attempts done in a very short amount of time.

Host logs can be a better indicator of an intrusion than a NIDS. A NIDS can tell you that an attack was attempted against a host, but usually cannot tell you whether the exploit was successful. In our example above, a NIDS could only detect that there had been a short ssh session, possibly that there were a very large number of sessions in a short amount of time, but would be unable to detect that authentication had failed, because a NIDS can only see what is happening on the wire. A host, if configured to log, can provide detail on what happened on the system. Of course this is not foolproof. You might log the wrong things or disks could fill up. Or the attacker could erase the log files. This is why it is critical to have your logs sent to a remote collection point. Even when the attacker covers his tracks we will have the initial log messages on the collection point which will help shed some light on what might have happened. In a more subtle example, here's a message from Snort, an open source NIDS:

```
Jan 2 16:19:23 host.example.com snort[1260]: RPC Info Query: 10.2.3.4
   -> host.example.com:111
Jan 2 16:19:31 host.example.com snort[1260]: spp_portscan: portscan
   status from 10.2.3.4: 2 connections across 1 hosts: TCP(2), UDP(0)
```

These messages show that an attacker did a port scan of the network looking for hosts running rcp.statd, which has had a number of vulnerabilities over the years. The messages also show that the scanner was successful in connecting to two hosts. But was the attack successful in gaining access to the machine? Was the connection dropped by TCP-Wrappers? Snort doesn't know. But more than likely the system on which TCP-Wrappers is running did log if the connection was dropped or not. If this system is set up to log, then you can correlate both the Snort log message and the TCP-Wrappers log message to come up with a better, more complementary picture of what is actually happening. Never underestimate the ability to combine log messages from multiple sources to paint a single, more informative picture.

Now look at this message found on one of the hosts:

```
Jan 02 16:19:45 host.example.com rpc.statd[351]: gethostbyname
   error for ^X÷ÿ¿^X÷ÿ¿^Y÷ÿ¿^Y÷ÿ¿^Z÷ÿ¿^Z÷ÿ¿^[÷ÿ¿^[÷ÿ¿bffff750
   804971090909090687465676274736f6d616e6e6f6e6e6f6e2065206f7220726f66
   bffff718 bffff719 bffff71a bffff71b_____



                                                                  _!
__!

_____

   _____
```

Well, it certainly looks like a buffer overflow was attempted or at the very least, some sort of error has occurred. We know this because of the gibberish that starts on the second line. This indicates that binary data is present, i.e. is non-printable characters, in the log message, which is usually a bad indicator.

But was it successful? The next message gives us a clue:

```
Jan 02 16:20:25 host.example.com adduser[12152]: new user: name=cgi,
   uid=0, gid=0, home=/home/cgi, shell=/bin/bash
```

This message shows an account being added to the system. The account has the username *cgi* but has a user ID of *0* (the root uid). This is generally a bad sign. Attackers like to create accounts that they can use to log back into the machine, and they like to pick benign names that might go unnoticed on the

> **WARNING**
>
> **Buffer Overflow**
>
> A buffer overflow is a type of attack that exploits a flaw in an application. The person exploits the flaw by entering more data than the application can handle. This extra data injection can have unwanted side effects like a crash or even, in extreme cases, where the perpetrator gains control of the systems processor for arbitrary code execution (Peikari & Chuvakin, 2004).

system—names that look like they belong there. But the intruder wants to keep his privileged access, so the account has to have the same uid (0) as root.

Now, the next message reads:

```
Jan 02 16:22:02 host.example.com PAM_pwdb[12154]: password for (cgi/0)
    changed by ((null)/0)
```

The interesting part about this line is that it shows that the account password was changed by a user with a null username, which is also a pretty bad sign, as a user who had logged in using normal methods would have an actual username ("root" in this case).

So, in the example above, the NIDS was not able to tell us whether the attack was successful, only that maybe an attack was attempted. The real information on the attack was logged on the host. The NIDS can be good for telling you about especially good times to look at your logs, but by itself does not give you a complete picture. Now it's certainly the case that host logs won't always indicate what happened, but it's pretty clear that NIDS and logs combined can be better than NIDS alone. Recall the example from the introduction? Never underestimate the power in combing log data together to find the proverbial needle in the haystack.

Logs tell you what is actually happening on your system(s). NIDS usually can't tell you about users attempting local exploits on a host, or users merely violating policy or committing some other undesirable activity. This is where host intrusion detection systems (HIDS) fill the gap. HIDS monitor the running state of a computer system. Things like users, directories, binaries, log files themselves, and other objects are monitored via checksums and other techniques to detect when they have been altered by malicious users or compromised and/or altered applications. As you may have guessed, HIDS systems emit log data whenever suspected alteration of system resources may have occurred.

And with the increasing use of encrypted transport protocols, such as Secure Sockets Layer (SSL), Internet Protocol Security (IPSEC), and other VPN technologies, it is becoming harder and harder for a NIDS to see the "interesting" parts of network traffic.

As alluded to above, user behavior is also contained in system logs. When a user logs in and out, where from, etc. some logs such as process accounting logs, tell you something about what the user did. And system "auditing" tools such as the BSM can provide even more fine-grained detail as to user and system activity.

Troubleshooting

Logs are also invaluable for troubleshooting. Syslog was actually designed for just that purpose. Diagnosing problems with daemons which are not connected to a console or tty can be quite difficult without logfiles to examine. Plus Syslog is often where the kernel provides information about what it's doing.

Forensics

Forensics is the process of building a picture of "what happened" after the event is over. The picture is often built off of incomplete information, but the credibility of the information available is critical. Logs can be an essential part of the forensic process.

Logs, once recorded, are not altered through the course of normal use of the system, meaning that they are a sort of "permanent" record. As such, they can provide a somewhat accurate complement to other data on the system which may be more susceptible to alteration or corruption.

Since logs usually have timestamps on each record, they provide a chronological sequence of events, not only showing what happened, but when it happened and in what order.

And logs forward to another host (usually a central log collector), also provide a source of evidence that is separate from the originating source. If the accuracy of the information on the original source is called into question (such as the issue of an intruder who may have altered or deleted logs), the separate source of information may be considered an additional, more reliable source.

Likewise, logs from different sources, even different sites, can corroborate other evidence and reinforce the accuracy of each source.

Logs serve to reinforce other evidence that is collected. Often, recreating the picture of an event is not based on one piece or source of information, but data from a variety of sources: files and their respective timestamps on the system, user command history, network data, and logs. Occasionally logs may refute other evidence, which in itself may indicate that other sources have been corrupted (e.g. by an intruder).

HOW LOGS CAUGHT AN INTRUDER

Several years ago, a company had their Web server crash. The Web server logs showed what looked like an attack that exploited a then-recently-announced Denial of Service (DoS) vulnerability. The incoming connection was from another company in town. Someone in the IT group remembered that a recently departed employee had started working for that company, and the employee had not left on the best of terms. Now, their logs only showed the attack coming from that company, but the accused attacker could have claimed that the logs were forged to "frame" him. But in addition to the Web server logs, firewall logs at both companies showed the same connections happening at the identical time, corroborating the logs. And the logs from the attacker's new company showed that it came from his desk computer. The final nail in the coffin was that one of the people at the victim company called the ex-employee at his new job, and he answered the phone, which placed him in front of his computer at the time of the attack. The attacker eventually pled guilty to a misdemeanor.

Had the victim company only had their Web server logs, they might not have had enough evidence to prove their case. Having supporting data from multiple sources, especially those under control of different groups, makes it much harder to claim the evidence is incorrect or fabricated.

The evidence shown in logs is at times indirect or incomplete. For example, a log entry might show a particular activity, but not who did it. Or, as an example, process accounting logs show what commands a user has run, but not the arguments to those commands. So logs can't always be relied on as a sole source of information. Although, when a host is compromised, the logs may be the only source of reliable information, provided the host has been forwarding logs to a central log server. The logs up to the point when the host was compromised can be trusted, but logs after the compromise are suspect at best. But the logs you collected up to the event might help shed light on what happened or point you in the right direction.

Boring Audit, Fun Discovery

Auditing is a process that verifies a system or process is working as expected. Logs are a part of any audit process, forming a part of the audit trail used.

Auditing is often done for policy or regulatory compliance. For instance, companies routinely have to do financial audits to make sure that what their financial statements say match what their books say, and that the numbers all add up. In the US laws such as Sarbanes-Oxley and HIPAA essentially require certain types of transaction logging, and an audit trail that can be used to verify user access to financial, respectively, patient data. Another example is the Payment Card Industry Data Security Standard (PCI DSS), a mandate that covers logging around credit card transactions and cardholder data access. We will discuss PCI in Chapter 16.

Logs can also be used for compliance to technical policies, such as a security policy. For example, if you have policies about what services are allowed on your network, an audit of various logs can be used to verify that only those services are running. For example, Windows has an Application event log which contains log messages of services that are started and stopped by the operating system.

Audit trails are also used for accountability, as such, logs can be used for non-repudiation. For instance, if someone claims that they never received a particular email, mail logs can be used to verify that claim and show the message was either delivered or not, much like having a signed receipt from a mail carrier. Or, in another example, if a user claims that they were not logged in when a certain event occurred, logs can show whether or not that statement was true.

Having an organized approach to log analysis can also turn a boring audit into "fun discovery." What does that mean? Well, for example, we'll show you tools you can use to extract from your logs a list of all the services running on a host. You might be surprised to find out some of the things that you are running (didn't know you had an IRC server on your network, eh?). Sometimes such discoveries show policy violations and on occasion, they show an intruder who's silly enough to start a service that leaves log records behind.

Auditing user activity can show you things you didn't know about. In the Unix environment, there is a utility called sudo. It allows you, as a regular user, to execute administrator commands without needing to know the administrator password. Looking at sudo, logs can show you who has been running administrator commands. That information can be invaluable when someone accidentally erases an entire filesystem and you're trying to figure out who did it.

If you allow users to log in remotely, you might find it quite interesting to see where they're logging in from. If you see a user logging in from two places at the same time that are geographically distant from each other, that might be something you want to investigate. (We've heard that cell phone companies do exactly that to detect cloned cell phones.)

Let's shift gears away from how useful logs are to how effective people, process and technology are in the overall log analysis picture.

PEOPLE, PROCESS, TECHNOLOGY

An effective log analysis strategy is not just a set of tools but a combination of people, process, and technology.

The technology is the combination of tools you use. But it's not enough to have a collection of the latest hip tools, you need to know what to do with them.

Process determines what you do with those tools. How are you going to manage the log data, make sure it contains the information you want, and be able to extract the information you need? A process is required for doing those things.

A documented process for handling log data can be essential for using logs as evidence in court. Being able to show how you regularly collect and preserve log data may make the difference as to whether your log data is admissible as evidence. Reporting can aid in this and Chapter 12 touches on this.

And it takes people to drive and execute on the process. Human intelligence is also required to decide what particular log messages mean in the context of a particular situation.

In the intrusion example, is an example of the human involvement required. The computer doesn't know that those log records indicate an intrusion. It takes a person to look at them and say "Wait, that's not quite right, why is an account being created with a uid of 0?" Another example of such a situation is when a host suddenly becomes unreachable. Since you were in a morning meeting where it was announced that network maintenance was going to occur at 3pm, you use that information to determine if the outage is related to this work or not.

SECURITY INFORMATION AND EVENT MANAGEMENT (SIEM)

No book on log management would be complete without a discussion on SIEM. SIEM is an industry in its own. SIEM tools provide a means to analyze, in real time, security events. It also provides mechanism for reporting, visualization, long-term storage, etc. We will not spend a lot of time on SIEM in this book. But Chapter 15 discusses some open source SIEM tools.

The following two case studies explain how log data helped solve to real-world problems.

TRACKING AN ATTACKER THROUGH FIREWALL LOGS

In a recent investigation, one of the authors had to look at a compromised server that was running at a small internet service provider (ISP). The system was apparently destroyed by the attacker, possibly due to frustration stemming from his inability to penetrate further into the network, or out of sheer malevolence.

One morning, company support team was alerted by a customer who was trying to download a driver update. He reported that the FTP server "was not responding" to his connection attempts. Upon failing to login to the FTP server remotely via secure shell, the support team member walked to a server room only to discover that the machine crashed and would not reboot. The reason was simple—no operating system was found on the disk.

While the machine itself was apparently compromised and all host-side evidence, including logs, were gone (yes, the logs may have been recoverable using "forensic" tools, but that's outside the scope of this book). But the network segment on which the server was located was behind a firewall, and the firewall was set to log at maximum level.

The firewall logs were searched for any messages occurring over the previous 24h which contained the IP address of the compromised server, providing a record of all connections to and from the server for the previous day. From those logs, they were able to establish that:

- Several hours prior to the time of the crash, someone probed the IP addresses of the FTP server from the outside. There were several connection attempts to various ports on the server, some not successful (such as TCP port 25) and some successful (port TCP 21—FTP).
- The attacker connected several times to the FTP port, with TCP session times ranging from several seconds up to ten minutes.
- The attacker uploaded a file to the FTP server.
- It appeared that the attacker managed to establish an interactive command session with the server. The firewall logs did not give any detail about the contents of the TCP session, so it was impossible to determine exactly what the attacker did. But it appears highly likely that he managed to exploit the FTP server and install his own software on it.
- The logs then showed connection attempts from the FTP server to outside hosts, which were blocked by the firewall as a result of rules on the firewall restricting outbound traffic. These failed attempts were most likely the intruder unsuccessfully attempting to access other machines from the compromised server.

So, even simple firewall logs can shed significant light on an incident where there would otherwise be no useful information. This example would have benefitted from a central loghost as well. The logs would have been stored off host and could have been retrieved.

Virus Tracking Through Antivirus Logs

Antivirus logs are often seen as mundane and useless. However, AV logs can prove invaluable as a piece of evidence to prove that the system is infected or compromised. Different AV vendors log their messages in different ways. In the case of the AV data used in this example, the AV system logged to the Windows Event Log.

In one case, a Windows system was showing unusual behavior:

- Slow system response for local programs.
- Slow networking on the same LAN segment as the system in question.
- Extraneous processes running even when no user is using the systems.

Logs from a network security monitoring tool also revealed that the system was a source of significant scanning activity. At that stage the machine was disconnected from the network.

The system administrators suspected some sort of malware (e.g. virus, worm, etc.), but the system was running an antivirus program that was believed to be up to date.

A review of antivirus logs on the system revealed a number of interesting things. First, there were a number of messages indicating failed updates due to low disk space. That explained why the system was not fully protected.

Then there were some messages showing the AV software responding to viruses:

> *Virus Found!Virus name: W32.Welchia.B.Worm in File: C:\WINNT*
> *system32\drivers\svchost.exe by: Manual scan. Action: Quarantine*
> *succeeded:*
>
> *Virus Found!Virus name: W32.Randex.gen in File: C:\WINNT\system32*
> *wumgrd.exe by: Manual scan. Action: Quarantine succeeded:*
>
> These messages indicate viruses which were found and "quarantined" or stopped:
>
> *Virus Found!Virus name: Backdoor.IRC.Bot in File: C:\WINNT\system32*
> *mfm\msrll.exe by: Manual scan. Action: Clean failed: Quarantine*
> *failed:*
>
> But this message shows a "backdoor" called "Backdoor.IRC.Bot" was detected, but not stopped.

NOTE

Backdoor

A backdoor is a piece of software or application program that allows a user to gain access to a computer system without being noticed. It is often the case that backdoors are used for malicious purposes (Skoudis & Zeltser, 2004)

The interesting thing about the above message is that while the first two malware instances were dealt with, the last was only detected but not cleaned out. The malware (an IRC backdoor bot) enabled the attackers to gain control over the system and to use it to scan other hosts for vulnerabilities.

Figure 1.6 shows a subset of the antivirus logs imported into Excel, showing just the actions taken with regard to Backdoor.IRC.Bot. Excel is being used here to more easily show the AV log messages.

The example indicates that the backdoor may have been on the system since at least May. It also confirms that the backdoor was not quarantined by the antivirus software.

The highlighted messages in Figure 1.7 show that around the time the backdoor appeared in May, the system was infected by both the Welchia and W32. Randex.gen worms, either of which could have installed the backdoor. In fact,

	A	B	C	E	G	H	J	M
1	Date	Filename	Virus Name	Action Taken	User	Original Location	Current Location	Scan Type
2	7/2/2004 1:07	msrll.exe	Backdoor.IRC.Bot	Left alone	Administrator	C:\WINNT\system32\mfm\	C:\WINNT\system32\mfm\	Scheduled scan
4	7/1/2004 1:07	msrll.exe	Backdoor.IRC.Bot	Left alone	Administrator	C:\WINNT\system32\mfm\	C:\WINNT\system32\mfm\	Scheduled scan
5	6/30/2004 19:45	msrll.exe	Backdoor.IRC.Bot	Left alone	Administrator	C:\WINNT\system32\mfm\	C:\WINNT\system32\mfm\	Realtime scan
6	6/30/2004 19:45	msrll.exe	Backdoor.IRC.Bot	Left alone	Administrator	C:\WINNT\system32\mfm\	C:\WINNT\system32\mfm\	Realtime scan
7	6/30/2004 19:44	msrll.exe	Backdoor.IRC.Bot	Left alone	Administrator	C:\WINNT\system32\mfm\	C:\WINNT\system32\mfm\	Realtime scan
8	6/30/2004 1:07	msrll.exe	Backdoor.IRC.Bot	Left alone	Administrator	C:\WINNT\system32\mfm\	C:\WINNT\system32\mfm\	Scheduled scan
9	6/29/2004 18:29	msrll.exe	Backdoor.IRC.Bot	Left alone	Administrator	C:\WINNT\system32\mfm\	C:\WINNT\system32\mfm\	Manual scan
16	5/28/2004 21:55	msrll.exe	Backdoor.IRC.Bot	Left alone	Administrator	C:\WINNT\system32\mfm\	C:\WINNT\system32\mfm\	Manual scan

FIGURE 1.6 Sample Antivirus Logs

	A	B	C	E	G	H	J	
1	Date	Filename	Virus Name	Action Taken	User	Original Location	Current Location	Scan T
14	6/4/2004 20:23	wumgrd.exe	W32.Randex.gen	Left alone in Quaranti	SYSTEM	C:\WINNT\system32\	Quarantine	Defwat
15	6/4/2004 20:23	svchost.exe	W32.Welchia.B.Worm	Left alone in Quaranti	SYSTEM	C:\WINNT\system32\drivers\	Quarantine	Defwat
16	5/28/2004 21:55	msrll.exe	Backdoor.IRC.Bot	Left alone	Administrator	C:\WINNT\system32\mfm\	C:\WINNT\system32\mfm\	Manual
17	5/28/2004 21:51	wumgrd.exe	W32.Randex.gen	Quarantined	Administrator	C:\WINNT\system32\	Quarantine	Manual
18	5/28/2004 19:21	svchost.exe	W32.Welchia.B.Worm	Quarantined	Administrator	C:\WINNT\system32\drivers\	Quarantine	Manual
19	5/17/2004 12:06	25227_up.exe	W32.Sasser.C.Worm	Left alone in Quaranti	SYSTEM	C:\winnt\system32\	Quarantine	Defwat
20	5/17/2004 12:06	25227_up.exe	W32.Sasser.C.Worm	Left alone in Quaranti	SYSTEM	C:\winnt\system32\	Quarantine	Defwat
21	5/17/2004 12:06	svchost.exe	W32.Welchia.B.Worm	Left alone in Quaranti	SYSTEM	C:\winnt\system32\drivers\	Quarantine	Defwat
22	5/17/2004 12:06	TFTP988	W32.Randex.gen	Left alone in Quaranti	SYSTEM	C:\winnt\system32\	Quarantine	Defwat
23	5/17/2004 12:06	svchost.exe	W32.Welchia.B.Worm	Left alone in Quaranti	SYSTEM	C:\winnt\system32\drivers\	Quarantine	Defwat
24	5/17/2004 12:06	TFTP1256	W32.Randex.gen	Left alone in Quaranti	SYSTEM	C:\winnt\system32\	Quarantine	Defwat
25	5/17/2004 12:06	svchost.exe	W32.Welchia.B.Worm	Left alone in Quaranti	SYSTEM	C:\winnt\system32\drivers\	Quarantine	Defwat
26	5/17/2004 12:06	TFTP1128	W32.Welchia.Worm	Left alone in Quaranti	SYSTEM	C:\winnt\system32\	Quarantine	Defwat
27	5/17/2004 12:06	TFTP328	W32.Welchia.Worm	Left alone in Quaranti	SYSTEM	C:\winnt\system32\	Quarantine	Defwat
28	5/17/2004 12:06	svchost.exe	W32.Welchia.B.Worm	Left alone in Quaranti	SYSTEM	C:\winnt\system32\drivers\	Quarantine	Defwat
29	5/17/2004 12:06	svchost.exe	W32.Welchia.B.Worm	Left alone in Quaranti	SYSTEM	C:\winnt\system32\drivers\	Quarantine	Defwat
30	5/17/2004 12:06	svchost.exe	W32.Welchia.B.Worm	Left alone in Quaranti	SYSTEM	C:\winnt\system32\drivers\	Quarantine	Defwat
31	5/17/2004 12:06	WksPatch[1].exe	W32.Welchia.B.Worm	Left alone in Quaranti	SYSTEM	C:\Documents and Settings\D	Quarantine	Defwat
32	5/17/2004 12:06	WksPatch[1].exe	W32.Welchia.B.Worm	Left alone in Quaranti	SYSTEM	C:\Documents and Settings\D	Quarantine	Defwat
33	5/17/2004 12:06	WksPatch[1].exe	W32.Welchia.B.Worm	Left alone in Quaranti	SYSTEM	C:\Documents and Settings\D	Quarantine	Defwat
34	5/17/2004 12:06	svchost.exe	W32.Welchia.B.Worm	Left alone in Quaranti	SYSTEM	C:\winnt\system32\drivers\	Quarantine	Defwat
35	5/17/2004 12:06	WksPatch[1].exe	W32.Welchia.B.Worm	Left alone in Quaranti	SYSTEM	C:\Documents and Settings\D	Quarantine	Defwat
36	5/17/2004 12:06	WksPatch[1].exe	W32.Welchia.B.Worm	Left alone in Quaranti	SYSTEM	C:\Documents and Settings\D	Quarantine	Defwat

FIGURE 1.7 Sample Antivirus Logs for a Specific Time Period

the reference for W32.Randex.gen (http://securityresponse.symantec.com/avcenter/venc/data/w32.randex.gen.html#technicaldetails) says that the worm is known to "open backdoor ports and open connections to predetermined IRC servers and wait for commands from an attacker."

The log entries above also show that the system was a "rats nest" of malware, only some of which was successfully cleaned (albeit often after the successful infection and system modification).

So, in this situation, without the antivirus logs, it would have been difficult or impossible to determine when the infection happened, or that the antivirus software had failed to update itself.

SUMMARY

This chapter presented concepts surrounding logging, logs, log messages, and log data. The piece parts of a logging ecosystem were discussed including log message generation, filtering and normalization, collection, analysis, and long-term storage. These concepts set the ground work for what is to come in the rest of the book. Additionally examples of how useful log data can be were presented, along with ways logs helped solve two real-world problems.

REFERENCES

Mauro, D. R., & Schmidt, K. J. (2005). *Essential SNMP* (2nd ed.) Beijing: O'Reilly.

Peikari, C., & Chuvakin, A. (2004). Overflow attacks. In *Security warrior* (p. 161). Beijing: O'Reilly & Associates, Inc.

Skoudis, Ed., & Zeltser, L. (2004). Backdoors. In *Malware: Fighting malicious code* (p. 124). Upper Saddle River, NJ: Prentice Hall PTR, 2004.

What is a Log?

What is a log? A secret

Let's crack it now!

Resist it will furiously

Haiku 2: Anton

INTRODUCTION

In Chapter 1 we talked about logs, but what are we actually talking about? We're not talking about trees, mathematics, nor ship's logs...so let's start from the definitions. Having a clear definitions around logging data is important because so many discussions in this area and that being high level and fuzzy, thus not useful for security analysts and network engineers.

Definitions

Many of the terms used in logging, log analysis, and log management—including these very terms we just used—have vague, misleading, or multiple meanings. In some cases, the terms are "borrowed" from other disciplines (and we use that word loosely), in some cases, they're just used differently by different people. In other cases, they used to be specific, but then got corrupted by tool vendor marketing departments. This vagueness only muddies the waters of what is already a difficult sea to navigate.

So, what should the logs convey? Are logs here to warn us or to be ignored? If logs are so important, how can it happen that they are ignored so often (and they are!)? The blatant cases of organizations that were compromised by hackers and never knew it, despite having all the evidence in their logs for months and occasionally years after the breach. Do we have to look at logs if everything is seemingly going fine with our computers, related software running on them as well as network devices?

Ideally, logs should not only serve for answering the ever-important "what's wrong" question. They are also useful for answering many other questions, including "how well we are doing?" "will anything be wrong in the near future?," "did we do enough to protect something?" as well as they whole slew of audit-related questions such as "who did what." Note that the latter are useful not only when we know that something wrong has happened.

Thus, logs analysis tools should not be broken out of their shrink wraps only when something goes wrong. Ongoing log review must eventually become a habit, a daily routine—something akin to brushing one's teeth. Regulations today compel organization to adopt such good hygiene habits, while many organization are resisting.

So, is it OK to only look at logs when all hell breaks loose? The best answer to that is "that is the least you should do" but there are lots of other ways of using the log contents beyond that.

Here are the definitions of the terms that we will be using them throughout this book.

"An event is a single occurrence within an environment, usually involving an attempted state change. An event usually includes a notion of time, the occurrence, and any details the explicitly pertain to the event or environment that may help explain or understand the event's causes or effects" (source: http:/cee.mitre.org and specifically http://cee.mitre.org/docs/CEE_Architecture_ Overview-v0.5.pdf).

Event categories group events based upon one or more event categorization methodologies. Example methodologies include organization based upon what happened during the event, the involved parties, device types impacted, etc.

"An event field describes one characteristic of an event. Examples of an event field include date, time, source IP, user identification, and host identification." (source: http://cee.mitre.org/docs/CEE_Architecture_Overview-v0.5.pdf)

"An event record is a collection of event fields that, together, describe a single event. Terms synonymous to event record include "audit record" and "log entry"" (source: http://cee.mitre.org/docs/CEE_Architecture_Overview-v0.5.pdf)

A log is a collection of event records. Terms such as "data log," "activity log," "audit log," "audit trail," "log file," and "event log" are often used to mean the same thing as log. (source: http://cee.mitre.org/docs/ CEE_Architecture_Overview-v0.5.pdf)

An audit is the process of evaluating logs within an environment (e.g. within an electronic system). The typical goal of an audit is to assess the overall status or identify any notable or problematic activity. (source: http://cee.mitre.org/ docs/CEE_Architecture_Overview-v0.5.pdf)

Recording is the act of saving the event fields associated with a single event as an event record. (source: http://cee.mitre.org/docs/CEE_Architecture_Overview-v0.5.pdf))

"Logging is the act of collecting event records into logs. Examples of logging include storing log entries into a text log file, or storing audit record data in binary files or databases." (source: CEE Architecture Document 2011) (source: http://cee.mitre.org/docs/CEE_Architecture_Overview-v0.5.pdf)

On the other hand, a security incident is an occurrence of one or more security events that indicate that Something Bad happened in the environment. The Something Bad might be unauthorized access to a system, theft of information, denial or service, or a range of other, sometimes organization-specific activities. Security incidents also often involve being woken up at odd hours of the morning, and are usually unwelcome (sometimes at the cost of "we'd rather not know" delusion).

On the audit side, log records may be used as all or part of an audit, and as we will show throughout this book, good logging will help with auditing. But logging alone is not auditing, and log messages are not necessarily an audit trail.

It should be noted that sometimes people differentiate between logging and auditing based on trust factor. Logging can be produced by system and user applications, servers, OS components, while auditing is produced by more trusted components such as the kernel or trusted computing based (TCB). Such a distinction is used in Windows operating systems.

"Alert or Alarm" is an action taken in response to an event, usually intended to get the attention of someone (or something). Sometimes people say that log files contain alerts. Specifically, some intrusion detection logs are actually collection of IDS alerts. In our book, we will treat an alert as an action taken when a particular log message needs to be relayed to a user quickly. We will treat alarms to mean the same as alerts.

Also, by now the reader recognized that logs are produced by various entities, such as dedicated security devices, application software, operating systems, network infrastructure components, etc. We will adopt a generic term device to indicate a source of security-relevant logs. Thus, a security NIPS appliance and Apache Web server become devices for the purposes of this definition. There are reasons to believe that some of the Internet-enabled home appliance of the future will also have logs and the nightmare scenario of "my toaster crashed again" will be resolved by looking at its log file…

Now that we are armed with the terms, let's look at some examples and thus into the nature of log and logging.

LOGS? WHAT LOGS?

Most operating systems have some type of logging capability and generate log messages. However, many computer users (and this include system administrators, however surprising it might sound) don't know the logs exist, let alone look at them. Let's study three primary reasons for logging across the entire spectrum of log sources.

First, *Security logging* is focused on detecting and responding to attacks, malware infection, data theft, and other security issues. The classic example of security-focused logging is recording of user authentication (login) and other access decisions with the purpose of analyzing whether anybody has access to the resource without proper authorization.

Next, *Operational logging* is performed to provide useful information to system operators such as to notify them of failures and potentially actionable conditions. Operational logging might also be used for service provisioning and even financial decisions (access-based pricing, Web server access logs are a common example of logs used for business not just for IT operations). This category is extremely broad and covers a very large number of log types.

Also, *Compliance logging* often overlaps significantly with security logging since regulations are commonly written to improve security of systems and data. It is important to know the difference between two types of compliance logging: regulations and mandates that affect the IT such as PCI DSS, HIPAA, ISO, ITIL, etc,. AND system regulations such as common criteria and other mandates on system design and security.

Finally, *Application debug logging* is a special type of logging that is useful to application/system developers and not system operators. Such logging is typically disabled in production systems but can be enabled on request. Many of the messages in debugging logs can already be analyzed by the application developer with full knowledge of application internals and sometimes also with possession of application source code.

These four types of logging are produced by nearly all log sources (event producers), but are analyzed and consumed differently and by different systems (event consumers).

Operating system produce logs from the above spectrum. For example, Windows XP as well as Vista and Windows 7 have a logging system, called the Event Log. When particular things happen on the system, the operating system or an application will write some information to the Event Log. For example, when a Windows program crashes, there is often an option to see "More details," which most users cheerfully ignore. That information is what ends up in the Event Log.

Savvy "power users" have known where to find the Event Viewer (Figure 2.1) since the "bad old days" of Windows NT 3.5.

Unix systems have a logging technology called syslog, that harks from the days of early Unix sendmail program in the 1980s. Like Windows, the operating system itself and some applications write message to syslog. If the system administrator has not disabled logging or removed the logs files ("because the disk was getting full"), he/she might see entries like this:

```
Nov 11 22:41:00 ns1 named[765]: sysquery: findns error (NXDOMAIN) on
   ns2.example.edu?
```

The entry contains a date, host name, name of the service that generated the message as well as the message itself. This particular message indicates an attempt to do a DNS lookup on a non-existent domain.

Some applications generate their own logs. Web site administrators may be familiar with Web server logs.

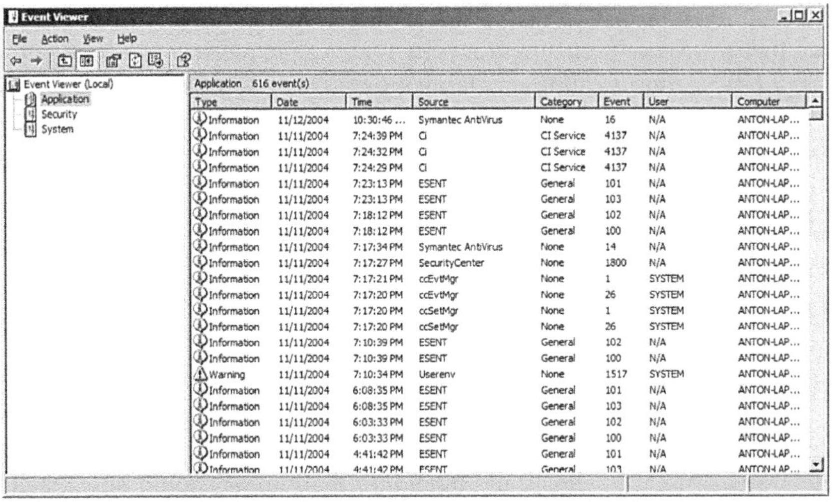

FIGURE 2.1 Windows Event Log Shown in Event Viewer

```
10.239.46.105 - - [09/Oct/2001:11:43:34 -0400] "GET /resume/ HTTP/1.0"
   200 1100
10.222.104.178 - - [09/Oct/2001:11:48:31 -0400] "GET /security
   HTTP/1.1" 301 322
10.222.104.178 - - [09/Oct/2001:11:48:31 -0400] "GET /security/
   HTTP/1.1" 200 759
10.222.104.178 - - [09/Oct/2001:11:52:20 -0400] "GET / HTTP/1.1" 200
   1014
```

This set of log entries show requests to a Web server from various sources (left) with the date and time of the request, locations of requested documents, and response codes (200,301, etc.) indicating the status of document delivery. Specifically, 200 indicates that the document was shown ("OK" code) and 301 indicates that its is moved to another location (Google for "http response codes" to find the detailed into on them!)

Web server logs are commonly analyzed for utilization and other ecommerce, marketing and others reasons. Web site administrators often mine Web server logs to study customer profiles and learn about their behavior, as well as other marketing-related tasks. In addition, Web server logs are used to study Web server performance and Web site usability.

The following is an example of a Snort NIDS "alert" log message.

```
Nov 14 13:04:14 ns1 snort: [111:16:1] (spp_stream4) TCP CHECKSUM
   CHANGED ON RETRANSMISSION (possible fragroute) detection {TCP}
   10.15.23.130:1682 -> 10.26.50.3:25
```

Note that in case of Snort these messages are called alerts, while some other NIDS / NIPS vendors call them alarms or even something else entirely. In all cases, they are actually just log messages that one might want to use to raise an alert to an operator or security analyst on duty.

All of the logging systems shown above are useful for security log analysis. Unix, Windows, and Web server logs can contain important clues about the organization's security posture.

These are just a few example of common logging systems. We will talk at length about these and other systems in Chapters 9 and 15.

Log Formats and Types

Before we discuss the formats and other information, we should note that any logging mechanism used for purposes listed above can be logically defined as four components:

- Log transport.
- Log syntax and format.
- Log event taxonomy.
- Logging settings, configuration, and recommendations.

These primary distinctions will be used throughout this report as well as other documentation produced under this project. Let's review their key concepts in detail.

Log transport is simply a way of moving log messages from one place to another.

There are many event transport protocols in existence—syslog, WS-Management, and numerous proprietary and product-specific log transport protocols—as well as logging mechanisms without its own transport method (e.g., local log file only). A proper log transport mechanism must preserve the integrity, and availability and (if required) confidentiality of log data, preserve log format and meaning as well as allow for an accurate representation of all the events that occurred, with correct timings and event sequence. The most important requirement for log transport is to preserve the integrity of individual logs—event records—and of the event stream/log as a whole.[1] Even more important is the preservation of each log entry correct time stamp.

Here is some well-known log transport mechanisms:

- syslog UDP.
- syslog TCP.
- encrypted syslog.
- SOAP over HTTP.
- SNMP.
- Regular file transfer such as FTPS or SCP.

For example, syslog UDP is by far the most popular log transport mechanism today used by millions of Unix-derived systems and Network Devices. Despite having multiple extreme weaknesses (such as lack of guaranteed message and availability), syslog is still the #1 way to move log data around.

Log syntax and format defines how the log messages are formed, transported, stored, reviewed, and analyzed. In the most trivial case, each event record could be treated as a text string and the event consumer could perform a full text search on the log and hope for consistency. But for reliable automated event analysis, it's necessary that event consumers and producers understand and agree on the syntax of the event record.

---

[1] As you can notice, some of the historical a popular mechanisms for transporting log data do not fit this requirement—such as syslog UDP.

Here is some well-known log formats:

- W3C Extended Log File Format (ELF) (http://www.w3.org/TR/WD-logfile. html).
- Apache access log (http://httpd.apache.org/docs/current/logs.html).
- Cisco SDEE/CIDEE (http://www.cisco.com/en/US/docs/security/ips/ specs/CIDEE_Specification.htm).
- ArcSight common event format (CEF) (http://www.arcsight.com/ solutions/solutions-cef/).
- Syslog (RFC3195 and newer RFC5424).
- IDMEF, an XML-based format (http://www.ietf.org/rfc/rfc4765.txt).

Regarding the last item, the term "syslog" is commonly applied to both a way to move messages over port 514 UDP (syslog transport) and to create log messages with a few structured elements (syslog format).

In particular, each field of every formatted event record contains some information in some representation. Although perhaps obvious to a human being, it's not at all clear that "Sun 12 3 2010 11:11pm" and "2010-12-03T11:11:00Z" represent the same time. Moreover, in the first example, the time is not really known due to lack of time zone information, and the date is ambiguous due to regional date order preference concerns (March 12 or December 3). Here are a few examples of various format that log files:

```
CEF:
CEF:0|security|threatmanager|1.0|100|detected a \| in
message|10|src=10.0.0.1 act=blocked a | dst=1.1.1.1
Apache CLF:
192.168.1.3 - - [18/Feb/2000:13:33:37 -0600] "GET / HTTP/1.0" 200 5073
127.0.0.1 - frank [10/Oct/2000:13:55:36 -0700] "GET /apache_pb.gif
    HTTP/1.0" 200 2326
W3C ELF:
#Version: 1.0
#Date: 12-Jan-1996 00:00:00
#Fields: time cs-method cs-uri
00:34:23 GET /foo/bar.html
12:21:16 GET /foo/bar.html
IDMEF:
<?xml version="1.0" encoding="UTF-8"?>
<!DOCTYPE IDMEF-Message PUBLIC "-//IETF//DTD RFC XXXX IDMEF v1.0//EN"
"idmef-message.dtd">
<IDMEF-Message version="1.0" xmlns="urn:iana:xml:ns:idmef">
```

```
<Alert messageid="abc123456789">
 <Analyzer analyzerid="hq-dmz-analyzer01">
  <Node category="dns">
   <location>Headquarters DMZ Network</location>
   <name>analyzer01.example.com</name>
  </Node>
 </Analyzer>
<CreateTime ntpstamp="0xbc723b45.0xef449129">
2000-03-09T10:01:25.93464-05:00
</CreateTime>
<Source ident="a1b2c3d4">
 <Node ident="a1b2c3d4-001" category="dns">
  <name>badguy.example.net</name>
  <Address ident="a1b2c3d4-002" category="ipv4-net-mask">
   <address>192.0.2.50</address>
   <netmask>255.255.255.255</netmask>
  </Address>
 </Node>
</Source>
<Target ident="d1c2b3a4">
 <Node ident="d1c2b3a4-001" category="dns">
  <Address category="ipv4-addr-hex">
   <address>0xde796f70</address>
  </Address>
 </Node>
</Target>
<Classification text="Teardrop detected">
 <Reference origin="bugtraqid">
  <name>124</name>
  <url>http://www.securityfocus.com/bid/124</url>
 </Reference>
</Classification>
</Alert>
</IDMEF-Message>
```

Most logs today, sadly, do not follow any specific or predetermined format (or only followed for a very small part of the message, such as timestamp) and can be considered free-form text.

There are various aspect of log formats. First, is the file in binary or ASCII format? Can a read the log file with a simple text browser or editor, or will he or she need a conversion tools to get to the information?

The obvious example of a human readable or ASCII log is Unix syslog. If you opened the book to this section, here is an example:

```
Nov 15 23:16:26 ns1 sshd2[12579]: connection from "10.85.179.198"
```

Web servers, firewalls, and many applications on all platforms log to text files which can be easily viewed.

Note however that human-readable, text, and ASCII log formats are not exactly synonymous. Unicode text (not ASCII) is not uncommon, and not every human can (or ever will be willing to!) read a complicated nested XML-formatted log file with long lines and numerous tags, etc.

The most common example of a binary file is Windows Event log. The reader might object that the Event Log is easily readable. But reading the Event Log requires using the Event Viewer. This utility converts the binary log (typically stored in files with an Evt extension in c:\WINDOWS\SYSTEM32\CONFIG\ directory) into a human-readable event, as shown in Figure 2.2.

Some other common binary formats are the Unix wtmp file, which contains login records and the *pacct* which contains process accounting information. While strictly not a log format, Tcpdump binary format can be defined as a format for logging network packet data, thus falling in the same category.

Why do programmers choose to log data in binary format? It sure would be simpler for us humans if all logs were text-based and easy to read! But there are compelling reasons for binary logging: Performance and space. If one has to log many thousands of records per second, the task could strain even modern CPUs. And system users usually have a reasonable expectation that logging will not disrupt system performance. In fact, one of the most common arguments against logging is that "it will impact performance." Our response to that is usually "and what will performance be like when the system crashes and you have no idea why?"

Binary format log entries are usually smaller (have less entropy), thus take less processing to format and write. Since the messages are usually smaller than ASCII message, the log files take up less disk space, and less IO when being transported.

Also, binary logs usually require less processing to parse, and have clearly delineated fields and data types, making analysis more efficient. An ASCII log parser has to process more data, and often has to use pattern matching to extract the useful bits of information.

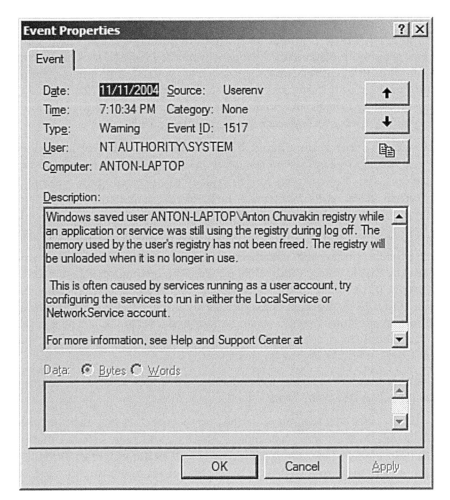

FIGURE 2.2 Windows XP Event Log

A compressed log is by definition a binary log, which provides further reasons for binary logging: it can be compressed. Just as obvious, if a log file is in an encrypted format, it has to be binary as well. Another reason for binary logs is that they are harder to read. How is that an advantage? Due to "security by obscurity," many believe that it makes their log files "more secure."

Another type of log format is the relational database, which isn't really text nor binary, or could be considered a very fancy binary format. A relational database stores binary records in a table for high-performance addition (called "insertion") and retrieval (called "selection"), defined by a database schema. A database schema is simply a method of defining records in a table and tables in the entire database.

Another important distinction between log types is whether the format is open or proprietary. An open format means that the format is documented somewhere, possibly in a standard document (such as ISO, ANSI, or an Internet Standard) or in a reference document (such as an RFC). A proprietary format may or may not be documented and is usually used by one specific device vendor. Proprietary formats are often undocumented, however, and one is at the mercy of the vendor for log reading and processing tools.

One might be able to understand a proprietary text format just by studying it ("reverse-engineering"—even though the term is more commonly used for binary formats). However, one runs the risk of misinterpreting the meaning of a particular fields, or it's data type, or range of values, and end up with rather useless or misleading results.

Logging settings, configuration, and recommendations is a common way for event producers and system operators to decide on what events to log and what logging to enable on each individual device. With a common way of expressing events, it is possible to advocate for what events products should generate. While it should be expected that a firewall should log events such as blocked connection attempts, there is no standard logging rules today. It is also important to not only be concerned with what events to log, but also what information details should be logged for each event.

There's no industry-wide recommendation in this area today. One common example is PCI DSS compliance.

Specifically, PCI DSS logging prescribes (see Figure 2.3) that each log entry at least contain user name, type of an event, date and time, success or failure indication, name of affected component as well as the system that originate in the event (these in fact present a very useful set of commonly used log details).

Many other industry organizations have created their own recommendations in regards to events and details to be logged. There is a way to generalize and summarize some of these recommendations, as done below in this report.

Log Syntax

Every log file of any format also has a syntax. Log syntax is conceptually similar to a syntax of a language, such as English. A sentence in human language syntax typically contains a subject, a predicate, sometimes a predicative, as well as complements and attributes. Sentence syntax covers the relations between the sentence members and their meaning. Note that syntax does not address the message contents. In other words, syntax deals with how we structure what we choose to say, and not what specific words we use.

10.2 Implement automated audit trails for all system components to reconstruct the following events:	**10.3** Record at least the following audit trail entries for all system components for each event:
10.2.1 All individual accesses to cardholder data	**10.3.1** User identification
10.2.2 All actions taken by any individual with root or administrative privileges	**10.3.2** Type of event
10.2.3 Access to all audit trails	**10.3.3** Date and time
10.2.4 Invalid logical access attempts	**10.3.4** Success or failure indication
10.2 5 Use of identification and authentication mechanisms	**10.3.5** Origination of event
10.2.6 Initialization of the audit logs	**10.3.6** Identity or name of affected data, system component, or resource.
10.2.7 Creation and deletion of system-level objects	

FIGURE 2.3 PCI DSS Requirement
Source: PCI DSS Standard, v 2.0

So what does syntax mean in the context of log messages? Well, each log message has a structure to it. Some types of log messages have portions of human language in them. Regardless, log messages each consist of patterns of information of various types. Based on regulations, one can define a common set of log fields that have to be present in every log entry for it to be useful. For example, a very common set of fields is:

1. Date/time (and, ideally, a time zone as well).
2. Type of log entry.
3. System that produced it.
4. Application or component that produced in.
5. Successful failure indication.
6. Severity, priority, or importance of a log message (typically present in all syslog messages).
7. For logs related to user activities in any way, a username recorded as well.

Network device manufacturers commonly follow the above in most of their logs, but they are notable exceptions where logs out lacking some of the details.

What is there in a log sentence? Let's try a "syntactic analysis" of a single syslog line. We will use a syslog message as an example of one of the most flexible (and chaotic) log formats.

```
Nov 16 00:26:24 ns1 named[765]: check_hints: A records for J.ROOT-
    SERVERS.NET class 1 do not match hint records
```

Isn't that nicely obscure! We purposefully choose a fairly long and esoteric line. We can say that a "subject" (answers "what" question) is a named process that noted that the user should "check_hints" ("predicate") for a specific DNS server and that this happened around 00:26 on November 16 (appallingly, syslog does not have a year in its timestamp, as will be explained in more detail in Chapter 2). Just for the curious, what really happened here is one of the root DNS servers has its IP address changed, but this DNS server in question (the one that produced the above log line) still has the old information in its configuration files (see, for example, an article "Some error messages and problems with DNS" at http://www.reedmedia.net/misc/dns/errors.html).

Why does the syntax of a log message matter? Log syntax is important for any kind of automated analysis of log data—which is the main subject of this book. Before the intelligent conclusions can be made from log data we need to split the log into its parts, according to its syntax.

Some log analysis-related software products (commercial and open-source) have developed "message schemas" to define the syntax of various types of logs. Such schema is designed to fit just about any message that can occur in various log files from devices, systems, application and other sources.

It may be obvious to the reader how most of our log message examples above fit into such schema. For example, this Dragon NIDS message:

```
2004-09-11 23:01:40|dralion1|IIS:DECODE-
    BUG|10.208.231.102|10.1.1.3|2611|80|T||6|tcp,dp=80,sp=2611|
```

easily fits into the general schema as shown in Table 2.1. The message indicates that a server 10.1.1.3 was hit by a IIS Web server exploit (either launched by a hacker or malware, such as a worm) from 10.208.231.102. The exploit is related to Unicode decoding by the Internet Information Services (IIS)—a standard Windows Web server.

Note that some data is also added when the message is collected (by the log analysis solution).

Note that EVENT, EVENT_TYPE, and various names (DNS, NetBIOS, etc.) were added by a log analysis system to complete the picture drawn by the Dragon intrusion detection system.

What about those data that are specified to a particular type of a log source such as from an unusual applications (although we're not sure if we've seen any "usual" application logs lately). In this case one might get away with using generic "custom" fields for storing such data. It's messy, but unfortunately that's the nature of log analysis today.

Table 2.1 Example Event Attributes

Fields	Example
EVENT	eid656539475ha1
DEVICE_TYPE	Dragon NIDS
DEVICE	*dralion1*
IMPORTANCE	High
EVENT_TYPE	Web Attack
DEVICE_EVENT_TYPE	*IIS:DECODE-BUG*
OCCUR_TIMESTAMP	*2004-09-11 23:01:40*
COLLECT_TIMESTAMP	*2004-09-11 23:01:43*
PROTOCOL_NET	TCP
PROTOCOL_APP	HTTP
SOURCE_IP	*10.208.231.102*
SOURCE_DNS	Evil.attacker.com
SOURCE_NBT	
SOURCE_MAC	
SOURCE_PORT	2611
DESTINATION_IP	*10.1.1.3*
DESTINATION_DNS	Poor.Webserver.com
DESTINATION _NBT	Poor-Web
DESTINATION_MAC	
DESTINATION_PORT	80
NETWORK	
BYTES_XFERRED	
EVENT_COUNT	1
STATUS	

Overall, knowing log file syntax is critical before any kind of analysis is approached. The fact that some people can do such analysis in their heads doesn't discount its value; it just shows one trivial case where such thing is possible (as well as highlights some advantages humans have over machines). In most cases, the automated system analyzing logs need to have an understanding of a log syntax, usually encoded in some template.

Overall, various system and device vendors use a few select types of logging coupled to a few common syntax choices (defined in the previous section). For example, some security logging is done in XML for easier and more information-rich integration with. A lot of operational logging is done via syslog and using unstructured text or semi-structured messages. Similarly, a lot of debugging logs is either syslog or even temporary text files. High-performance logging is often binary and in proprietary format.

Common device logging options are summarized in Table 2.2.

Table 2.2 Pros/Cons of Logging Mechanisms

	XML logging	Syslog text logging	Text file logging	Proprietary logging
Consumption mode	Mostly machine reading	Mostly manual reading	Only manual reading	Only machine reading
Common use case	Security logging	Operational logging, debugging logging	Debugging logging (enabled temporarily)	High-performance logging
Example	Cisco IPS security appliance	Most routers and switches	Most application debugging	Checkpoint firewall logging, packet capture
Recommendation	Use when a rich set of structure information need to be transferred from producing to consumer and then analyzed	Add structure such as name=value to simplify automated analysis; use for most operational uses	Add structure to enable automated analysis, if the logs are to be left enabled during operations	Use for super high performance uses only
Disadvantages	Relatively low performance, large log message sizes	Lack of log message structure makes automated analysis complicated and expensive	Typically the logs can only be understood by the application developers	Not human readable without a dedicated application that can convert binary into text

Among other notable logging methods, a few network devices log into comma-separated (CSV) or ELF formats (mentioned above). These are relatively less common.

Log Content

So we have talked about log format and syntax, but the real meat in is their content. Content of logs is commonly defined a taxonomy of what the logs actually mean. As a result, log event taxonomy is an unambiguous way of classifying logged events. If multiple systems log the same event, it should be expected that their taxonomy description of that event are identical. A computer should be able to immediately determine whether two logs refer to the same type of event. In order to make this happen, there needs to be a collection of well-defined words that can be combined in a predictable fashion—a log taxonomy. Presumably these words would describe the type of activity, the actors involved, the outcome, and other relevant event data.

There are no well-defined public standards on event taxonomies yet, even though some are in development. However, most security information and event management and some log management vendors on the market today have developed a log taxonomy that is utilized inside their products. Sadly, every vendor has used slightly different foundational principles for their taxonomy.

Content is a difficult topic, there's a lot of stuff to look at, sometimes it's inconsistent, incomplete, or misleading. We'll be looking at log content in Chapters 8, 9, and 11 starting with the next chapter. In this section we'll give an overview of the types of information that one can expect to find, what one might want to find, and what one could only dream of having logged.

Logs can contain information about user activity: who's logged in, what they were doing, mail they received and sent, etc. Logs can tell you about things that are broken or are going to break, such as disk errors. Logs can tell you that things are working fine and give you information about resource utilization and performance. Logs can contain information about status changes, starts and stops, etc. And logs can sometimes tell you about intrusion attempts, and occasionally indicate a successful intrusion.

The types below cover the entire spectrum of security, operations and debugging messages, these are:

1. *Change Management*: Records of system changes, component changes, updates, account changes, and anything else that might be subject to a change management process; these logs typically split into add, delete, update, and modify records. These can cross the line between security and operational types.
2. *Authentication and Authorization*: Records of authentication and authorization decisions (such as successful or failed logins to the device) and especially privileged user logins of the most common security messages and should be produced by every application and every network device. These are the security messages that often find operational uses as well (such as to track who utilized a particular system).
3. *Data and System Access*: Related to the previous types, records of access to application components, data (such as file or database tables) find common security as well as performance/operational uses. In some cases these messages are not enabled all the time and are only generated insensitive environments.
4. *Threat Management*: From traditional intrusion alerts to other activities that violate security policies, this types of messages is produced by Network Devices that have a dedicated security function (such as firewalls).
5. *Performance + Capacity Management*: A broad category of messages related to system performance and capacity management, including various

thresholds, memory and computing capability utilization and other finite resource utilization. These are very common operational messages that sometimes find security use as well.

6. *Business Continuity + Availability Management*: Most systems will produce a log when the system is being shutdown or started; other types of continuing tea and availability messages related to backups, redundancy or utilization of business continue itty features. These are very common operational messages with infrequent security use.

7. *Miscellaneous errors and failures*: Other types of system errors that the designers decided to bring to users attention are classified here; these are not critical operational messages that might or might not require an action by the device administrator.

8. *Miscellaneous debugging messages*: Debugging logs are typically created at the discretion of individual developers and are extremely hard to classify; most debugging logs are not left enabled in operational production environments.

CRITERIA OF GOOD LOGGING

As we will show in various examples throughout this book, there are many cases where the information logged is incomplete or sometimes just useless. So what makes a "good" log? What information is necessary for a log message to be usable for intrusion detection, resource management, or auditing? There are many kinds of logs and even more kinds of log-producing devices 5, so it is hard to define a single criterion.

In general, logs should tell you:

- What happened (with appropriate detail; "Something happened" is not usually particularly useful).
- When did it happen (and when did it start and end, if relevant).
- Where did it happen (on what host, what file system, which network interface, etc.).
- Who was involved.
- Where he, she or it came from.

The above list is the set of absolute essentials—the "5 W's of Logging". These are taken from other disciplines where they are used: journalism, criminal investigation, and other disciplines. For icing on the cake, many people would also like to see:

- Where do I get more information.
- How certain should I be that the above is really what happened?
- What is affected.

And since we are allowed to dream, one would also like to know:

- What will happen next.
- What else happened that I should care about.
- What should I do about it.

Of course, in some cases the latter items are dependent on the particular environment—what your site should do about a particular event might not be the same as what another site should do.

As organizations have finally taking network device and—to an extent—server logging under control, the next battle front is clearly in application logging. After getting used to neat Cisco ASA or other firewall logs and Linux "password accepted" messages, security incident investigators have been thrust into horrific world application logging while trying to respond to the next wave of attacks. These logs might miss details here and there and not always be useful, but at least they are familiar.

Problems with many today's application logs are truly staggering: logs are often simply missing, critical details are omitted, no standard form or content are anywhere to be found. On top of this, many security practitioners had to deal with debugging logs masquerading as security audit logs.

Table 2.3 illustrates the key difference between two types of application logs.

While debugging logs are present in application frameworks more frequently than well-designed security audit logs, using them for investigations often presents an exercise in frustration since key details needed for incident response and forensics might not be recorded in debug logs. Chapter 18 provides more detail on this topic.

Ideal Logging Scenario

So if we could have logging just the way we wanted it, what information we would like to see in logs and how should it be presented?

Table 2.3 Logging and Timing Issues

	Audit Logs	Debug Logs
Intended consumer	Security, audit	System operator, developer
Condition for logging	Always on	Sometimes on
Content of log messages	Attacks, activities, faults	Faults, failures, errors
Scope of what should be logged	Known in advance	Not known
Time scope	Useful for years	Useful for hours/days

Table 2.4 Critical Versus Accounting Logs	
Critical log / "act now"	**Accounting log / "keep in mind"**
Faults that can affect system operations	System status messages
Attacks that are successful	Attack attempts and probes
Attacks that have a high chance of being successful	Low impact attacks
System reaching capacity or maximum of some value	System reaching a relatively high value of some parameter
System changes possibly leading to security and availability problems	Various system changes
System crash	System startup/shutdown
Failed login	Successful login
Hardware failure	Hardware status message
Security-relevant configuration change	Routine and automated configuration change
Unauthorized connection detected	Connection established/terminated

We would like to see only the stuff we need to know about at the moment, no more—no less. Of course this is a pipe dream, so we will settle for having more information than that—events of various severities so that log analysts can make a decision based on the circumstances.

On a high-level, we would prefer to separate information into two categories: Deal with now (urgent), and deal with later (not urgent). The first is a high priority log that is clear and actionable. Wherever an entry is added to that log, it should be conveyed to the operator or analyst for immediate action. There should also be no confusion about what action to take.

The second log contains records that don't necessarily require immediate action. These events will, however, provide important information when summarized, over time, or for auditing or forensic analysis.

To summarize, we would like to see:

Table 2.4 is not a comprehensive list, but it gives an idea of things that ideally should be logged and how. It is possible to come up with more than two priority levels, but the concept continues to the be same. In fact, in reality there are usually at least three, the third being the "ignore" log—messages that are useless or unimportant.

SUMMARY

This chapter introduced the reader to general concepts log files, audit trails, and other log related things.

- Logs come in all shapes and forms, but you can look at the similarly by looking at the common denominators in them.
- There's a big difference between what logs actually contain and what we would like the to contain, which make log analysis a challenge.

In addition to that very basic conclusion—YOU MUST LOG!—we have to remind our readers that the importance of logging will ONLY GROW. In particular, the need to analyze application behavior for security issues across distributed and also cloud-based application calls for us to finally get logging under control.

Software architects and developer need to "get" logging—there is NO other way since infrastructure logging from network devices and operating systems won't cut it for detecting and investigating application level threats. Security teams will need to guide developers and architects tours useful and effective logging.

REFERENCES

Common event expression. Web, September 26, 2011. <http://cee.mitre.org/docs/CEE_Architecture_Overview-v0.5.pdf>.

Event log monitoring, event log management, syslog monitoring. Web, September 26, 2011. <http://www.prismmicrosys.com/EventSourceNewsletters-July10.php>.

Log analysis mailing list "World Domination" thread. <http://lists.jammed.com/loganalysis/2002/08/0012.html>.

Some error messages and problems with DNS. <http://www.reedmedia.net/misc/dns/errors.html>).

Syntax resources on the web. <http://www.utexas.edu/courses/linguistics/resources/syntax/>.

Log Data Sources

INFORMATION IN THIS CHAPTER:

- Logging Sources
- Log Source Classification

INTRODUCTION

The first step of the log analysis process is to understand what a log source is. Some applications and systems log by default, some do not. In some cases, the application may be sending log data, but there is nothing to receive it. In this chapter, we are going to show how to get basic logging enabled for systems and applications. Since the default settings for some applications/systems are not necessarily sufficient, we are also going to show how you can improve the quality of your logs by tuning application settings. And in a few cases, we show tools that you can use to augment the logs with information not provided by the application. The overall goal is to provide examples that will help get you thinking about how you can set up logging in your environment and also augment what you already have.

LOGGING SOURCES

We'll first look at various logging systems and the format of the data they collect. Log sources fall into two general categories:

Push-based.

Pull-based.

With push-based log sources, the device or application emits a message either to local disk or over the network. If it's over the network, you must have a log collector ready to receive this message. The three main push-based sources are

CONFIGURATION

Configuring Log Data Sources
This chapter will provide an example syslog configuration for Unix. We will not provide examples of different log source types. The reason being is most log sources will either have ample documentation provided by the vendor or, in the case of open source log sources, Google searches can provide guidance on configuring such tools.

Syslog, SNMP, and the Windows Event Log. These are protocols over which log message are transmitted. Technically, the Windows Event Log encompases the protocol, transport mechanism, storage, and retrieval.

With pull-based, an application pulls the log message from the source. This method almost always relies on a client-server model. Most systems which operate in this manner store their log data in some proprietary format. For example, Checkpoint offers the OPSEC C library which developers can use to write applications to pull Checkpoint firewall logs. Other products use databases like MSSQL, Oracle, MySQL, etc. to store their data. Pulling logs from a database is somewhat easy and can be done in a script or program.

Let's take a look at the three most common log source protocols. Up first is a look at the syslog protocol.

Syslog

You have already seen syslog message examples in Chapters 1 and 2. This section is more about the protocol itself. Syslog is used on Unix system by the kernel and many applications for logging messages. Syslog was originally built for collecting debugging information. As a result, it has some limitations that are not optimal for security log analysis. Regardless, syslog has become the most common method of recording application events on UNIX based systems.

Syslog consists of the syslog daemon (syslogd). It is normally started and stopped at boot and shutdown, respectively. Applications communicate with syslogd via the syslog(3) library calls. Syslogd receives log records from applications and the kernel via a Unix domain socket. Syslogd can also optionally receive data from remote hosts via UDP messages on port 514. Modern versions and syslog replacements such as rsyslog and syslog-ng also work with TCP.

Syslogd behavior is controlled by a configuration file, usually /etc/syslog.conf. The daemon reads log messages from the Unix domain socket /dev/log (the name may vary between flavors of Unix/Linux), and writes to one or more output files or forwards the logs via UDP to a collection host. Changes to the configuration file require sending a SIGHUP to the syslogd process to re-read the new configuration.

Syslogd is normally started at boot time, but to start it manually, just run "syslogd." Standard arguments to syslogd allow specifying the location of the configuration file, the "mark interval" (explained below), whether or not to accept data from the network, and the path to the Unix domain socket. The particular names for the options vary with different flavors of Unix/Linux. For instance, Linux uses "-r" to enable accepting logs from other hosts ("remote"), whereas OSX uses "-u" for the same thing. Some versions of syslogd accept remote messages automatically, without requiring any command-line arguments. These options usually have default values, the command-line arguments are used to override the defaults. Consult your local man page for information specific to your operating system.

The content of the default syslogd configuration file (/etc/syslog.conf) also varies between distributions. Most configurations do not log everything by default, and some log different things to different files. You should always examine the syslog configuration file to determine if it is logging the things you want it to log.

Basic Logging with syslogd

So, how to get started logging with syslogd? We recommend a simple approach: log everything to a single file on the local host (we'll talk much later on about whether or not logging everything is a good idea in the long run). Logging everything to a single file has two advantages. First, you can browse one file and see what's being logged. And if you don't know what's being logged, how are you going to make decisions on what should be logged where, anyways? Second, since later we're going to be forwarding this message to a central loghost, the local copy remains for troubleshooting and backup purposes.

To get everything logged in one file, put this in syslog.conf (the meaning and syntax of this is explained later):

```
*.debug      /var/log/messages
```

You can use a different pathname if you like, this is the one we're going to use as an example. If you do, you may have to create the (empty) file before syslog will write to it (we'll say more about that later in the chapter).

You can comment out other lines in the file, to avoid redundantly writing the same information to more than one file. Place a "#" in front of the lines that you want to comment out or disable.

Use ps to get the process-ID of your syslog daemon (syslogd)

```
# ps -ef | grep syslog
root  3344  1 0 Oct20 ?        00:00:01 syslogd -m 0
```

send a SIGHUP to the process:

```
kill -HUP 3344
```

and look in the file /var/log/messages. You should see a message like this:

```
Oct 23 17:08:22 somehost syslogd 1.4.1: restart.
```

possibly followed by (a lot of) other messages. Voila! You are now recording everything that is being sent to the syslog daemon. It is important to note that on some versions of Unix, the syslog daemon does not listen for incoming requests from remote systems by default. This means that remote systems that have application that can emit Syslog log messages will not be able to log to a central place, i.e. a central log server. In most cases a special flag will need to be passed to the syslog daemon at startup. Recall that on most flavors of Linux this is the −r option, while OS-X uses a −u option. Consult your syslog daemon's manual to be certain.

Soon we'll discuss what the messages that you are seeing in your log file mean. But right now we're going to explain what you just did from a configuration standpoint.

Syslog Message Classification

Syslog messages have two attributes used by syslogd to decide how to route them: a facility and a priority. The facility is intended to give a general classification of where the message was generated. The priority ...

The facility is one of a fixed set—you can't make up your own facility and just start using it. The set of facilities you can use are:

auth	Non-sensitive authentication information. On Linux, the name "security" can also be used.
Authpriv	Sensitive authentication information (things that you might not want in a generally readable log file)
Cron	Cron activity
Daemon	Messages from any daemon
Kern	Messages generated by the kernel
Lpr	Messages from the printing system
Mail	Messages from the mail transport agent
Mark	Internal messages generated at a regular interval
News	Messages from the Usenet news system
Syslog	Messages from the syslog daemon
User	Messages from command-line utilities (e.g. logger)

| Uucp | Messages from the uucp system |
| local0 through local7 | Messages from "custom" applications. Intended for things like in-house applications. |

The names of these facilities vary slightly between different Unix/Linux distributions, and some OSes have a few categories that the others don't. For example, OS-X also has a facility called "install." Solaris 9 does not have the "syslog" or "authpriv" facilities. Consult your man pages for your operating system.

Note that the application programmer chooses the facility, and there are no restrictions on the choice. A programmer could choose to use the mail facility or the kern facility, even if her programs were neither a mail program nor a kernel program.

The "Mark" Facility

There is one special facility called "mark." This facility is used internally by syslog, which generates a mark message at regular intervals like the following:

```
Oct 23 17:54:00 somehost -- MARK -
```

The purpose of the mark facility is to verify that the syslog daemon is working even if no messages have been received by it. Mark messages are useful for monitoring whether a system is up and running, and for determining when a host has crashed—you use the time of the last mark message before the crash to determine (approximately) the time of failure.

The default interval, if not specified on the command line, is twenty minutes, but some distributions have startup scripts which turn off the mark messages completely (with a mark interval of zero).

Syslog Priority

The priority of a message is ostensibly to indicate the importance of a message. The set of available priorities is (in increasing order of severity):

- debug.
- info.
- notice.
- warn.
- err.
- crit.
- alert.
- emerg.

Again, the priority attached to any given event is chosen by the application programmer, so there are no guarantees that the severity is actually meaningful.

The practical application of the combination of facility and priority is that it is used by the syslog daemon for a rudimentary form of filtering of messages. This filtering is specified in the syslog.conf file.

Syslog.conf

The syslog.conf file contains one or more lines with the following format

<selector>... <tab> ... <action>

The <selector> specifies which types of messages to which the given line applies, and <action> specifies what to do with that message.

The <selector> is a combination of a facility and a priority separated by a period, e.g. daemon.debug. A given selector will match all messages of that facility at the specified priority or higher. This means that kern.info matches kern.info up though kern.crit (or whatever the highest priority is). Traditional syslog does not allow you to specify only a single priority to match, only the lowest priority to match. Multiple facilities can be given for a single priority by separating them with commas, e.g. daemon,lpr.debug specifies both daemon.debug and lpr.debug. "*" can be used in place of a facility name to specify all facilities. Multiple selectors can be given on the same line by separating them with a ";", e.g. daemon,info;mail.crit. Finally, the keyword "none" can be given as a priority, which negates any previous selectors on the same line, which can be used with a wildcard to select everything except a particular facility, e.g. *.info;mail.none" will select everything at the info priority, except for messages for the mail facility.

The selector and the action are separated by the <tab> character. While newer versions of syslogd will accept <space> in addition to <tab>, older versions die a rather ugly death if <space> is found on the line.

The action taken for a selector can be one of three things: append the message to a file or a pipe, forward the message to syslogd on another host, and/or write the message to a user's terminal.

The most common action used is to append the message to a file, by specifying the full path to the file. For example:

```
mail.debug  /var/log/mail.log
```

On many versions of syslogd, the file has to already exist for syslogd to write to it; syslogd will not create the file if it does not exist. If the file does not exist, you can create the file with `touch <filename>` or if you prefer, `cp /dev/null <filename>` (the advantage of using `touch` is that <filename> will not be destroyed if it already exists, which is useful for shell scripts).

The same action can be used to write messages to devices. The most common example is to write to the system console (/dev/console). In ancient times, consoles were actually hardcopy terminals (e.g. decwriters), and "important" messages would be written to the console so that when the system crashed, the administrators could go look at the printout and try and deduce what was happening at the time of the crash. Of course, in those days, systems were much slower, and fewer services were running, so the amount of information printed on the console was manageable. Plus, in those days, disks were expensive, and paper was relatively inexpensive.

Forwarding log messages to another host is done by giving a hostname with "@" prepended to it as the action, e.g.

```
*.info    @loghost.mydomain
```

The loghost may be a hostname or an IP address. The advantage of specifying an IP address is that messages will be forwarded even if DNS is not working when the syslog daemon is started. Messages to the remote host are sent via UDP, and no response is expected, so a failure of the remote host will not prevent syslogd from running on the local host (this is both good and bad, we will discuss it more below).

Finally, the third possible action is to write the message to a user's terminal. The user, of course, must be logged in for the message to appear. This is done by just specifying the username in the action, e.g.:

```
kern.crit              kjs
```

This example will cause all kernel messages of priority crit and higher to be written to any tty owned by anton. Note that this action should be used judiciously, sending *.debug to user "anton" will probably make anton rather unhappy. Messages can be sent to all users by specifying "*" as the action. This special case is usually reserved for very critical events, normally those which indicate an impending system crash, e.g.:

```
kern.emerg      *
```

Some syslog daemons have additional features which can be controlled through the configuration file. For example, some syslogds allow you to limit from which hosts the loghost will accept syslog messages. We recommend you Read the Fine Man page for your system(s) to find out what extra features you might have.

The Mark Interval
As we mentioned above, the frequency of the "mark" message can usually be set as a command-line argument, with a granularity of one minute. The default is usually twenty minutes. There are trade-offs in determining the "right"

interval for mark messages. A small value such as one minute will give you pretty precise timing as to when a host (or at least, the syslog daemon) is up or down. However, if you have thousands of hosts sending mark messages to your central loghost every minute, you're going to have an awful lot of traffic on your network just for those messages. But you'll probably want to have some mark interval, so that you can verify that syslog is actually working.

Syslogd Output

Syslogd writes messages as ASCII text, terminated with newlines. So no special viewer is needed for reading the files, any text viewer will work. However, we do not recommend using "vi" or any other editor for examining the log files. For one thing, log files can get really big, and your editor may very well choke on them. But more importantly, reading log files with a text editor creates the risk that you'll inadvertently modify the log file, which can be a big no-no if you need the log data for legal or business purposes. And it's good system administration practice to not use a text editor on a file unless you intend to modify the file.

The Syslog Protocol

For many years, the standard RFC for the Syslog protocol was RFC3194 (http://www.ietf.org/rfc/rfc3164.txt). Now RFC5424 (http://tools.ietf.org/search/rfc5424) is the new proposed draft standard for the Syslog protocol. In other words, RFC5424 obsoletes RFC3194.

RFC5424 is a much-needed revamp of the older Syslog protocol. One of the biggest changes to the protocol is the specification of timestamps that adhere to RFC3339 (http://tools.ietf.org/search/rfc3339). The older protocol didn't specify much in the way of a timestamps. If you were lucky the log message you received contained the bare minimum of month, day, hour and, second. Typically there was no year in the timestamp and time zone information was nonexistent. This made it very difficult from an analysis standpoint. RFC5424 also adds structured data such as name=value pairs to syslog which promises to dramatically simplify automated log analysis.

We encourage you to review the RFCs presented and get a basic feel for what the protocol is and has to offer.

SNMP

SNMP was designed to meet the growing needs of network managers. Since the early 1990s, SNMP has been integrated into almost every network-able system you can think of, including many network security systems. SNMP is a protocol for querying and configuring devices. SNMP traps and notifications are a particular type of SNMP message which is generated by a device when a particular event occurs. While the SNMP protocol as a whole is not a logging system, SNMP traps or notifications can be considered types of log messages. While many network devices are capable of sending event information via syslog, some are not, especially some older devices, thus SNMP traps and notifications are a method of getting event information from devices which you otherwise could not collect. And in some cases, the type of information sent via SNMP is different than that sent over Syslog.

There are multiple versions of SNMP, versions 1, 2, and 3, commonly known as SNMPv1, SNMPv2, and SNMPv3. Covering SNMP in fine detail is beyond the scope of this book, so we'll just focus on traps/notifications, gets and sets. The following sections introduce these topics, but first we need to discuss the concept of managers and agents.

Managers and Agents

SNMP managed devices are typically controlled by a network management station (NMS). The NMS polls devices periodically, querying for status information, sends configuration changes as necessary. The NMS also listens for traps or notifications. In this manner, the NMS functions similarly to a centralized log collector. The primary reason to support SNMP is so log events can be exported to traditional NMS's like HP's OpenView. But they can also be exported to log collection systems.

The exact manner of configuring SNMP traps varies with each device. This document at the following link describes in more detail how to configure all aspects of SNMP on IOS 12: http://www.cisco.com/en/US/docs/ios/12_2/configfun/configuration/guide/fcf014.html.

This document is a good mix of general introduction to SNMP as well as practical guide to configuring SNMP which, while geared toward IOS, is general enough that it can be used as a guide to other systems.

As with syslog, something has to be listening for the SNMP traps. The receiver can be a NMS, or you can run some SNMP daemon on your favorite flavor of Unix. Net-SNMP is the most popular open source SNMP toolkit. It is comprised of useful command-line tools and an SNMP trap daemon (snmpd) which runs on most flavors of Unix and Windows. The official Web site is http://www.net-snmp.org/

SNMP Traps and Notifications

SNMP traps are part of the SNMPv1 protocol. SNMP notifications are part of the SNMPv2 and SNMPv3 protocols. The key difference between traps and notifications is that notifications include the ability for the receiver to send an acknowledgement back to the sender. The device has to be configured to generate the message, including which events generate messages, and where to send the messages.

As with Syslog, SNMP is implemented over UDP, and thusly suffers from the same reliability issues as Syslog. In 2002, CERT found vulnerabilities with many commercial implementations of SNMP. Today this is largely a forgotten issue, and vendors have tried to put their best foot forward in addressing these security issues. But it is nonetheless worthwhile to be aware of its existence. SNMPv2 notifications allow for an acknowledgement to be sent back from the receiver, at least providing more reliable message delivery than unidirectional UDP messages.

Also as with syslog, SNMPv1 traps are sent in clear text and are not authenticated. They are therefore subject to the same types of spoofing attacks. SNMPv2 notifications are also sent in clear text. SNMPv3 has optional authentication of messages, which protects against spoofing attacks at the cost of some CPU cycles at both the sender and receiver.

SNMP Get

The SNMP protocol allows for a *get* operation which allows you to retrieve information from a device or system. What exactly can you get? This varies greatly depending on what the device in question has implemented. For example, routers will track things like bytes sent and received for each interface. Operating systems will often allow you to get information on CPU usage, memory usage, etc. It is possible for you to get information from a device or system which can aid you in log analysis. But, in reality, this is neither practical nor a reality. In the network management world there is a concept called *trap-directed polling*. This means that when you receive an SNMP trap of some sort, you initiate a poll of the device using an SNMP get to retrieve additional information to further correlate or validate the trap you just received. But, in general, security devices which send traps do just that: they send traps but don't track anything which can be "gotten."

SNMP Set

For completeness we will briefly discuss the SNMP *set*. As its name implies, the SNMP set allows you to change the value of something on a remote system. For example, network bridges implement a certain specification which allows you to use and SNMP set to turn a switch port up and down. In order to do this you need to know the MAC address of the host attached to the particular port.

Issues with SNMP as a Log Data Alternative

As mentioned earlier, one big problem with Syslog messages is that there is no standardized format. This means that vendor ABC's log messages will more than likely be different than vendor XYZ's. With SNMP, however, the situation is only slightly better. SNMP makes use of what is called a MIB, or Management Information Base. At a high level this is a definition of, among other things, which traps or notifications a particular system supports. The following is a notification from the Snort MIB:

```
sidaAlertGeneric NOTIFICATION-TYPE
    OBJECTS { sidaSensorVersion,
        sidaSensorAddressType, sidaSensorAddress,
        sidaAlertTimeStamp, sidaAlertActionsTaken,
        sidaAlertMsg,
        sidaAlertMoreInfo, sidaAlertSrcAddressType,
        sidaAlertSrcAddress, sidaAlertDstAddressType,
        sidaAlertDstAddress, sidaAlertSrcPort,
        sidaAlertDstPort, sidaAlertImpact,
        sidaAlertEventPriority, sidaAlertSrcMacAddress,
        sidaAlertDstMacAddress }
    STATUS current
    DESCRIPTION
        "The Sida Alert Generic Trap is sent whenever an
        event is detected by snort (rules) and no specific
        Alert is found applicable."
    ::= { sidaAlertTypes 1 }
```

It's not important to look at the details of the structure and meaning of this notification. We just want to give a general idea of what SNMP is about. One thing to point out is the OBJECTS section of the definition. These are the individual event details that will be sent in the notification. For example, the sidaSensorVersion is defined in the same MIB as:

```
sidaSensorVersion OBJECT-TYPE
    SYNTAX SnmpAdminString
    MAX-ACCESS read-only
    STATUS current
    DESCRIPTION
    " the version number of the sensor that detected the event."
    ::= { sidaSensorEntry 3}
```

This gives us an idea of what this particular detail may look like, in this case it's a string that represents the version of Snort which reported the notification.

Unfortunately, even though MIBs provide a strong framework for providing well formatted, understandable messages, vendors rarely provide such. There are a number of ways in which vendors screw it up. For example, the MIB may not match up with the actual trap or notification sent by the device or system. Or, changes are made to the underlying SNMP implementation, and the MIB is not updates and quickly gets out of sync. Then when end users like us go to use the MIB to figure out what the traps might look like, they are at best confused, if not completely misled.

Finally, instead of spending time creating a MIB much like the Snort one above, a vendor will create a trap that sends a single variable in the trap, as a free-form text string. The result is equally difficult to parse as Syslog messages. In fact, many vendors just take the exact same message they would send as a Syslog message and wrapper it in an SNMP trap.

So SNMP may not be the best thing for collecting log information, but it may be the only way to get it from some devices.

The Windows Event Log

Microsoft decided a long time ago to invent their own log sourcing and collection system. This system is called the Event Log. It has evolved over the years and has been around almost as long as Windows. Today's Event Log has some advanced features. The Event Log is used to collect and review primarily two types of logs:

Windows Logs.

Application Logs.

Windows Logs encompasses at least Application, Security, and System. Of importance is the Security log. This is where logons, logoffs, resource access (shares, files, etc.) are logged. The Application Logs are pretty self-explanatory. Applications can write to this log to relay status, errors, and other noteworthy items.

Let's take a quick look at an Event Log. To launch the viewer you can run by going here: Control Panel->System and Security->Administrative Tools->View Event Logs. This brings up the Event Viewer. Figure 3.1 shows the viewer.

On the left pane of the window are the various log message types. In the middle are the actual log message for the type you have selected (in this case Security). Below the log message in the middle are the details for the log message. If you double-click the log message, you will get a pop-up message similar to that in Figure 3.2.

Figure 3.2 shows details of the log message you selected. Depending on the type of log message you will see things like the following:

Event Id (4624 in Figure 3.2).
Account name.
Domain.
Resource (in the case of file or directory access).
Status (was the request successful or not).

While what the built-in log viewer shows you is great, http://eventid.net/ is a resource you can use to get more insight into what a given event means. If you have the Event Id you can use this Web site to pull up more detail on the event. Figure 3.3 is a snippet from this Web site for the Event Id 4624.

As you can see, there is more content beyond that found in the actual log detail in Figure 3.2.

Chapters 8 and 15 discuss the Windows Event Viewer in terms of ease of management of this invaluable resource.

LOG SOURCE CLASSIFICATION

The following sections provide examples of applications and systems which generate log data.

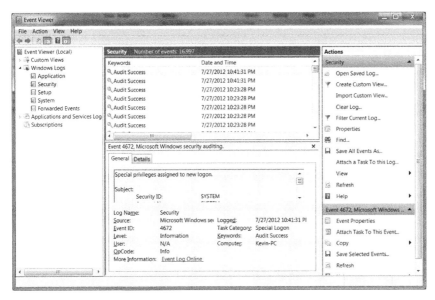

FIGURE 3.1 Windows Event Viewer

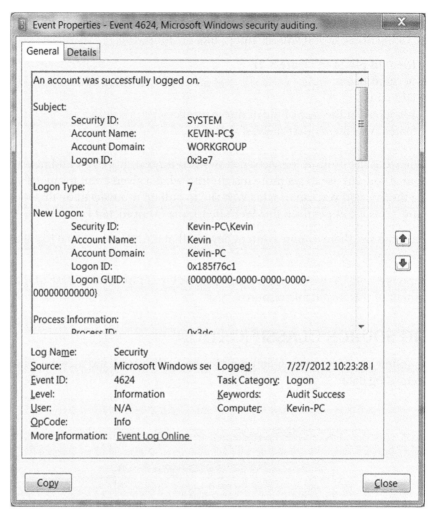

FIGURE 3.2 Event Detail For Event 4624

Security-Related Host Logs

This category covers host logs produced by operating system components, various network services logs as well as other applications running on the system. While many of the messages are only or primarily produced for performance tracking, audit or troubleshooting reasons, a vast majority of them is also useful for security.

Operating System Logs

Operating systems log an amazing variety of messages. Let's review some of the security relevant types of messages produced by the operating systems:

```
Event ID: 4624

Source: Microsoft-Windows-Security-Auditing

Type: Success Audit

Description:
An account was successfully logged on.

Subject:
Security ID: NULL SID
Account Name: -
Account Domain: -
Logon ID: 0x0

Logon Type: 3

New Logon:
Security ID: SYSTEM
Account Name: JDOE$
Account Domain: CONTOSO
Logon ID: 0x2b5a1cc
Logon GUID: {8d290146-94c0-cb12-53e0-fc3f3e7fa143}

Process Information:
Process ID: 0x0
Process Name: -

Network Information:
Workstation Name:
Source Network Address: ::1
Source Port: 54076

Detailed Authentication Information:
Logon Process: Kerberos
Authentication Package: Kerberos
Transited Services: -
Package Name (NTLM only): -
Key Length: 0

This event is generated when a logon session is created. It is generated on the computer that was accessed.

The subject fields indicate the account on the local system which requested the logon. This is most commonly a service such as
the Server service or a local process such as Winlogon.exe or Services.exe.

The logon type field indicates the kind of logon that occurred. The most common types are 2 (interactive) and 3 (network).

The New Logon fields indicate the account for whom the new logon was created i.e. the account that was logged on
```

FIGURE 3.3 Windows Event Viewer

■ Authentication: user logged, failed to log and so on.

Example (Linux syslog):

```
Jan 2 08:44:54 ns1 sshd2[23661]: User anton, coming from 65.211.15.100,
    authenticated.
```

This example is a Linux syslog line related to remote user authenticating with Secure Shell (SSH) daemon:

■ System startup, shutdown, and reboot.

Example (Linux syslog):

```
Nov 4 00:34:08 localhost shutdown: shutting down for system reboot
```

This example is a Linux syslog line related to system shutdown:

■ Service startup, shutdown and status change.

Example (Solaris syslog):

```
Nov 5 13:13:24 solinst sendmail[412]: [ID 702911 mail.info] starting
    daemon (8.11.6+Sun): SMTP+queueing@00:15:00
```

This example is a Linux syslog line related to sendmail daemon starting up:

■ Service crash.

Example (Linux syslog):

```
Jan 3 12:20:28 ns1 ftpd: service shut down
```

This example is a Linux syslog line related to FTP server shutting down involuntarily (it might be due to a crash or a kill command):

■ Miscellaneous status messages.

Example (Linux syslog):

```
Nov 20 15:45:59 localhost ntpd[1002]: precision = 24 usec
```

This example is a Linux syslog line related to a time synchronization daemon (NTPD)

Overall, the operating system messages are considered security-relevant for two main reasons:

1. They are useful for *intrusion detection*, since successful and failed attacks often leave unique traces in the logs. Host intrusion detection systems (HIDS) and security information and event management systems (SIEMs) collect the messages and can make judgments about the past and upcoming (in case of seeing traces of attacker's reconnaissance activity in logs) threats.
2. They are also useful for *incident response*, (see Chapter 16) since successful attacks will happen despite the presence of various security safeguards. As we noted in many chapters, logs are paramount for incident response since they allow the investigators to "piece together" the disjoint pieces of the intrusion puzzle.

Network Daemon Logs

Network daemons usually log security-relevant messages of the following categories:

■ Connection established to the service.

Example (Linux syslog):

```
Dec 26 06:45:14 ns1 popper[14251]: (v4.0.5) POP login by user "anton"
  at (10.192.17.92) 10.192.17.92
```

This message from a Linux syslog shows a successful connection to a POP3 mail daemon by a remote user "anton."

■ Connection failed to server.

Example (Linux syslog):

```
Dec 28 01:54:16 ns1 xinetd[14923]: FAIL: telnet libwrap
  from=210.93.83.28
```

This message from a Linux syslog shows a connection failure (due to access controls) to a telnet service.

■ Connection was established, but access was not allowed.

Example (Linux syslog):

```
Dec 13 08:45:00 ns1 sshd2[18120]: connection lost: 'Connection closed.'
```

This message from a Linux syslog shows an unsuccessful connection to the Secure Shell server.

■ Various failure messages.

Example (Linux syslog):

```
Dec 26 06:47:12 ns1 sendmail[14259]: iBQBkZc14259: lost input channel
  from [10.8.206.4] to MTA after rcpt
```

This message from a Linux syslog shows a failure of a sendmail daemon to continue talking to a client (likely a spam program).

■ Various status messages.

Example (Linux syslog):

```
Dec 26 06:47:12 ns1 sendmail[14259]: iBQBkZc14259: from=<cqywejwywwno@
  fghjgh.com>, size=0, class=0, nrcpts=2, proto=SMTP, daemon=MTA,
  relay=[10.10.206.4]
```

This message from a Linux syslog indicates a successful Email tranfer.

The network daemon logs are usually as useful as the general operating system logs. In fact, they are commonly logged to the same place; for example, on Unix and Windows the same logging mechanism is commonly used.

Network daemons present of the most common entryways into the system remotely and many of the attacks are targeted against them. Thus, having robust logging is crucial in this environment.

Application Logs

Applications also log an amazing variety of messages. We can boil down the types of things applications log to a single list:

- Application user activity.
- Privileged user activity.
- Routine but critical activity.
- Reconfiguration.

Security-Related Network Logs

This category covers network logs generated by network infrastructure. Routers and switches generate an amazing variety of log messages, which are related to their operation as well as traffic passing through them.

Network Infrastructure Logs

Network infrastructure includes routers, switches and other devices that comprise networks and tie desktops and servers together. Logs from such devices play a critical role in security.

The most common messages fall into the following categories:

- Logins and logouts.
- Connection established to the service.
- Bytes transferred in and out.
- Reboots.
- Configuration changes.

Security Host Logs

This category covers host logs from applications with a security mission running on a host for protection. Unlike the above logs that might or might not be relevant to security in each specific case, these security logs are always interesting since they relate to attacks, intrusions, compromises infections, etc. However, in many cases the security gear will be lying to you, producing false alarms of various types (such as the well-known "false positives.")

Host Intrusion Detection and Prevention

Host intrusion detection systems (HIDS) and intrusion prevention systems (HIPS) definition and mission have evolved since early 1990s when the first commercial systems of that type were introduced. By the way, the first systems actually looked at logs and tried to apply intrusion trace signatures to those logs. The HIDS mission was extended to also watch for file systems changes and other unauthorized system modifications.

Nowadays, such systems detect and block a wide variety of network, operating system and application attacks. While HIDS only alert, HIPS can also block attacks based on signatures, dynamic rules or other mechanisms.

Most of the event records generated by such systems are related to:

- Reconnaissance or probe detected.
- Changes to executable files.

Example (Dragon HIDS):

```
2002-10-11|10:38:38|labdragon-hids|FTP:NESSUS-
PROBE|0.0.0.0|146.127.94.13|0|0|I||0|target:146.127.94.13,file:messages|
```

This message from a Dragon host sensor (formerly known as Dragon Squire) shows a Nessus vulnerability scanner probe detected by watching the FTP log.

- Attack detected.

Example (Linux syslog):

```
Dec 26 06:47:12 ns1 sendmail[14259]: iBQBkZc14259: lost input channel
    from [10.8.206.4] to MTA after rcpt
```

This message from a Linux syslog shows:

- Attack detected and blocked.

Example (Linux syslog):

```
Dec 26 06:47:12 ns1 sendmail[14259]: iBQBkZc14259: lost input channel
    from [10.8.206.4] to MTA after rcpt
```

This message from a Linux syslog shows:

- Successful intrusion detected.

Example (Linux syslog):

```
Dec 26 06:47:12 ns1 sendmail[14259]: iBQBkZc14259: lost input channel
    from [10.8.206.4] to MTA after rcpt
```

This message from a Linux syslog shows:

- Insecure system reconfiguration or corruption.

Example (Dragon HIDS):

```
2002-10-11|10:32:11|labdragon-
hids|FILE:DELETED|0.0.0.0|146.127.94.13|0|0|I||0|target:146.127.94.13,f
ile:/etc/inetd.conf|
```

This message from a Dragon host sensor (formerly known as Dragon Squire) shows a critical system file deletion alert.

- Authentication or authorization failed.

Example (Dragon HIDS):

```
2002-10-11|10:38:38|labdragon-hids|LOGIN-
FAILED|0.0.0.0|146.127.94.13|0|0|I||0|target:146.127.94.13,file:messag
es|
```

SUMMARY

This chapter covered a lot of ground. The focus was on presenting concepts by way of example. The ideas presented in this chapter are by no means exhaustive. They are meant to give you a basis for what is possible so you can go on to solve problems in your own environment.

Log Storage Technologies

INFORMATION IN THIS CHAPTER:

- Log Retention Policy
- Log Storage Formats
- Database Storage of Log Data
- Hadoop Log Storage
- The Cloud and Hadoop
- Log Data Retrieval and Archiving

INTRODUCTION

Storage of logs and being able to quickly retrieve and analyze logs is a critical issue within an organization. Log records retained by small- to medium-sized businesses can grow into the size of terabytes or petabytes of data very quickly. This data is stored in a variety of formats in an organization and we will explore the numerous retention strategies to match environmental and compliance needs.

LOG RETENTION POLICY

Developing a log retention policy will lay the groundwork for reviewing the retention topics covered in this chapter. The policy that you design for your organization will drive many of the decisions that will need to be made about the type of storage, size, cost, retrieval speed, and archive and destruction requirements for your log data.

We will go through a process of creating a retention strategy, based on the following factors explained below. A number of stakeholders from the security, compliance, and business management groups in your organization should be involved in the plan creation process to end up with a logical, useful, and appropriately scoped plan that will not be overly cost prohibitive, but still meet the needs of the organization. The following items should be reviewed when developing your log retention policy:

1. *Assess applicable compliance requirements:*

   ▪ There a number of robust compliance requirements placed on many industries today. Examples include the Payment Card Industry Data Security Standard (PCI DSS) with a very specific log retention period of one year, PCI DSS section 10.7 (PCI Security Standards Council, 2010); the North American Electric Reliability Corporation (NERC) rules mention specific times for specific types of logs; other regulations call for retention of specific types of logs but do not state a time period. This guidance helps lay the foundation and minimum requirements for a retention policy.

2. *Review the organization's risk posture:*

   ▪ Internal versus external risks drive the retention period for various parts of your network. The length of time and importance of the logs may vary wildly in each of these risk areas for an organization. Keep in mind that if you focus on using logs for investigating the internal threats, the retention period needs to be longer, as such incidents are often not discovered for years, but when discovered, cause an urgent need to "get to the bottom of it!"

3. *Look at various log sources and the size of the logs generated:*

   ▪ Firewalls, servers, databases, web proxies—not only based on need, but also on the typical log volume and the size and type of each log record generated. There is a wide variety on the volume of logs you will get from each type of device or application. For example, logs from the main firewalls will generate a massive volume of logs and as such should most likely only be stored for 30 days simply due to the storage requirements of long-term retention of this log data. However, an organization's compliance needs, such as PCI DSS, and the criticality of the main firewall should be closely evaluated to determine if a longer retention period is required. Also you may have log sources that produce logs that you don't have the tools necessary to analyze the logs, like custom applications and unsupported operating systems.

4. *Review available storage options:*

   ▪ Log storage options range from disks, DVDs, WORMs, tape, RDBMS, log-specific storage, and cloud-based storage. A decision on this is mostly about price, capacity, and speed of access and—what is VERY important is the ability to get to the right log records in a reasonable period of time. Tape is known to be a cheap option, but is notorious for its inability to efficiently search the stored records and may require human intervention to locate the proper tape and restore the data for analysis. The longevity of the media will need to be considered here as well and how often the media should be rewritten to meet a retention period requirement. For example, seven years for cheap writable CDs or DVDs is probably a stretch. Technology formats age and the availability to purchase drives for reading tapes and disks may become scarce.

Table 4.1 is an example of an online business that focused most of the security strategy outwards.

Table 4.1 Example Retention Policy for an Online Business (Chuvakin, 2011)

Type	Network	Storage Tier	Retention Period
Intrusion Prevention System (IPS)	Demilitarized Zone (DMZ)	Online	90 days
Firewall	Demilitarized Zone (DMZ)	Online	30 days
Servers	Internal	Online	90 days
All	Demilitarized Zone (DMZ)	Archive	3 years
Critical	Internal	Archive	5 years
Other	Internal	Archive	1 year

The retention time and the space requirements to retain the logs in an organization can be overwhelming at first. The rest of this chapter will review the types of log formats that will be encountered and strategies to maintain and store log files in accordance with the policy for your organization.

LOG STORAGE FORMATS

In this section, we will cover a number of log storage formats. Our network devices, applications, and operating systems produce a multitude of different formats and in many cases the logs will be stored in a text-based, binary, or compressed format.

Text-Based Log Files

Text-based logging is the most abundant type of log found due to low cost for systems to generate these types of logs and the inclusion of frameworks in many existing computer languages that ease the generation of text-based logs. The popularity and abundance of systems that log to text-based files is a result of the many benefits to this format.

Benefits:

- It is a very inexpensive operation in terms of CPU and I/O resources for an application to write to a text-based log file.
- The format is typically human readable and can be processed and reviewed with common text manipulation tools, such as grep and awk, that are native to many flavors of the Unix/Linux operating systems.
- A number of common text-based log formats exist, such as syslog, that ease operational and security team's ability to centralize and parse logs in a common way and create a more powerful log management system.

Flat Text Files

Flat text files are in many ways as the name implies, a flat schema-less file that may follow a common pattern or be free form. Typically a system will create a new log file and continue to append to this file as long as there is disk space or until a system process, like logrotate that we will discuss later, instructs the system to begin a new log file and archive the current one. This format tends to be in chronological order with the oldest events at the beginning of the file and the most current activity at the end.

One of the more common formats adopted by many systems is the syslog format. From Chapters 1, 2, and 3, we learned that many servers are configured to send their logs via syslog on port 514 utilizing the User Datagram Protocol (UDP) or Transmission Control Protocol (TCP). The logs sent via syslog exist on disk prior to being sent and have a very simple and specific format. The following is a typical syslog formatted log message:

```
May 1 00:14:54 Mac-mini kernel[0]: HFS: Very Low Disk: freeblks: 0,
    dangerlimit: 334
May 1 00:30:47 Mac-mini kernel[0]: add_fsevent: unable to get path for
    vp 0xffffff80154a3d10 (system.log; ret 22; type 4)
May 1 00:30:47 Mac-mini kernel[0]: add_fsevent: unabled to get a path
    for vp 0xffffff80154a3d10. dropping the event.
May 1 06:45:55 Mac-mini kernel[0]: IOSurface: buffer allocation size is
    zero
May 1 15:15:20 Mac-mini kernel[0]: 0 0 AppleUSBCDC: start - initDevice
    failed
May 1 15:15:20 Mac-mini kernel[0]: USBMSC Identifier (non-unique):
    000A2700229F4191 0x5ac 0x1266 0x1
```

A notable benefit of long-term storage of log data in flat text files is the abundance of tools to read and review data in this format. There are many tools on every platform that can easily access and read data in this format. This becomes an important feature if you will need to read and review the data 5,7, or 10

SYSLOG

Syslog is a very widely used logging format and is the defacto logging format across many systems including Unix/Linux. Though it is heavily used, it has not been formally standardized. Due to the lack of standardization, implementations may vary widely across systems and may make cross-platform correlation of events difficult in some environments. The more common use of syslog is the BSD syslog protocol and is defined at http://www.ietf.org/rfc/rfc3164.txt. Though not a true standard, this reference can be used to help correlate data across systems that adhere to this RFC.

years in the future and will need tools capable of processing and correlating events.

Indexed Flat Text Files

One of the limitations organizations quickly run into with flat text files is the ability to query, sort, and retrieve key elements from a flat text quickly to find meaningful trends across the platforms they are managing. Also, as the log files quickly grow into gigabytes, terabytes, and petabytes of data, using traditional grep, awk, and text-based search tools because an exercise in patience and quickly becomes a very time-intensive process.

Indexed flat text files are a way of organizing data from the log files so the key elements of the logs can be queried more quickly. Many organizations may start off adopting indexed flat text log files as their organizations grow and they begin centralizing their log information and quickly realize they need structure to generate reports and to aid in the destruction of log data once it has aged beyond the required retention period. Indexed flat files share many of the advantages of flat text files with quick data insertion and maintaining a human-readable format to the data.

An example of flat file indexing is a strategy used by a log retention utility which we will discuss in Chapter 15, OSSEC. OSSEC organizes logs it receives in the following directory structure:

```
/var/ossec/logs/alerts/2011
/var/ossec/logs/alerts/2011/Jan
/var/ossec/logs/alerts/2011/Feb
/var/ossec/logs/alerts/2011/Mar

...
```

From the structure, it is noted that logs are organized based on the year and month the log event was received. So if we wanted to review the web server logs from January 2011, we could go to the directory "/var/ossec/logs/alerts/2011/Jan" and begin using our analysis tools on the January logs.

There are also a number of utilities designed to generate indexes to speed the searching and analysis of logs. One of the more powerful utilities is Apache Lucene Core at http://lucene.apache.org/core/. Lucene is a Java-based framework that aids in the generation of indexes to enable full text search logging and integrating into utilities to aid in the searching and analysis of logs.

Binary Files

Binary log files as the name indicates are machine-readable log files that applications generate that require special utilities or tools to read and process them. Some examples of the more common binary log files you will encounter in environments are Microsoft Internet Information Server (IIS) logs and Windows Event logs. In many environments with mainframes or custom applications, the log files may also be encoded in binary or machine-specific formats like Extended Binary Coded Decimal Interchange Code (EBCDIC) that will need tools to decode them and read them on Intel and PC hardware platforms.

The long-term storage of binary log files will pose a number of challenges to your organization. Items to consider before storing and retaining binary log files in their native format are:

- The availability of tools to read the log files 5, 7, or 10 years in the future. It is probably highly unlikely that you will keep a Windows NT server around 10 years from now to read and perform forensics on your legacy IIS 6.0 web server logs!
- Binary log files tend to be efficient in terms of usage of disk space. However, they also do not compress well. Compressed binary files can occupy 90% of their original size. By contrast, text-based files may only occupy 10% of their original size when compressed. This may increase the storage space needs for binary files compared to text-based logging.

Compressed Files

Most of the systems that generate logs will typically begin a new log file once a log grows to a specific size, or a configured time period of daily, weekly, monthly, etc (Kent and Souppaya, 2006). The previous log file is typically renamed and archived on the system's disks in an uncompressed format so it can still be easily accessed and queried. As a log file ages, a log file becomes less relevant for day-to-day reports, and log review tasks, but is still critical for meeting the compliance retention period and in performing forensics. In many cases we will still want the log files to be quickly accessible, but with a smaller footprint on disk to save precious space for additional logging and other system process needs. Compressing the log files on the system is a mechanism that will address these needs and save precious disk space.

On Unix/Linux systems, there is a handy utility called logrotate that will help manage the number of log files you retain and additionally compress logs. The following shows an example configuration file for logrotate to rotate syslog messages. There is additional information on this utility for the reader at http://linuxcommand.org/man_pages/logrotate8.html: (Troan and Brown, 2002)

```
# sample logrotate configuration file
compress
/var/log/messages {
    rotate 5
    weekly
    postrotate
      /sbin/killall -HUP syslogd
    endscript
}
```

Let's review the settings and how they help us rotate, compress, and maintain our syslog events.

Table 4.2 Logrotate Settings, Example for Compressing and Retaining Syslog Messages (Chuvakin, 2011)

Setting	Configuration Value	Notes
Rotate	5	The setting will retain the latest five message files before removing the log files from the system.
Weekly	N/A	The log will be rotated once a week. Other options in logrotate are monthly and daily rotations.
postrotate / endscript	/sbin/killall-HUP syslogd	This allows a script to be run after log rotation occurs. In this example, we need to restart syslogd to get it to start a new log file.

Table 4.2 shows the analysis of logrotate configuration script.

Unix/Linux systems have compression toolset equivalents for many of the standard tools. The tools zgrep and zcat can read and retrieve data from compressed files just like their cousins grep and cat can work on uncompressed files. However, there are a number of tools that will not be able to work on compressed files natively. To utilize the full set of tools many times, the file will need to be decompressed and space should be allocated to meet this analysis need. To avoid obsolescence when choosing a compression format, it is good to pick a compression format that has several years of use and is available on multiple platforms. On Unix/Linux tar and zip formats have had a long history of use and PKZip format compression files are a common format on Windows. Just like with binary files, we want to limit the obsolesce of the toolsets used to decompress and access log data in the future.

DATABASE STORAGE OF LOG DATA

Many of the storage techniques discussed till this point require direct access to systems and specialized toolsets for log review. This is fast and efficient, but in many cases our ability to create summary reports, filter, and correlate log data across hosts is severely limited. Many organizations find that writing log information to a database is useful in opening access to stakeholders that need log information in a format that can be quickly searched and queried, and to facilitate the setup and use of front-end tools in the log review process.

Advantages

One of the primary advantages of using a database for log retention is the ease with which you can use standard SQL queries to search and retrieve log records quickly. Database systems have robust user access and permission systems for accessing data and may already be part of your organization's backup and recovery plan. Many standard tools exist to query databases. These tools allow log data to be queried via a common toolset to retrieve data rather than using platform-specific tools on each individual system that may require specialized knowledge and access. Built-in support in many programming languages for working with data in databases allows front-end tools to be developed for real-time viewing and analysis of log data. In chapter 15, we will discuss a number of tools that already have built-in support for writing directly to a database. This reduces the need to develop and maintain specialized in-house systems to load log data into a database. Also, this will aid in centralizing log data into a database system and a number of tools we explore in Chapter 15 already have tools that can be used for front-end analysis and review.

Disadvantages

Storing log information into a database system is not without its own set of issues and risks though. Writing log messages to a database comes at a significant cost. Writing data to the database will be significantly slower than writing to a local on disk text file due to network latency, database SQL parsing, index updates, and committing the information to disk. Disk space requirements for log storage will also be higher in a database due to the number of index files needed to perform fast search and retrieval, and the limited options available to compress the data in the database. Database systems are used for many purposes in an organization and are subject to the risk of data loss when there is a database outage, maintenance, or upgrade to support logging or other internal systems. When log entries are no longer needed based on our retention policy, data destruction can also be problematic. If not properly planned or partitioned, deleting log data can take a very long time. Log data is typically very large and log data destruction could instruct the database system to remove millions or billions or more rows individually and update all indexes for the removed data.

Defining Database Storage Goals

The key in avoiding a number of disadvantages we laid out is developing storage goals when moving data into a database. A plan should be defined to align the storage needs with the organization's log retention plan we discussed earlier in this chapter. A good plan upfront will reduce future maintenance outages, data restores and rebuilds, and deployment and operations resource needs in the future. We will review a number of critical areas to focus on in developing your database log storage plan.

What to Store?

A critical question in designing the storage of logs into a database is "What to store?" When using the database as the central repository and online tool for daily log review and analysis, you will want to retain all the log entries and log fields in the database. A number of syslog replacements in Chapter 15, rsyslog and syslog-ng, come with pre-built database schemas and configuration options to directly move syslog into database storage and store all the fields of the syslog message. You may need to write your own utilities and develop your own database schema for less common binary and application logs to maintain your log data in the database. Good analysis and an effort to retain all fields will avoid the situation in reviewing a critical system breach and realizing that there is critical information missing to do a full analysis.

In many organizations, the disadvantages of using a database as the primary log storage are too great from a log security or infrastructure perspective. It is also possible that the volume of data cannot be supported by the database infrastructure without impacting customers or other critical systems. A hybrid storage approach may work best in these situations where the original log data is retained on the source system or a centralized syslog server, but one or more of the following is stored in the database to facilitate analysis and reporting systems:

- Header Info—Typically includes the timestamp of an event and the IP addresses involved in the event. Storage of this information alone is useful in building trending information to determine hosts that are overreporting, underreporting, or linkages of event trends between systems.

- Body—Typically the message of the event. Storage of this information in a database system is useful in building a real-time alerting system. For example, seeing the same failed login message in high frequency could be queried and reported on quickly.
- Analysis and summary results—Custom scripts and tools may be in use on each system to determine trends and summarize results. Storage of this analysis in a central repository would ease reporting of event analysis across the enterprise and ease the development of centralized auditing and summary reports for an organization with lower overall database storage and scalability requirements.

Fast Retrieval

After defining what will be stored, some analysis and review will need to be done to optimize the database for fast retrieval of relevant data. A critical item will be to define the columns in the database that will be used for daily review or part of common queries for reporting and alerting. A recommended approach when storing syslog data would be to create database indexes on these common syslog fields:

- Priority—severity or relative importance of the message.
- Date and Time—indicate when an event occurred.
- Generating Host—system generating the event.
- Message—details on the event that occurred.

A recurring theme with log data is that the storage size will continue to grow. Even in a database that is indexed and optimized for your queries, searching over trillions and trillions of rows can become slow and cumbersome. Many database systems support partitioning. Partitioning allows a logically single database table to be split into smaller chunks. With log data, partitioning a database table based on date and time is a logical approach and will provide the following benefits:

- Improved data insertion speed as a smaller physical file will be appended to and smaller index files are updated on each insertion.
- Query performance can be improved for some queries as small chunks of data are reviewed and filtered by the database system.
- Bulk deletion can be accomplished by removing a data partition when a set of log data is beyond the retention period. This dramatically improves the destruction of log data over individual deletes in a single large database.

- Some systems allow seldom used partitions to be migrated to slower cheaper storage options.
- Individual partitions can be taken offline for database maintenance. This can allow the database to be maintained for optimal performance without affecting the insertion of new log data.

Reporting

Organizations will typically need to generate reports off of log data to support the auditing and review of log data with external auditors and internal stakeholders. Additional sets of reporting tables are usually necessary to allow reports to be generated quickly and on demand. These tables should include summary counts of key items relevant to the organization and can be calculated by backend processes on a timed basis to speed front-end tool data retrieval. Generating this information on the fly can take a significant amount of time and changes to the reporting structure can be expensive. The following are areas to consider generating summary reporting data on and should be included as possible additions to the storage system to facilitate reporting:

- Analysis results—these are typically a combination of log entries that indicate something interesting that needed to be reviewed or acted on.
- Number of events by severity per host—this can be useful in finding attack patterns in an organization or pinpointing trouble areas quickly.
- Time-based summary counts—many organizations will need to have a daily, weekly, or monthly report to share with the organization and rollup summaries counts based on these time periods will automate and speed up this reporting.
- Reporting based on network or device type—certain portions of your network may require different reporting needs or fall under different compliance frameworks. PCI is common use case where only payment card processing segment of the network may have special reporting and auditing needs. This requires additional reporting tables to support separate auditing requirements.

HADOOP LOG STORAGE

Many of the challenges with a traditional database are the scalability of the system as log data increases and spikes in activity require excess storage and system capacity. Hadoop is a relatively new alternative to a traditional database system. Traditional database systems are built utilizing fast high-end hardware with fast SAN storage to support a large number of simultaneous users and requests, and meet data storage needs. Hadoop systems by contrast are typically built utilizing commodity PC Intel hardware running Linux and a few terabytes of local storage on each node of a cluster of machines with no RAID. A Hadoop cluster consists of a few slave nodes and at least one master node. Additional space and capacity can be added by simply adding another node to the cluster. Companies like Yahoo and Facebook use Hadoop today to support their applications with petabytes of information quickly being processed and searched with end-user status updates and search queries.

Advantages

Hadoop shares many of the advantages of a traditional database system. Hadoop allows for the quick retrieval and searching of log data rather than using platform-specific query tools on each system. Hadoop scales well as data size grows by distributing search requests to cluster nodes to quickly find, process, and retrieve results. Hadoop is built primarily in Java and tools can be developed for real-time viewing and analysis of log data. Hadoop stores data as a structured set of flat files in Hadoop's Distributed File System (HDFS) across the nodes in the Hadoop cluster. This allows Hadoop to support faster data insertion rates than traditional database systems. Hadoop is also fault tolerant making multiple copies of data across the cluster nodes so if a single node fails the data can still be retrieved from other nodes in the cluster.

Disadvantages

Hadoop is a powerful system for log storage, but has a number of shortcomings that may impact your organization. There is currently limited direct support for Hadoop by many of the existing logging tools. Rsyslog has recently added the ability to write syslog messages to a Hadoop cluster, but for most other log sources a tool will need to be developed to insert your log data into Hadoop. The set of tools available to directly query and report on data in Hadoop is also very limited. Organizations will need to develop and maintain custom front-end systems for real-time analysis and review as few options already exist to meet this need.

THE CLOUD AND HADOOP

Amazon has recently added a new offering called the Amazon Elastic MapReduce (Amazon EMR). This system combines many services from Amazon's Elastic Compute Cloud (Amazon EC2) and Amazon Simple Storage Service (Amazon S3) to provide an in the cloud Hadoop instance. This offering allows organizations to pay for only the computing and storage options they need. This option can be an alternative for organizations that do not want to build and invest in an in-house instance of Hadoop. However, a careful evaluation should be made in reviewing this as an option. Most notable the time to write data to an in the cloud solution will be significantly higher as the data is no longer in close proximity to many of the hosts generating logs. Also, organizations with long log retention periods may find that the costs are greater due to the growing storage size and long-term storage period.

Getting Started with Amazon Elastic MapReduce

In the next sections, we will walk through a simple example of getting log data into Amazon EMR, parsing the logs using Pig language MapReduce Job, evaluating and reviewing the analysis output of this job. To go through these examples, you will need an Amazon Web Services (AWS) account. To get started, sign up for an account at http://aws.amazon.com/.

Navigating the Amazon

To utilize Amazon EMR for log retention and analysis, we will be using several services available from Amazon to load our data in the cloud, and to parse and analyze it.

We will load our log data into the Amazon Simple Storage Service (S3) from our individual servers. Amazon S3 is an online storage web service that allows us to store an unlimited amount of data, at a cost of course, that is very scalable and provides data security and redundancy. The data we upload into Amazon S3 will be stored in named buckets. Buckets are a method in Amazon S3 that allows us to create separate named data storage area for the data we upload.

Once we have uploaded our data into Amazon's S3 storage, we will create a MapReduce job to process our log data using the Hadoop Pig language. MapReduce is the Hadoop framework for distributing the computational work of processing large data sets into a set of jobs. Amazon EMR is the Amazon in the cloud implementation of MapReduce that runs on the Amazon Web Services (AWS) framework. We will write our MapReduce jobs utilizing Pig

AMAZON WEB SERVICES ACCOUNT

Charges and your account
The examples and steps illustrated in this section will incur charges to your Amazon Web Services account. There will be charges for storage of log files uploaded to the Amazon S3 storage buckets and compute costs for the execution time needed to process the logs in Amazon EC2. The costs of running the examples will depend on the time you spend on the examples and the amount of storage you use. For more details on Amazon Web Service pricing, review the information at http://aws.amazon.com/pricing before running and experimenting with the examples below.

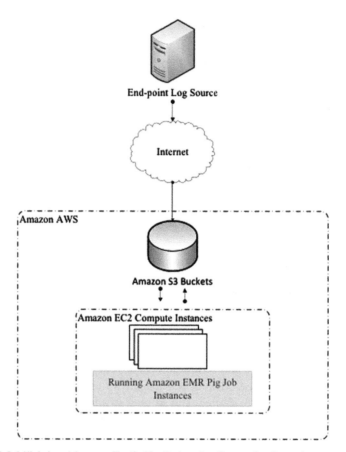

FIGURE 4.1 High-Level Amazon Elastic MapReduce Log Processing Example

and its Pig Latin job language for manipulating our log data. Pig is a utility from the Apache project that is a subproject of Hadoop that aids in the creation of MapReduce programs utilizing its simple language Pig Latin. Amazon EMR includes Pig to aid in processing the data we will upload to the S3 data infrastructure. The high-level diagram in Figure 4.1 illustrates the flow of the processes involved in our example.

Uploading Logs to Amazon Simple Storage Services (S3)

We will need to load our log data into Amazon S3 so that we can process the data with our Pig script. There are numerous ways to get your data loaded into Amazon S3 and Amazon provides an API for organizations that would like to integrate Amazon S3 storage into their existing applications. For our example, we will be using a third-party command line utility s3cmd.

S3CMD AND AMAZON

Support for s3cmd

s3cmd is not an officially supported utility by Amazon and is currently in beta. For more information about the utility and information on the setup, use, and configuration of it, visit the tool's website at http://s3tools.org/s3cmd

We will create a bucket in the Amazon S3 storage console named "apache-accesslog-bucket." This will be the storage location for our web server access logs, pig parsing script, and the resulting reports. We create the storage bucket and upload our Apache webserver access log via the following commands:

```
$ s3cmd mb s3://apache-accesslog-bucket
Bucket 's3://apache-accesslog-bucket/' created
$ s3cmd put /var/log/httpd/access_log s3://apache-accesslog-bucket/
    accesslog
/var/log/httpd/access_log -> s3://apache-accesslog-bucket/accesslog [1
    of 1]
1203 of 1203 100% in 0s 1825.23 B/s done.
```

We now have our log data loaded in the cloud! We can review the log data we have uploaded to Amazon in our S3 management console from https://console.aws.amazon.com/s3/home.

Figure 4.2 shows Apache access log loaded into Amazon S3.

This was a simple example of loading the data into Amazon's S3 storage. The s3cmd command line utility can be integrated into a logrotate script

FIGURE 4.2 Apache Access Log Loaded into Amazon S3

like the one we discussed earlier in the chapter. This approach would help automate the process of loading log information off of an end point server to the Amazon cloud once a log file has been rotated. Amazon S3 does not natively accept syslog feeds. However, Amazon does have an extensive API to build your own utilities and in Chapter 15 we will discuss a syslog alternative, rsyslog, which has built-in support for Hadoop that can be used for your own private Hadoop infrastructure and perhaps extended to Amazon EMR.

Create a Pig Script to Analyze an Apache Access Log

We would like to parse our data and get useful intelligence about what is going on in our environment. In web access logs, it is often useful to research remote hosts that are generating a larger number of HTTP access errors. Access and other HTTP errors have a status code of 400 or greater. We can create a script in Pig's language Pig Latin to parse our log we uploaded, and provide us counts by IP address of all the remote hosts in the log generating these types of errors. The following Pig script will perform the heavy lifting to generate us a report:

```
--
-- setup piggyback functions. Useful pig function library
--
register file:/home/hadoop/lib/pig/piggybank.jar
DEFINE ApacheCommonLogLoader
org.apache.pig.piggybank.storage.apachelog.CommonLogLoader();
--
-- import log file and parse into individual components
--
logs = LOAD '$INPUT' USING ApacheCommonLogLoader as (remoteHost,
    hyphen, user, time, method, uri, protocol, statusCode,
    responseSize);
--
-- Filter Apache GET requests from the log where the HTTP status code
    is 400 or greater
--
logsfiltered = FILTER logs BY method == 'GET' AND statusCode >= 400;
--
```

```
-- Retrieve the remote host list that generated the HTTP errors
--
logsremoteaddr = FOREACH logsfiltered GENERATE remoteHost;
--
-- Group parsed information by the remote hosts performing GET requests
--    and create counts on the number of times the host generated an
   error
--
groupedByRemote = GROUP logsremoteaddr BY remoteHost;
statusCounts = FOREACH groupedByRemote GENERATE group AS remoteHost,
   COUNT(logsremoteaddr) AS numStatus;
--
--Store HTTP status error report to S3
--
STORE statusCounts INTO '$OUTPUT';
```

In order to use this script, we will need to upload our Pig script to Amazon S3. To follow along in later sections, upload the script to our Amazon S3 bucket at s3://apache-accesslog-bucket/HttpStatusCodeReport.pig.

Processing Log Data in Amazon Elastic MapReduce (EMR)

Now that we have our data loaded in Amazon S3 and our report script, we can create an Amazon EMR job to process our log data. A new job can be created from the Amazon EMR console at https://console.aws.amazon.com/elasticma-preduce/home. From the Elastic MapReduce console, choose "Create New Job Flow" to define a new job to process our Apache access log. We will create a job called "Apache Log Parse Job" and utilize our own pig application to generate a report.

LEARN MORE ABOUT PIG LATING

Pig Latin
To learn more about the Pig Latin language go to http://pig.apache.org/docs/r0.7.0/piglatin_ref1.html.

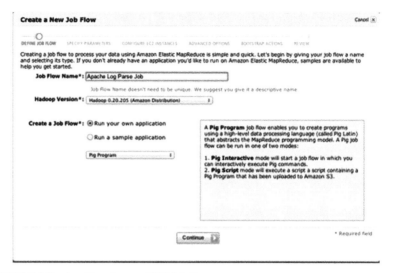

FIGURE 4.3 Create a New Amazon EMR Job Flow

Figure 4.3 shows how to create a new Amazon EMR Job Flow.

Next, we will use the pig script HttpStatusCodeReport.pig to process our log. We set the parameters of the script to run, our log file to parse, and where we would like our report to be stored.

Figure 4.4 shows how to configure the Amazon EMR Job Flow parameters.

FIGURE 4.4 Amazon EMR Job Flow parameters

FIGURE 4.5 Running Amazon EMR Job Flow Instance

In configuring our Amazon Elastic Compute (EC2) instances, we will configure the lowest setting with only an instance count of one. For larger environments processing gigabytes of logs, you will want to configure multiple jobs for the different log types and multiple instances to keep up with the volume of logs you receive on a daily basis. This will take some research and experimentation for your environment, but fortunately Amazon EMR has the scalability and flexibility to accommodate a wide range of computing needs. The remaining settings we will leave at their defaults for this example. At the end, we will choose "Create Job Flow" to create and start our processing of our access log.

Figure 4.5 shows a running Amazon EMR Job Flow instance.

After our Job Flow has completed, we have a report generated on Amazon S3 in a directory called "access-error-by-ip." The log file uploaded for this example generates the following report:

```
192.168.0.6 3
192.168.0.25 3
192.168.0.26 1
```

From the results, we can see remote host IP addresses 192.168.0.6, 192.168.0.25, and 192.168.0.26 generated an HTTP status error and the number of times an error occurred for each IP.

LOG DATA RETRIEVAL AND ARCHIVING

There are multiple options available for the physical storage of logs. A key in reviewing each option will be the retrieval and access speed of each medium. In general, the higher access speed options also have the highest cost. In log management we discuss online, near-line, and offline storage of logs and their relative costs and access speed.

Online

Online log information is information that can be immediately accessed and retrieved. This is typically the most expensive option, as dedicated hardware must by powered on and available for immediate retrieval. Online storage can be the physically attached disks to a server, a database system, or storage area network (SAN) systems. Typical storage costs for online storage systems are roughly $1.30 per gigabyte.

Near-line

Near-line storage is the in between state between online and offline storage. Near-line systems typically do not require human intervention and data is retrieved as part of an optical storage jukebox or robotic tape system. Access times for this type of storage are typically high and can range from a few seconds to a few minutes depending on the system. The costs vary widely for near-line storage systems, but are typically half the cost of online storage options. Near-line storage is also highly scalable by adding additional tapes or optical disks to increase capacity.

Offline

Offline storage is the slowest and cheapest option. Offline systems typically require human intervention to retrieve an optical disk or tape, and restore the data onto online or near-line storage systems for data access. Offline storage is highly scalable with the purchase of additional optical disks or tapes and systems are typically cheaper than near-line storage. The issue for both near-line and offline storage will be the expected shelf life of the storage medium. The generally accepted shelf life of a CD/DVD is roughly 2 to 5 years and roughly the same life span for tape (National Archives). As you approach the end of the media life span, you will need to rerecord data to media if you have a longer retention policy than the life of the media.

SUMMARY

Log storage is an important consideration when it comes to logging. This chapter introduced you to the concepts surrounding the storage of logs. Many examples were given, including an introduction to Amazon's Hadoop interface.

REFERENCES

Chuvakin, A. (2011). SANS Sec434 Log Management Course Material, slide 108.

Kent, K., & Souppaya, M. (2006). Guide to computer security log management. <http://csrc.nist.gov/publications/nistpubs/800-92/SP800-92.pdf>.

National Archives. Frequently asked questions (FAQs) about optical storage media: Storing temporary records on CDs and DVDs. <http://www.archives.gov/records-mgmt/initiatives/temp-opmedia-faq.html>.

PCI Security Standards Council (2010). *PCI DSS v2.0*. Retrieved July 7, 2012 from PCI Security Standards, October. <https://www.pcisecuritystandards.org/documents/pci_dss_v2.pdf>.

Troan, E., & Brown, P (2002). logrotate. <http://linuxcommand.org/man_pages/logrotate8.html>.

syslog-ng Case Study

INFORMATION IN THIS CHAPTER:

- Obtaining syslog-ng
- What Is syslog-ngsyslog-ng?
- Example Deployment
- Troubleshooting syslog-ng

INTRODUCTION

You might be asking, "Why do I need a new or different syslog daemon?" That's a good question. For many years the standard syslog protocol found on Unix systems was good enough for its purposes. As time went on, and the needs of users, applications, systems, and organizations changed, it became clear that something new was needed. syslog-ng began as an attempt to provide users with more options and features than could be found in a stock syslog daemon. It has grown over the years from open source software to a full-fledged, commercial-grade software with varying levels of enterprise-level support options available. This chapter will provide high-level details on some of its more useful features, as well as a discussion of a real-world deployment. It should be noted that syslog-ng comes in a free and enterprise edition. The enterprise edition is not free and it enables features that you cannot use with the free version.

OBTAINING SYSLOG-NG

The best place to obtain the latest version of syslog-ng for your particular platform is to visit this Web site: http://www.balabit.com/network-security/syslog-ng/opensource-logging-system/downloads/upgrade.

Providing step-by-step installation instructions is really beyond the scope of this chapter. Earlier versions of syslog-ng required supplemental libraries and tools installed. Today's syslog-ng comes with everything bundled in a single download. The syslog-ng Web site contains many sources of information to aid you in installation, setup and administration at http://www.balabit.com/network-security/syslog-ng/opensource-logging-system/support/documentation/.

WHAT IS SYSLOG-NGSYSLOG-NG?

As we stressed before, classic syslog has multiple problems. For example, UDP is used as the transport. UDP is unreliable. But sometimes a conscious decision is made to forgo guaranteed delivery for the non-blocking and low-overhead nature of UDP. It might be the case that this is more important to you than the features of TCP, which do incur some overhead because of its connection-oriented nature.

Another issue is security. The standard Syslog protocol neither supports secure transmission of log data, nor does it specify authentication.

syslog-ngsyslog-ng one of the options out there that attempts to solve many of them without "changing the world." To this end, some of the more noteworthy syslog-ng features include:

- TCP support: This allows for more reliable transmission of syslog data.
- Transport Layer Security (TLS): syslog-ng natively supports the TLS protocol. This feature allows for both the secure transmission of syslog messages as well as mutual authentication of the source sender and the recipient of syslog messages. These are critical features in today's environments where log data must not be tampered and often has to be kept confidential due to regulatory compliance issues, legal issues, etc. It should be noted that TLS can only be used over TCP.
- Database support: syslog-ng supports sending syslog messages to a remote database. As of version 3.3, MySQL, Oracle, MSSQL, PostgreSQL, and SQLite 3 are supported. A major advantage to this feature is that it allows for log data to be stored in a relational database. This makes reporting, searching, and other analysis techniques very easy. The downside to this, however, is that the raw log message is not preserved in the database. This can have an impact on chain of custody if your log data is ever needed for criminal prosecution.
- IPv4 and IPv6 support: syslog-ng supports sending and receiving syslog to and from both types of networks.
- Flexible filtering: syslog-ng is able to filter on various fields in the syslog message. Macros are created from what is filtered, which can be used to write messages to files or directories.
- Message rewriting: It is possible to create rules to rewrite fields in a syslog message. For example, you can supplement missing or incomplete data in a message.

- Processing the message body: syslog-ng allows you to process and parse the actual log message. The current version of syslog-ng (3.3) can separate the columns of CSV-formatted log messages, that is, columns separated by commas, tabulators, or other delimiters, for example, Apache logs.
- High performance: syslog-ng is geared towards handling high message rates, and—of course, depending on the exact configuration and processing requirements—can reliably handle hundreds of thousand messages per second.

Let's look brief example of one of the more advanced features of syslog-ng. It can process the message using a fast and flexible pattern matching engine to extract the useful information from the message body. For example, a login message of an OpenSSH server looks like the following:

```
Accepted password for joe from 10.50.0.247 port 42156 ssh2.
```

This can be described with a syslog-ng pattern like:

```
Accepted @QSTRING:authentication_method: @ for @QSTRING:username:
    @ from @QSTRING:client_address: @ port @NUMBER:port:@ @
    QSTRING:protocol_version: @
```

As you can see, the changing parts of the log message are parsed using special variables. The names assigned to the parsed message parts become syslog-ng macros, and can be used in filters, file names, database column names, and so on. The advantage of this pattern matching method over others (for example, regular expressions) is that it is much faster, more scalable, and the patterns are easier to read, understand, and maintain. It is also possible to trigger actions if a log message matches a pattern: with some tweaking, this can be used to send out alerts when specific events are detected. For a complete reference of this feature, see chapter *Processing message content with a pattern database* in The syslog-ng Administrator Guide.

These features and many other concepts are covered in detail in the 3.0 Administration guide: http://www.balabit.com/sites/default/files/syslog-ng-v3.0-guide-admin-en_0.pdf.

EXAMPLE DEPLOYMENT

In this example setup there are three components to the deployment:

1. Client machines which send syslog via UDP to local collection server. The client machines are running stock syslog daemons.

2. Local collection server which receives syslog from client machines. This system is running syslog-ng.
3. Global collection server which receives logs from the local collection server over TCP with TLS enabled.

Figure 5.1 depicts the deployment.

The local syslog-ng server will channel all the collected data to a remote site, where another syslog-ng server is installed. Such a site might be the globally centralization site, a backup "log drop" or some other environment, connected to our syslog-ng collection server via a WAN. Due to this, log data transfer needs to be protected by encryption. The easiest way to accomplish it will be by using syslog-ng's built-in TLS support.

So, after we deploy syslog-ng on both syslog-ng servers, it's time to start configuring logging on all the systems.

Configurations

In this section we cover the basics required to configure our setup. A thorough treatment of configuring syslog-ng is beyond the scope of this chapter; see the syslog-ng Administration guide for complete details on using syslog-ng.

For consistency, we will refer to our central log server that collected logs over UDP as 10.10.10.1 and the remote log server will be called 10.11.11.1. In this scenario we will assume that all logs are being collected. In real life, filters can be applied at multiple locations to curb the flood of data.

Log Sources

For modern Linux systems running vanilla syslog, we need just this line in /
```
etc/syslog.conf*.*              @10.10.10.1
```

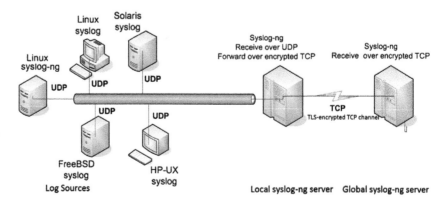

FIGURE 5.1 Shows Our Example Deployment

Syslog daemon needs to be restarted; which is usually accomplished by

```
/etc/init.d/syslog restart
```

For older Solaris 7 or 8 systems, the changes are similar

```
*.debug        @10.10.10.1
```

And then restart via:

```
/etc/init.d/syslog stop ; /etc/init.d/syslog start
```

For recent FreeBSD systems, the changes are similar.

For recent OpenBSD systems, the changes are similar to Linux:

```
*.*        @10.10.10.1
```

And restart:

```
kill-SIGHUP 'cat /var/run/syslog.pid'
```

For HP-UX systems, the changes are:

```
*.debug        @10.10.10.1
```

And restart.

Finally, syslog-ng needs the following configuration file implemented:

```
source src { unix-stream("/dev/log"); internal(); };
destination loghost { udp("10.10.10.1"); };
log { source(src); destination(loghost); };
```

In case of an existing syslog-ng configuration the above needs to be merged in. As you can guess, the daemon (in the case, the syslog-ng daemon) needs a restart.

Local syslog-ng Server

This system will receive UDP messages from various sources and will forward them over the TCP-based tunnel to the other machines. TLS is the best way to accomplish this (Schroder, 2010). The following list outlines the basic steps required in getting this feature working:

1. Create an X.509 certificate using a tool like openssl.
2. Copy the certificate to the local syslog-ng server.
3. Using a tool like openssl, create a hash file based on the X.509 certificate.
4. Create a TLS configuration statement which uses the following syslog-ng configuration block.

```
destination demo_tls_destination {
tcp("10.11.11.1" port(6514)
tls(ca_dir("/opt/syslog-ng/etc/syslog-ng/ca.d"))); };
```

Section 3.13 of the 3.0 Administration guide provides more detail on these and all features of syslog-ng.

Global syslog-ng Server

The global server will receive message encrypted using TLS. The basic steps to configure it to receive such messages are as follows:

1. Copy the X.509 certificate to the server.
2. Copy the private key of the certificate to the server.
3. Configure the global server to receive encrypted log messages.

```
source demo_tls_source {
tcp(ip(0.0.0.0) port(6514)
tls(key_file("/opt/syslog-ng/etc/syslog-ng/key.d/syslog-ng.key")
cert_file("/opt/syslog-ng/etc/syslog-ng/cert.d/syslog-ng.cert"))
); };
```

Again, be sure to see Section 3.13 of the 3.0 Administration guide for more details.

Database logging

The global syslog-ng forwards copies of the log messages it receives to a MySQL database. The database serves as a structured and searchable store of what is received from remote log collection points. The main advantage of this kind of setup is that analysis and searching can be performed without impacting remote systems, or needing to remotely log into these systems and search log file by hand. A second advantage is that you have yet another place where log data is stored. This can be ideal in situations where the global collection server crashes or becomes unavailable.

The following is a sample syslog-ng configuration for MySQL:

```
options {
   use_fqdn(yes);
};
destination d_sql {
   sql(
        type(mysql)
        host("127.0.0.1") username("root") password("")
        database("logs")
```

```
        table("messages_${FULLHOST_FROM}_${R_YEAR}${R_MONTH}${R_DAY}")
        columns("datetime", "host", "program", "pid", "message")
        values("$R_DATE", "$FULLHOST_FROM", "$PROGRAM", "$PID",
"$MSGONLY")
        indexes()
    );
};
log {
    destination(d_sql);
};
```

Some items are worth pointing out.

- The database name is logs.
- syslog-ng will automatically create a table named
  messages_${FULLHOST_FROM}_${R_YEAR}${R_MONTH}${R_DAY},
  which means each host that sends log messages will have its own set of
  tables, segmented by the year, month, and day the log messages are sent.
- syslog-ng will also automatically create the columns for the table, namely
  datetime, host, program, pid, and message. By default the SQL type used
  for each column will text. You can override the default type.
- In the options section of the configuration, use_fqdn(yes); is specified. Without this option set and without DNS in use, the source of your
  messages, which will be an IP address, would only record the first octet of
  the IP address. With this option specified, the full IP address will be used
  in the table name as well as the record itself.

Section 8.2.5 of the 3.0 Administration guide discusses this feature in great
detail.

TROUBLESHOOTING SYSLOG-NG

One the most important things to keep an eye on is when syslog-ng begins to
drop packets (Open Source Information Security, 2010). This can be an indicator that your syslog-ng server is getting overloaded with incoming messages. In
order to keep any eye on this, you first need to enable stats collection in syslog-
ng. The following global configuration options are needed to control this:

```
options {
    stats_freq(10);
    stats_level(2);
};
```

The first statement turns on stats generation in the form of a syslog message. The variable passed to the option is the number of seconds that syslog-ng will write the message to whatever destination you have specified in your configuration. Here we are emitting stats every 10 s. The second option specifies the level. There are three levels, 1, 2, and 3. The default is 1, but in order to get the particular data we need, we need to specify 2. The following is a sample stats message generated by syslog-ng:

```
Nov 30 12:32:35 172 syslog-ng[1343]: Log statistics;
   processed='source(s_net)=0', processed='src.file(s_local#2,/
   proc/kmsg)=0', stamp='src.file(s_local#2,/proc/kmsg)=0',
   processed='source(s_local)=1', processed='src.host(172)=1',
   stamp='src.host(172)=1291138345', processed='src.udp(s_
   net#0)=0', stamp='src.udp(s_net#0)=0', processed='src.
   internal(s_local#0)=1', stamp='src.internal(s_
   local#0)=1291138345', dropped='dst.file(d_messages#0,/
   var/log/messages)=0', processed='dst.file(d_messages#0,/
   var/log/messages)=1', stored='dst.file(d_messages#0,/
   var/log/messages)=0', processed='center(received)=0',
   processed='destination(d_messages)=1', processed='center(queu
   ed)=0'
```

The item we are interested in is the dropped= item. It shows, for the given destination, if it had to drop any messages. Each destination you have specified in your configuration will be represented here.

There is a downside to enabling this feature. Per the syslog-ng manual, levels 2 and 3 can cause increased CPU and memory usage by the syslog-ng process. On top of this, enabling these features requires a restart of syslog-ng, which may not be feasible if you run in a highly available environment. There is an alternative way to detect if UDP packets are getting dropped: using the netstaty command:

```
# netstat -us
Udp:
    169412 packets received
    170 packets to unknown port received.
    0 packet receive errors
    167002 packets sent
#
```

The output of this command shows if any UDP packets were dropped. This is a simple but effective way to troubleshoot things.

SUMMARY

syslog-ng provides many advanced features which take log data transmission and collection to a new level. With features like TCP transmission support, TLS, and logging to a database, syslog-ng is an excellent replacement for the stock Unix syslog daemons that are featureless and don't provide much value. The example deployment presented in this chapter provides a glimpse into a real-world setup.

REFERENCES

Schroder, C. (n.d.). Build a secure logging server with syslog-ng (Part 2). *EnterpriseNetworking-Planet—News, trends and advice for network managers.* N.p. Web. November 29, 2010. <http://www.enterprisenetworkingplanet.com/netsysm/article.php/3598146/Build-a-Secure-Logging-Server-with-syslog-ng-Part-2.htm>.

Open source information security: Syslog-NG performance tuning. *Open Source Information Security.* N.p., n.d. Web. November 29, 2010. <http://15cards.blogspot.com/2007/11/syslog-ng-performance-tuning.html>.

Covert Logging

INFORMATION IN THIS CHAPTER:

- Complete Stealthy Log Setup
- Logging in Honeypots
- Covert Channels for Logging Brief

Evil can be covert

Can good be?

It can, for a reason

Haiku 8: Anton

INTRODUCTION

While common sense and various regulations compel us to focus on protecting logs from various attacks, one of the protection methods that we can use is making the log files and logging infrastructure hidden from the attackers, who seek to undermine it. Encryption, secure agent-based log collection and integrity checking are useful (and, in many cases, also mandatory), hiding your logging and log collection architecture from the attacker has a unique appeal of "winning the battle" for secure logging without firing a single shot. After all, encryptions and other measures will be your fallback mechanism, if an attacker discovers that he is being covertly logged. However, years of running honeypots and even whole networks of them—honeynets—leads the chapter author to believe that it is unlikely for most attackers. Such cover infrastructure is one rare case in security technology where the defender might actually score an advantage.

This section covers this specific methodology. It is singled out due to its importance, ability to be combined with other techniques, its use in honeypots as well as a number of myths surrounding hidden logging.

The idea of stealthy logging is certainly appealing, especially if it is sometimes interpreted like this: why secure, encrypt and protect log collection components if we can just hide them from the would-be attackers and they will be completely immune. Others, on the other hand, play the "security by obscurity" argument and say that hiding logging is futile, since the attackers can always find it. As usual, both extreme points of view are the farthest from the truth.

For it to become clear, let us briefly digress a bit and explain why "security by obscurity" is considered to be bad security. First, "security by obscurity" should really be known as "security by obscurity ONLY." If your protective measures are solely reliant on attackers' not knowing some critical piece of information about your infrastructure, said security measure, security technology in use, etc. what happens if they do learn it?

Security wall comes thumbing down! On the other hand, security of the environment can be significantly enhanced by hiding important information from plain view, but still not relying on them being secret. The trivial example is: what if your computers are not connected to the internet and armed guards are posted next to each terminal. Does it mean that you have to use Post-It notes to "broadcast" your password? No, it still makes sense to keep them secret even though their disclosure will no break your security.

Similarly, hiding the pieces of your logging infrastructure help to improve security of your otherwise solid security measures such as hardened log servers, cryptographic tunneling, and trusted access controls.

Now, let's review what logs can we hide and where. We will start from an insightful example of "hidden" logging encountered and then utilized by one of the authors early in his security career. It worked surprisingly well for the task at hand.

It is well known that an amateur attacker breaking into Unix and Linux systems will first kill the syslog daemon to prevent logging from being accumulated locally and sent to a remote log server. This will be done by something similar to "killall syslogd" command. So, in this small company network, the system administrator has compiled another copy of a syslog daemon, named it "cachefd" (or some other similarly obscure, "Unix-sounding" process name) and let it run using a configuration file in his home directory. This file configured log files to be accumulated in some non-standard directory (such as, for example, an obscure /usr/src/kernel). Thus, the amateur attackers (who were perceived to be the main threat to this particular company—and, as we know, to most companies nowadays as well) were effectively prevented from terminating logging. Admittedly, such scheme relies on the company actually looking at the log files and having a periodic log review or near-real-time log monitoring capability.

Now, advanced security practitioners (authors included) may laugh at such "secure logging," but amateur attackers observed in honeypots never went beyond killing the syslog daemon and never looked for any other logging mechanisms, hidden or otherwise. Thus, the above measure would have been in fact 100% effective…

We will start our journey into hidden logging from a classic example of a stealthy sniffer for syslog pickup. It is used by one of the authors in the honeynet and was also reported to be effectively used in production environments as well (see, for example, Bauer, 2002).

COMPLETE STEALTHY LOG SETUP

In this section we will discuss a complete stealthy log setup using syslog and log pickup using a sniffer. We'll cover log generation, transfer, and pick up.

Stealthy Log Generation

Stealthy log generation presents a challenge since it is that very likely that the program producing logs will reside on a compromised information asset. Picking logs via packet capture is nearly always stealthy, but generation of logs is harder to hide.

In general, there are two options that they can exploit:

- Hide logging altogether.
- Hide logging and present a fake logging daemon for the attacker to kill and feel good about.

Obviously, there are other techniques as well such as making a log daemon unkillable logging via kernel privileges.

Hiding Logging

Hidden daemons via kernel capabilities or a dedicated loadable kernel module (LKM) on Unix and Linux is well known. Essentially, we are talking about a rootkit for logging. There are two additional choices:

- A separate hiding module or a general-purpose hiding program that can obscure other running processes (such as our logging). Most root kits work using this principle.
- A dedicated hidden login module. Honeynet Project Sebek tool works on this method, even though it can also hide other programs.

Finally it should be noted that if an attacker deploys a rootkit based on similar principles it might interfere with our log hiding.

Hiding Logging with Misdirection

If we utilized the above techniques but also leave default logging infrastructure in place—for the attacker to kill—it is very likely that most attackers will not beat further and would assume that there is no more login going on.

This simply requires creating a separate instance of syslog connecting it to the infrastructure (see next section) and then leaving the default one in place, with some functionality is able so that it does not interfere with real logging.

Stealthy Pickup of Logs

Here is how one can set up a somewhat covert pickup of NIDS, firewall, or other syslog-based logs. We will use a sniffer to pick up the logs on the log server.

First, what do we protect? This method will defend against attacks on the central log collection servers by hiding their identity or even redirecting the wrath of the attacker onto a different server of our choosing (possibly, a "log server" honeypot, configured to log and analyze attacks aimed at log servers). Used in combination with the above stealthy logging, it can also defend against the attacks on local logging capabilities.

The main idea is that we will not be using a listening daemon to pick-up User Datagram Protocol (UDP)-based syslogs, but use a sniffer off a stealth interface (i.e. one with no IP configured) instead. In combination with some other tricks, it will allow us to deflect the interest of the attacker away from the valuable log collection server. Now, in light of our description of "security by obscurity," it does not mean that the log server should not be hardened to the best of our ability and protected against unauthorized access and malicious attacks.

Let's consider what we should configure on each of the above:

IDS Log Source

Here we will configure the destination for syslog-based logs. We will need to forward the logs somewhere; instead of sending them to the collection server we will send them to either the "fake" server or to a random IP address on our network (that has no host sitting on it)—or, better, a honeypot.

If we are sending the system logs or other logs we will modify the standard /etc/syslog.conf file, such as by adding:

```
*.*     @fakeserver
```

Where 'fakeserver' stands for the name or IP address of our decoy server (hopefully, it will have of a telltale name). Or:

```
*.*     @10.10.10.10
```

where "10.10.10.10" is an IP on the same LAN segment which has no host on it.

The above will likely work only on Linux and modern BSD variants. On older Solaris systems we will need to specify message priorities (which cannot be a wildcard, like on Linux) like:

```
*.crit    @fakeserver
```

In case of a popular Snort IDS running on Unix or Linux as a fake logging source, the above recipe works as the alert forwarding is performed by a syslog daemon and not by Snort. The same trick can be performed on a commercial Sourcefire Snort appliance, for as long as syslog is the mechanism of choice.

In case of a Snort IDS running on Windows (not really common but still seen in some environments) as a fake logging source, we will modify its own configuration file snort.conf wherever it is located. It will be edited to have:

```
output alert_syslog: host=10.10.10.10, LOG_AUTH LOG_ALERT
```

Thus, the configuration on a log server will be no different from the normal. However, should the attacker want to attack the log server upon compromising this system or an IDS sensor, it will be redirected down the wrong track or, in fact, "the right track" for us to study their behavior…

Log Collection Server

This is where most of the important changes occur. Here we will pick up the logs off the network by using a sniffer program. There are several choices to make here. First is: should this server have an IP address? If it has two network cards (the ideal choice) we can make one a management interface (with an IP address) while the other will be the sniffing interface (with no IP address, but a sniffer program running on it). This configuration provides the best combination of manageability and security. We will describe such a configuration here.

On the management interface we will configure access controls via a firewall (such as Linux iptables, a standard firewall code included in every Linux system). This interface will have some remote access service running (ssh is the standard for Unix remote management).

On a sniffing interface with no IP address (often called a stealth interface), we install the sniffer program. There are many choices, here but the main one boils down to: should we use a general-purpose sniffer (such as tcpdump packet sniffer) to pick up the logs off the wire and then extract them from the recorded traffic manually or use a purpose-built sniffer.

The drawbacks of the former are numerous. We will need some mechanism to extract logs from capture traffic and convert them back to some standard format such as syslog and then combine them with other logs. Also, such sniffer will record data in binary format and we will need to convert it to text before we can analyze it. However, many popular sniffers are well audited for security flaws and might provide a better solution to be exposed to a hostile network. One might argue about the word "exposed" here, since there is seemingly no way for an attacker to know that there is sniffing going on and thus attack it. Unfortunately, the truth is different. Exploits against sniffers running on stealth interfaces are known and even tcpdump, the grand-daddy of all sniffers, has not escaped this fate.

Using a dedicated log sniffer allows for easy integration with other logging infrastructure pieces. For example, we can pick up the syslog logs off the wire and immediately send them to another system, such as an analysis server.

We will discuss two such logging solutions: plog (written by Marcus Ranum a few years ago) and passlogd (written by Christian Void). Plog can be obtained at http://www.ranum.com/security/computer_security/code/ and passlogd can be downloaded from http://freecode.com/projects/passlogd.

Plog is a tool to sniff the traffic for syslog messages and forward them to /dev/log (a syslog devices used for application to forward messages to a syslog daemon running on a Unix system).

While we try to stay away from rephrasing manuals and listing command line options, we will make an exception for these important tools. Here is an example of plog in action on the honeynet system:

```
# ./plog -i eth1
```

The above command line starts the plog (it forks and becomes a daemon process) and makes it sniff the eth1 network interface for syslog-formatted messages on UDP port 514 directed toward any system. The downside of the above configuration is that the messages will appear to originate from the system running plog and not from the actual source of the messages on the network.

It is used to pick up logs emitted from the honeypot victim server onto the LAN. The messages are aimed at the other system that is not even equipped with a syslog daemon. This is done to confuse the attacker!

Passlogd is a similar tool that can be used for the same purpose. The main differences lie in having more options and an added ability to associate messages with sources and destinations as captured on the wire. For example:

```
Mon May 5 14:22:42 2001 baby to mama: <23> su[821]: Authentication
    succeeded for user 'anton'
```

Before using passlogd one should keep in mind that the versions before 0.1e have serious bug that can be exploited even on the sniffing stealth interface (just as we hinted above). Not only is the vulnerability known, but the working exploit is actually posted publicly.

Here is how a modified passlogd sniffer program was used by one of the authors on the honeynet:

```
$ passlogd [...]
```

The above command captured all the syslog messages sent from the victim server in the honeypot to another system (which had to syslog daemon installed). Both can be setup on the log collection server to sniff logs and immediately send them somewhere else or integrate with other collected log files.

One more important comment needs to be made about sending logs to non-existing servers. For the UDP packet to be sent, the sending server needs to hear a response from some server on the network that it is willing to receive IP connection. Since this is accomplished via ARP (Address Resolution Protocol, that maps IP to MAC hardware addresses), a little ARP spoofing is in order. This is how it can be done:

```
# arp -s 00-05-00-e5-8a-28 10.10.10.10
```

The above command needs to be run on the server that runs the sniffer, but the MAC address can belong to any machine on the network. IP address does not even have to exist on the network.

"Fake" Server or Honeypot

This particular server is not required for the setup, but it is a very good idea to have it. The reason is that if the attacker will see that there is no server listening for the logs, there has to be something "funny" going on and that security of this environment is much stronger than initially suspected (on the other hand, an amateur attacker might thing that the syslog server crashed or was misconfigured by the administrators.)

There are several options for this server. It can have a minimum secure syslog daemon running and nothing else. In this can it may or may not be configured for actual log pickup, but its real purpose will be to provide a extremely hardened target to waste attackers resources.

The second option is to set up a full-blown honeypot on this IP address. That sounds like a good idea since the advanced attackers have a chance of being stuck in its "honey" after compromising the system sending logs to it. Guidelines on setting up honeypots go beyond this book. Look at the references section for some books with information on the subject. In this chapter we will address some honeypots logging issues, but not the detailed setup guidelines.

LOGGING IN HONEYPOTS

While the references in the end provide a lot of material on the honeypots, we will provide some brief definition and background.

A honeypot is a "dummy" target machine set up to observe hacker attacks. A honeynet is a network built around such dummy machines in order to lure and track hackers as they step through the attack process. By studying real-world attacks, researchers hope to predict emerging trends in order to develop advance defenses. Lance Spitzner, the founder of one such tracking endeavor known as the Honeynet Project (http://www.honeynet.org), defines a honeypot as "a security resource whose value lies in being probed, attacked or compromised." The Honeynet Project, that one of the authors works with, differentiates between research and production honeypots. The former are focused on gaining intelligence about attackers and their techniques, while the latter are aimed at decreasing the risk to IT resources and providing advance warning of incoming attacks on the network infrastructure as well as possibly diverting attacks from real "crown jewels."

As we mentioned above, honeypots are the environment where logs are the most likely to be attacked, corrupted, and prevented. And it is also the environment where protecting logs by hiding the logging technology makes the most sense as other honeynet infrastructure is also hidden from the attacker. On the other hand, the environment has added difficulties as well since we need to log much more details on the honeypot activities than in most production environments.

What do we log in the honeypot?

1. Network transaction recording
2. Network traffic recording
3. Host activity recording
4. IDS alerts

Let's briefly look at the above log types.

Network transaction recording in a honeypot includes network layers 3 and 4 data such as source and destination IP addresses, protocols, and ports. This data is usually capture by a honeynet's firewall and a network monitoring tools (such as flow collector) as well as a network IDS. Network transactions include inbound communication and connection attempts from the Internet, internal connections between the machines within the honeynet, and the most ominous outbound communications initiated from the honeypot.

Network traffic recording logs can be considered an exclusive feature of honeypots as compared to production networks, as very few can afford to log all the packets traversing the network. It includes a complete recording of network communication in raw binary format.

Host activity recording includes the recording of the attacker's activities (such as keystrokes and attacker's impact on the system) as well as other host process activities, occurring at the same time (standard application and operating system logs files).

IDS alerts, the last log category emanating from a honeypot, are the main method of becoming aware of what is going on in the honeypot. They add structure to network traffic analysis and allow you to take action based on what is going on in the honeypot.

Obviously, all the above logs need to be protected.

First, we need to make sure that the events occurring on the honeypot are logged even after system standard non-stealthy logging capabilities are destroyed by the attacker. As we mentioned before, in most Unix honeynet compromises the attackers kills the logging daemon as one of his first actions.

Honeynet's Shell Covert Keystroke Logger

A simple example of honeypot logger is a Honeynet Project's bash shell patch, improved by one of the authors. It can be downloaded from the Honeynet Project tool pages http://www.honeynet.org/tools/index.html.

The tool allows to log the keystrokes typed in a "bash" shell prompt (the most important to capture on the honeypot since they show what the attacker did on the system) and to transfer them from the honeypot to a collection server. For those from the Windows part of the world, "bash" shell is the standard command line interpreter on most Linux systems and is the main mechanism used by remote (and many local) users to interact with the system.

Since we are discussing covert logging we will focus on the covert properties of this tool. The main protection it can muster against the honeypot "guest" or attacker is that its presence is hidden. Amateur attackers who are caught in the honeypots usually do not suspect that the very system shell is working against them. They usually disable history logging and think that their keystrokes are not saved anywhere.

Bash shell forwards the commands to a remote machine directly via the UDP protocol without utilizing any host programs. The bash binary itself contains a UDP sender, which sends the packets to the wire. UDP communication is ideally suitable for the covert log transfer task at hand (to remind, UDP is also used by a standard syslog logger). UDP is somewhat harder to detect than Transmission Control Protocol (TCP) (for example, UDP communication will not always show in netstat), does not require "root" privileges (unlike more esoteric covert data transmission methods such as Internet Control Message Protocol (ICMP) payloads or connectionless TCP data transfer discussed in the works on network covert channels), and thus can be used straight by the shell binary run by the attacker, even if he does not possess "root" privileges.

Another protection of this logging channel is "destination spoofing" (described above). UDP destination is hardcoded to be a non-relevant server or even another honeypot, as described above. Note that this spoofing does not refer to the usual IP spoofing (that can be called "source spoofing"), but just sending the UDP datagrams to non-existent or non-listening hosts and picking them up via a sniffer. This allows you to mask the position of the receiving log server. This is possible since UDP protocol is connectionless and the log packets can be sent to a machine that does not explicitly choose to accept them.

Here is the example bash log:

```
T=17:19:15-12222004. PI=11354 UI=0 ./dumbscan -B 10.11
```

The format includes time and date of the command execution (17:19 am on December 22, 2004 in the above example), UNIX process ID of the shell (it can be used to track different shell sessions), the UNIX user ID (0 means that the user is "root"), and the executed command. "./dumbscan –B 10.11" (an attempt to scan a B class of IP addresses from 10.11.0.0 to 10.11.255.255 for whatever exploit).

This covert logger can also be used to monitor users in production environments.

The stealthiness of such logging mechanism is not that high, since it can be easily sniffed by the attacker on the honeypot. Also, it can be detected by looking at the "bash" shell binary. To resolve these problems, Honeynet Project came up with Sebek2 covert logger, briefly covered in the next section.

Honeynet's Sebek2 Case Study

Sebek by the Honeynet Project (http://www.honeynet.org/papers/sebek.pdf) is the best example of a covert logger. It has facilities for both covert audit collection and log information transfer from the source systems to the log collection server. Sebek2 can be obtained at the Honeynet project's tools' page, referenced above.

It can collect much more information, including keystrokes entered in applications as well as entered passwords. What is more interesting for us in this chapter is its protection measures, presenting the ultimate in stealthy logging (this side of "white hat–black hat divide," of course).

These are the protections available in Sebek2 (as of 12/2004):

- Hidden process: Sebek2 doesn't modify any program on the system, but exists as a hidden kernel module. It can also exist in a compiled-in form, embedded in the main kernel code during compilation, presenting the extra-stealthy option.
- Hidden content: unlike the bash shell above, Sebek2 encrypt all the data transmitted off the system, using SSL.
- Sniffing protection: Sebek modifies the kernel to block its packets from being sniffed by the honeypot. Thus, even the rare attacker who tries to monitor the local network will now know that he is being watched.

For more details on Sebek architecture and use refer to the whitepaper "Know Your Enemy: Sebek" located at http://www.honeynet.org/papers/sebek.pdf.

Sebek can be used in production environments for user and potential intruder activity monitoring in a highly clandestine manner. There are several benefits for that type of hidden logging in a production environment. Those include an obvious bonus to forensics analysis (a lot of evidence is available) and an ability to watch trusted users (such as system administrators). The latter comes very handy when the possibility of audit destruction by a trusted attacker is high.

On the other hand, the main disadvantage is a sheer volume of logged data. Such logging is much more detailed and granular than most standard auditing system mechanisms.

COVERT CHANNELS FOR LOGGING BRIEF

Going beyond Sebek places us firmly in the realm of covert channels, an exciting area but the one likely outside the scope of this book. We will briefly discuss the modern covert channels and their use for logging.

The classic notion of "covert channels" (first formalized in the "Light Pink Book" from the NSA Rainbow Series) is all but irrelevant today. The more modern instances of covert channels deal with covert information transfer using basic TCP/IP protocols as well as common application protocols. Admittedly, the protocols from lower layers (such as CDP mentioned below) can also be used.

For example, many of the fields in the TCP (also UDP) and IP headers are somewhat undefined (e.g. The type of service (TOS)/Explicit Congestion Notification (ECN)TOS/ECN field), unset (padding), set to random values (like the initial sequence number), set to varied values (IP ID), or are optional (such as options). This very important fact creates possibilities for covertly adding the information to transmit without breaking the TCP/IP standard (and thus losing the packet) and making the packet appear anomalous (and thus triggering the detection systems). Also, many of the higher layer protocols, such as HTTP can be configured to carry data (such as via the HTTP tunnel tool) that is used to channel a shell session through a sequence of web accesses.

More specifically, there are tools to transfer data, possibly log data, over Cisco Discovery Protocol (CDP)—a non-routable protocol that is used for network device communication.

Where one might choose to use such degree of stealth for logging? Honeynets or closely monitored production servers in high-security environments are two possibilities.

SUMMARY

This sectioned covered the covert and stealthy logging. It can be used to enhance the protection of logging infrastructure in addition (to avoid being "security by obscurity") to other security measures.

The important lessons of this chapter are:

- Stealthy logging tools can be used for beneficial purposes.
- Honeypots are an environment where stealthy logging is usually found.
- Stealthy logging can ultimately be discovered, that is why it should not be the only protection available.

REFERENCES

A guide to understanding covert channel analysis of trusted systems (ncsc-tg-030 version-1, "Light Pink Book") <http://www.fas.org/irp/nsa/rainbow/tg030.htm>, National Computer Security Center, November 1993.

Bauer, M. (2002). Stealthful sniffing, intrusion detection and logging. <http://www.linuxjournal.com/article/6222>.

Honeynet Project (2004). *Know Your Enemy*. (2nd ed.). AWL.

Know Your Enemy: Sebek <http://www.honeynet.org/papers/sebek.pdf>.

Spitzner, L. (xxxx). Honeypots: tracking hackers.

## CHAPTER 7

Analysis Goals, Planning, and Preparation: What Are We Looking For?

CONTENTS

INTRODUCTION

So far we've covered the basics of what log data is, log data architectures, centralized logging, log retention, and a few other topics. Now it's time to get into log analysis. But before we can start talking about techniques and approaches, we need to set some groundwork for what it takes to get to the point where you can actually begin analyzing log data. This chapter will cover three important topics: Goals, Planning, and Preparation. Log analysis goals are, as the name implies, the goals of what you want to accomplish via log analysis. Planning is the next step in the process of getting to log analysis. We plan out our approach to log analysis. Finally we will cover Preparation. This deals with preparing your log data and environment to handle the activity of log analysis.

GOALS

The goals of analysis can be varied depending on your particular needs. If you are a banking institution you will have different goals from those of a restaurant chain. There are however a set of higher level goals which can apply to mostly everyone.

Past Bad Things

The primary goal is to be cognizant of things which have already happened and be able to alert on them. This section provides sample past bad things.

Creating New User (Windows):

```
EvntSLog:423: [AUS] Fri Oct 05 11:59:09 2001: HANDCUFFS/Security
    (624) - "User Account Created: New Account Name: tbird New Domain:
    HANDCUFFS New Account ID: S-1-5-21-1647595427-22557637-1039276024-
    1001 Caller User Name: Administrator Caller Domain: HANDCUFFS Caller
    Logon ID: (0x0,0x2B79) Privileges- "

EvntSLog:424: [AUS] Fri Oct 05 11:59:09 2001: HANDCUFFS/Security
    (626) - "User Account Enabled: Target Account Name: tbird Target
    Domain: HANDCUFFS Target Account ID: S-1-5-21-1647595427-22557637-
    1039276024-1001 Caller User Name: Administrator Caller Domain:
    HANDCUFFS Caller Logon ID: (0x0,0x2B79) "

EvntSLog:425: [AUS] Fri Oct 05 11:59:09 2001: HANDCUFFS/Security (628)
    - "User Account password set: Target Account Name: tbird Target
    Domain: HANDCUFFS Target Account ID: S-1-5-21-1647595427-22557637-
    1039276024-1001 Caller User Name: Administrator Caller Domain:
    HANDCUFFS Caller Logon ID: (0x0,0x2B79) "
```

SSH CRS-32 Attack:

```
sshd[6169]: fatal: Local: Corrupted check bytes on input.
sshd[6253]: fatal: Local: crc32 compensation attack: network attack
    detected
```

sendmail Exploits:

```
Jul 21 01:25:49 ariel sendmail[308]: BAA00307: to=lamarbroc@delphi.
    com, ctladdr=":/bin/mail root@ariel.sdsc.edu </etc/passwd",
    delay=00:00:34, mailer=smtp, relay=bos1h.delphi.com. (192.80.63.8),
    stat=Sent (Ok.)

Jul 21 01:35:40 ariel sendmail[545]: setsender: "/bin/mail root@
    ariel.sdsc.edu </etc/passwd": invalid or unparseable, received from
    [205.133.101.5]

Jul 21 13:13:04 ariel sendmail[784]: NAA00783: to=\tsutomu,
    ctladdr=tsutomu@ariel.sdsc.edu, delay=00:03:09, mailer=local,
    stat=Sent
```

Cisco IOS Change:

```
%SYS-5-CONFIG: Configured from host1-config by rcp from 172.16.101.101
```

FW-1 MAD Port Scan:

```
Feb 26 17:47:28 host.example.com root: 26Feb2001 17:47:28 accept
    localhost >daemon useralert product MAD proto ip src elendil dst
    host additionals: attack=blocked_connection_port_scanning
```

Chapter 9 will show you how correlation can be used to tackle this problem with ease.

Future Bad Things, Never Before Seen Things, and All But the Known Good Things

Aside from being able to recognize things that are known bad things, you will want to be able to detect things that you don't know about, have never seen before, or are outside of what you already know about. Why is this critical? As attackers evolve their techniques, normal means of detecting outside-the-norm behavior, e.g. looking at your log data for things you know about, will eventually become the attacker's way into your environment. This sort of analysis is generally not easily accomplished by manual review of logs. It requires more sophisticated techniques. Chapter 11 discusses using data mining techniques while Chapter 10 shows how statistical analysis can be used to identify things you have never seen, among other things.

PLANNING

Requirements for log analysis systems are as critical as what your goals are. If you don't understand the key concepts in planning an analysis system, you will sort of be lost. This section will focus on higher level concerns about the planning of a system. These concerns will serve as a blueprint of sorts which you can refer to when logging at commercial and open source solutions, managed security providers, or even if you want to build your own system.

Accuracy

Accuracy is the cornerstone of any logging system. But what exactly are the implications on a logging system? Accuracy, quite frankly, is ensuring that any log data received, processed, archived, etc. is free from defects or misleading information in any way. In other words, the data that received is what you or your logging systems intended it to be. One issue is that of false positives. Intrusion Detection Systems (IDS) are one source of false positives. For example, an IDS may report malicious traffic that either isn't malicious or may not represent a true vulnerability on the target system. One solution to this would be for the IDS to consult a vulnerability database to cross reference possible malicious behavior. Further yet, your IDS could also implement a policy scheme whereby user and group profiles are used to create acceptable network usage of individuals.

Cutting down on false positives can help keep clutter down to a minimum. Obviously if you are consuming log data from vendors, you have almost no control over what is transmitted. But in the event that you are planning to write a custom logging system, keep in mind that, much like human conversations and interactions, it is often useful to keep things brief and to the point.

One final area regarding accuracy involves the notion of timestamps. A timestamp is the date and time that some event occurred. Almost every security application on the planet uses timestamps. Furthermore, most of these applications send along a timestamp with any log messages they forward upstream. The problem is that different vendors use differing formats. Some use a UNIX epoch, while others either use a standard formatted string for date and time or, worse yet, make up their own. The main standard with regard to timestamps is the ISO 8601 standard. An example ISO 8601 timestamp follows:

> 2004-07-21T11:44:44+00:00

The format is YYYY-MM-DDTHH:MM:SS.SSS+/−H. There is a literal "T" in the timestamp in order to delineate between the date and time. The +/− is an offset for GMT. Additionally, RFC 3339 defines date and time formats for use on the Internet.

Finally, here are a few samples of log timestamps from various systems:

- Fri Aug 31 15:44:13 2007
- 10/Jul/2006:00:02:20 −0400
- Jan 11 10:36:21
- 10/21/2005 11:11:38
- 2004-08-06 10:32:53
- 12/2/2003,3:29:05 PM
- 07-06-200400:00:49
- <time offset="0" timeZone="GMT">1041880724715825000</time>

As you can see, log timestamp formats are a real problem. Sadly, you will most likely have to deal with timestamps in formats like this.

Integrity

Integrity deals with trusting the source, and sometimes the content, of log messages. If you are relying on log data from commercial log data, then you are at the mercy of the vendor. Some vendors get it. For example, some commercial products already make use of the Secure Sockets Layer (SSL) to not only authenticate clients and servers, but also for encryption of data itself. Other vendors rely on plain-old syslog or making use of the SNMP. Sure, the latest version of SNMP (version 3) makes allowances for security and encryption, but many vendors do not support it as of yet. In the event that you are relying on a vendor's insecure log data, you can use something like STunnel (http://www.stunnel.org). STunnel is a generic application (written in C) that allows you to forward and receive any type of data over an SSL tunnel. It does come in handy when you need secure communication but either don't have control over the data itself, or you don't have time to figure out a particular SSL API.

Yet another solution is to send data in clear, but make use of dedicated network links which you know are free from prying eyes and hands. This is an expensive proposition, however, since you may already have network links that are multi use. Obviously you can't use these links for sensitive data transmission.

One last tidbit of information regarding integrity deals with digital signatures. If you digitally sign your log data, you can be assured that it is authentic. Some regulatory bodies may require this level of integrity within your system, if log data ends up being used as evidence in a criminal investigation.

Confidence

We are reminded of the scene from the movie *War Games* where, just as Joshua tried to convince NORAD that nuclear destruction was fast approaching, an operator at some console announces over a loudspeaker that confidence was high. Confidence has to do with how sure you are that what happened, or is happening, is an actual event worth caring about. Some products attempt to do this by placing a priority or severity on a given event. This conceptual notion might be in the form of high, medium, or low, or it may be a sliding scale from 0 to 99. Many Cisco devices, for example, use a scale of 0 through 7.

Confidence in reality goes a bit deeper than a simple priority scheme. True confidence is derived from knowing all you can about your network and infrastructure. SIEM systems are useful in this regard. The SIEM marketplace is one that is fairly new and ever evolving. SIEMs are typically enterprise applications that sit atop all the security devices in a network. This includes, but is not limited to, firewalls, IDSes, vulnerability scanners, databases, and applications. All these systems feed into the SIEM, where the SIEM can either use statistical algorithms to analyze log data or allow an operator to create custom rules that look for specific patterns in the log data. The benefit of creating custom rules is that it allows for an abstraction of a potential security threat to be caught based on heterogeneous log data. (firewalls and IDSes for example). This is at the heart of confidence: the taking inputs from many areas (often disjoint) and deriving a more mature (and accurate) fact from the set of all inputs.

Preservation

Preservation is the idea that log data should not be altered in any way whatsoever. This is a must if you ever plan to use a piece of log data to prosecute malicious actions. For example, many security device vendors provide their own notion of the type of potential attack, e.g. a firewall drop, an IDS port sweep, and so forth. It is critical this information not get altered at all during any point of the log system receipt, processing, analysis and archival.

The argument has been made time and time again that some vendors classify events poorly. Some savvy network security engineer may feel that she knows best and wants to rename a given event's type description from that of the vendor supplied one, which the engineer is confident is more expressive of the "real" intrusion, threat, breach, etc. The motive is pure, however the method may not be. In this scenario, the engineer should have a log system that allows for this mapping to occur independent of the original data.

Sanitization

Confidentiality of log data can sometimes be a concern when dealing with log systems. For example, you may have user account information or IP addresses that you don't want transmitted over a network link. Or possibly you are transmitting logs to a third-party vendor and you want to keep certain things private. There are two main techniques for log sanitization. The first is to detect and either replace or remove the entries you want sanitized. For example, and IP address of 10.0.3.4 may become xxx.xxx.xxx.xxx. This alerts someone viewing the sanitized log entry that there was an IP address in the log file. The other technique is based on a scheme where the removed log data can be reconstructed at some later point. For example, the sanitized information may be extracted and placed into a secure file.

Normalization

Normalization, as it pertains to log and analysis systems, is an interesting topic. What we are now concerned with is normalizing vendor data into a format we as security and network analysts can manipulate, report on, etc. In other words we are concerned with creating a well-known log event format. Many security vendors choose their own logging format regardless if Syslog or SNMP is used. To make matters worse, some vendors choose to provide a proprietary software development kit (SDK) to access their application's internal data formats. This can be a real problem mainly when you actually want to process log messages to extract pieces of data like IP addresses and port information. Normalization, sometimes referred to as unification, is essentially the act of mapping many different vendors' log data format to one that is well known, i.e. one that you have come up with.

As we saw in Chapter 4, defining a logical scheme for storing data is one piece of the normalization puzzle. By coming up with a data schema which meets the needs of your application or organization, you can easily map almost any vendor's log event data, no matter how verbose or unwieldy, to your own. This makes things like forensic mining and historical searching much easier since you know the format of the data up front. Chapter 9 expands on this topic by discussing parsing and normalization.

Challenges with Time

Our final topic in the planning section is that of time synchronization. Time is a very critical component of investigation after the fact. Logs can show with exact certainty that something happened. Here are some challenges with time and log data:

- Completely false timestamp in logs—a dead battery or another hardware failure is a common reason for seeing time stamps that have no connection to reality whatsoever.
- It's always 5PM somewhere: which time zone are your logs in? Many log files will contain no time zone in the logs themselves; one needs to take care of noting down in which time zone the logging system was located.
- Are you in drift? Your clock might be—admittedly NTP clock drift cause time deviations at the order of seconds, but even this might change the sequence of events (e.g. did he launched an attack first or did he try to login first—thus seeing the login banner?) Using UTC time on all systems might resolve this issue.
- Syslog forwarder mysteries: his time vs. my time—less common more likely in the future as people adopt buffering syslog servers (such as syslog-ng or commercial systems that can store-and-forward logs). In this case, one needs to make sure that a syslog message contains the time of the event and not the time of the delayed log transmission.
- So, which one is right? Systems with two timestamps! Some of the systems will have more than one timestamp and one will possess a high degree of certainty about which is the time of the event.
- If something got logged at 5:17AM, when did it happen? Log lag is real as well, especially for logging processes or programs execution. For example, some systems will log the process execution when the program terminates or exits and not when it is launched.
- 5:17 in logs, sadly, may mean 5:17AM or 5:17PM (17:17). Some older systems make that mistake.
- Finally, can you trust your NTP time source? Do you have an SLA with the time provider? The answer to this is likely "no." This is admittedly very esoteric but needs to be at least considered briefly.

Here are some rules of thumb to abide by to mitigate these challenges.

- NTP religiously; run a time server that synchronizes with a guaranteed time server (e.g. time.nist.gov).
- Implement time synchronization across all the logging systems with the above NTP server.
- Note down the time zone when receiving and centralizing logs (make sure to use EST, EST, PDT, or GMT+/−N format).

- If timing mechanism fails and you end up with January 1970, you can try to use other logs to correlate—however, justifying the timing procedure in court will be an uphill battle.
- To account for log lag mentioned above—know the system that logs!
- For higher levels of assurance investigate trusted time protocols (look up ANSI X9.95:2005).

PREPARATION

Our final topic is that of preparation. Preparation deals with gearing up to get down, so to speak. Here we want to make sure we have prepared our environment and log data so we can not only analyze it, but store it, report on it, etc.

Separating Log Messages

If you can separate your log messages by host and then by service, this can make analysis much easier. It can also make the following tasks much easier, too:

Develop a set of unique patterns: Easier to do if you separate messages by service.
Identify the "variables" in each pattern: Type and range.
Check for false positives (in pattern matches) and corrupt data.
Storing patterns: Can be a flat text file, database, etc.

Parsing

Parsing deals with taking a raw log message and extracting feature information from it. These features include the source of the log message, timestamp of when the log occurred, source and destination IP information, user information, etc. This allows you to gain a greater understanding of your log data because you can work with the piece parts of the log message for detailed analysis, reporting and so on. Chapter 9 goes into detail about parsing and the concepts surrounding it.

Data Reduction

It is important to understand data reduction techniques in order to not only efficiently transmit log data from its source to an intermediate processing server, but to also store the data efficiently as well. Some of these techniques, however, do come at a price. Some impact the CPU performance of the source host system, receiving host system, or both. The gains had by some of these techniques sometimes outweights the system impact. If you are able to send less data over your network, i.e. you utilize less bandwidth, which could be a gain if you have limits of how much data you can transmit over your network.

Data Compression

Data compression deals with taking a sting of bytes and compressing it down to a smaller set of bytes, whereby it takes either less bandwidth to transmit the string or to store it to disk. The compressed string is then re-inflated by the receiving side or application. The downside is that there is a performance impact on both the sender and receiver when the data has to be compressed and then inflated on the other end.

There are two ways in which compression can be applied to log analysis. One is when we transmit our normalized events from the log aggregator to the processing server for analysis and/or archival. The other way to use compression is at the database level. This is largely a function of what your particular database vendor supports.

Data De-duplication

In the normal course of log data collection, duplicate event data is often received. Technically speaking, the notion of duplicate event data almost never applies to security log data. What you end up with is the same sort of event that has some variable characteristic. For example, let's say an attacker is port scanning hosts on your network. For each of these probe attempts, your IDS will more than likely create separate events. The event type may be the same (port sweep or some such type), but the attacker's source IP address and port may differ for each event, especially if spoofing is employed, but the destination IP address (the attacked host) will be the same for each event.

Security log events fall into two main categories: those which are informational and those which are of real operational and/or tactical value. Informational messages are things like system start up or shut down. Operational or tactical log data are events reported from your IDS, firewall and such. SSH login failure attempts, for example, are of particular operational interest.

The goal is to come up with a unique identifier for an event which will allow for seemingly disparate events to be lumped together logically into a single event, differentiated only by a count of how many times the event in question. This count allows hundreds and thousands of events to occur with a single event representing all occurrences. This saves a tremendous amount of space.

There are several pieces of information in log data which can help you with de-duplication. They are:

- Source of the Log Event (IDS, FW, etc.)
- Source IP Address

- Source Port
- Destination IP Address
- Destination Port.

Source of the Log Event: The source of the log event is the device, software, etc. which generated the event. This has several implications. Many security products are moving toward management server architecture. This means that instead of every device reporting individually to a log server, each device will report to a management system which forwards events to the log server on behalf of one or more devices. This is a more efficient and scalable way for vendors to transmit log events to third-party receivers. The downside is that, whether SNMP or Syslog is used, the physical source of the log event is the management server, i.e. the IP address of the management server will be what we see in the Syslog message. In order to identify the sensor which actually generated the event, the management server will place the origin of the event inside the log message it emits to the log server. Note that we are using the term sensor in a general sense; a sensor could be a firewall, IDS and so forth. Now, much like the non-standardization of event log formats, the format of the origin field is vendor specific. It may be the IP address or hostname of the sensor, or it could be some unique identifier. This is a fact to be aware of when you may want to use the source of the log event as part of your de-duplication uniqueness key.

Source IP Address: The source IP address is from where the attack originated. In practice, this is not enough to guarantee uniqueness. This is due mainly to the fact that attackers may spoof one or more source IP address.

Source Port: The source port is the randomly created port of the origin of the source system. Again, due to spoofing this is generally not reliable enough for de-duplication.

Destination IP Address: The destination IP address is the IP of the target system. This is generally the one thing that will remain static during the duration of an attack. This is a good candidate to aid in our de-duplication efforts.

Destination Port: In the event that a port scan attack is happening, the IDS will report many different ports for the same destination IP address. For many attacks, there will be one destination IP address and one destination port. Destination port is a somewhat good candidate for inclusion into our de-duplication process.

After Hours Data Transmission
This topic is not technically a data reduction technique, but it does bare mention in this chapter. This technique works well for transmission from your aggregator to the main/analysis server. The basic principal is that you determine

a time of day to transmit events for which you don't necessarily wish to have analyzed, but you do want to archive the data. For example, if you have very strict firewall rules in place, you may not care about seeing or analyzing firewall accepts, permits, and so on, but you still have a need to archive all of these events. With after-hours transmission, you could send these firewall events at some time, say 3AM, when network traffic is at a minimum. Also not analyzing these events on your server can reduce the load and leave CPU cycles available for events of a more dire nature to be dealt with.

The steps to accomplish this technique are quite straightforward. First, you need to have a way to detect and segregate the log messages you wish to transmit at a later time. This can be done via using built-in facilities in syslog-ng or whatever your system supports. These messages need to be kept on the log aggregation point, but stored in a place where they can't impact the coming-and-going of higher priority events. Second, a date and/or time will need to be declared in order to define when events should be transmitted. Finally, when the time comes, transmit events to the main server for analysis and/or archival. You will also need to a way to communicate to the server that these events are not to be analyzed; it doesn't always make sense to process these events if you are transmitting them at some later date and time. It should be noted that if your particular log analysis tool doesn't support this concept, you might have to create your own solution using scp, rsync, or some other tool.

One issue to be aware of is that if you allow for time ranges to be specified, e.g. 3AM to 4AM, you may have the situation where an hour is not enough time to transmit all the segregated event data. You now must make a decision: do you stop sending the events, or do you keep going regardless of the time, until all the events are sent? It really depends on your particular requirements, or simply what your gut tells you is the right thing to do.

SUMMARY

Before log analysis can commence, you need to make sure you have your ducks in a row. This includes setting your goals, planning your log analysis system, and preparing your log data for analysis. The remaining chapters in this book will go into more detail on many of the concepts introduced in this chapter.

Simple Analysis Techniques

INTRODUCTION

Manually reading logs should be reserved as a punishment in the appropriate circle of Hell. However, lacking good, automated tools, one will always fall back to manual review, thus we are reviewing it in this chapter. Having a firm foundation in the basics will serve you well. Additionally we will provide insight into responding to the results of log analysis.

But why do we perform log analysis? Here are some of the reasons:

- Compliance and Regulatory Concerns.
- Situational Awareness on Your Network.
- Infrastructure ROI.
- Measuring Security.
- Incident Response.

LINE BY LINE: ROAD TO DESPAIR

As we are starting up with a subject of manual analysis, let's try to go through a log file from a Nokia IPSO platform (a variant of BSD Unix) that is used for a Checkpoint Firewall-1, line by line, as a beginner system administrator or a security analyst just to get a feel for the process:

```
Mar 25 15:56:42 cp41 [LOG_NOTICE] xpand[370]: Sending trap request
   (to default addresses)..
Mar 25 15:56:42 cp41 [LOG_NOTICE] xpand[370]: Trap sent
Mar 25 15:56:42 cp41 [LOG_NOTICE] xpand[370]: Configuration changed
   from 172.16.10.55 by user admin for page /opt/syswatch/templates/
   configuration
Mar 25 15:57:00 cp41 [LOG_INFO] /USR/SBIN/CRON[18212]: (root) CMD
   (/etc/hourly 2>&1 >>/var/log/hourly)
Mar 25 15:58:11 cp41 [LOG_NOTICE] xpand[370]: Configuration changed
   from localhost by user admin
Mar 25 15:58:24 cp41 [LOG_INFO] sshd-x[16837]: Generating new 768 bit
   RSA key.
Mar 25 15:58:25 cp41 [LOG_INFO] sshd-x[16837]: RSA key generation
   complete.
Mar 25 15:59:05 cp41 [LOG_INFO] sshd-x[18383]: Accepted publickey for
   ROOT from 172.16.10.55 port 36710 ssh2
```

Let's quickly analyze the log file now:

1. OK, so the first line indicates sending of an SNMP trap. Looks perfectly normal.
2. Second, same thing, looks like a success status that a trap was sent.
3. Next, looks like some configuration change done by "admin" from an IP address 172.16.10.55. Might or might not be normal, depends upon what else we know.
4. The next line indicates that a process was run from *cron*, a facility to run programs periodically in the background. This looks normal.
5. Line five is also a configuration change, although unattributed to a specific user, can't tell whether it's important, but looks like IPSO considers it a low priority.
6. Next two messages are related to a routine activity by a *sshd* remote access daemon, that regenerates the encryption key every predefined time period. To be ignored.
7. The last of our batch indicates that the "root" has connected from the same IP that we observed the above change from. This might be normal, unless the previous configuration change was by itself malicious.

Aren't you getting frustrated? And we just analyzed about 3 min from the life of this specific computer systems; just eight lines of logs or 762 bytes. Now, imagine that we had a month of logs from this busy system. We will be talking about gigabytes and millions of lines of logs. Suddenly, a manual reviews sounds like a deeply troubled process. Indeed, manual log review doesn't scale, to put it mildly. However, we will still fall back to it in some circumstance, such as lacking tools or needing a quick glance on something very specific.

As an additional complication, we were familiar with this log format and had general environment knowledge of Unix, IPSO, etc. Often the analyst will have to learn all that from scratch. As we pointed out in earlier chapters, binary and other non-readable format will also complicate the situation significantly. Thus, logs might be hard to read as well as hard to understand, which hampers manual analysis.

SIMPLE LOG VIEWERS

Let's now look at some simple viewers in Unix and Windows and how they help.

Real-Time Review

On most Unix and Linux flavors, there are several tools that can assist with log analysis. Some of them help with real-time log viewing, while others help with reviewing historical logs.

We will start from the classic:

```
# tail -f /var/log/messages
```

This command will show the last lines in the standard Unix messages file and the new lines that appear after the command is launched. This is by far the simplest real-time log viewer, albeit the least useful in most circumstances. However, it is quite handy if all that is needed is a look at the system log records as they appear, for example, during a new program test or a daemon crash.

The above command may be enhanced with filtering by using the standard Unix string matching utility—*grep*:

```
# tail -f /var/log/messages | grep sshd
```

This command will only show messages produced by the secure shell daemon, such as:

```
Dec 12 17:31:56 ns1 sshd[4095]: refused connect from 80.92.67.68
Dec 12 17:37:34 ns1 sshd[484]: Generating new 768 bit RSA key.
Dec 12 17:37:34 ns1 sshd[484]: RSA key generation complete.
```

To further enhance the above real-time log viewing, we can throw in a *tee* command that will help us to look at the data as well as send it to a file:

```
# tail -f /var/log/messages | grep sshd | tee file-of-latest-sshd-logs.
   txt
```

This command shows log lines will also be recorded to a file "file-of-latest-sshd-logs.txt."

For the fans of *less*, they can use this Unix command in wait mode to perform the same feat:

```
# less /var/log/messages
```

Now, press "F" for the *less* to go into the "tail" mode and show the latest and newly arriving data.

In Windows environment, a bundled Event Viewer can be run to monitor newly arriving log records in each of the three logs. It will be covered in the next section on simple historical log viewers.

Historical Log Review

Now that we mentioned *less*, we can start talking about looking at stored logs. Obviously, any text editor on your platform of choice can be used to look at the plain text logs. There is one caveat however! Some log files are very large, as we mentioned before. Thus, not every text editor will handle them efficiently (if at all). Just try loading a 1 GB file in Windows notepad (without success) and you'd get the point. Other editors will work, but operation will be extremely slow. Thus, you'd want to have something lightweight, but, on the other hand, with search and other useful features.

On Unix, *more* and *less* utilities usually fit the bill. They can handle large files (gigabyte sizes) as well as have search. Following our policy not to rephrase manual pages, we refer the reader to the output of a *man* command on his or her Unix/Linux system. Typing *man more* and *man less* will show the information. Sometimes, more details help can be obtained by an *info* command, such as:

```
$ info less
```

On Windows, the only bundled tool is an Event Viewer. Here we will mention that it allows perusing the three standard Windows logs (Application, Systems, and Security), waiting for new events and displaying them as they arrive (by clicking "Refresh"), as well as filtering and sorting. Figure 8.1 shows the viewer.

As described,[1] some of the more interesting features of the Windows 7 Event Viewer include:

- Working with individual events as XML.
- Subscribing to events on remote machines using event subscriptions.
- Saving filters as custom views.

---

[1] http://www.razorleaf.com/2009/11/event-viewer-top-5/.

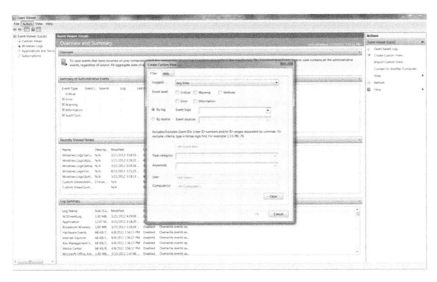

FIGURE 8.1 Windows 7 Event Log Viewer

- Logging your own custom events in the application log.
- Running a task in response to an event.

The above tools will show you logs, but most likely you will start wishing for more right away. Can we filter for that? Summarize like this? Slightly change format? This is where some tools will help.

Simple Log Manipulation

We will start from Unix, since it has more tools for that purpose, and will go to Windows afterwards.

We established that we can look at logs in real time on Unix using *tail* and *less* and use many of the file viewing tools (such as *cat*, *more*, or *less*) for looking at stored files.

Let's first summarize what are we aiming at while using the simple tools and then we will show how to do it:

1. *Log filtering:* We want to only see specific stuff.
2. *Log reformatting:* Modifying the way we see it.
3. *Log summarization:* Seeing a condensed view.

As we mentioned above, grep in combination with *tail* allows for simple filtering. *Grep* can also help with more advanced filtering on large log files. Here is a scatter of examples of common log filtering tasks with *grep*:

```
# grep -ev 'ssh|telnet' /var/log/messages
```

See all messages with the exception of those containing *ssh* and *telnet*:

```
| # grep -f patterns /var/log/messages
```

See all messages matching the patterns from a file "patterns."

Other tools enhance the power of grep are *tail* and *head*. They are used to look at the front and end parts of a log file. For example:

```
# tail - 1000 /var/log/messages | grep ailed
```

The above looks for records with a string "ailed" (aiming to catch both "Failed" and "failed" since *grep* is case-sensitive) in the last 1000 lines of a messages file. Similarly,

```
# head - 1000 /var/log/messages | grep ailed
```

looks for records with a string "ailed" in the first 1000 lines of a messages file.

If you add *awk* and *sort* tool to the mix, we can do a lot more with the logs. For example, we can view what devices and systems has logged to our file:

```
# cat messages | awk '{print $4}' | sort -u
```

On our test system the above gives:

```
ns1
ns2
ns-backup
```

Those are the names of three Unix systems logging to the server, we just extracted this summary information from a bunch of logs. This example brings us into sorting and simple summaries of logs. In fact, *awk* allows writing complicated (both in functionality and in comprehension) scripts to process the log files, but we will focus only on commands used here.

Log Parser and Log Parser Lizard: A Better Way to Sift Through Windows Logs

On Windows, the Event Viewer allows us to filter, sort, and extract logs to files. On a typical Windows system filtering is limited to:

- Event type.
- Event category.
- Event ID.
- Source computer.
- Source application or system component name.

- User name.
- Date and time range.

For somewhat more advanced analysis of Windows logs we can use Log Parser with Log Lizard. Log Parser is a Microsoft Windows add-on which gives you an SQL-like interface to the Windows Event Log. For example, here is a query which will retrieve all rows from the System Windows event log:

```
SELECT * FROM System
```

By itself it is a command-line tool, which makes it difficult to use in any analytical way. This is where Log Lizard comes in. It's a GUI which puts a nice interface around Log Parser. Installation of the two tools is very easy and straightforward. You can obtain them from the following places:

1. *Log Parser:* http://www.microsoft.com/download/en/details.aspx?displayla ng=en&id=24659.
2. *Log Parser Lizard:* http://www.lizard-labs.net/log_parser_lizard.aspx.

Figure 8.2 shows the Log Parser Lizard GUI.

Some of the features of Log Parser combines with Log Parser Lizard include:

- Charting.
- Customized searching.
- Limiting the rows returned.

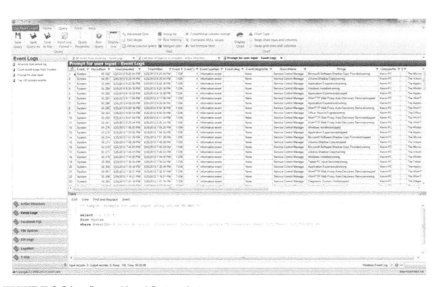

FIGURE 8.2 Log Parser Lizard Screenshot

- Export of results returned *via* queries.
- And many more.

The Microsoft Log Parser Toolkit provides a great introduction to Log Parser (Giuseppini and Burnett, 2004). You can use this reference to understand how it works and what features are available *via* the query language.

Log Parser Lizard has online documentation and forums which both provide a good starting point to learn more about this useful tool.

LIMITATIONS OF MANUAL LOG REVIEW

At this stage it should become clear that while manual log review and using simple tools and commands certainly has its place in log analysis, it should not be relied upon as a main mechanism for log analysis.

The obvious limitations include:

- Manual log review just doesn't scale up with the increasing log file sizes: we looked at eight lines, but a more realistic task is to look at 8 million. In large-scale enterprise environments, logs are often produced at the rate of 20,000 log records *per second*. Manual log analysis will break and become ineffective and inefficient at a much lower logging rate.
- Manual log review is easy for easy logs: when the file is pretty-much self-explanatory and tells you that something specific has failed it can be interpreted manually, but in case of a more obscure and undocumented log source, the approach fails flat on its face. The effort needed to interpret each line will go from a second of quick thinking to hours of research online and in other sources.
- Simple tools and manual review will likely never yield a big picture of what is going on in the computing environment, but more advanced tools can produce such a picture from log data.
- In addition to confusing and obscure formats, in many cases the analysis will require relating logs from multiple sources together. Such activity can indeed be performed manually but the time needed will go up by a large margin (compared to just looking at one log file). Such correlated should better be left to the automated tools.
- Last but not least, such activity is usually extremely *boring*. While this is a problem by itself, boredom usually saps the efficiency of an analyst faster than he can say "beer."

Overall, as long as we don't ask too much of our manual log review activities, they definitely have this place. We summarize the results of this in the summary section at the end of the chapter.

RESPONDING TO THE RESULTS OF ANALYSIS

One might think that since the book is about log analysis, we will stop when the analysis is complete and we know for sure what was going on. However, the only real practical purpose of the analysis is to *act* after it is complete. While the emphasis of the book is obviously on the analysis itself, this brief chapter reviews a spectrum of actions, which are usually performed based on log analysis. In particular, relevance of logs to incident response will be discussed, since sometimes the logs reveal that the incident has taken place.

Up to this point, we have pursued log analysis for various, now it is time to tie various reasons we analyzed logs to real-world actions. We will deal with actions on two levels: a micro level (what to do if you see a specific line or an indication in a log file) and macro level (what kind of process improvements needs to be implemented as a result of log analysis).

Acting on Critical Logs

If you see something like this in your network intrusion detection logs:

```
2004-12-02|00:46:58|dralion1|SSL:COMPROMISE-
SHELL|10.2.3.4|213.190.36.144|443|2328|X||6|tcp,dp=2328,sp=443|
```

which is then followed by this:

```
2004-12-02|00:47:02|dralion1|HIPORT:SHELL-
UNAME|10.2.3.4|213.190.36.144|443|2328|X||6|tcp,dp=2328,sp=443|
```

your action should be swift, decisive as well as planned and prepared. For those who didn't know, the above messages from the Enterasys Dragon Network Intrusion Detection system reliably indicate that the target server (with an address 10.2.3.4) has been compromised by an attacker (from 213.190.36.144). Note that in the Dragon messages above the source and destination are reversed since the NIDS detected the response from the victim system to the attacker that indicates that an attacker has obtained interactive access to the target Web server. Just for reference, the above Dragon messages are interpreted in Table 8.1.

This example aims to indicate that for some messages the required action is obvious: jump to your incident response plan right away. What are some of the log files, messages that usually trigger an *immediate* action that does not require much deliberation (or, rather, all deliberation can happen in advance)? Table 8.2 has specific examples of actions to take on critical logs.

Note that the actions in Table 8.2 are not provided as a comprehensive "What to Do Guide" for all the circumstances in life, but to illustrate that logs can often be actionable.

Table 8.1 Definition of Dragon Log Message Fields

Field	Meaning
2004-12-02|	Date of the logged event
00:46:58|	Time of the logged event
dralion1|	Host name of the log producing machine
SSL:COMPROMISE-SHELL|	Attack name as classified by the NIDS vendor
10.2.3.4|	Source IP
213.190.36.144|	Destination IP
443|	Source port
2328|	Destination port
X||	Unused in this case
6|	Protocol (where 6 stands for TCP
tcp,dp=2328,sp=443|	Other information

Table 8.2 Summary of Actions to Take on Critical Log Messages

Critical Log	Required Action
Faults that can affect system operations	If system operation is lost, a backup system needs to be brought up
Attacks that are successful	Initiate the incident response and recovery process for the compromised machine
Attacks that have a high chance of being successful	Initiate the incident response and recovery process for the compromised machine
System reaching capacity or maximum of some value	Bring additional capacity or risk losing the entire system
System changes possibly leading to security and availability problems	Reverse the changes if unauthorized to avoid the problems
System crash	A backup system needs to be brought up
Numerous failed logins	Check for signs of compromise if an attacker managed to guess the password
Hardware failure	If system operation is lost, a backup system needs to be brought up
Security-relevant configuration change	Reverse the changes if unauthorized
Unauthorized connection detected	Investigate who accessed the system and why

In this section we looked at a simple case of acting on logs, since we didn't have to design and implement a complicated plan. In addition, we only provided a summary of actions. In real-life, for example, "Investigate who accessed the system and why" might evolve into a prolonged multi-day investigative process.

Acting on Summaries of Non-Critical Logs

This section touches upon acting on aggregates of non-critical logs. The volume of firewall, router, or host messages does not invoke such an immediate response as the above critical messages from Dragon NIDS do. Just the fact that a connection was denied by a firewall usually does not map into instantaneous action by the user watching the logs (it is also unlikely that somebody is viewing those logs in near real time). However, a combination of such messages will often invoke an indirect action (otherwise, why even analyze the stuff that never leads to an action?).

As was pointed by Marcus Ranum "most log files are useless, and that most organizations are better off deleting their files and saving the disk space for something that's actually productive" (Garfinkel, 2005). The reason this was proclaimed is that if you never look at your log files (and thus, never act), there is absolutely no sense in keeping them. While nowadays in this regulatory compliance era one can claim that he keeps the logs "for compliance reasons," the above argument still applies since if neither you nor the compliance auditor looks at the logs and acts based on what they find—they are still useless. In the 2011 Verizion Data Breach Report, it was discovered that very high percentage of incidents had evidence in log messages of the breach, but no one was paying attention to the logs. This is a clear-cut proof that log analysis can indeed pay off.

We hope by that time the reader is already convinced that he not only needs to retain log files, not only to review and analyze them, but also act on them in order to derive the maximum value out of them.

There are several paths from seemingly non-actionable logs to action. We summarize some of the most common ones below:

1. *Acting on a summary or trend*: A lot of non-actionable messages often translate into action due to a developing trend or some new knowledge deduced from the summary.
2. *Acting on a correlated event or a group of events*: Often, a known combination of non-critical events falls into a critical pattern due to their sequence and timing.
3. *Acting on a discovered pattern* or *unusual sequence of non-critical events:* Using advanced log analysis tools, one can sometimes mine a new suspicious pattern out of otherwise normal and harmless log records.

Let's consider examples of the above three possibilities in detail.

Summaries and trends are a common result of log analysis. A long log file might be summarized into a brief "Top 10 Attacks" or "Top Suspicious IP Addresses" or an infinite number of other useful summaries. Often, such summary view will prompt an action. For example, it might become obvious from a "Top Bandwidth Users" report that the top three users in the company utilize 90% of available bandwidth. This can quickly lead to a disciplinary action, especially if such bandwidth is used to share files on P2P or to download non-work related materials. Similarly, an observation of a router CPU utilization log over a long period of time might reveal periods of unusually high activity, leading to an investigation possibly discovering attacker communication with a compromised system.

Correlation (described in Chapter 9) will often lead to groups of unimportant events to be flagged. A connection here, a failed login there, and an application launch in some other place might mean a system compromise or insider abuse of system privileges. For example, if an administrator access to a system is spotted at 3 AM, it might not mean anything bad, just slightly suspicious. If the administrator then tries to access several applications and then connects to a database and starts loading data, it might raise a flag, but still not mean anything bad. If, however, the final action is a large data download attempted from the same system, we know that an intrusion have likely taken place and it is time to act. Thus, by putting together a rule to watch for such activity, we can provide a (much needed!) action on relatively unimportant events.

Pattern discovery in logs is a novel area in log analysis (described in Chapters 10 and 11). It provides a highly effective and automated way of discovering new knowledge in logs and thus making ultimately boring and routine logs into actions. For example, a log file might be discovered to contain a repeating pattern of connections from a seemingly diverse set of source IP addresses. When presented, this pattern might be interpreted as a new exploitation tools, covertly tried on a company network. It can then lead to a set of actions by a security team and even community at large.

Table 8.3 summarizes more examples of how actions are associated with non-actionable logs.

Table 8.3 shows that even innocuous and routine events will often require an action if they are analyzed appropriately and can save a lot of headache by predicting the trouble early.

Developing an Action Plan

The above examples allow us to generalize and come to a valuable "Last step of log analyses"—action.

Such a plan will incorporate all possible results of analysis (as well as actions if the result doesn't fit the defined results) and cover both critical and informational alerts.

Table 8.3 Summary of Actions Associated With Non-Actionable Logs

Accounting Log / "keep in mind"	Path to Action	Action Needed
System status messages	Correlated	A pattern of system status messages might indicate unauthorized system use, leading to an investigation and then disciplinary action
Attack attempts and probes	Correlated summary	A pattern of probing might indicate that an advanced attacker is seeking to break in and strengthening of security defenses (an action!) is needed
Low impact attacks	Trend	A growth in low impact attack might coincide with an increase of more damaging attacks, that need to be acted on
System reaching a relatively high value of some parameter	Trend	A sharp increase in such messages indicates either an intrusion or overall system instability; both need an action to restore performance
Various system changes	Correlated	A pattern of system change messages might indicate unauthorized system reconfiguration, leading to an investigation and then disciplinary action
System startup/shutdown	Summary	A large number of system shutdowns in a certain time period might indicate that system became unstable and needs fixing
Successful login	Correlated	A successful logging coming at the heels of a long string of failed login indicates that a brute forcing password attack has succeeded.
Hardware status message	Summary	Summarizing hardware status messages across various systems might help pinpoint systems having the most problem, leading to overall optimization program and improved performance
Connection established/terminated	Discovery	Log mining can help to discovery an connection pattern indicative of a new hacking tool, leading to a need to strengthen security defenses

Admittedly, a plan will have a close relation to an incident response plan (see Chapter 16), but will also cover some of the early signs of danger (not constituting the incident) as well as changes in normal patterns of activity. A typical incident response plan will include communication, escalation, and response. Chapter 16 shows how to develop such a plan based around log data, along with insights in how to tailor it toward your environment.

Automated Actions

We covered the planning and different types of actions, but one critical action possibility was left outside the scope: automated action. Why plan and have people execute that action if you can program a system to do them automatically? While this is very tempting, real-life implementation of it faces a large number of challenges.

What are some of the possible automated actions? What kind of environment and what kind of circumstances call for their implementation?

In many cases of critical logged events, automated action is certainly appropriate. For example, here is how one of the authors uses log-driven automated action in the honeynet. Admittedly, the criticality of a honeypot environment is lower than that of the production system, however the risks are often the same or even higher. One of the most critical requirements for the honeypot is that it is always monitored. Thus, if some monitoring features fail, the operation of the honeypot should be halted. This is logically similar to the feature of several operating systems that can be configured to fail gracefully if audit collected stops workings.

Since the honeypot uses multiple monitoring mechanisms, the main failure scenario is the disk space exhaustion: if there is no space, no monitoring can function and record the attacker's steps. Thus, a script runs a "df" command AND watches the */var/log/messages* file for the traces of "wite failure—check your disk space," "n space left on device," "disk full" or "insufficient storage available at the moment" messages. In case such messages appear in the syslog or the "df" command shows that partitions holding log data are 100% full, the script will run and block all access to and from honeypot network *via* a special firewall configuration request.

EXAMPLES

This section will cover two examples of action on logs: log analysis in emergency incident response and routine analysis conclusions review.

Incident Response Scenario

This scenario deals with a company that was attacked. Incident investigators have analyzed (or, rather, tried to analyze, as logs were destroyed). "Rats R Us" is a global leader in end-to-end rat management for business and consumers. The Web site provides a significant part of the company revenue they have built a DMZ architecture with two firewalls that protects publicly available servers (Web, Email, etc.). One sunny day of May 2005, the intrusion prevention system started generating a huge volume of alerts related to IRC (Internet Relay Chat) program use on the company network.

The first action from the above log observation was to take a machine online—a drastic action indeed. This provides an example of acting on a critical log, similar to the above case of Dragon NIDS alert. The incident investigators have tried looking for the logs, but all were erased. Next, the analysts have tried looking at the external connectivity logs on a firewall.

As you know from above, such logs are not immediately actionable, but need to be summarized, correlated, or mined. However, summaries didn't really help in this case and no advanced log analysis tools were available to the investigators. The firewall contained its normal noise and, even though there might have been some interesting events, discovering them would have required having a starting point. Otherwise, it was just a mix of random IP addresses connecting through the firewall and no indication of which one was the attacker. Thus, they were unable to take action based on such logs and the incident remained largely unresolved.

The overall and final action taken was to formulate generic security recommendation. That included installing a security information and event management (SIEM) product, so that even routine logs can be analyzed proactively and acted upon.

Routine Log Review

Now, let's take a look at the same company after all the incident findings and lessons learned have been implemented and the company is more proactive in log analysis and review. To remind, the company made sure that the logs were configured to be sent to a commercial log collection and analysis product—SIEM—that can securely transfer and preserve them as well as perform advanced analytics on logs in real time and over the long term. For all practical purposes, "Rats R Us" was now in logging paradise. Let's take an example of how they now act on logs, routine, and others.

The company now has a clear plan to act on logs. Every day the company runs various log summaries and trends to observe the "big picture" of security. Those include "Top Attacked Ports," "Top Event Types," "Top Growing Event Types," as well as "Top Bandwidth Users" inside the company. Those are acted if some unusual things are observed in them or if whatever metric is growing dramatically. Similarly, if the number of connection events goes down ("Summary of Network Connection" report), another action is defined since it might indicate that the servers' performance is affected.

Other, less-common but very effective summaries include "Least Common Event Types," "Previously Unseen Events," and "Correlated Events." These help to discover rare but critical events in logs.

SUMMARY

This chapter looked at trying to assault the log problem by force: using manual log review and simple tools. In reality, this is similar to trying to attack a well-defended fortress with just clubs and not siege weapons: theoretically, it can be done, but it will take a huge crowd or a lot of time (and, likely both). In addition, a lot of attackers will die in the process and this is not something you want happening with your valuable IT personnel. The next chapter focuses on more automate analysis tools and techniques.

The important points to remember from this chapter are:

- *The time to use* the methods and techniques from this chapter:
  - A quick glance at the logs is all that is needed (such as to check something quickly).
  - A log volume is not too large.
  - The analyst is familiar with the log formats to be reviewed.
  - The log files to be analyzed contain high-severity critical alerts, that are immediately actionable without any further analysis.

- *The time not to use* the methods a techniques from this chapter:

  - A big picture view or a trend is needed (such as for a senior manager).
  - A high degree of automation and intelligence is needed in log analysis.
  - Logs are diverse and located in different places.
  - A large volume of sparse and non-critical logs needs to be distilled into something actionable.

REFERENCES

Garfinkel, S. (2005, April 1). Another look at log files. CSO. Web March 25, 2012. <http://www.csoonline.com/article/220233/another-look-at-log-files>.

Giuseppini, G., & Burnett, M. (2004). *Microsoft log parser toolkit*. Rockland, MA: Syngress.

Verizion 2011 data breach report. Verizion. Web June 1, 2012. <http://www.verizonbusiness.com/resources/reports/rp_data-breach-investigations-report-2011_en_xg.pdf>.

Filtering, Normalization, and Correlation

CONTENTS

INTRODUCTION

In the world of logging and log management, a large part of an administrator's time is spent reviewing logs for potential problems. In the past, this task was largely manual. Log analysis systems today provide automated mechanisms to help alleviate this burden. This chapter provides insight into this process. While no particular product is used, plenty of examples are given on the topics of filtering, correlation, parsing, rules, and so on. The goal is to provide you with the necessary concepts so you can use them no matter what logging system you use.

At the heart of this chapter are three large concepts: *filtering, normalization,* and *correlation*. Filtering is the act of taking in raw log data, determining if you want to keep it. The output of filtering is a normalized log data. This data is an input to correlation. Correlation is the act of matching a single normalized piece of data, or a series of pieces data, for the purpose of taking an action. Figure 9.1 shows the logical flow of this process.

Let's briefly describe each step in the process:

1. *Raw Log Data:* This is what you start with. This is the first input into the process.
2. *Filter:* In the filter stage we look for log messages that we care about and don't care about. The ones we don't care about can be "dropped" in order

to reduce load on the overall system. In Figure 9.1, this is shown with an arrow going to an exceptions store. This can be used to review the less-interesting log messages at a later time.

3. *Normalization:* In this step we take the raw log data and map its various elements (source and destination IP, etc.) to a common format. This is important for the correlation step. When a raw log message is normalized, the typical term for what results is an *event*. This term will be used throughout this chapter to denote a normalized log message. Another step in the normalization process is that of categorization. This means that a log message is transformed into a more meaningful piece of information. For example, a vendor might only provide something like "ID=6856" in the log message. But this sting of characters, per the vendor, is a login failure. It is the job of the person writing the normalization steps to do this transformation. A nice side effect of doing this is that it makes writing correlation rules more robust and intuitive. More on this later.

4. *Correlation:* Correlation will often lead to groups of individually unimportant events to be flagged. A connection here, a failed login there and an application launch in some other place might mean a system compromise or insider abuse of system privileges. The two basic forms of correlation are rules-based and statistical.

5. *Action:* An action is generally what you do after a correlation has occurred. Figure 9.1 shows several kinds (this list is by no means exhaustive):

   a. *To Analysts:* If you have a log monitoring interface (generally some sort of GUI), this is where you send your high-priority events that require immediate attention.

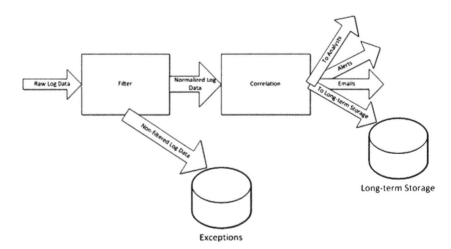

FIGURE 9.1 Basic Flow for Filtering and Correlation

CORRELATION CONCEPTS

General concepts
The authors of this book have a combined experience in this space approaching 20 years. We present the concepts in a general so as to provide you with the foundation needed when it comes to selecting or using a logging system. Of course, we do show some actual tools which can be used to solve correlation needs.

   b. *Alerts:* This is generally a hybrid of sending an event to an analyst. In this scenario an alert might be a grouping of events which indicate something at a high level has occurred.
   c. *Email:* This can be used as a means to alert on-call staff after hours.
   d. *Long-term Storage:* Long-term storage is where you keep your log data and normalized events. This is a prerequisite for reporting, auditing, long-term analysis, etc.

Let's now take a look at what is involved in filtering.

FILTERING

Filtering boils down to the following operations:

1. Keeping or discarding log data you care about.
2. Parsing the raw log message into a common format so you can more easily analyze the data.

As you may already know, vendors do not standardize log message formats between each other. For example, Cisco's log message format is totally different from Palo Alto Networks or Sonicwall, and so on regardless of the fact that each vendor may use Syslog as the underlying message transport. The power of step number 2 allows for disparate log data formats to be in one common normalization format. This is the key for efficient analysis and correlation (more on this later). But how do you go about knowing what you want to keep or not keep? Let's look at a high-level example.

Artificial Ignorance
The Great Marcus Ranum coined the phrase "Artificial Ignorance" back in 1997. At the heart of this concept is a mechanism for finding log data that you are familiar with so that you can find things you don't yet know about. He provided the following UNIX shell commands to aid in this process: (Ranum, 1997).

```
cd /var/log
cat * | \
   sed -e 's/^.*demo//' -e 's/\[[0-9]*\]//' | \
   sort | uniq -c | \
   sort -r -n > /tmp/xx
```

In the sed command, the "demo" string is the name of the system on which the commands are running. The idea is to strip this and the preceding timestamps in the log messages so we can reduce the variability in the log data. This is the key!

When you run this command you will see output similar to the following:

```
297 cron: (root) CMD (/usr/bin/at)
167 sendmail: alias database /etc/aliases.db out of date
120 ftpd: PORT
61 lpd: restarted
48 kernel: wdpi0: transfer size=2048 intr cmd DRQ
... etc
```

The number preceding the log message shows how many times the log message was seen in log files. As you get to the bottom of the output, you will notice the numbers getting smaller and smaller. The idea is that these are log messages you may not know about because they occur less frequently than the others. As he shows in his article, you can take the things you know about, place them in an ignore file so you can exclude things you know about.

Most log analysis systems provide mechanisms to perform filtering. But it is important to err on the side of keeping more data than filtering it out. The example provided in this section was merely to acquaint you with the concept so you know about it and understand its usefulness. The next section on normalization takes us to the next step in the process.

NORMALIZATION

The next step after filtering is normalization. It is assumed that at this point you already know what log data you would like to keep. Normalization means we take known log messages, parse them for piece part components (timestamps, IP addresses, etc.) and turn them into a common format. This common format has historically been arrived at via the use of a Relational Database System (RDBMS) or some other lower level format (binary on disk, etc.). However, in today's big data and No SQL movements, more and more vendors are moving away from databases because they do not scale.

The steps to normalizing a raw log message are:

1. Get documentation for product or products you are using.
2. Read the documentation for descriptions of what the raw log data looks like and what each field is.
3. Come up with the proper parsing expression to normalize the data. Most log analysis systems utilize a regular expression implementation to parse the data.
4. Test the parsing logic on sample raw log data.
5. Deploy the parsing logic.

Regardless of the ending storage mechanism used for normalized events, certain fields are more common and useful than others. These include:

- *Source and Destination IP addresses:* These are very useful during the correlation process.
- *Source and Destination Ports:* These are used to understand what services are trying to be accessed or are accessed.
- *Taxonomy:* A taxonomy is a way to categorize and codify a log message's meaning. For example, all device vendors generate some sort of login message. These typically map to login successes, failures, attempts, etc. An example taxonomy for a login success might be: login.success. The reason a taxonomy is critical is because it allows you to group like messages together (from an analysis standpoint) without caring about the particular vendor who generated the log message.
- *Timestamps:* In the world of log data, we typically care about two types of timestamps: the time the log message was generated on the device and the time the logging system received the log message.
- *User Information*: If provided, it is often good to capture any user information (username, command, directory location, etc.).
- *Priority:* Some log messages come with some sort of priority contained in the log message. This is obviously the vendor's assessment of the priority of the log message, but this might not match up with your thoughts on the matter. So as part of normalization, you need to understand how a particular log message impacts your environment. Typical values for priority are low, medium, and high.
- *Raw Log:* As part of the normalization process, you want to keep the raw log data around. This is used to ensure the validity of the normalized event. Another use case is that of log retention. You might have a requirement to keep your raw log data for X period of time. There are two solutions to this. You can store the raw log as part of the normalized event or you can store it on disk and provide for a means to "get back to" the raw log message from the normalized event.

Let's run through a few examples on normalization which will help drive the concept home.

IP Address Validation

It is often important to be able to recognize an IP address. We have seen the following used many times:

```
\d+\.\d+\.\d+\.\d+
```

While this will catch IP addresses like 10.0.3.1, it will also catch an invalid IP address like 300.500.27.900. The key to coming up with a regular expression for matching IP addresses is to not only detect the dotted-quad, but also make sure that each octet is in the proper range. The following regular expression will validate an IP address:

```
^([01]?\d\d?|2[0-4]\d|25[0-5])\.([01]?\d\d?|2[0-4]\d|25[0-5])\. ([01]?\
    d\d?|2[0-4]\d|25[0-5])\.([01]?\d\d?|2[0-4]\d|25[0-5])$
```

Note that the expression is broken up onto two lines, however, it should be all on one line. Further note that this expression will detect an IP address of 0.0.0.0, which some network types might say is invalid. However, some security systems report spoofed IP addresses as 0.0.0.0, so detecting this IP is valid in certain contexts.

Snort

Snort (www.snort.org) is an open source intrusion detection system. Here's a sample Syslog message generated by Snort:

```
Feb 24 12:05:03 10.0.0.25 snort: [1:1002:2] WEB-IIS cmd.exe access
    [Classification: Web Application Attack] [Priority: 1]: {TCP}
    10.0.0.15:16936 -> 10.0.0.21:80
```

It's a Microsoft IIS exploit. The following Perl snippet will parse the data:

```
my($a,$b,$c,$type,$class,$priority,$proto,$srcip,$srcport,$dstip,$dst
    port) = $message =~ /\[(.*?):(.*?):(.*?)\] (.*?)\[Classification:
    (.*?)\]\[Priority: (.*?)\]: {(.*?)} (.*?):(.*?) -> (.*?):(.*?)$/;
```

Of course you will want to verify any IP addresses against the regular expression supplied in the previous section.

Windows Snare

Snare (http://www.intersectalliance.com/projects/BackLogNT/) is an agent-based tool for finding and detecting abnormal system usage. Windows Snare is an agent for Microsoft Windows which is capable of reading Windows Event Log and forwarding Syslog messages to a host. The following is a sample of Windows Snare event:

```
Oct 29 13:54:50 10.0.1.2 MSWinEventLog 0 Security 238 Fri Oct 29
    13:54:50 2011 593 Security kjs User Success Audit KJS600 Detailed
    Tracking A process has exited: Process ID: 1452 Image File Name: C:\
    windows\system32\ssbezier.scr User Name: kjs Domain: GUARDED Logon
    ID: (0x0,0x2577F) 181
```

According to the Snare manual, each item in the Syslog message is separated via a tab character. The following Perl snippet will parse Windows Snare messages:

```
my($cruft,$criticality,$sourceName1,$count,$dateTime,$eventId,$sourceN
    ame2,
$user,$sidType,$eventLogType,$computerName,$categoryString,$dataString,
$expandedString,$md5) = split(/\t/,$message);
```

We use the split() function since everything is delimited by a tab. The names of the variables returned by split() are pretty self-explanatory as to what each of the items are. A good variable for setting a type might be $eventLogType, which is "Success Audit" in the example event. However, the Snare documentation provides definitions for all the possible event IDs which are generated by Snare; the event ID (variable $eventId) above is 593. It might make more sense to create a Perl hash with the keys being all the event IDs Snare knows about. You can obtain Snare from http://sourceforge.net/projects/snare/. Also see Chapter 15 for an example of Snare installation.

Generic Cisco IOS Messages

Cisco IOS is the operating system used to run Cisco routers, switches, and other devices. It can emit an impressive amount of varying log messages. The following is an example of an IOS SecurityEvent:

```
Nov 19 15:32:33 10.4.9.1%SEC-6-IPACCESSLOGP: list 110 denied tcp
    10.0.0.2(113) -> 10.0.0.15(34237), 1 packet
```

The following Perl snippet will parse this event:

```
my($category,$severity,$type,$srcip,$srcport,$dstip,$dstport) = $x =~
    /%(.*?)-(.*?)-(.*?):.* (.*?) \((.*?)\) -> (.*?) \((.*?)\) /g;
```

Almost all IOS messages contain an identifier of the form%category-severity-type. The code above shows a severity of six. Cisco defines the following severities:

{0 | emergencies} System is unusable.
{1 | alerts}Immediate action needed.

{2 | critical} Critical conditions.
{3 | errors} Error conditions.
{4 | warnings} Warning conditions.
{5 | notifications} Normal but significant conditions.
{6 | informational} Informational messages.
{7 | debugging} Debugging messages.

A more generic way to parse IOS message would be as follows:

```
my($category,$severity,$type,$rest) = $x =~ /%(.*?)-(.*?)-
    (.*?):(.*?)$/g;
```

This will capture the category, severity, and type, and place the remainder of the message in the $rest variable.

Go to http://www.cisco.com/web/about/security/intelligence/identify-incidents-via-syslog.html for a discussion on identifying incidents with Cisco firewalls and IOS routers.

Regular Expression Performance Concerns

Due to the fact that regular expressions are based on the computer science concept of Non-deterministic Finite Automata (NFA), you need to be aware of the fact that writing regular expressions could impact performance for tasks you perform over and over again. For example, if you want to extract a substring from many log messages you are normalizing, you can craft a regular expression that will pull out the text you want. This is useful if you kind of know where the string appears in the message, but is not entirely sure. For example, look at the following Perl script:

```
#!/usr/bin/perl
my $text = "I would like to get the following IP address: 10.0.0.2";
for(my $a=0; $a<100000; $a++)
{
    my($IP) = $text =~ m/: (.*)$/;
}
```

We know that the IP address appears after the colon. So We crafted a regular expression which grabs all characters after the colon. Since We use parentheses around the regular expression, Perl will return what it matches, if anything, in array context. This is why We use the syntax my($IP) = ... When We time the run of this script, here is what We get:

```
$ time ./regex.pl
real 0m0.727s
```

```
user 0m0.724s
sys 0m0.003s
```

This may seem like a good time (0.727 s) for performing this regular expression match 100,000 times. A sub-second runtime is great. However, there is a way to get even better performance, and it doesn't involve any regular expressions at all. Perl has a substr() function which will return a substring from a text string, given and offset. Let's now consider the following modified script:

```
#!/usr/bin/perl
my $text = "I would like to get the following IP address: 10.0.0.2";
for(my $a=0; $a<100000; $a++)
{
    my $IP = substr $text, 46;
}
```

We now use the substr() function since We know the IP address starts at offset position 46. When We time this run, here is what We see:

```
$ time ./substr.pl
real 0m0.103s
user 0m0.100s
sys 0m0.003s
```

This run time (0.103 s) is much better. This is because the substr() function goes directly to the position we wish. It doesn't have to search the string for pattern matches. Using substr() only works if the data you wish to extract always appears at the same offset position in the string. Unfortunately, things are not always this easy in real-world processing. Vendors have a tendency to have many different event formats, and things like IP addresses, ports, etc. will often appear in different positions in the message. This is a real pain to deal with to say the least.

For those of you who may be inclined to write your own parsing system using a language like Java, you can use its overloaded indexOf() method for the String class which allows for finding the beginning portion of a substring. This can make finding arbitrary portions of a substring, no matter where it lies in the string, pretty easy.

The next section takes to the next crucial step in the process: correlation.

CORRELATION

The goal of this section is to provide plenty of examples using tools and concepts so you can get a feel for what correlation is about. It is beyond the scope of this chapter to provide an exhaustive set of correlation examples. Part of the process of creating correlations is to understand your own environment and the specific needs of your users, analysts, and so on.

Alright, now let's define what is meant by the term *correlation*. One of Merriam-Webster's definitions for correlation is as follows:

the state or relation of being correlated; specifically: a relation existing between phenomena or things or between mathematical or statistical variables which tend to vary, be associated, or occur together in a way not expected on the basis of chance alone.

This definition is sort of vague and doesn't fully capture the intent of correlation as it relates to log data analysis. Alright, so what does correlation means to system and network professionals? Well, what it means to log analysis is that we are interested in tying together several similar or dissimilar events in a single piece of knowledge that something much larger is happening, as opposed to getting an incomplete view of what's happening by simply looking at single events. This is accomplished by the creation of rules in some sort of a language, which model situations that are of interest to security and network administrators and analysts.

For example, if we receive log data from firewalls and IDSes, we can capture reconnaissance attempts followed by a firewall policy violation with the following rule:

> **If the system sees an event E1 where E1.eventType=portscan**
> **followed by**
> **an event E2 where E2.srcip=E1.srcip and E2.dstip=E1.dstip and**
> **E2.eventType=fw.reject then**
> **doSomething**

This rule, expressed in pseudocode, details how two disjoint events can be tied together. The rule looks at two different events from two different network security systems. The first one is a portscan, which would be detected by IDS. The next event, denoted by E2, is generated by a firewall. It reflects that an attempt was made to access a host that has a firewall policy to exclude all but certain trusted hosts. Note that the rule contains the phrase "followed by," this doesn't necessarily mean that this event has to follow immediately, although it could. What is meant by this is that at some point in the future the fw.reject event must occur in order for the rule to perform the doSomething action (Email, alert, etc.). It should be noted that using fw.reject and portscan for the two E1 and E2 eventTypes are simply arbitrary categorizations (taxonomy) for these event types.

What we have seen is how useful *stateful rule engine* (SREs) are. They afford the administrator and analyst the ability to create rules which can detect arbitrary sequences or patterns. This is where simply looking at Syslog files and trying to correlate these events yourself is next to impossible. The downside is that, as the name indicates, there is a notion of state that must be maintained in order to perform the tests. This is seen in the rule above when we compare event E1's srcip to event E2's srcip. You cannot do this unless you have some way to keep events in some sort of peripheral view or storage layer.

One way this can be accomplished is to naively use your archival data store as the persistence layer. The SBR engine can simply mine the database for event sequences which match one or more rules. This is a very costly proposition, because to do it right requires vast amounts of SQL queries and in-memory manipulation of event data. You will take a good I/O hit, as well as impact other applications which may be trying to use the archival database.

A better solution is to cut a feed of the event data prior to it that goes to long-term storage. As the data is received either at the aggregator (if this is also where you are performing your analysis) or on the analysis server itself, you feed the data some sort of system message queue like a System V queue, where it is consumed and processed by the SBR engine. As the SBR consumes event data, it has to keep these events around in memory so it can apply rules to these events. The problem is that if we never age these events out of memory then we can eat up the RAM on the system. So this is why it is imperative that we age out events as the data itself becomes invalid.

One way to accomplish this is to set a time-to-live (TTL) for each rule in the engine. More specifically, we could set TTL's for each step in the rule. For example, in the rule above, we would not start tracking events until we get an event with an eventType of portscan. Once this happens our TTL starts ticking. If we don't see an event that meets the requirements of the next stage of the rule by the time the TTL is reached, we can reset the rule and discard all the events that we are tracking for this rule.

Micro-Level Correlation

Micro-Level correlation is concerned with correlating fields within a single event or set of events. Micro-Level correlation is sometimes referred to as atomic correlation. This is where normalization of raw event data is crucial to effectively perform atomic correlation. The remainder of this section will present topics pertaining to atomic correlation, along with examples.

Field Correlation

Field correlation provides a mechanism for discovering items of interest in one or more fields within normalized event data. For example, you may be interested when your IDS detect activity targeting your Web server. The most logical thing to do is to look for events which have port 80 or 443 as the destination port.

Event types are yet another valuable source for field correlation. Many firewalls emit event types like accept, drop, and so forth. It is often times useful to be able to correlate events based on event type names. If you are concerned about unwanted access attempts to a particular server, you can correlate events which have an event type of drop and a destination IP address of the server in question.

Rule Correlation

Rule correlation deals with crafting a rule which is able to model a certain behavior. Recall the pseudocode example from before:

> **If the system sees an event E1 where E1.eventType=portscan**
> **followed by**
> **an event E2 where E2.srcip=E1.srcip and E2.dstip=E1.dstip and**
> **E2.eventType=fw.reject**
> **then**
> **doSomething**

This rule models a behavior pattern. While it is pseudocode, you can see that the rule is trying to find the situation where an attacker is port scaning a host and at the same time is causing a firewall to reject his attempts.

In order for rule correlation to be affective, the following is a minimum functionality list for a rule engines:

- *Stateful Behavior:* Systems which implement correlation are sometimes referred to as engines. Furthermore, rule correlation engines are sometimes referred to as stateful rule engines or stateful business rule engines. This stateful operation is exhibited by modeling behavior which is of interest to a security engineer. A single stateful rule may consist of one or more states. For example, one state may look for all events with destination port 80 (HTTP). If an event comes into the engine which matches this criteria, then a next state in the rule might now look for all events which have a certain source IP address (maybe to look for unauthorized Web server access). If this second state is reached then we perform some action.
- *Counting:* One very useful tool is also a simple one: counting. This basically allows you to create a rule which waits for an event to occur a

number of times before an action is taken. There is also counting unique occurrences of an event. This is also very useful because it can be used to detect situations where someone is scanning the same port across a bunch of different destination hosts.

■ *Timeout:* Most, if not all stateful rule engine implementations use memory to perform their analysis, etc. This allows for speed and efficiency. We'll call the memory an engine uses *working memory.* As you add more and more data to the engine's working memory, this can cause not only the engine to slow down, but impact the overall performance of the host system. Timing or aging out events which haven't matched a rule in a certain time period is very critical to maintaining an effective engine. For example, you may want to set a default age-out period of five minutes.

■ *Rule Reuse:* You obviously want to lessen the burden of creating rules. From the example rule above, the following is a single condition in the rule itself: If the system sees an event E1 where E1.eventType=portscan. A rule can have many conditional statements. It is always beneficial to be able to reuse components like these in other rules create.

■ *Priorities:* Priorities are useful in that they can dictate the order in which a rule or set of rules will be performed.

■ *Language:* All rule engines implement some sort of language or pseudo language for specifying rules. What's en vogue today is using XML as a pseudo language, but We have seen rule engines also use Lisp. Some use proprietary formats. The thing to keep in mind is that you want to have a language which is easy to learn and use.

■ *Action:* It almost goes without saying that performing actions is what rule correlation is all about. There has to be a mechanism in your rules engine to do something. Just knowing something happened is often not good enough. As with rule reuse, there should be a mechanism in place to create actions which can be reused by many rule sets.

Not all rules engines will have these features. Even if you decide to build your own implementation of an engine, you may choose to have some of these features, but not all. It is good to be aware of the things which are crucial to successful rules processing. A few of the later sections discuss building your own rule engine.

Macro-Level Correlation

Macro-Level correlation is concerned with pulling in other sources of information in order to further validate or gain intelligence on your event stream. This technique is sometimes referred to as fusion correlation. One example of macro-correlation is taking vulnerability scan data into account and comparing it inline with event data coming into your analysis system.

If your IDS detect port scans to a series of hosts on your networks, it would be nice to know if these hosts actually exist, and if so do any vulnerabilities exist on these hosts. As with micro-correlation, normalization of your raw event data is important. This also extends to the other data sets you would like to bring into the correlation process. For example, having username to full name mappings can be very useful, as can a user's roles on a particular system. This data is referred to as context data. Operating systems like Windows or Unix will insert some context information into the log messages they generate. If you want to get more detailed information for a user, you will need to do a second gathering step by pulling it out of an LDAP server or Active Directory server.

The remainder of this section will preset concepts and examples of fusion correlation.

Rule Correlation

Much like micro-level correlation, macro-level correlation makes use of rule correlation. One of the main differences is that rule correlation in micro-level correlation systems can often transition to a rule in macro-level correlation which can be used either as input back into other micro-level rules or simply actions which write to text files, create help desk tickets, etc.

Vulnerability Correlation

Vulnerability scanners help find hosts and other systems which are vulnerable to known attacks. All scanners provide at least the following information:

> *Vulnerable Host:* Hostname or IP Address.
> *Vulnerable Service or Port:* Sendmail Port (25), etc.
> *Remediation Steps:* Patch version of Sendmail, etc.

Most scanners (commercial or otherwise) are designed to be run on a daily, weekly, or monthly basis. It is up to the user to run the scan by hand or to schedule it to run at a preset time and date. The notion of real-time vulnerability scanning has recently begun to get addressed by IDS vendors like Sourcefire (http://www.sourcefire.com). Sourcefire employs Real-time Network Awareness (RNA) as a form of real-time vulnerability analysis.

In threat analysis, we can combine vulnerability scan data with real-time event data, in order to help reduce false positives. For example, if your IDS detect a port scan is occurring across several hosts in your network, then the chances are that it will report a range of ports which have been scanned. Furthermore, it is likely that some of these reported ports may not be active. If you routinely scan your network for vulnerabilities, you can use this information along with the IDS messages you get in real time to verify if there is indeed an open port on the host in question and whether or not it's vulnerable.

Profile (Fingerprint) Correlation

Information gathered through banner snatching, OS fingerprints, vulner-ability scans, and remote port scans can be beneficial from a forensic stand-point. Moreover, this data can be used to gain better insight into who might be attacking you and also aid in prosecution. As part of normal correlation (rule correlation, for example), an action can be setup to initiate one of these forensic-gathering tasks as events of a particular nature come into the system. This gathered information can then be stored to a database for later use.

Nmap is a tool which is able to perform OS fingerprinting, among other things. Nmap is available at http://www.insecure.org/nmap. Here is a basic fingerprinting run of Nmap:

```
$ sudo nmap -A 192.168.1.6
Starting Nmap 5.21 (http://nmap.org) at 2012-03-25 18:03 EDT
Nmap scan report for 192.168.1.6
Host is up (0.00038s latency).
Not shown: 991 closed ports
PORT STATE SERVICE VERSION
135/tcp open msrpc Microsoft Windows RPC
139/tcp open netbios-ssn
445/tcp open netbios-ssn
2869/tcp open http Microsoft HTTPAPI httpd 2.0 (SSDP/UPnP)
|_html-title: Service Unavailable
49152/tcp open msrpc Microsoft Windows RPC
49153/tcp open msrpc Microsoft Windows RPC
49154/tcp open msrpc Microsoft Windows RPC
49158/tcp open msrpc Microsoft Windows RPC
49160/tcp open msrpc Microsoft Windows RPC
MAC Address: 68:A3:C4:4D:4A:FF (Unknown)
Device type: general purpose
Running: Microsoft Windows Vista|2008|7
OS details: Microsoft Windows Vista SP0 - SP2, Server 2008, or Windows
    7 Ultimate (build 7000)
Network Distance: 1 hop
Service Info: OS: Windows
Host script results:
|_nbstat: NetBIOS name: KEVIN-PC, NetBIOS user: <unknown>, NetBIOS MAC:
    68:a3:c4:4d:4a:ff
| smb-os-discovery:
```

```
| OS: Windows 7 Professional 7600 (Windows 7 Professional 6.1)
| Name: WORKGROUP\KEVIN-PC
|_ System time: 2012-03-25 18:04:10 UTC-4
|_smbv2-enabled: Server supports SMBv2 protocol
HOP RTT ADDRESS
1 0.38 ms 192.168.1.6
OS and Service detection performed. Please report any incorrect results
    at http://nmap.org/submit/ .
Nmap done: 1 IP address (1 host up) scanned in 56.55 seconds
$
```

The—A option instructs Nmap to perform fingerprinting.

Anti-Port Correlation

Most, if not all firewalls emit log messages based on allowed or denied packets and other events. Anti-port correlation deals with using open port information along with firewall data to be able to detect attacks in the slow or low category. Nmap can be used to track open ports on your systems. The following pseudo-code shows the basic idea:

> if (event E1.dstport != (Known_Open_Ports on event E1.dstip))
> then
> doSomething

One attack this technique can help detect is worm activity. In general, however, it can help detect when an attacker is trying to access a system's ports or services which don't exist. There are several ways to track open port information. One way is to regularly run Nmap and keep track of open ports. As you receive events you can compare the destination ports from both firewalls and IDSs against the known open ports. Another way to do this is to keep a list of hosts and ports up to date by hand, rather than relying on Nmap. This technique is only viable if you have a fairly static environment.

Watch List Correlation

It is sometimes beneficial to be able to know when events are received which target a host or even a network. The opposite is often true; you may want to place the source of an attack on a watch list, i.e. the attacker.

Often times this can be in the form of external intelligence gathered from different places such as Dshield (http://www.dshield.org/). Dshield has a list of top 10 attackers which you can place on your own watchlist. SANS also has similar information: http://isc.sans.org.

Geographic Location Correlation

Many network management platforms employ the use of a network map to visualize devices in the enterprise. As alarms and such are generated, nodes on the map light up to indicate trouble. While this type of map in the security world is of marginal value, what is really valuable is the ability to graph threats in real time as they occur. This requires some unusual processing. The American Registry for Internet Numbers (ARIN) is one resource that can help with this. ARIN (http://www.arin.net) is the Internet number registry for North America, the Caribbean, and sub-equatorial Africa. Internet providers, companies, etc. go through ARIN for networks. ARIN collects contact information on these organizations. ARIN does not collect latitude and longitude information, but you can obtain airport codes or reverse lookup of IP addresses from WHOIS records. The ARIN Web site has tools which you can use to query its services for information on IP addresses and networks, especially contact information. While plotting attacks on a map based on this information isn't 100% accurate, it does go a long way to helping track down evil doers. VisualRoute is a tool which can be used to visualize which routes packets take from one place to another. See http://www.visualware.com/personal/products/visualroute/index.html for information.

Using Data in your Environment

Using data about your environment is one of the best sources of correlated data you can use. As was mentioned in the Macro-Level Correlation section, this data is considered context. For example, if you know your company's holiday schedule, you can use this information to raise an alert when you see access to internal resources when everyone is at home. Some of the more common environmental triggers you can use include:

- Vacation schedules.
- Business hours.
- Holiday schedule.
- Access rights to internal resources.
- Repeating network "events," e.g. vulnerability scans.
- Scheduled backups of systems, data stores, etc.
- Maintenance schedule, e.g. router configuration changes and reboots, OS patching, etc.

These things can be used to aid in determining if some behavior is legitimate or outside of normal boundaries.

Simple Event Correlator (SEC)

The Simple Event Correlator (SEC) is a Perl-based tool which implements a simple correlation system. It is available at http://kodu.neti.ee/~risto/sec/.

SEC was developed to fill the gap between open source log analysis tools and commercial systems. It has robust syntax for creating rules which can do simple things to very complex things. Rules can be chained together to form models of behavior, which can be used to detect known situations or help diagnose or discover unknown situations. At the heart of SEC's engine is the notion of *contexts*. A context can be thought of as a place holder for some occurrence of an event or series of events. It is the context notion which allows SEC act in a stateful manner. This is a very critical feature for being able to detect multiple log message patterns which when combined indicate something of interest. We'll see some useful examples soon.

SEC Basics

The purpose of this section is not to present SEC in its entirety, but rather to present the key features. The installation of SEC is very straightforward, so instead of showing this, I'll present practical SEC rule examples. But for now, let's look at the various rule types which SEC supports:

- *Single*—Single matches an event and performs an action.
- *SingleWithScript*—SingleWithScript matches an event and gets the return code from a script or program it runs.
- *SingleWithSuppress*—SingleWithSuppress matches an event and then ignores any subsequent matches for *t* seconds.
- *Pair*—Pair combines two or more events into a single event, within a given time range.
- *PairWithWindow*—PairWithWindow is similar to Pair, but it waits *t* seconds for the next event to arrive.
- *SingleWithThreshold*—SingleWithThreshold counts matching events within a time window and up to a threshold. An action is fired once the threshold is met, and no other events will be considered during the remainder of the time window.
- *SingleWith2Thresholds*—SingleWith2Thresholds counts matching events within time window *t1* and executes an action when the first threshold is reached. The count is reset and matched events are counted for *t2* seconds. Execute another action if the count falls below the second threshold within time window *t2*.
- *Suppress*—Suppress doesn't match events and cannot execute actions.
- *Calendar*—Calendar executes actions at specific time, via a configuration similar to UNIX crontab entries.

SEC rules have the following basic format:

```
type= <Rule Type>
ptype=RegExp
pattern= <regular expression pattern>
```

```
desc= <description text>
action= <semicolon separate action list>
```

We'll see some actual examples in a little bit. SEC supports many actions, but only the more generic ones will be presented here:

write <filename> [<event text>]: The write command will write event text to filename. A dash ("-") can be used to write to standard out.

shellcmd <shellcmd>: A shell command or program will be executed.

spawn <shellcmd>: This is identical to shellcmd, except the output of the shell command or program is fed back into SEC. This means you can write SEC rules to correlate this output.

event [<time>] [<event text>]: This causes an internal SEC event to be created. This can be used as feedback into SEC. Time is the amount of time SEC waits before it feeds event text back into SEC. Note that if you use a nonzero value for time, SEC will wait until time has expired before it does anything else. In most instances, a zero value could be used and SEC will not hold up its processing.

Real-World Examples
What We would like to do now is present how to use SEC in a few real-world examples. All of these examples can easily be extended by you to fit your own environment.

Stateful Rule Example
Recall the pseudocode rule from earlier in the chapter:

> **If the system sees an event E1 where E1.eventType=portscan**
> **followed by**
> **an event E2 where E2.srcip=E1.srcip and E2.dstip=E1.dstip and**
> **E2.eventType=fw.reject**
> **then doSomething**

What we are interested in catching are two separate events. One is an IDS portscan event and the other is a firewall reject event. If the source and destination IP addresses in both events are the same, we want to do something. The SEC rule set for this is as follows:

```
#
# Rule 1: Catch a portscan from source IP address to destination IP
# address. It will then create a dynamic context based on whatever the
# source and destination IP addresses are.
#
type=Single
```

```
ptype=RegExp
pattern=portscan (\d+\.\d+\.\d+\.\d+) -> (\d+\.\d+\.\d+\.\d+)
desc=$0
action= create PORTSCAN_$1_$2;
#
# Rule 2: Catch a firewall reject from source IP address to destination
  IP
# address. If the portscan context already exists, we have a situation
# where an attacker is portscanning AND getting a reject from a
  firewall, all
# from the same source IP address to the same destination IP address.
#
type=Single
ptype=RegExp
pattern=reject (\d+\.\d+\.\d+\.\d+) -> (\d+\.\d+\.\d+\.\d+)
context=PORTSCAN_$1_$2
desc=$0
action= write - Portscan and firewall reject from $1 to $2;
```

There are two rules. At first glance, you may be wondering why We didn't use the Pair rule. The problem with the Pair rule is that it only detects one event followed immediately by another event. We want to be able to find the first occurrence of an event and then find a second event at some later point in time, not necessarily right after the first.

At any rate, the comments describe what's happening pretty well. The first rule catches a portscan event and gets the source and destination IP address. It then creates a dynamic context which will take the form of PORTSCAN_SRCIP_ DSTIP, where, of course, SRCIP and DSTIP are actual IP addresses. It also uses the special SEC variable $0, which is the entire log message which matched the pattern. The second rule looks for a reject, extracts the source and destination IP addresses and uses these to see if a portscan context exists with the same source and destination IP addresses. A message is written to standard out if this is indeed the case. Let's run through an example run of SEC. A good way to test rules is to run SEC so that it accepts input from standard in. This is accomplished with the command-line parameter –input=-. You specify a rules file with the –conf=filename option. In the example below, our input to SEC is in boldface:

```
$ ./sec.pl -conf=portscan-reject.rule -input=-
Simple Event Correlator version 2.2.5
Reading configuration from portscan-reject.rule
```

```
2 rules loaded from portscan-reject.rule
portscan 10.0.0.2 -> 10.0.0.3
portscan 10.0.0.2 -> 10.0.0.4
portscan 10.0.0.2 -> 10.0.0.5
portscan 10.0.0.2 -> 10.0.0.6
Some random text
More text..
reject 10.0.0.2 -> 10.0.0.4
reject 10.0.0.2 -> 10.0.0.6
reject 10.0.0.2 -> 10.0.0.5
reject 10.0.0.2 -> 10.0.0.3
Almost done..
There..
Creating context 'PORTSCAN_10.0.0.2_10.0.0.3'
Creating context 'PORTSCAN_10.0.0.2_10.0.0.4'
Creating context 'PORTSCAN_10.0.0.2_10.0.0.5'
Creating context 'PORTSCAN_10.0.0.2_10.0.0.6'
Writing event 'Portscan and firewall reject from 10.0.0.2 to 10.0.0.4'
    to file -
Portscan and firewall reject from 10.0.0.2 to 10.0.0.4
Writing event 'Portscan and firewall reject from 10.0.0.2 to 10.0.0.6'
    to file -
Portscan and firewall reject from 10.0.0.2 to 10.0.0.6
Writing event 'Portscan and firewall reject from 10.0.0.2 to 10.0.0.5'
    to file -
Portscan and firewall reject from 10.0.0.2 to 10.0.0.5
Writing event 'Portscan and firewall reject from 10.0.0.2 to 10.0.0.3'
    to file -
Portscan and firewall reject from 10.0.0.2 to 10.0.0.3
```

We simply placed our input data in a file and cut and pasted from this file into the standard in of SEC. After our input we see that SEC creates four unique contexts, one for each of the four portscan events. As each of the reject events comes into SEC, it begins emitting the messages for each one of the distinct portscan and reject event pairs. This is a valuable distinction in that SEC can detect this situation regardless of what type of events occur between matching portscan and reject events. It should be pointed out that the format of the portscan and reject events are contrived and used only to simplify the example. In real life you will need to write more elaborate regular expressions to capture this information.

Vulnerability Correlation Example

Let's say you want to narrow down false positives by performing vulnerability correlation. This means that you use a tool like Nessus to periodically scan your network for vulnerable systems. Output from your scanner is placed into a database. We can write a rule in SEC that can detect portscans, run a program which queries the vulnerability database and returns whether or not the attacked system is vulnerable. Here's the SEC rule which accomplishes this:

```
#
# Rule 1: Check to see if the attacked system is vulnerable
#
type=SingleWithScript
ptype=RegExp
pattern=portscan \d+\.\d+\.\d+\.\d+ -> (\d+\.\d+\.\d+\.\d+)
script=./vulnCheck.pl $1
desc=$0
action=write - $1 is vulnerable!
action2=write - $1 is NOT vulnerable
```

The SingleWithScript rule executes a script or program. If the exit code of the program is 0, then action is performed. If the exit code is anything other than 0 action2 is performed. The Perl script vulnCheck.pl simply performs an exit(0) which will cause action to be performed, i.e. we have a vulnerable system. Here's an example run:

```
$ ./sec.pl -conf=vulnerability.rule -input=-
Simple Event Correlator version 2.2.5
Reading configuration from vulnerability.rule
1 rules loaded from vulnerability.rule
portscan 10.0.0.2 -> 10.0.3.4
Child 25163 created for command './vulnCheck.pl 10.0.3.4'
Child 25163 terminated with exitcode 0
Writing event '10.0.3.4 is vulnerable!' to file -
10.0.3.4 is vulnerable!
```

Cisco IOS Configuration Changes

Many environments have some sort of configuration change controls in place. For example, all hardware or software changes are done between certain hours. This can be used to your advantage in that if you receive router configuration changes outside of normal hours, then you may have something to worry about. SEC can be used to detect such occurrences. Let's look at an example configuration of how this would be caught:

```
type=Single
ptype=RegExp
pattern=%SYS-\d+-CONFIG
desc=$0
action= write - A configuration change has occurred!
```

At first glance, this is an alright way to deal with it. But do we really want to have it trigger during ever configuration time, even during your maintenance hours? If you don't mind, then you can leave the SEC configuration as is. But for those who would like to limit the alerts, this configuration may be on interest to you:

```
type=SingleWithScript
ptype=RegExp
pattern=%SYS-\d+-CONFIG
script=./isItMaintTime.pl
desc=$0
action=write - Configuration during non-maintenance period!
action2=write - Configuration attempt during maintenance period!
```

This SEC configuration block will now run a Perl script which will check to see if the date and time the event is received coincides with maintenance time. We can take this one more step:

```
type=SingleWithScript
ptype=RegExp
pattern=^.* (\d+\.\d+\.\d+\d+) .*%SYS-\d+-CONFIG: .* from (.*?)$
script=./isItMaintTime.pl $1
desc=$0
action=write - $1 Configured during non-maintenance period from $2!
action2=write - $1 Configured during maintenance period from $2!
```

We now extract the host from which the configuration attempt was made. We then pass this to the isItMaintTime.pl script. The goal is to look up (maybe in a database) to see if the router in question is scheduled to be configured during the current maintenance period. Most, if not all Syslog messages include the host which generated the message early on in the message itself. The first regular expression attempts to gather this information. Note that you may need to turn off DNS resolution in order to not convert the router's IP address to a hostname. Finally, the source of the configuration is gathered so this can be reported, too.

Promiscuous Mode Detection

When a network interface is placed into promiscuous mode, all packets are sent to the kernel for processing, including packets not destined for the MAC address of the network interface card. The one main reason that this is a bad thing is because users on the system with a promiscuous mode network interface can now use a tool like a sniffer to view any and all network packets. Let's look at how to detect an interface going into promiscuous mode on Linux:

```
type=Single
ptype=RegExp
pattern=^.*(\d+\.\d+\.\d+\.\d+).* (.*?) entered promiscuous mode$
desc=$0
action= write - Interface $2 on $1 entered promiscuous mode
```

Here the SEC rule will detect the host and the host's network interface which went to promiscuous mode.

Keywords to Watch For

The following SEC examples show some keywords that are noteworthy.

Kernel panics generally mean some sort of hardware is failing or some such event. SEC can detect these with the following:

```
type=Single
ptype=RegExp
pattern=panic
desc=$0
action= write - A potential kernel panic has occurred
```

Messages with fatal in them should probably be captured. The following SEC rule will catch these:

```
type=Single
ptype=RegExp
pattern=fatal
desc=$0
action= write - A fatal error may have occurred
```

Finally, keeping an eye out for messages which contain the string password or passwd in them are noteworthy because they can be indicative of malicious attempts to subvert normal channels for password maintenance. The following will detect password messages:

```
type=Single
ptype=RegExp
```

```
pattern=password|passwd
desc=$0
action= write - Password operation detected
```

Application Exit Codes

When applications exit, they generally return an error code to the operating system. This code is generally zero (0) for normal program termination. An exit status of one (1) is generally used to denote some sort of an abnormal operation has occurred which caused the application to terminate abruptly. The following SEC rule will detect such error codes:

```
type=Single
ptype=RegExp
pattern=exit status 1
desc=$0
action= write - An application exited with status of 1
```

Of course we could extend this rule to the following:

```
type=Single
ptype=RegExp
pattern=exit status (\d+)
desc=$0
action= write - An application exited with a status of $1
```

This has the benefit of actually getting the exit code so we can perform finer-grained analysis on it.

Final Words on SEC

There is one last thing We should point out. For most of this chapter I have been saying that you need to normalize your raw data in order to correlate it. With SEC this isn't the case. SEC works best by reading log files. But you can pass data into SEC via alternate methods. So you can either use it to correlate your log data, or use it to correlate data after you have gathered and normalized it.

Building Your Own Rules Engine

What if you are using a log analysis system which doesn't have a rules engine? If you are interested in writing your own engine, and you are Java inclined, this section covers two frameworks which allow you to write two somewhat different kinds of processing engines:

- Rules-based.
- Stream-based.

Rules-Based Engine Using Jess

Jess is maintained by Sandia National Labs (http://herzberg.ca.sandia.gov/Jess/). Jess is not open source, but it is free for non-commercial and academic use. Still, the commercial licensing model is not cost prohibitive for most organizations.

One of the best resources for getting to know Jess is a book called *Jess In Action*. It was written by the author and maintainer of Jess, Dr. Ernest Friedman-Hill. This section merely introduces Jess in the context of using it for security log analysis, so you should see this book for a detailed and well-written explanation of how to use Jess in a general sense.

Jess is written in Java. You don't actually need to know Java in order to use Jess, as Jess has its own rule language and can function as a shell (hence the name). However, in order to use it in a manner consistent with how log data is gathered and normalized, you will need to do some Java development. So, this section assumes you have some understanding of Java development. You don't need to be a guru, but you should be familiar with it.

Jess and the Rete Algorithm

Central to Jess' ability to perform its duty as a rules engine is the fact that it implements the *Rete* algorithm (note that Rete is pronounced ree-tee). The Rete algorithm was invented by Dr. Charles L. Forgy. The algorithm came about in order to solve the problem of pattern matching. Traditional pattern matching can be fairly inefficient, when used in the context of rules or rules engines. According to Dr. Friedman-Hill, the Rete algorithm accomplishes its goal by remembering data that are asserted or retracted into working memory (more on these in a moment). This means that the rules engine only tests (or fires) rules against the data items which have actually changed. This reduces the amount of work the engine has to perform. Rules generally have what is termed a left-hand side (LHS) and a right-hand side (RHS). The LHS of a rule is the condition, similar to if-then-else statements you are used to. The RHS is the action to take if the LHS evaluates to true. It's that simple.

The Rete algorithm organizes its data in a tree-like structure. Each node in the tree represents a test which will get performed against data being added or removed from memory. Each node will have one or two inputs and possibly many outputs. As a new piece of data enters the tree, it is filtered through the tree until it reaches a terminal node. If a terminal node is reached, this means that a new activation record is created with all the data points which caused the rule to be true. Rules in Rete systems work best if you can be as explicit as possible. This means you should write rules that look for very detailed items in a given piece of data. This causes a path in the Rete tree to be traversed in a somewhat determinant manner, which exposes the efficiencies inherent to the Rete algorithm.

Many Rete-based rule engines exist. Certain terminology is commonly used when talking about such engines, so We would like to discuss these now.

Forward- and Backward-Chaining. A forward-chaining system is one where rules are executed against a set of data. In other words it's data driven. Backward-chaining is one where a data set is queried for truth values. The data set is almost always pre-existing, so backward-chaining is not necessarily data-driven. Prolog is the classic example for a backward-chaining system. Jess can operate in both modes.

Working Memory. Working memory (WM) is the area in a rule engine where data, to be processed by one or many rules, is kept. This area is sometimes referred to as the fact space. The key to maintaining a high-performance rules engine is to keep the number of facts in WM low. You cannot continually place facts into WM without clearing them out. This will cause not only the Java process to consume memory and possible cause swapping out to disk, but the Rete algorithm will begin to perform poorly.

Object Assertion. Data is placed into WM via a process called assertion. We use the term object because the example We provide in this section places Java objects into WM. This can be done programmatically or from the rule language itself.

Object Retraction. Data in WM is removed via a process called retraction. This can be done programmatically or from within the rule language itself.

Agenda. The agenda is the list of rules which have RHSs which will be executed/ fired.

Conflict Resolution. Conflict resolution is the process by which the actions in the agenda are picked to fire. The programmer doesn't entirely have direct control over this process, but one way he or she can affect this is by setting salience values. Salience is a form of priority. You may have rules which have similar conditions. The rules engine will have to decide which rule to fire if the same fact in WM would satisfy both rules. Setting a higher salience value (typically a signed integer) for one rule will influence the engine to execute the rule as opposed to another one which may also be a candidate for execution.

Jess Rule Language

Jess uses a LISP-like language for crafting rules. You do have to work with it a bit to wrap your mind around it, but once you do you will see that it's quite expressive and powerful. We are only going to briefly present it. The *Jess In Action* book does a great job of describing the language. There is also a freely available manual on the Jess Web site which describes the syntax details, too.

JAVABEANS CONVENTIONS

Getters and Setters

Note that the naming conventions for getters (getType(), getDstPort(), etc.) is actually the common JavaBeans convention for naming properties. Jess uses the property name corresponding to the getter method name—sometimes it can be "is" instead of "get," for example, with boolean properties.

For our purposes here, We are only going to present the barest of syntactical details to illustrate how to accomplish our goal of security log data analysis:

```
(defrule find-port-80
?event1 <- (event (dstport 80))
=>
(printout t "Found an event with dst port of 80: " (fact-slot-value
   ?event1 type) crlf)
(retract ?event1))
```

I'll describe each of the piece-parts of the rule. First off, the defrule tag gives a name to your rule. The code ?event1 <- (event (dstport 80)) is the LHS of the rule. It takes an object called event, calls the getter method getDstport(), checks to see if it is 80, and assigns (binds) the event object to a variable called ?event1. Note that We left off the get portion of the getter. In Jess, you simply use the portion after the get or your getter method. So this means all your getters, in your Java code, need to be prefixed with get.

The => symbol defines the RHS of the rule. For those of you who took a logic or discrete math course in school, think of the => operator as a conclusion, therefore, or implies statement in a proof or argument. If the LHS evaluates to true, then everything after the conclusion is executed. In the example above, some text is printed using the printout operator. In the printout command, the fact-slot-value operator is used to access a member of our event object. As with dstport, type is the property name for getType() in the event object. Finally, we remove the object from WM by calling the retract operation on the? event1.

Jess in the Real World

In order to use Jess for analyzing log data, we need to do some Java programming. First off, We are going to assume that log aggregation and normalization is already being done. The following Java Class, called SecurityEvent, is a barebones object to represent a single log event:

```
public class SecurityEvent
```

```
{
    private String mSrcip;
    private String mDstip;
    private int mSrcport = 0;
    private int mDstport = 0;
    private String mType;
    private String mHostname;
    /*
    Constructor
    */
    public SecurityEvent(String hostname,
         String dstip,
         String srcip,
         int dstport,
         int srcport,
         String type)
    {
    mSrcip = srcip;
    mDstip = dstip;
    mHostname = hostname;
    mDstport = dstport;
    mSrcport = srcport;
    mType = type;
    }
    /* member data getters */
       public String getType()
    {
       return mType;
    }
       public String getHostname()
    {
       return mHostname;
    }
       public String getSrcip()
    {
       return mSrcip;
    }
       public String getDstip()
```

```
    {
       return mDstip;
    }
       public int getDstport()
    {
       return mDstport;
    }
       public int getSrcport()
    {
       return mSrcport;
    }
  }
```

The class has the usually private members and getters for these members. We have omitted any setters, as you normally don't want to alter log event details. However, you can freely add them if you need this functionality.

The next bit of code shows how to use Jess and this event object:

```
import Jess.*;
public class Main
{
   public static void main(String[] argv)
   {
      try
      {
         //Create new Rete instance
            Rete rete = new Rete();
         //Read in the rules file from file
         rete.executeCommand("(batch myrules.clp)");
         //Define our Java SecurityClass as a Jess class called event
         rete.defclass("event," "SecurityEvent," null);
         //Create an new instance of a SecurityEvent and assert it
      rete.definstance("event,"
                  new SecurityEvent("webserver," //hostname
                           "10.0.0.2," //dst ip
                           "10.0.0.3," //src ip
                           80, //dst port
                           5512, //src port
                           "Web-Access-Event" // event type
                           ), false);
```

```
      // Run the engine
      rete.run();
  }
  catch(JessException jex)
  {
  jex.printStackTrace();
  }
 }
}
```

The in-line comments are pretty much self-explanatory. Basically, we load the rules file from a disk file; this is done with the executeCommand() method. It will attempt to load a file called myrules.clp. The defclass() method tells Jess about our event class. The first parameter to this method defines how you will refer to the object in the rules file. The definstance() method asserts an new SecurityEvent object into WM. Finally, the run() method runs the engine. In a production rule engine, you will want to assert objects and run the engine in loop, maybe getting your event objects from some sort of queue or database. Depending on the number of events you plan to assert per second, you may want to run the engine with every object assertion, or you may want to assert a certain number of events first and then run the engine.

Another alternative is to assert the events in one thread, and run the engine continuously using Rete.runUntilHalt() in a dedicated thread. This is all highly dependant on your event rate, how many rules you have, how many rules have partial matches (more on partial matches in a bit), and so forth. You may need to play with your own engine to see what works best for you and your environment.

Recall the rule from the previous section. Let's say you wanted to find one type of event followed by another, i.e. a stateful rule example:

```
(defrule find-portscan-followed-by-reject
?event1 <- (event (type portscan) (srcip ?sip))
?event2 <- (event (type reject) (srcip ?sip))
=>
(printout t "Portscan followed by Firewall Reject from: ?sip" crlf)
(retract ?event1 ?event2))
```

This rule has two states. One looks for an event of type portscan. The second state looks for an event of reject. The first state gets the source IP of the event and assigns it to ?sip. The second state uses ?sip and compares it to the source IP of the second event, and if they match, i.e. the same person caused the portscan and reject events to occur, then the rule fires. The final action in the LHS is to retract both ?event1 and ?event2 from WM.

We mentioned something about partial matches. This is an issue to be aware of with any Rete-based engine. Let's say in the rule above we get 5000 events coming through the engine which match the first state. This means the engine has to keep around these 5000 partial event matches in WM. When an event comes into the engine that matches the second condition in the RHS, the rule is complete and it fires.

This example is not entirely perfect. This rule will only match a portscan event followed immediately by a reject event. In some cases this may be what you want, but you will definitely want to be more flexible than this. The reject event may not occur until several minutes after the portscan event. To remedy this you will need to add a timestamp to your SecurityEvent object. This timestamp should be of type long. You can use the System.currentTimeMillis() Java call to set the value. You also need to add a corresponding getter. Once you do this, the rule now looks like the following:

```
(defrule find-portscan-followed-by-reject
?event1 <- (event (type portscan) (srcip ?sip) (timestamp ?time1))
?event2 <- (event (type reject) (srcip ?sip) (timestamp ?time2))
(test (>= ?time2 ?time1))
=>
(printout t "Portscan followed by Firewall Reject from: ?sip" crlf)
(retract ?event1 ?event2))
```

The first state in the rule gets the object's timestamp and assigns it to ?time1. The second state assigns? event2's timestamp to? time2. The new rule introduces the test function, which used the >= operator to determine if ?event2 happens at the same time or later than ?event1.

Jess Performance

According to Friedman-Hill, determining the exact performance characteristic of a Rete engine is difficult. He writes that the runtime of the engine will be proportional to approximately the following: $R'F'^{P'}$. R' is a number less than the number of rules. F' is the number of facts which change on each iteration through the engine. P' is a number greater than one but less than the average number of patterns per rule.

Final Words on Jess

This section on Jess presented only the barest details regarding Jess. The emphasis was on using Jess in a capacity consistent with security log analysis.

Jess has a very small system footprint and can easily be embedded in any Java application, including J2EE.

Stream-Based Engine Using Esper

The final of the two developer-centric examples deals with stream-based processing or Complex Event Processing (CEP). The idea behind stream-based processing is that streams of data (or events) are passed through a CEP engine, whereby complex patterns can be discovered across multiple events. CEP engines employ query languages which allow you to define the patterns you are interested in discovering. The best and easiest way to understand a CEP engine is to compare it to a database. Databases use queries to sift through data. CEP engines stream data through queries to find interesting things. CEP engines tend to be very fast with benchmarks in the range of hundreds of thousands of events per second which get evaluated by thousands of rules (queries). How is this? CEP engines do much of what they do by executing in memory, rather than disk. This has the advantage of being fast, but means you need lots of RAM and CPU if you anticipate lots of events and queries. This section is going to introduce the basics on CEP. There are many great resources online which will go into greater depth.

Let's look at Figure 9.2. It depicts the basic flow through a CEP engine.

What we see in Figure 9.2 are events flowing in the CEP engine. What comes out are the events themselves along with any alerts or actions created based on patterns of discovery. The box labeled "Window" denotes the temporal aspect of stream processing. With *windowing* you are able to define constraints around how long you want to look for patterns of events before the engine nullifies any events it is keeping in memory.

The most well-known open source CEP engine is Esper (http://esper.codehaus.org/). Esper is a framework which allows you to rapidly build a CEP engine with very little in the way of code. Esper in a nutshell is:

- Pure Java.
- Embeddable into any Java application.
- Expressive via Esper Query Language (EQL), which is a SQL-like language for defining.

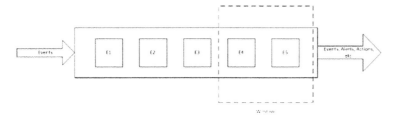

FIGURE 9.2 Basic CEP Engine Flow

- Well documented.

On top of all of this, there is a way to obtain commercial support for Esper.

By now you might be asking how CEP can help with correlation. Let's look at a quick example. Like Jess, you will need to create Java classes which model the kinds of normalized log messages you plan to analyze. In the following example, we use two separate objects for the example, but there are other options. OK, let's look at an EQL statement:

```
select * from pattern [every LoginFailure -> (timer:interval(10 sec)
    having count(*) >= 5 and LoginSuccess)]
```

The EQL statement is looking for a specific pattern. First, it is looking for LoginFailures. We set the window to be 10 s. Then we are looking for at least five LoginFailures to occur in this window. The five failures in 10 s must be followed by a LoginSuccess. Here is what we are looking for in English:

If 5 LoginFailures occur in 10 seconds followed by a LoginSuccess then alert.

This is a classic pattern for a brute-force login attempt. Of course in a real application, we would need to make sure the LoginFailures and LoginSuccess are mapped to each other via the source and user.

Stream processing is a viable alternative to using a rules-based engine. We have only scratched the surface of how to use CEP for correlation. Esper has lots of great documentation and has a ton of solution patterns found at http://esper.codehaus.org/tutorials/solution_patterns/solution_patterns. html.

COMMON PATTERNS TO LOOK FOR

There are some common patterns which correlation is uniquely positioned to help uncover. Table 9.1 presents some of the more common patterns.

THE FUTURE

What does the future hold? The future is pretty bright actually. The Big Data movement has brought a new way of storing and dealing with large volumes of data. In the Big Data world, you are able to store large volumes of data across commodity machines with on-board disk storage. Sifting through these stored data is accomplished by running jobs which are geared toward finding what you are interested in and then returning a result set which is narrowly focused to what you need. A logical use for these types of systems is in finding patterns of things you may or may not know about (sound familiar?).

Table 9.1 Common Patterns

Pattern	Discussion
X login failures followed by a login success.	This could be an indication of a brute-force login attempt. What value should X take? We have seen numbers like five or ten used. On Windows, when someone logs in, Windows will actually generate more than one login message. You will want to investigate this in your environment by logging into your workstation and looking at the number of login events which are generated. Once you identify all of the extra messages, you should use your log analysis tool to filter out these other log messages.
Non-admin account creation followed by privilege escalation.	This isn't the typical user administration path, i.e. non-admin accounts don't generally get their privileges escalated to admin or some other advanced user status.
Login by a VPN user outside/inside of work hours and a transfer of megabytes or more (at some point during the VPN connection) of data outside of the network.	This could be an indication of possible exfiltration of data. This one is a bit harder to accomplish because it would require the use of something like Netflow. It's not easy to collect, summarize, and correlation Netflow in a real-time manner. This might have to be done in a post-processing manner.
A host on your network begins attacking or probing other hosts on the network.	This could be an indication that the source host is infected with a worm/trojan/malware/etc. You can use firewall logs to determine this.
X attempts in close proximity to access a share/file/directory/etc. for which a user doesn't have access.	This could be an indication of user account compromise. If this happens after hours this should be investigated immediately.
Logins from multiple usernames from the same workstation.	This is pretty simple. Some is using several different user names to access multiple different resources on the network.
Multiple AV failures across several systems.	This pattern is more general, but if you begin seeing many AV failures across a wide swatch of your systems or hosts, this could be indicative of a virus outbreak.
Exploit against DMZ system followed by outbound connection (the classic!).	This could be indicative of a bot infection.
Exploit against DMZ system followed by a configuration change on same system.	An attacker has gained access to a system and altered.
Lots of Web 404s, 401s, 500 and other Web error codes within a few minutes.	This could be indicative of your Web server or applications not functioning properly to various causes.

SUMMARY

We covered a lot of materials in this chapter. The intent was to provide you with practical tools and concepts surrounding filtering, normalization, and correlation. Network and security administrators will find the topics presented in this chapter stimulating. A large part of dealing with log data, in a meaningful way at least, has to do with properly dealing with the data in a way which allows you to derive meaning and understanding of the data.

REFERENCE

Ranum, M. J. (1997). Artificial ignorance: how-to guide, September 23. Web, March 19, 2012. <http://www.ranum.com/security/computer_security/papers/ai/>.

Statistical Analysis

INFORMATION IN THIS CHAPTER:

- Frequency
- Baseline
- Machine Learning
- Combining Statistical Analysis with Rules-based Correlation

CONTENTS

INTRODUCTION

In Chapter 9 one of the topics discussed was rules-based correlation. Correlation of this type is very useful. Unfortunately, it is based on creating rules to catch things you already have some knowledge of. In order to catch things you don't yet know about, or catch things which look similar to other things, you need to employ some statistical methods. This chapter and Chapter 11 touch on some of the more common uses of statistical concepts to help discover or uncover things which are occurring, based on log data collection, in your environment. In this chapter we look at frequencies, baselines, machine learning, and how statistical analysis can be combined with rules-based correlation.

FREQUENCY

One very simple technique which can be used is to count source and destination IP addresses in incoming log flow, across all log sources. The idea is pretty simple: a spike in the number of occurrences of a destination IP address could be an early warning sign that something is occurring, e.g. someone is targeting an attack at this system. The same is also true of source IP addresses, too. The reason this works so well is because many security devices and systems emit source and destination IP addresses. Even when you don't get source IP information, you know the destination of the potential attack (you should, it's the device being monitored by a firewall, IDS or some other detection/control system), which is often times all you need for further investigation.

Time is a factor which also needs to be a consideration in this form of analysis. You don't want to simply continue to count destination IP addresses, occurrences forever. After some predefined time period (the shorter the better), any frequencies accumulated for a destination or source IP address should be considered null and void and accumulation should begin again, i.e. new occurrences of a particular destination IP address, for example, would begin all over again. This allows hosts which have lower frequencies to not show up on your radar, while others which have higher frequencies in the same amount of time to show up on the radar in a more prominent manner.

While frequencies are a simple analysis technique, it can fall short. What we need is a more automated technique for discovering when something occurs outside of the "norm." This is where baselines come into play. We will discuss this topic in the next section.

BASELINE

As its name implies, a baseline gives you a measure of the normalness of some set of data. Why do we need to baseline? There are several compelling reasons, including:

- The gain situational awareness (SA).
- New threat discovery.
- Get better return on investment (ROI) on the gear you already have in place.
- Extra meaning from your data so you can act upon it automatically.
- Measuring your security via metrics, trends, etc.

Some actual examples of baseline usage include:

- Hits on port 443 over the last week.
- User logins to a server X times per day.
- Use of su command per hour of day.
- Count of new ports hit on a firewall.
- Number of hosts touching servers in your environment per day.

In order to create baselines, we need lots of data, in normalized form, and expert feedback. The expert feedback is needed to discern what is normal from what is bad. In most cases, training data is not needed for baselines. The key baseline assumptions are as follows:

- There is data available.
- The past was not disastrous, i.e. there were no gaping outages and so forth in the data we plan to derive the baselines from.

- A baseline is the correct model; it won't work for erratic/random phenomena (this causes bad baselines).

The basic idea is you calculate a baseline over a period of time so you get to see how something operates normally. Then, once you've gathered enough data points, you can then begin using techniques to see when things happen outside of the baseline, thus indicating a possible issue. In order to improve your baseline, it is best to collect as much data as possible. The more data you have the accurate your results will be.

One of the big questions is how much data should you collect before you can say you have captured normalness? Ideally you will collect four to six weeks of data points. In some cases, as little as one to two weeks of data can be used. Let's take a look at the basic formulas used in calculating a baseline.

First, we use the mean, or average, to find the average value of the data points.

$$mean = \frac{\sum_{k=1}^{n} x_k}{n}.$$

This is simply where we add up all data points and divide by the number of data points collected. Next, we will want to use the standard deviation formula.

$$Standard\ deviation = \sqrt{\frac{\sum_{k=1}^{n} (x_k - \mu)^2}{n}}.$$

Standard deviation is used to measure the amount of variability in your data. The formula consists of taking the square root of each data point subtracted by the mean, then squared (to get rid of negative values), then divided by the number of data points in the sample. Finally, we need to cover the standard error formula.

$$Standard\ error = \frac{\sigma}{\sqrt{n}}.$$

Standard error is used to determine a confidence interval, and it's the standard deviation divided by the square root of the number of data points. In other words, we use this to denote an interval between which future values can fall and not be deemed statistically relevant. Generally a 95-percent confidence value is used (although 90 and 99 percent are also used). Refer to Kachigan (1986) for a more in-depth discussion on this topic.

Now that we have all the basics in place, let's outline the steps to calculating a baseline:

1. Obtain the mean for your data set.
2. Calculate the standard deviation.
3. Calculate the standard error.

> ## CONFIDENCE INTERVAL
>
> ### Normal Distribution
> It should be noted that the confidence interval only works if the data follows a Normal distribution (bell curve). If your data does not follow such a distribution, there are a few techniques which can be applied like transforming the data to something approximating normal. Please see some of the books in the reference section if you want to learn more about this.

4. Multiply your standard error by 1.96 (this is based on using a 95th percentile. Again, see Kachigan (1986) for a deeper dive). Some texts use a value of 2 rather than 1.96.
5. Add and subtract the number obtained in step 4 to define your 95th percentile confidence interval. You compare future data points against this interval. If future values fall within this range, they are not necessarily too different from the baseline. If they fall outside of this interval, they might be statistically different from the baseline.
6. Add new data to baseline and age out old data. This is critical since older data is, well, old and skew results. You also need new data to detect changes in behavior.

Figure 10.1 shows the lifecycle for baselines.

What sort of things should you baseline, i.e. what baselines well? In the world of log data, there are some key things to observe. Let's list out a few of these:

- User login and logoffs, both successes and failures.
- Network traffic bytes both inbound and outbound.
- Network traffic to particular ports/services/protocols.
- Administrative account usage/access.
- Processes running on a server.
- Hardware health statistics—depending on what instrumentation a particular hardware vendor supports, it is possible to look at error rates (error rates of the hardware) and try to determine when a particular piece of hardware might fail.
- Domain Name System (DNS) requests.
- Dynamic Host Configuration Protocol (DHCP) requests.
- Total amount of log data sent and received—this can be used to detect situations where your log data sources might be misbehaving or are under attack.
- New attack type.
- New usernames.
- Log message type per sensor per day.
- Log message type per protocol and port.
- Log message types (new ones).

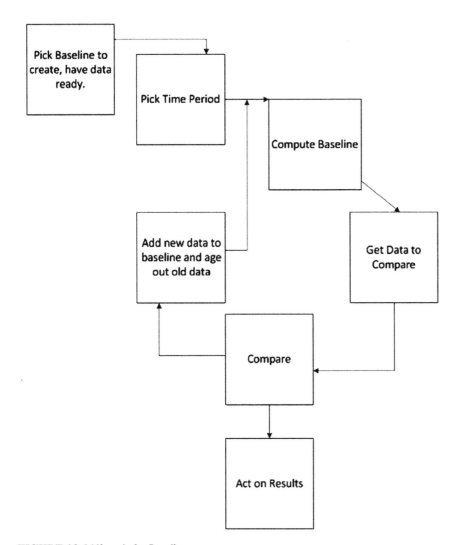

FIGURE 10.1 Lifecycle for Baselines

- Protocols per sensor per day.
- Count of unique alerts per source.
- Count of unique ports per source.

What sort of things do not baseline well?

- Random things which have no relation to what you are monitoring, from a log perspective, in your environment.

- Things which go up and down on their own, e.g. accesses to a document on a server.
- Sometimes only large deviations matter at all.
- Let's now delve into some topics which make use of baselines.

Thresholds

Thresholds are used for determining when something exceeds a baseline value. For example, let's say you know that a particular server normally receives an average of 10 failed logins per hour. If you suddenly see this number jump up to 23, then this is something you might want to investigate. This example also shows how time can factor into thresholds. Thresholds are typically not useful when are used with open-ended intervals of time. Overtime normal activity will eventually exceed any threshold. This is why placing a time bound on a threshold will help identifying things outside of the norm. But in some cases, your time bound might be fairly large. For example, if you want to catch low and slow attacks, you will need to cast your net over a wide time range, like several weeks or a month. And, on top of this, it is uniqueness which is the key here. You will likely be interested in looking at IPs which visited you more than X distinct days.

Automating the creation of thresholds can be useful. But how can automated threshold creation occur? An approach to this problem is that you can take a look at log data over a 24-h period (you really need to have your log data normalized at this point). Based on this, you can execute the following analysis:

1. Collect counts of log data / events which were not seen over the last 24 h period.
2. Collect counts of log data / events which were not seen over the previous week.

Based on the counts you collect, you can see what might be abnormal. This will give you a basic threshold to use, especially if your analysis shows that the sources of these events are not known to you. You can also use the same logic with destination IP addresses appearing in your DMZ, etc.

Anomaly Detection

Anomaly detection deals with detecting things which have never before been seen. Usage of a baseline, as described in the Baseline section, is a form of anomaly detection. This is true because we are keeping track of confidence intervals. What exactly is an example of anomaly detection? Think about a denial of service (DoS) attack. If someone is trying to attack your infrastructure to make them unavailable for your use, you can use statistical baseline to know when an increase in connections are being received by your infrastructure and possibly detect the DoS before it really becomes a problem.

Windowing

Let's say we want to be able to determine instances where users login either outside of their normally observed times, or maybe when a user, uncharacteristically, logs in from home after normal hours. One of the first things you will need to do is track login times for each user in your environment, per day. You can then establish a baseline of behavior and use steps 4 and 5 in the baseline section to determine if something warrants investigation. For example, if Bob all most never logs in after 9 pm and before 8 am, and he suddenly does, your baseline can help detect this so it can be further investigated.

Another technique, albeit simpler, is to divide the distance from one side of the baseline window by the size of the window. A small and arbitrary threshold can be used to determine if a deviation from a pattern, in this case login time, has occurred. More on this can be found in Singer and Bird (2004).

Windowing is very useful, but care must be taken. For example, simply tracking when someone logs in is fine, but it doesn't take into account things like sick days, vacation schedules, holidays, etc. These sorts of variables are called seasonal parameters. Discussing this is beyond the scope of this chapter. Just about any advanced book on statistics will cover this topic in detail, including Kachigan (1986).

MACHINE LEARNING

Machine learning (ML) is a branch of Artificial Intelligence (AI). ML uses algorithms and statistical methods to create systems which can learn. The basic concept of many ML algorithms is not unlike that of establishing a baseline. Data is used in conjunction with statistical methods to learn from past experiences and behaviors to accomplish tasks like pattern recognition, predictive systems, fraud detection, speech recognition, etc. ML algorithms basically fall into one of two categories: supervised and unsupervised. In supervised learning, a teacher is available to correct any mistakes made by the algorithm. With unsupervised learning there is no teacher. An algorithm of this type learns from available data and attempts to identify relationships in data sets.

A thorough treatment of ML is beyond the scope of this chapter. See some of the books references at the end of this chapter for more detail on the topic.

As for the topic of this book, log data, we can talk about one type of ML algorithm which might be of use. It's the k-Nearest Neighbor (kNN) technique.

k-Nearest Neighbor (kNN)

What is the kNN technique? It's a learning algorithm and it basically aims to classify unknown patterns against a set of a previously seen patterns. We are interested in uncovering a pattern in unlabeled data. The key to this is the distance used to determine which of the known patterns, the unknown one closely resembles. At the heart of this technique is a distance calculation. The most commonly used calculation is the Euclidean distance formula.

$$distance = \sqrt{\sum_{i=1}^{n}(p_i - q_i)^2}.$$

The basic premise behind k-NN is that you define features of different patterns. Each feature denotes something unique to the pattern. The more patterns and features you have, the more likely you will be able to detect unknown patterns. The patterns you have defined ahead of time, the better you will be able to detect unknown patterns. So how does the distance formula factor in? The formula makes use of two vectors of data: p and q. One is the set of known patterns and the other is the pattern we are trying to detect. As we loop through each set of vectors and the features of each pattern, we calculate the distance away from each known feature and the unknown feature. Where the k comes in is that we take the k closest neighbors and use a majority voting scheme. This has the advantage of reducing misclassification since more examples can impact the vote.

Let's run through an example to see how this works in practice.

Applying the k-NN Algorithm to Logs

Let's enumerate a set of features we want to use for our example:

1. Excessive Outbound Traffic: EOT.
2. Excessive Inbound Traffic: EIT.
3. VPN Login After Hours: VPNLI.
4. Firewall Accepts: FWA.
5. Firewall Drops: FWD.
6. Login Outside of Internal Network: LOIN.
7. Multiple Failed Logins in a Row: MFL.
8. At Least 1 Successful Login: SL.
9. Single Source Probing Multiple Destination IPs: SSPMD.
10. Single Source Probing Multiple Destination IPs and Ports: SSPMDP.

Table 10.1 shows a set of patterns along with what set of features each pattern has. A blank column means the pattern does not have the feature.

Table 10.1 Patterns and Features

Pattern	EOT	EIT	VPNLI	FWA	FWD	LOIN	MFL	SL	SSP-MD	SSP-MDP
Possible-Brute Force Login				Yes			Yes	Yes		
Possible-Brute Force Login				Yes			Yes	Yes	Yes	
Portscan			Yes						Yes	Yes
Portscan									Yes	Yes
Possible Exfiltration	Yes		Yes	Yes						
Possible Exfiltration	Yes		Yes			Yes				

Table 10.2 Unknown Patterns with k-NN Recognition Results

EOT	EIT	VPNLI	FWA	FWD	LOIN	MFL	SL	SSP-MD	SSP-MDP	Results
	Yes				Yes	Yes	Yes			Possible Brute Force Login
								Yes		Portscan
									Yes	Portscan
Yes										Possible Exfiltration Attempt
Yes		Yes								Possible Exfiltration Attempt

It should be noted that what we are trying to do is classify and detect scenarios which require multiple events in order to make up a higher level behavior, i.e. we are not simply classifying a single log message but multiple ones in order to define a pattern.

If we apply the k-NN algorithm as it's describe in k-Nearest Neighbor (kNN) section, we can generate some results. Table 10.2 shows the results of running a few unknown patterns through the k-NN algorithm.

The classifications of the unknown patterns were not bad. k-NN was chosen because it is easy to understand and implement. A quick Google search will turn up implementations in Java, C, Perl, etc. One of the drawbacks in using k-NN is that it can take a lot of computation time, if the features set and the unknown set are large. It can also require lots of memory for processing, too.

COMBINING STATISTICAL ANALYSIS WITH RULES-BASED CORRELATION

The final topic to cover is statistical analysis and rules-based correlation. More specifically, we want to look at how the two are typically combined to make each concept more powerful. In the section on k-NN, the outcome of the algorithm is very similar to rules process, except for the fact that k-NN allows for partial data to be present to make its determination. SIEM vendors have always employed statistical methods alongside the rule processing components. Figure 10.2 shows a high-level logical flow of correlation with statistics embedded.

What this shows is the end-to-end flow of a raw log message all the way through to its final resting place. Statistical calculations play an important role here. Whether you are looking to buy a commercial log analysis or SIEM platform, build one, etc. here are some things to keep in mind:

- How integrated is the statistical part of the system with the rules engine? Some platforms all correlation rules to be created which contain conditionals expressed as statistical calculations. Other platforms allow for statistical analysis pre- and post-rules correlation, and vice versa.

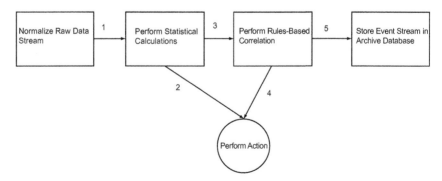

FIGURE 10.2 Conceptual Flow for Statistical and Rules-Based Correlation

- How easy is it to extend / enhance the statistical component of your platform? You want to be able to tweak the analysis component without needed a statistics degree.
- Is the statistical analysis adaptive in nature? The idea here is, simply, does it use some sort of ML or data mining techniques to help thwart the ever changing threat landscape of the hackers.

SUMMARY

This chapter introduced some of the most basic statistical analysis methods. While basic, they are quite powerful in usage when applied to log data analysis. Baselines are critical when it comes to understanding how something acts normally. We then apply techniques like thresholds and windows as specific applications of a baseline to find things which might not be so normal. Machine learning is an interesting area of statistical analysis which can be used to learn in either a supervised or unsupervised manner. It is suggested you learn more about statistical and ML concepts.

REFERENCES

Kachigan, S. K. (1986). *Statistical analysis: An interdisciplinary introduction to univariate & multivariate methods*. New York: Radius.

Singer, A., & Bird, T. (2004). *Building a logging infrastructure*. USENIX Association.

## CHAPTER 11

Log Data Mining

- Data Mining Intro
- Log Mining Intro
- Log Mining Requirements
- What We Mine for?
- Deeper into Interesting

CONTENTS

INTRODUCTION

A vast majority of log analysis techniques require that an analyst know something specific about what he or she is looking for in the logs. For example, he might "scan" the server logs for "known bad" log entries (just as OSSEC does. See Chapter 15 for information on this tool.) which indicate attacks, exploits, server failures, or whatever other infraction of interest by using string matching or regular expressions. One can observe that it requires significant domain knowledge; in this case, expertise in security and specific type of logs available for analysis on all stages of the log analysis process, from reviewing the data to running queries and searches all the way from interpreting the results to acting on the conclusions. In other words, you have to know what questions to ask before you get the answer you want—a tricky proposition at best. In addition, it requires an immense amount of patience to even start the task, since one can be going through logs for a long time without finding the aberrant line or a group of lines; or, it might not even be there.

In this chapter, we will describe methods for discovering interesting patterns in log files for security without specifically knowing what we look for and thus without the onerous "patience requirement" and without the expensive "expertise requirement" on all analysis stages. We will review some practical results of such methods, demonstrate the tools, and discuss how they can be used in various scenarios that occur in the process of maintaining security and availability of IT operation as well as assisting with compliance initiatives.

Since the techniques we will cover are similar in many regards to data mining, we need to step back and provide a brief data mining overview for those readers not familiar with it.

DATA MINING INTRO

We will start from a "dictionary" definition of Data Mining (DM), that can be found in Encyclopedia Britannica Online (http://www.britannica.com/EBchecked/topic/1056150/data-mining). It succinctly states that: "data mining, also called knowledge discovery in databases, in computer science, the process of discovering interesting and useful patterns and relationships in large volumes of data. The field combines tools from statistics and artificial intelligence (such as neural networks and machine learning) with database management to analyze large digital collections, known as data sets."

Two other definitions will also be useful for our purposes. They are: "The nontrivial extraction of implicit, previously unknown, and potentially useful information from data"[1] and "The science of extracting useful information from large data sets or databases."[2] Yet another definition useful for our purposes is: "An information extraction activity whose goal is to discover hidden facts contained in databases."

Notice what is in common among those:

- Data Mining (further DM for brevity) deals with a pool of data, possibly very large.
- Such data exists on a computer system in machine-readable format (such as a relational database system); in other words, it is structured data.[3]
- Available data might lead us to some interesting conclusion, but, then again, it might not.
- There is some useful outcome that we are trying to get to, which requires searching or otherwise analyzing the data.

Structuring the DM using the above items reveals definite similarities between it and log analysis. We have a large pool of log records and we need to

---

[1] Frawley, Piatetsky-Shapiro, and Matheus (1992).
[2] Hand, Mannila, and Smyth (2001).
[3] Data mining on unstructured data is called "text mining." Many logs nowadays are more similar to unstructured, text data and thus text mining techniques will be useful. Even though the author is conducting active research in this area, this chapter will focus on structure data mining, not text mining.

understand what the computer systems are trying to tell us by producing those logs. What they are trying to say is sometimes on the surface, but in other cases is hidden within a deluge of meaningless or irrelevant information. Thus, likeness between log analysis and DM leads us to believe that DM can be useful for our challenge at hand: making sense of logs.

Let's dive a bit deeper into data mining. The realm of data mining covers a broad range of scientific methods, software applications, and usage scenarios. Here we will try to show you the parts of data mining related to security log analysis. Consequentially, DM finds uses in many areas of business, from retail to fraud analysis and risk management.

In general, there are two broad types of data mining methods: predictive and descriptive. While everybody will rush to trying to peek into the future by using predictive DM, descriptive is just as useful since it can reveal the hidden truths applicable to past and present, a no mean feat by itself. Descriptive DM also serves to describe data sets in an informative way, thus almost "explaining" what is going on. Predictive DM, on the other hand, allows making forecasts about the not-yet-available data based on whatever is already here.

Since DM finds so many uses in retail, our illustrative DM examples—before we move to mining the logs—will be from that area. Descriptive DM may reveal what else you have likely bought if you just bought a car CD player (for example, disks, cable kit, speakers), thus allowing the store to position them closer to the player. On the other hand, predictive DM might help the store to figure out what you will buy next (or when you will go broke from buying too much already…)

Individual DM techniques are numerous, Table 11.1 shows some that find common use.

Data mining process is often described as having the following steps:

1. *Acquiring subject matter expertise* in the area that the data relates to—it is essential to "know what you are doing" in data mining, as much (or more) than in other areas. DM tools do not "perform magic" and will likely not produce the results unless the user understands the data to be mined.[4]
2. *Defining the goal* is an obvious but critical step. While explorative techniques are known, we still need to know why we want to collect, prepare, and mine the data and what will be done with the results.

---

[4] This "limitation" killed many worthwhile data mining projects …

Table 11.1 Data Mining Techniques in Common Usage

Type	Technique	Example
Descriptive	Clustering	Group people with common hobbies together
Descriptive	Association Rule Discovery	Discover what parameters in data are associated with other
Descriptive	Frequent Itemsets Discovery	Finding what objects occur in groups
Descriptive	Sequential Pattern Discovery	Finding what objects occur in a specific sequence
Predictive	Classification	Sorting out the data bits into classes
Predictive	Regression	Predicting the behavior of a data set, similar to the one being mined.
Predictive	Deviation Detection	Discovering whether the data points actually fit the profile, mined previously

3. Planning for collection and then *collecting data*—this sets the foundation for future DM endeavors. Data also has a nasty tendency to grow beyond control, just as we observed with audit log data.

4. *Data preprocessing and cleaning* are often needed for the DM process to be effective or even to happen at all. Sometimes, DM experts estimate that this stage takes 60% of all the mining effort. This stage usually involves dealing with missing bits of information as well as possibly duplicate data points, smoothing "noisy" data, identifying, and correcting other inconsistencies in the data set. Sometimes this step is also called "data cleansing."

5. *Data reduction and transformation* involves things such as dropping extra dimensions of data as well as applying algorithms aimed at making the data more manageable by removing parts of the data set.

6. *Choosing the method* to apply is the next step. Do we want to cluster the data or look for sequences? Do we baseline or uncover associative rules? The method chosen is likely to be driven by the goals, defined several steps above.

7. Are we done yet? No, we need to *choose a specific algorithm* that implements the method chosen above. Researchers as well as tool vendors are constantly working on new algorithm to look for patterns as well as on the performance of the existing algorithms. The right choice might make a difference between an efficient 10 min run versus a multi-day database abusing disaster.

8. *Run the mining software* and get the results. That might refer to seeing picture (when the results are visualized) or a table or other textual representation of data.
9. And now, as some estimate, the hard part starts: *figuring out what the results actually mean*. From simple text reports to fancy visualizations, this stage is where we can actually understand whether all the previous steps actually brought the gold.

As one can see, the above steps fit closely to a normal log analysis process. That is why in the next section we will start illustrating how one can use DM-like techniques for log analysis.

Let us focus on the last step and discuss an interesting problem of "interestingness."[5] Provided the DM succeeded and the results returned are correct (meaning that the methodology and utilized application do not have flaws), where are the assurances that we actually care to see them?

For example, one of the author's experiments with associative rule discovery on log data brought up the following bit of DM wisdom: if the protocol of the connection is DNS (Domain Name System), then there is a high probability that the ports where it was sent is 53. "Duh!" would be the appropriate response here, since the mining algorithm did its job but we didn't really care to see the results. For the analyst, it is fairly obvious that most if not all DNS traffic always occurs on port 53. This shows that DM techniques can discover "hidden" patterns, but why are we so sure that the user will care to see them? "Interestingness" measure is an attempt by the researchers to quantify that. Another useful definition of it is: "A pattern is interesting if it is easily understood by humans, valid on new or test data with some degree of certainty, potentially useful, novel, or validates some hypothesis that a user seeks to confirm." The measure is sometimes classified into objective and subjective interestingness. The former is determined by the computer using whatever "interestingness" algorithm while the latter is defined by the human expert. This distinction is obviously useful for log analysis, since in many regards it is "an art, not science" and the human analyst is the ultimate judge of any technique's usefulness.

The main reason we wanted to highlight the "interestingness" at this stage, is that when looking into data mining people often expect miracles. For example, "let me put my logs into the systems and it will tell me everything I need to know at the moment." Such thing will hardly ever happen, since, even if system has

---

[5] Yes, that is a data mining term. Specifically, it is defined at ftp://ftp.gte.com/pub/kdd/kdd-terms.html#Interest as "a pattern instance measures its quality and has several dimensions. The main dimensions are the validation on the sample set, the reliability on the universe, the degree of redundancy with respect to other already known pattern instances, the generality, the simplicity, and the usefulness."

perfectly tuned data mining capabilities, it will likely have no idea of what you are interested in at the moment. However, the good news is that DM is a technology that allows one to approach the above idea closer than any other method.

After this review, we are ready to see how data mining techniques can be applied for our purposes of analyzing logs.

LOG MINING INTRO

While log mining is technically a kind of analysis, we want to show that it starts where the usual log analysis ends, thus the differentiation. In addition, the author would hate to say "log anomaly detection" since it is often (such as in academic publication on information security) another way of saying "it doesn't work, but it well might one day if the moons are aligned and the appropriate animal is sacrificed to the appropriate deity."

Knowing a bit about the data mining methods and technologies, let's step back from it and review what are we trying to achieve by applying the data mining to log data. In general, we are seeking to:

- Improve the quality of log analysis to provide better answers and predictive power.
- Make the advanced and effective methods available without requiring rare and expensive human expertise.

Richard Bejtlich in his book "Tao of Security Monitoring" described his view on network monitoring for security. The monitoring obviously covers logs (such as from intrusion detection or prevention systems) as well as network traffic information, such as neftlow[6] and full packet captures. The main tenet of his NSM approach is that highly skilled analysts follow a well-optimized analysis process and run tools in order to gain insight from the incoming data such as logs, alerts, and packet dumps. A *minor* problem with this is that such analysts might be simply unavailable or, at the very least, unaffordable for the task at hand. As a result, the entire methodology breaks down ungracefully, since it relies on having trained, intelligent, and motivated human analyst (or even "expert") in front of the console all the time. Thus, this approach will likely remain in the realm of well-funded and security-minded organizations.

By using data mining and other advanced automated analytics, we will try to move as much of the "analysis burden" (or "glory," depending who you ask)

---

[6] Cisco netflow format is used to collect network traffic information from the infrastructure devices (see more at "Cisco IOS NetFlow" http://www.cisco.com/en/US/products/ps6601/products_ios_protocol_group_home.html).

to software and automated systems, away from exceptionally skilled—and just as exceptionally hard to find—human analysts. At least, we will prefer that the involvement of such analysis will be critical only at the early stages of the process, when we designed the specific mining methods, as we outlined in the previous section. In this case, the experts might define the specifics of the mining process and then let the less-skilled operations stuff to run the algorithm and act on the results with no reduction in efficiency.

Let's briefly look at how DM techniques are applied to logs, why do it and what are the benefits. We coin the term "log mining" to mean "application of data mining techniques to advanced log analysis."

We will start by asking "why mine the logs?" Ideally, our vision is to reduce the human effort needed and increase the role of the automated system in log analysis. Log mining, in brief, is one of the ways to get there. In fact, it is likely to be the most promising, as we mentioned before. So, log analysis faces challenges such as these:

- *Too much data:* A volume of log data floods the log analysis systems as well as the human analyst, thus destroying any possibility to get the answers out. Indeed, logs can go into gigabytes and then crawl into terabytes; so you need tools to deal with the deluge.
- *Not enough data:* Critical piece of data is missing for various reasons, making log analysis more of a challenge that it should be.
- *Diverse records:* Too many different and dissimilar log sources need to be analyzed to get to truth. This problem is due to the lack of the universal audit standard; most applications log in whatever formats developed by their creators, thus leading to the massive analysis challenge. Future standard efforts such as MITRE's Common Event Expression (CEE) (see http://cee.mitre.org) will resolve this.
- *False alarms:* Logs are full of messages that do not reflect reality in any measurable way (network IDS "false positives" largely occupy this category).
- *Duplicate data:* Different logs refer to the same events without any indication of that; this situation is often further complicated by missing time synchronization between different log sources.
- *Hard to get data:* While a device might create perfectly useful log records in a proprietary format, it will not "cooperate" with centralized log collection by lacking "standard"[7] log formats such as syslog or Windows NT event log. Similarly, getting the detailed mainframe audit records may be a challenge.

---

[7] From reading this book, you already know that these standard are not real, but just common formats used by many systems.

Many techniques have been developed to deal with the challenges. So, why mine the logs, if we have all those other approaches? Here are the top reasons:

- *Reduce the reliance on skilled analysts* by enabling more human-like pattern recognition and only necessitating such expertise at the early stages of the analysis.
- *Deal with sparse data* that cannot be effectively analyzed by other, more conventional means. Looking at gigabytes or even terabytes of data is better left to fully automated approaches, such as log mining.
- *Detect things* that sneak "below the radar" of other methods. Yes, log mining promises to increase the efficiency of detecting the intrusion traces.
- Offload *conclusion generation* to machines; so that this so far human-only task can also be automated. Human will still act on the conclusions, but they won't need to wrack their brains by trying to figure out what is going on.
- Attempt to *predict problems*, rather than find ways to deal with things that already occurred. While DM does not provide an easy guaranteed way to such prediction, it certainly comes closer than any other method.

We should note that even though the trend will likely go toward "replacing" humans, the algorithms will always need to be defined and tuned by experts. However, DM techniques will clearly reduce the skill requirements on the operational staff.

In case of some early implementations seen by the author, the users of DM-based log analysis systems have commented that after a relatively brief tuning period the systems become "better than junior analysts." In this scenario, the systems that used DM-like log analysis methods were implemented at a bank to look at the detailed audit data from multiple intrusion detection and firewall devices, deployed across the enterprise. The system developers and senior analysts have utilized the systems during the initial phase; the same people also trained the junior analysts who used to just watch the consoles with log records flowing by and perform the initial alert investigation. Now, with tuned DM-based log analysis system in place, the analysts focused on investigation only since the systems picked the signification alerts and episodes as good as those analysts.

Let's look at what is necessary before we can apply data mining to log data.

LOG MINING REQUIREMENTS

It is important to note up front that many requirements for log mining are the same as needed for any significant log analysis. However, there are some added factors that either appear to make log data suitable for mining or convert from optional to mandatory requirements:

1. *Data centralization:* To look in just one place is nice to have for regular log analysis such as filtering and summarization, but becomes critical for log mining, since mining algorithms can crunch much more data than any single human analyst.
2. *Normalized:* To look across the data sources centralized as described above requires a uniform information format. It might not be the real standard, just the uniform way of representing the log data.
3. *Relational storage:* Relational data storage such as a RDMBS is essential here, but can be left out if only simple analysis and filtering is performed.[8] Such normalization is accomplished by looking for common fields in logs. Those commonly include:

- Time.
- Source.
- Destination.
- Protocol.
- Port(s).
- User name.
- Event/attack type.
- Bytes exchanged.
- *Others.*

Thus, normalized and centralized data can be subjected to the log data mining algorithms. Now, we are ready to review what we will look for by applying the data mining.

WHAT WE MINE FOR?

As we established, DM methods are most useful when we are not sure what we look for (otherwise, we can just filter or search for what we need) How about we find something "interesting," as we hinted in the previous section? As we mentioned above, interesting likely includes being unexpected to the user and actionable.

What are some of the common examples that a system administrator or a security analyst will find "interesting" and can use some help with finding?

- *Infected system spreading malware:* While obvious in many cases, systems that get infected and then spread the infection enterprise-wide and even

---

[8] Text mining that was mentioned above certainly does not need the two of the mentioned requirements. Text mining methods will work on mere piles of log data.

Internet-wide are high on the priority list of every security administrator. Despite antivirus and other dedicated solutions, mining logs proves invaluable in tracking that perky initial system that brought down the house.

- *Compromised system:* Every security pro worth his weight in paper certificates, should be interested in knowing that attackers or their minions—"malware"—have taken over a system or systems in their network.
- *Successful attack:* If the attacker just succeeded in breaching your system, it will likely be "interesting" to know (to put it mildly); while this actually relates to the previous item, it usually describes the earlier stages of the attack as it develops from an attempt to a full-blown compromise and system utilization by the attackers.
- *Insider abuse and intellectual property theft:* While evil hackers and worms steal all the glory, internal network abuse seems primitive by comparison. However, insiders hold all the keys for the kingdom and have potential for dealing much more damage; to add insult to injury, detecting their exploits is much harder than average malware. Clear evidence of insider attacks, even failed, will certainly be of interest to the administrators and analysts.
- *Covert channel/hidden backdoor communication:* Unless you are "into that sort of thing," covert channels are probably not in regular use on your network; thus, it is highly likely that network security administrators will be interested in knowing this.
- *Increase in probing:* While all but few sensitive government networks now discount Internet probing activity as mere noise, certain increases in such activity, reflected in logs, are known to serve as precursors to attacks, thus becoming interesting.
- *System crash:* While "denial service detection" always causes a chuckle (by definition, you detect it by noticing that you happen to not have any service), a system administrator might not be monitoring for uptime of all the systems.

Thus, the above summary shows some of the universally interesting things that we can hope to discovery by mining the logs.

Criteria of what is *interesting* is very hard to define for a computer, but it is possible with log mining! Let's also look at common examples of *not* interesting, that do not match the above "interestingness" criteria of unexpected and actionable:

- *Probe* (*not unexpected*): Network probes and scans happen all the time and people grew to expect them. One should be mindful of those, but will not be likely to spend resources looking for them. At the same time, change in the number of such probes (per day, week, month, etc.) has a higher chance of being interesting.

- *Common failed attack* (*not unexpected*): If your security architecture is solid you can expect to see failed attacks; those occur for various reasons (attacker skill is one of them). Similar to probes, one should know about them, but not spend resources looking for them.
- *Normal message* (*not unexpected*): Logs are full of messages indicating completion of some routine process and other perfectly normal events, recorded for audit and other purposes. Those are obviously not unexpected and we do not mine for them. However, changes matter here as well: normal messages that stop coming or the ones that start appearing more/less frequently might well be interesting.
- *Blocked attack* (*not actionable*): Similar to a failed attack, if your security countermeasures block an attack, even an interesting one that you do not expect, no prompt action is truly necessary. Indeed, an investigation might be in order, but this still fails to match the "interestingness" criteria.
- *System status update* (*not actionable*): Similar to a normal event, those likely invoke no action. At the same time, system status updates happening at some unusual time might well be of high interest…

Let's look at finding interesting things via log mining in more detail.

DEEPER INTO INTERESTING

Let's look back at our data mining preview and again review some of the methods to see how they apply to the task at hand. Here are the things that we can mine for and have a reasonable hope of finding interesting things:

- *Rare* things: maybe it doesn't happen frequently for a reason! If something just hasn't happened before, it well might be malicious. Thus, rare events are prime candidates for our mining. Rare attacks, rare system messages, users that almost never logging are all fun to detect!
- *Different* things: while we do not advocate total "log xenophobia," one should be on the lookout for things differing from what they were. This is where the baselining methods of data mining come into play.
- *"Out of character"* things: while being closely related to the above category, log records that appear "out of character" need to be mined for, since they are more likely to be interesting.
- *Weird-looking* things: if something just looks weird, it might be a sign of trouble. There is a subtle difference here between the above two types that we look for. To see something weird, such as your DNS system going to packetstorm.com and downloading exploit tools all by itself, does not require any baseline or prior data collection.

- Things goings in the unusual *direction:* some log records completely change their relevance to the analysts and administrators depending on the communication direction. As in the above example, a connection to your server is perfectly legitimate, while the server going out and connecting (even on an innocent port such as TCP port 80) will likely raise some eyebrows, at the very least.
- *Top* things: while sitting in the realm of summarization and reporting and not strictly data mining, "Top X of Anything" remains useful for finding interesting log records and their patterns. After all, if it climbed up there to be (example: "top use by bandwidth transferred"), it well might be interesting for that.
- *Bottom* things: similar to rare things (which as simply, "bottom by occurrence"), this "evil sister" to "Top X of Anything" is even more useful to look at. It is well known that often systems that attract the smallest amount of attention become the stepping stones to future attacks and losses.
- *Strange combinations* of uninteresting things: this roughly follows a formula of "good" + "good" = "evil." Yes, even a bunch of perfectly normal log record might form something malignant in aggregate. The simplest example is a port scan, that is simply a set (often, a very large one) of benign connection requests.
- *Counts* of an otherwise uninteresting things: count of something uninteresting might well generate some interest. Moreover, *a change* in such count will often be even more significant. A sudden surge in a number of "ping" ICMP packets even outside the firewall might well mean a denial of service, especially if such ICMP flood came suddenly without warning.

Let's give an example here that illustrates this. In this example, a hacking incident involving unauthorized use of a vulnerability scanner is discovered. As we all know, network IDS (also referred to as "NIDS") are deployed by a large percentage of companies, but many have failed to realize value from such purchases. Some reasons for such misfortune include high volumes of false alarms in their logs, undermining trust people have in such systems. That especially applies to signature-based systems that are supposed to flag packets and connections having specific patterns in them. To realize value from NIDS we can use log mining methods, aimed at flagging real attacks over routine noise and false alarms. Note, that in this case we might not learn about the attack success, but just the persistence and focus of the attacker as well as distinguish attacks from benign and erroneous triggering of the NIDS.

When a legitimate connection is recorded by network infrastructure components or whatever misuse detection systems (such as IDS), they usually produce a small number of unique event types in the logs. For example, a connection through a firewall generates one connection message. Even a scan of a firewall will likely generate one event per connecting session and likely one event type (*connection_denied*) for the whole scan (this event will be repeated many times, but they will all be of the same type). Similarly, a "false positive" will *not* commonly be associated with other suspicious activity between the same hosts, such as recon scanning or other exploits. On the opposite, false alarms are more likely to happen in complete isolation or in large numbers of the same log record type with no other, "related" records. Here, by session we mean a *unique combination* of:

- Source.
- Destination.
- Protocol.
- Source port.
- Destination port.

Thus, if we organize events collected in the database by session and record the number of unique events (often the same as number of attack types) in each session we will have a way of distinguishing real attack from legit traffic and false alarms. This log mining approach uses a generic pattern to arrive at a specific and interesting outcome of a potentially damaging attack. Again, we give no indication of the attack's success, but just qualify it as real or false.

SUMMARY

This chapter cast a brief look upon using data mining methods for practical log analysis. We illustrated that log mining and knowledge discovery in logs is a novel way of looking at log data, which actually works in real life! Many types of logs can be subjected to such mining with useful results. While data mining is indeed a truly esoteric area, log mining (at least some of its methods) are not that hard and can be implemented within many environments. Moreover, log mining can help where common analysis methods that requires skilled analysts working long hours fail.

Finally, active research in the area—including mining of unstructured log via text mining—is likely to bring more useful methods that people can use.

REFERENCES

Frawley, W., Piatetsky-Shapiro, G., & Matheus, C. (1992). Knowledge discovery in databases: An overview. *AI Magazine*, 213–228.

Hand, D., Mannila, H., & Smyth, P. (2001). *Principles of data mining*. Cambridge, MA: MIT Press. ISBN: 0-262-08290-X.

Reporting and Summarization

INFORMATION IN THIS CHAPTER:

- Defining the Best Reports
- Network Activity Reports
- Resource Access Reports
- Malware Activity Reports
- Critical Errors and Failures Reports

INTRODUCTION

Anybody who had to look at log data for any period of time knows that nothing works by looking at the actual raw logs. However, as last majority of log analysis tasks involve looking at summaries—reports—of log data over a period of time or across a particular set of systems. The more data we have to analyze, the more summarization and aggregation we have to do. In fact, most people's first experience reviewing logs likely happens to reports be on log data—all the venerable "top 10 users," "top attacks over time", and other reports.

Indeed, summarization and reports are the mainstay of log analysis: *Top Connection by Bandwidth, Top Attacks by Country, Top Users with Authentication Failures,* and other reports based on logs are what most people think about when they think about log analysis today. Even commercial log analysis and SIEM tool users will look at reports more often than they look at original log data.

Summarization works and reduces the amount of data you need to see, but by summarizing data we kill it—there is a loss of useful information; in addition, data might be lost due to the type of summaries we choose to utilize. For example, if you look at top 10 users, don't forget that your bottom 10 users might be just as interesting.

Finally, reports are typically pretty numerous, and there is the challenge of which report to pick. As a fine example, one of the vendors used to tout having "13,000 reports" in their product—as if it can be a good thing...

On top of this, many organization struggle with multiple regulatory compliance frameworks (PCI DSS, HIPAA/HITECH, FISMA, and many others discussed in other chapters of this book) as well as with advanced threats (malware, criminal hackers, mobile threats, cloud security challenges, etc.). Also, malicious insiders now get additional opportunities to harm or defraud a business. At the same time, the importance of information technology for businesses and government organizations has grown tremendously and will grow even more.

DEFINING THE BEST REPORTS

In light of the broad usefulness of reporting for log analysis, as well as other large number of possible reports, it is important to try to create a list of "the best" reports or at least the ones with the broadest applicability in the industry.

This chapter is an attempt to create just such a list. The reports are organized into six broad categories or report types with specific examples applicable to most organizations. They designed to be a technology agnostic and can be produced with commercial, open source or homegrown log management, and analysis tools. More advanced SIEM tools can be used as well.

The top report categories are:

1. Authentication and Authorization Reports.
2. Systems and Data Change Reports.
3. Network Activity Reports.
4. Resource Access Reports.
5. Malware Activity Reports.
6. Failure and Critical Error Reports.

In the rest of the document, we will cover each category with specific examples.

Authentication and Authorization Reports

These reports identify successful and failed attempts to access various systems at various user privilege levels (authentication) as well as specific privileged user activities and attempts to use privileged capabilities (authorization).

Why They Are Important

Authentication is the main barrier and means of controlling access to today's systems. From simple passwords to tokens and cryptographic mechanisms, reviewing authentication activity across the organization is one of the key security activities.

Specifics Reports

Key reports in this category are:

- *All login failures and successes by user, system, business unit:* this may be one report or multiple reports showing login successes and login failures across various systems, access methods (local, remote), and user. Not that to be valuable, this report requires that you log both login successes and not just failures.
- *Login attempts (successes, failures) to disabled/service/non-existing/default/ suspended accounts:* this report group covers attempted access to accounts and services that should not be accessed, ever. Both failures and successes are of interest to security professionals.
- *All logins after office hours / "off" hours:* similar to the above report, such activity is commonly of interest especially if access attempt is successful. However, such events have to be investigated especially in environments where system administrators work 24/7.
- *Users failing to authentication by count of unique systems they tried:* this aggregate report has to detect account scans where a single machine checks for the same or different account across many systems. It is a little similar to an old school "host scan."
- *VPN authentication and other remote access logins (success, failure):* while all login attempts might be of interest under the right circumstances, remote login attempts such as via VPN or other remote connectivity methods are of escalated interest and should be tracked carefully.
- *Privileged account access (successes, failures):* *root* or *administrator* logins, *su* use, Run As use, as well as relevant equivalents for other platforms and systems have to be accounted for, since a privileged user can typically do much more damage than a normal user.
- *Multiple login failures followed by success by same account:* while rule-based (SIEM-style) correlation is needed to produce this report, tracking for multiple account failures immediately followed by a successful connection would be of obvious interest, since it almost always indicates attempts to guess login credentials (source: http://chuvakin. blogspot.com/2010/08/updated-with-community-feedback-sans_ 06.html).

Who Can Use These Reports

These reports have universal applicability, depending on scope of systems covered. A chief security officer (CSO) may review authentication summaries across the entire organization, security analyst may use these reports during daily log review, incident responders may run them while investigating an incident, and system administrators can run these reports on their own systems.

Example

Table 12.1 shows login attempts to systems.

Change Reports

These reports identify various system and security critical changes—configuration files, accounts, regulated and sensitive data, and other components of the system or applications.

Why They Are Important

Unauthorized changes to information systems lead to many costly crashes, data losses, and security incidents. On top of this, attackers will often modify your systems in order to enable their access in the future. Being diligent with tracking changes will also improve your overall IT operation.

Specifics Reports

Key reports in this category are:

- *Additions/changes/deletions to users, groups:* attackers will frequently add new act now owns and then sometimes delete them after access. These activities should have been performed in an authorized manner.
- *Additions of accounts to administrator / privileged groups:* in particular, changes to the administrator accounts and other privileged users should be at the top of the list of tracked account changes.
- *Password changes and resets—by users and by admins to users:* password changes are often just as important as new account creations. These can be performed by users as well as by administrators. In addition, this report can be used to make sure that if authorized password changes are performed according to policy schedule.
- *Additions/changes/deletions to network services:* new services that allow network connectivity may open your network to additional attacks; they also are frequently performed by attackers.
- *Changes to system files—binaries, configurations:* changes to system files such as buying at ease and configuration files—whether accidental, planned or malicious—needed to be carefully tracked.

Table 12.1 Sample Report Showing Login Attempts

System	Account Name	Source IP	Status	Method	Count
Venus	administrator	10.1.1.2	Failure	Local	1
Jupiter	anton	10.11.12.13	Success	Local	1
Mercury	root	10.1.2.3	Failure	SSH	893765

- *Changes to other key files:* various systems might have broad lists of key files in addition to binary executables and configuration files; track access to these as well.
- *Changes in file access permissions:* a sneakier variety of a risky change is a change in file permissions; if not accounted for, such changes have led to sensitive data compromise.
- *Changes to sensitive files:* or downloading/copying of sensitive documents.
- *Application installs and updates (success, failure) by system, application, user:* all application installs and updates need to be logged across all systems; at the very least, these logs will be incredibly useful during incident response.

Who Can Use These Reports

These reports have universal applicability, depending on scope of systems covered. A chief security officer (CSO) may review change summaries across the entire organization, security analyst may use these reports during daily log review, incident responders may run them while investigating an incident, and system administrators can run these reports on their own systems.

Example

Table 12.2 shows all account and group additions on a Linux system.

NETWORK ACTIVITY REPORTS

These reports identify various system suspicious and potentially dangerous network activities as well as activities that need to be tracked for common regulations.

Why They Are Important

Network is the main way for threats to arrive at information assets. Obviously, the network is also the main way to steal information assets from today's organizations.

Table 12.2 Sample Report Showing Account and Group Additions

Date	System	Account Name	Operation	Object	Status
1/10/11 11:11AM PST	Venus	root	Account Added	anton	Success
1/11/11 11:11AM PST	Jupiter	anton	Group Added	sudoers	Success
1/10/11 11:11AM PST	Venus	root	Account Added	root1	Failure

Specifics Reports

Key reports in this category are:

- *All outbound connections from internal and DMZ systems by system, connection count, user, bandwidth, count of unique destinations:* there are multiple ways to slice the information on outbound connections from your environment, but the main essence remains the same: tracking who is connecting from your network outside is the way to detect intrusions and compromises and malicious software—as well as users abusing network access.
- *All outbound connections from internal and DMZ systems during "off" hours:* using firewall and web proxy logs, one can use a more targeted version of the above report and only track outbound access during unusual hours.
- *Top largest file transfers (inbound, outbound) OR Top largest sessions by bytes transferred:* either of the two reports allows organizations to track blatant data theft and bandwidth abuse.
- *Web file uploads to external sites:* based on proxy logs, one can track what files are being uploaded to external sites as well as being attached to Webmail.
- *All file downloads with by content type (exe, dll, scr, upx, etc.) and protocol (HTTP, IM, etc.):* tracking what files enter your environment from the Web is also important and can be done by tracking files across protocols and methods.
- *Internal systems using many different protocols/ports:* while there is no reliable way to always know malware activity from legitimate, internal systems, suddenly starting to "talk" over many new ports and protocols, are a known telltale sign of malicious activity.
- *Top internal systems as sources of multiple types of NIDS, NIPS or WAF Alerts:* one of the most useful reports is tracking internal information assets that "light up" like a holiday tree by generating many different types.
- *VPN network activity by username, total session bytes, count of sessions, usage of internal resources:* we highlighted the need to track VPN logins in the above section, but VPN usage should also be tracked in order to spot the VPN access and traffic anomalies.
- *P2P use by internal systems:* while user-breaking AUP might be the focus of this effort, P2P software was also implicated in accidental and malicious data theft and loss.
- *Wireless network activity:* wireless network devices can record many different events but it is useful to treat them as VPNs and other remote access network mechanisms above and track access (with username or Windows name); another useful report on wireless data will include rogue AP presence detection and rogue AP association logs.
- *Log volume trend over days:* while not strictly an example of network activity report, reviewing of a role lab volume produced on your network is extremely useful as a big picture view across the entire pool of log data.

Who Can Use These Reports

These reports have universal applicability, depending on scope of systems covered. A chief security officer (CSO) may review network activity summaries across the entire organization, security analyst may use these reports during daily log review, incident responders may run them while investigating an incident, and system administrators can run these reports on their own systems.

Example

Table 12.3 shows a report on all VPN account access and activities across the organization network.

RESOURCE ACCESS REPORTS

These reports identify various system, application, and database resource access patterns across the organization and can be used for both activity audit, trending, and incident detection.

Why They Are Important

Tracking resource access can be used to reveal insider abuse and even fraud. They are valuable during incident response for determining which resources the attacker has accessed and possibly corrupted or modified (see section Change Reports). In addition, resource access can be used for purposes outside of security, such as capacity planning and other purposes.

Specifics Reports

Key reports in this category are:

- *Access to resources on critical systems after office hours / "off" hours:* similar to the above "off" of network access and Logins, this report can be used to track access and activities on critical and regulated system during unusual times.
- *Top internal users blocked by proxy from accessing prohibited sites, malware sources, etc.:* this versatile Web access report can be used for our multiple

Table 12.3 VPN Account Access and Activities

Date	VPN	UserName	System	Action	Status	Count
1/11/11	VPN1	anton	antonlaptop	Login	Success	2
1/12/11	VPN1	antom	antonlaptop	Login	Failure	1
1/13/11	VPN2	root	Lapt19847	Login	Failure	77

purposes from tracking compromised systems to the data leakage tracking to improved productivity.

- *File, network share, or resource access (success, failure):* this report can only be useful if run for specific audited resources; enabling logging of file access (Windows) and system calls (Unix) will always lead to data overflow.
- *Top database users:* to be useful for security activity tracking it must exclude known application access to the database; ideally, a production database should have no direct access from users or developers.
- *Summary of query types:* similarly, excluding known application queries have turned this report into anomaly detection tool that show anomalous database access.
- *All privileged database user access:* as with servers and application, all privileged user activities should be recorded and analyzed periodically.
- *All users executing INSERT, DELETE database commands:* in addition to tracking application and user access, it makes sense to separately track more damaging commands that can destroy data; excluding known application queries is a useful practice here.
- *All users executing CREATE, GRANT, schema changes on a database:* in addition to tracking application and user access, it makes sense to separately track more damaging commands that can destroy data and change the database instance itself.
- *Summary of database backups:* backups present a clean way to extract massive quantities of data from a database and thus commit data theft; this report will allow you to review which are the old database backups and catch those who performed without authorization.
- *Top internal Email addresses sending attachments to outside:* across many email access reports, this stands out in the it's less a teller key and usefulness for both detecting and investigating insider abuse and data theft.
- *All Emailed attachment content types, sizes, names:* similar to the above report, this can be used to track information leakage as well as detect users emailing potentially sensitive information.
- *All internal systems sending mail excluding known mail servers:* a basic way to find systems infected with spam-sending bots across your environment.
- *Log access summary:* logging and then reviewing access to logs is prescribed by regulations; this basic report should allow you to exclude your own viewing of log data.

Who Can Use These Reports

These reports have universal applicability, depending on scope of systems covered. A chief security officer (CSO) may review resource access summaries across the entire organization, security analyst may use these reports during daily log review, and incident responders may run them while investigating an incident. Resource owners can use these reports to plan capacity and make other business decisions.

Example

Table 12.4 shows a report on all file access across multiple servers.

MALWARE ACTIVITY REPORTS

These reports summarize various malicious software activities and events likely related to malicious software.

Why They Are Important

Malicious software in various forms remains one of the key threat vectors for today's organizations, large and small. Given that anti-virus tools have been dropping in efficiency of stopping malware for the last few years, other information sources such as logs must be used for fighting malware.

Specific Reports

Key reports in this category are:

- *Malware detection trends with outcomes*: a basic report with a summary or a trend of malicious software detection, also showing the system and the outcome (cleaned or left alone) is a good starting point.
- *Detect-only events from anti-virus tools*: all anti-malware tools log the cases where malicious software was detected but not cleaned (for various reasons); such logged "leave-alones" have helped many organization to avoid massive damage.
- *All anti-virus protection failures*: given that today's malicious software is well equipped for fighting anti-virus tools, all crashes, protecting engine unloads, update failures, etc. must be logged and reviewed.
- *Internal connections to known malware IP addresses*: one can run this incredibly useful report using their logs (such firewall or other) and a public

Table 12.4 File Access Across Multiple Servers

Date	Server	UserName	File Name	Access Type	Status	Count
1/11/11	Win1	anton	Expenses.xlsx	Read	Success	1
1/12/11	Win2	anton	Roadmap.ppt	Read	Success	1
1/13/11	NFS	anton	Blank.docx	Write	Failure	37

blacklist of IP address; such simple approach can stop the organization from losing valuable data to malware operators.

- *Least common malware types:* along with other "Bottom 10" (as opposed to "Top 10") reports, this presents a useful insight into unusual and thus possibly damaging malicious software in your organization.

Who Can Use These Reports

These reports are useful for all security professionals, from a junior administrator in charge of desktop anti-virus to a CSO in charge all entire organization security. Such reports are also useful for incident response and malware infection investigations.

Example

Table 12.5 shows virus types across a network and over a week of log data, sorted by ascending count.

CRITICAL ERRORS AND FAILURES REPORTS

These reports summarize various significant errors and failure indications, often with direct security significance.

Why They Are Important

Errors and failure log messages often present valuable early indication of security threats, including advanced threats not captured by security-specific devices, such as IDS and IPS systems. Paying diligent attention to unusual error messages often pays off when a possibly damaging new threat factor manifests on your network.

Specifics Reports

Key reports in this category are:

- *Critical errors by system, application, business unit:* while on the surface not security significant, various error messages appearing in logs (especially for the first time) should be investigated as they often present a very early

Table 12.5 Virus Types Across a Network

Malware type	Status	Infected System Count
VirusX	Detected	1
VirusY	Detected	1
Botz	Quarantined	2

Table 12.6 Disk Full and High CPU Report

Server	Event Type	Date
Serv1	Disk Full	10/1/11
Sirius	Disk Full	1/1/11
VenusX	CPU Load 100%	1/2/11

indication of malicious activities; analytic reports in the next section can be used very effectively for managing these types of log messages.

- *System and application crashes, shutdowns, restarts*: whenever applications crash—due to failed attacks or other reasons—business functioning is likely to be affected; these events should not only be taken as having impact on availability but investigated as possible early indirect indication of attacks.
- *Backup failures* are critical events affecting business continuity and possibly regulatory compliance, in addition, unauthorized backups (failed, in this case) may be triggered by attacker's attempts to steal data.
- *Capacity / limit exhaustion events for memory, disk, CPU, and other system resources:* often stem from attacker's or other unauthorized use of business systems, high resource usage may also be caused by attack floods, denial of service, or brute force attacks.

Who Can Use These Reports

These reports are useful for all security professionals, from a junior administrator in charge of desktop anti-virus to a CSO in charge of all entire organization security. Such reports are also useful for incident response and malware infection investigations. Other IT personnel can benefit from them as well.

Example

Table 12.6 shows an example report on disk full and high CPU usage messages across a pool of Unix/Linux servers.

SUMMARY

As we stated in the introduction, it is impossible to create one list of reports that everybody would use across all log data. All attempts to create such a list are doomed to fail, no matter how compliance regulations will be mandated. However, it is useful to have a list of reports that almost everybody should use and adjust to their circumstances.

Visualizing Log Data

CONTENTS

INTRODUCTION

This chapter provides a brief introduction on the topic of log data visualization. A thorough treatment of this topic is beyond the scope of this book. Conti (2007) and Marty (2009a) provide in-depth treatment on this topic and we encourage you to explore these and all the other references.

VISUAL CORRELATION

Recall Chapters 7 and 8 which discussed log analysis techniques. It was apparent in that chapter we were leveraging the human eyeball for visualizing and finding anomalous behavior in our log data. If you have a small log data load, then Visual Correlation can be beneficial. You first need to begin gathering your log data to an aggregation point. The next step is to use a tool to simply watch your log data files for incoming events. Sometimes you can simply use the UNIX tail command, especially if you are gathering all of your log messages to a single file. The task becomes complicated very quickly if you have more than one log file to watch.

The downside to this technique is that you realistically can only visually correlate about five or so events per second. This means that you will end up spending more of your time going back through your log data in a non-real-time

FIGURE 13.1 OSSIM Real-Time Event Viewer

fashion, which defeats one of the main purpose of correlation: finding things in real-time.

REAL-TIME VISUALIZATION

There is, of course, and alternative. Most log analysis for SIEM platforms come with some sort of real-time interface for viewing events. Figure 13.1 shows the OSSIM[1] event viewer.

Tools such as this allow you to visually inspect normalized log data (i.e. events) as they flow from your remote log collection points into your analysis servers. Also, most of these tools allow you to perform actions like filter, correlation, and highlight events which might be of interest. Interfaces such as this are important for several reasons:

1. It allows for aggregation of disparate event data.
2. Multiple users can use the tool at a time, thereby increasing scale.
3. Unknown or never-before-seen log data is easier to spot.
4. Reclassification of signature data is easier to achieve.

---

[1] http://communities.alienvault.com

TREEMAPS

A treemap is a visualization technique whereby hierarchical data is displayed using colors to represent varying leaf nodes. This process allows for greater identification of patterns.

Figure 13.2 (taken from Marty, 2009b) shows firewall data in a treemap image.

Each box in Figure 13.2 with an IP address at the top represents a source. Then all the IP addresses contained within each box are the destinations along with the connections each source made. For example, 192.141.69.45 is a source IP and the sub boxes (like 192.134.0., 192.26.92., etc.) are the destinations 192.141.69.45 contacted.

It is hard to tell from the black and white image, but firewall accepts are green (light) and firewall drops are red (dark). This sort of visualization can be extremely useful in detecting when you need to add firewall rules, verify that rules are working, or even combine firewall logs with IDS logs to create a cross-sectional treemap view.

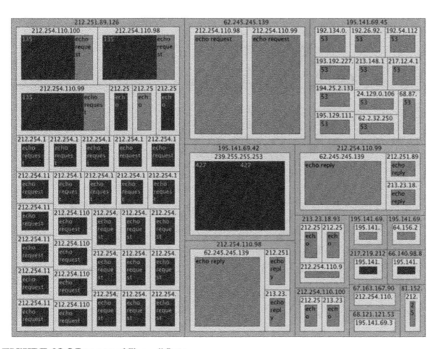

FIGURE 13.2 Treemap of Firewall Data

LOG DATA CONSTELLATIONS

Jimmy Alderson, a network security industry veteran, started working with GraphViz to create visual representations of log data. He coined the term *Constellations*. GraphViz is a tool for representing information via graphs and networks. The core distribution is available at http://www.graphviz.org/. This appendix, however, will present the GraphViz Perl module, which is available at http://search.cpan.org/CPAN/authors/id/R/RS/RSAVAGE/GraphViz-2.10.tgz. You need to install the GraphViz package before you can install and use the Graph-Viz Perl module. The module requires other Perl modules, and it will tell you which are missing.

Figure 13.3 shows an example of what GraphViz can do for you.

You now see where the name comes from. The figure, while probably not obvious from the black and white figure, does have color. The idea is to represent various services or servers in your infrastructure as nodes. As other systems

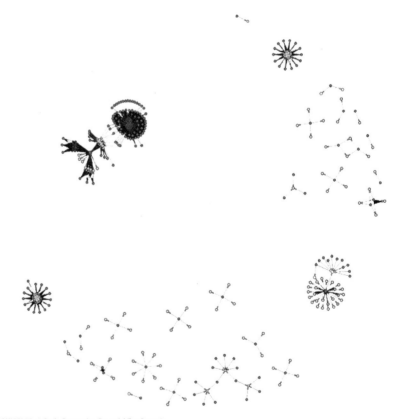

FIGURE 13.3 Sample GraphViz Graph

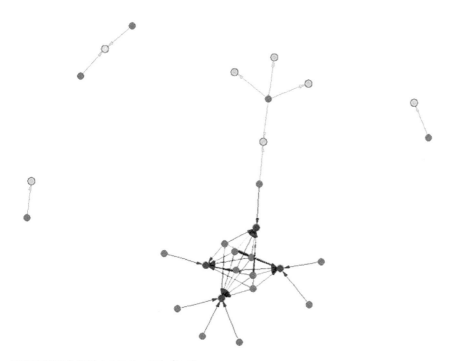

FIGURE 13.4 Clickable GraphViz Graph

initiate contact with these services, GraphViz can represent this communication as an edge from the source system to the destination system.

Figure 13.4 shows a GraphViz map for use in a browser.

In the interest of showing greater detail, the browser itself has been omitted. The map in Figure 13.4 is designed to be a clickable image. Each node in the map is either the destination or source of some kind of network communication. In essence, Figure 13.4 is a directed graph of nodes and edges. As you can see each node has an edge to another node, with an arrow which shows the direction of communication. The following Perl script creates not only the clickable map images, but an HTML file which can be used to browse the map:

```perl
#!/usr/bin/perl
#
# Author: Jimmy Alderson
#
use GraphViz::Small;
my %dst_hash = ();
my %edge_hash = ();
```

```perl
my $g = GraphViz::Small->new(layout => 'neato', bgcolor => 'black');
while ($line = <STDIN>){
   chomp($line);
   undef($sip);
   undef($dst);
   undef($count);
   if(($sip,$dst,$count) = $line =~ m/^([^ ]+) ([^ ]+) (\d+)/)
   {
      ($port) = $dst =~ m/:(\d+)/;
      ($dip) = $dst =~ m/(\d+):/;
      if(!exists($sip_hash{$sip}))
      {
         $g->add_node("$sip", URL =>  "$sip.html", tooltip =>
         "$sip", style => 'filled', fillcolor => 'red',);
         $sip_hash{$sip} = 1;
      }
      else
      {
         $sip_hash{$sip}++;
      }
      if(!exists($dst_hash{$dst}))
      {
         $color = get_fill_color($port);
         $color2 = get_border_color($port);
         $g->add_node(name =>"$dst", URL => "$dst.html",
         tooltip => "$dst", style => 'filled', color =>
   "$color2", fillcolor => "$color", cluster => "$port",      rank
=> "$port");
         $dst_hash{$dst} = 1;
      }
      else
      {
         $dst_hash{$dst}++;
      }
      $edge_hash{"$sip-$count#$dst"} = 1;
   }
}
foreach $edge (keys%edge_hash)
{
   if(($s, $c, $d) = $edge =~ m/([^-]+)-(\d+)\#(.+)/)
```

```perl
    {
        ($port) = $d =~ m/:(\d+)/;
        ($dip) = $d =~ m/(\d+):/;
        $color = get_fill_color($port);
        $g->add_edge("$s" => "$d", color => "$color", minlen => "$c");
    }
}
open(FH, ">map.html");
print FH '<HTML><BODY BGCOLOR=black><img src="map.png"
usemap="#map"><map name="map">';
print FH $g->as_cmap;
print FH '</map></body></html>';
close(FH);
print $g->as_png;
sub get_fill_color
{
    my $port = shift;
    my $control = 'magenta';
    my $web = 'white';
    my $email = 'yellow';
    my $encrypted = 'green';
    my $ftp = 'pink';
    my $netbios = 'blue';
    my $console = 'cyan';
    my $proxy = 'orange';
    my $db = 'green';
    my $suspect = 'red';
    my $chat = $suspect;
    my%colors = ();
    $colors{'0'} = $control;
    $colors{'21'} = $ftp;
    $colors{'20'} = $ftp;
    $colors{'23'} = $console;
    $colors{'25'} = $email;
    $colors{'53'} = '#00FF00';;
    $colors{'80'} = $web;
    $colors{'443'} = $web;
    $colors{'135'} = $netbios;
    $colors{'139'} = $netbios;
```

```perl
                    $colors{'161'} = $control;
                    $colors{'1433'} = $db;
                    $colors{'1434'} = $db;
                    $colors{'1080'} = $proxy;
                    $colors{'5190'} = $chat;
                    $colors{'8080'} = $proxy;
                    $colors{'6000'} = $console;
                    $colors{'6667'} = $chat;
                    $colors{'31337'} = 'gold';
                    if(exists($colors{$port}))
                    {
                        return $colors{$port};
                    }
                    return 'lightblue';
            }
            sub get_border_color
            {
                my $port = shift;
                my $encrypted = 'green';
                my $unencrypted = 'yellow';
                my%colors = ();
                $colors{'0'} = $unencrypted;
                $colors{'22'} = $encrypted;
                $colors{'23'} = $unencrypted;
                $colors{'25'} = $unencrypted;
                $colors{'53'} = $unencrypted;
                $colors{'80'} = $unencrypted;
                $colors{'443'} = $encrypted;
                $colors{'135'} = $unencrypted;
                $colors{'139'} = $unencrypted;
                $colors{'1433'} = $unencrypted;
                $colors{'5190'} = $unencrypted;
                $colors{'6000'} = $unencrypted;
                $colors{'6667'} = $unencrypted;
                if(exists($colors{$port}))
                {
                    return $colors{$port};
                }
            }
```

The script expects the input data to be in the following format:

```
source_ip destination_ip:port count
```

The source_ip is the source of communication to the destination_ip on the port specified. Count is the number of times source_ip communicated with destination_ip on port. This format mandates that you perform some sort of pre-processing of your log data. Firewall and IDS events are the most likely choices for graphing, however you could graph just about anything you want. One item to note about the script is that it uses different colors for the edges between nodes, based on whether the destination port's underlying service was encrypted or not and the type of service (Web, database, etc.).

An example run of the above script looks like the following:

```
$ ./graph_bloom.pl < data > map.png
```

We named the script above as graph_bloom.pl. The file data contains processed data in the format previously mentioned. Two files are output: map.html and map.png, which we specify as part of the command-line. Graphs of this nature may not be suitable for real-time, but they can be useful for near-real-time analysis or possibly forensics analysis. The main problem this tool solves is it creates another dimension to how you view and analyze log data. An interesting feature about these constellations is how different types of traffic manifest themselves in unique and recognizable patterns. For example, HTTP, SMTP, DNS, and Netbios each have their own unique constellation signature, making anomalies easy to spot for the trained eye.

TRADITIONAL LOG DATA GRAPHING

The graphs presented in the previous section are very interesting from the standpoint of being able to visualize traffic patterns and how different sources interact with your critical servers. The Multi Router Traffic Grapher (MRTG)[2] is used by many organizations across the world to analyze things like router interface usage (in and out octets), as well as operating system resources like memory and disk usage. It can be used to gather and graph just about anything. For example, you can graph things like firewall accepts and drops. You could also graph things like source and destination IP addresses.

The following MRTG configuration shows how to execute a script which returns the number of firewall accepts:

---

[2] www.mrtg.org

```
Target[fw.accepts]: '/usr/bin/perl /usr/local/bin/accepts.pl'
MaxBytes[fw.accepts]: 512
Options[fw.accepts]: gauge
Title[fw.accepts]: Number of firewall accepts
YLegend[fw.accepts]: FW Accepts
PageTop[fw.accepts]: <H1>FW Accepts </H1>
<TABLE>
   <TR><TD>System:</TD> <TD>My Firewall</TD></TR>
   <TR><TD>Maintainer:</TD> <TD>""</TD></TR>
</TABLE>
```

The script, accepts.pl, simply opens a data file and prints a single line from the file. In order for this process to work properly, you must pre-process your log data, much like we did in the previous section. MRTG is typically run periodically and automatically via the UNIX cron facility. So you will want to have a script or program pre-process your firewall data and dump out to a file the number of occurrences of accepts. Here is an example accepts.pl:

```
#!/usr/bin/perl
open(FILE,">processedFile");
while($line = <FILE>)
{
   chomp($line);
   print "$line\n";
}
#
# The following code prints the system uptime and the hostname. These two
# items need to be included in every script that you write and should be
   the
# very last thing that is printed.
#
chomp($uptime = '/usr/bin/uptime');
print "$uptime\n";
chomp($hostname = '/bin/hostname');
print "$hostname\n";
```

Here are some things to keep in mind:

- Since MRTG runs every 5 min (you can actually run it more or less often, but 5 min is a good sampling interval), your pre-processing script will need to be able to complete in less than 5 min in order for the next run of MRTG to complete properly.

- Your pre-process script should keep track of where it is in the original log data file, so it can pick up where it left off.
- For each firewall you wish to graph, you need a separate configuration block.

SUMMARY

We covered a few key topics on the area of visualization. Visual Correlation allows for a quick-and-dirty analysis of log data, but can be someone laborious and error-prone. Real-time Visualization provides more of a 10,000 foot view of your log analysis enterprise. Treemaps are an interesting way to visually see patterns in your log data. Log Data Constellations provide you with a point-to-point view of your log data. And finally, Traditional Log Data Graphing takes a more network management centric approach to visualizing log data.

REFERENCES

Conti, G. (2007). *Security data visualization: Graphical techniques for network analysis.* San Francisco: No Starch.

Marty, R. (2009a). *Applied security visualization.* Upper Saddle River, NJ: Addison-Wesley.

Marty, R. (2009b). Data visualization with treemaps—A hands-on tutorial. *Network World.* Network World, May 20. Web. June 17, 2012. <http://www.networkworld.com/community/node/42024>.

Logging Laws and Logging Mistakes

INFORMATION IN THIS CHAPTER:

- Logging Laws
- Logging Mistakes

INTRODUCTION

As we described in previous chapters, logs from information systems have been collected and analyzed for decades. It is not surprising, therefore, that certain general truths about avoiding have emerged. In this chapter we will call out such universal truths about logs and label them—with some degree of presumption—logging laws.

LOGGING LAWS

Our logging laws will cover the entire spectrum of dealing with this important source of IT data—from collection to analysis and decision-making. But before we do that it would like to introduce our inspiration in regards to defining universal logging truths—Ranum Laws of Logging and IDS.

Mentioned by Marcus Ranum (2012) in one of his security presentations back in the 1990s, these laws are:

> Ranum's First Law of Logging and IDS
> —Never collect more data than you can conceive of possibly using.
>
> Ranum's Second Law of Logging and IDS
> —The number of times an uninteresting thing happens is an interesting thing.

Ranum's Third Law of Logging and IDS

—Collect everything you can except for where you come into conflict with the first law.

Ranum's Fourth Law of Logging and IDS

—It doesn't matter how real-time your IDS is if you don't have real-time system administrators.

(source: http://ranum.com/security/computer_security/archives/logging-notes.pdf).

These laws definitely remain true today but will be expanded and accompanied by others.

Law 1—Law of Collection

The first law is similar in spirit to the above inspiration: *"Do NOT collect log data that you NEVER plan to use."*

This universal logging truths seem to contradict with recent calls to "collect 100% of data" and "never meeting the log one didn't like," promoted by some vendors. Indeed, this law simply states that for every message logged and retained, there has to be a reason.

In fact, reasons such as "I might need it to investigate an incident" are perfectly legitimate, while "eh…. I guess I might need it" are not.

In fact, this law also applies to generation of log data not just collection—*"Do NOT log what you NEVER plan to use."*

Law 2—Law of Retention

While more data can be collected, it is rarely used at this very moment. That's the subject of log retention, as we cover in this book, becomes an important consideration.

"Retain log data for as long as it is conceivable that it can be used—or longer if prescribed by regulations."

As we imply further in this chapter. When we talked about logging mistakes, situations where a log message is needed exactly one day after it has been purged by the retention routine are not as rare as you think. Storing the data for as long as it might be useful thus presents the subject of this law.

On the other hand, it is rather unlikely that a mere debugging message will be used for years after the application crashed. While we can manufacture an artificial situation where this will become the most important thing in the world, it is not a recommendation to store every single message for 7 years.

Law 3—Law of Monitoring

While the previous laws made one think that it would be wise to err on the side of more logging and longer log retention, the opposite truth emerges about the monitoring: *"Log all you can (which is as much as possible), but alert only on what you must respond (which is as little as possible)."*

Indeed, the universal truth of this statement comes to life when you realize that the system can easily store petabytes of data—trillions of log messages—but your security response personnel can barely address a dozen issues a day.

This is a trillion: 1,000,000,000,000

This is a dozen: 12

A big difference, right? That is the difference between logging and monitoring!

Just as an organization must log before it can start to monitor, the approaches are completely different. As we discussed elsewhere in the book the principle that an organization should follow is "Log all, store some, monitor what is needed."

Law 3—Law of Availability

"Don't pay to make your logging or monitoring system more available than your business systems" sounds counterintuitive at times. However, it only makes sense that security monitoring needs to be as available as business systems, but not more so.

Indeed, it is important to make sure that log data is being collected and analyzed, and can be available for future investigations or even court cases. However, most business leaders would tell you that it is even more important that business systems are available.

Law 4—Law of Security

If you understand the law of availability, you'd like the law of security as well: *"Don't pay to protect your log data more than you pay to protect your critical business data."*

Hard problem, is it? What should we protect better: a secret new fighter plans (ok, we'd settle for a secret customer list or a celebrity health record) or a nice set of syslog messages? Logs are indeed valuable—and sometimes can even be considered business records—but most businesses will be able to point at another data set that will be more valuable than the logs.

That is why few organizations actually choose to encrypt log data. Apart from operational challenges that encryption brings up, in many cases such controls will be clearly excessive. Some settle for hashing of log archives which reduces tampering of logs. Others prefer to rely on stringent access controls.

Law 5—Law of Constant Changes

One thing constant in the domain of logging, log management and log analysis is change. *"Logs sources, log types, and log messages change."*

While a legacy application has been checking alone for 20 years, it will not suddenly have different logs. However, the environment around this application will likely produce many different and new types of log messages. Today in the age of virtualization and cloud computing, there are more changes coming down the organizations, collecting and analyzing logs.

Thus organizations need to continually review the log review policies, procedures as well as operational tasks and system configurations. It is useful to document each step in the log collection process and keep it up to date—from the point the log is generated to its final resting place, show all the points in between it flowed through.

LOGGING MISTAKES

Ignoring the above laws of login happens at the peril of organizations and individuals doing so. However, there are more mistakes unrelated to laws, some originating many years ago, but still relevant today, while others more modern and specific to today's IT environments.

This section covers the typical mistakes organizations make while approaching management of information systems logs and other records produced by computers and network devices. These mistakes are sadly common in many organizations, even though awareness of them is growing.

As technology continues to spread and computers start playing even more important role in our business and personal lives, logs—the records that they produce—start to play bigger and bigger role. Thus, the cost of making those mistakes continues to increase. Twenty years ago making a mistake from this list would only hinder troubleshooting or other system related activity. In 10 years, when computers control an ever increasing parts of our lives, these mistakes—and we are not trying to over dramatize the situation—can cost somebody their life.

From firewalls and intrusion prevention systems (IPS) to databases and enterprise applications to wireless access points and VOIP gateways and virtualization platforms, logs are being spewed forth at an ever-increasing pace. Moreover, locations where such log sources may be present are expanding—from systems to cloud applications to mobile devices. Both security and other

IT components not only increase in numbers, but now often come with more logging enabled out of the box. Example of that trend include Linux systems as well as web servers that now ship with increased level of logging. Windows systems today also logs many more events than 10 years ago—and with more details for each event.

All those systems, both legacy and novel, traditional and virtual of cloud based, are known to generate copious amounts of logs, audit trails, records, and alerts, that beg for constant attention. Thus, many companies and government agencies are trying to set up repeatable log collection, centralization, and analysis processes and tools.

In fact, companies at the forefront of cloud computing are the ones drowning in logs. From the unique scale of Google and Facebook to other web companies, logs are no longer measured in gigabytes, but terabytes and even petabytes. Organizations where combined volume of logged data—security as well as debugging and operations—measures in terabytes a day are becoming more common.

However, when planning and implementing log collection and analysis infrastructure, the organizations often discover that they are not realizing the full promise of such a system and, in fact, sometimes notice that the efficiency is not gained but lost as a result.

We will start from the obvious, but unfortunately all are too common even in this age of regulations and mandates such as Sarbanes–Oxley and PCI DSS. This mistake destroys all possible chances of benefiting from logs.

Not Logging at All

The mistake #1 is simply not logging at all. A more exciting flavor of this mistake is: "not logging and not even knowing it until it is too late."

How can it be "too late," some say? "Its just logs!" Not having "just logs" can lead to losing your income (PCI DSS that contain explicit logging requirements implies that violations might lead to your credit card processing privileges being canceled by Visa or Mastercard and thus putting you out of business), reputation (somebody stole a few credit card number from your database, but the media reported that all of the 40 million credit card have been stolen since you were unable to prove otherwise), or even your freedom (see various Sarbanes-Oxley and HIPAA horror stories in the media).

Even better-prepared organizations fall for this one. Here is a recent example. Does your web server have logging enabled? Sure, it is a default option on both of the popular web servers: Apache and Microsoft IIS. Does your server operating system log messages? Sure, nobody canceled /var/log/messages. But does your database? Oops! Default option in Oracle is to not do any data access audit logging. Maybe MS SQL fares better? Nope, same thing, you need to dig deep in the system to even start a moderate level of audit trail generation (see more on this in our database logging paper).

To add more detail, let's review a common database type for what logs we can get out of this by default. Oracle (and, in fact, other databases) will have very minimum system logging, some database server access by DBA logging, and no data access logging whatsoever (by default).

So, where is data access audit records, schema and data change audit logs, configuration change audit logs? They can all be configured (you need to read the documents for this!), but are off by default.

In fact, it appears that many systems deployed in cloud computing environments not only lack logging configuration settings but often lack login at all. For example, at the time of this writing a popular cloud computing provider does not have any way of logging connections to and from its cloud environment.

Thus, to avoid this mistake one needs to sometimes go beyond the defaults and make sure that the software and hardware deployed does have some level of logging enabled. In case of working with systems that does not even have logging settings, the unfortunate choice is to either abandon the use of such system, negotiate with your provider (which is probably not an option if they are a much larger company), or add additional technology to record activities and actions.

Not Looking at Log Data

Not looking at the logs is the second mistake. While making sure that logs do exist and then collecting and storing them is important (yes, you can in fact benefit from heaven log data to be looked at when needed), it is only a means to an end—knowing what is going on in your environment and being able to respond to it as well as possibly predict what will happen later. Thus, once the technology is in place and logs are collected, there needs to be a process of ongoing monitoring and review that hooks into actions and possible escalations, if needed. In addition, personnel reviewing or monitoring logs should have enough information to be able to determine what they really mean and what—if any—action is required.

It is worthwhile to note that some organizations take a half-step in the right direction: they only review logs (provided they didn't commit the first mistake and they actually have something to review) after a major incident (be it a compromise, information leak ,or a mysterious server crash) and avoid ongoing monitoring and log review, often by quoting "the lack of resources." This gives them the reactive benefit of log analysis, which is important, but fails to realize the proactive one—knowing when bad stuff is about to happen or become worse. For example, if you review logs, you might learn that the failover was activated on a firewall, and, even though the connection stayed on, the incident is certainly worth looking into. If you don't and your network connectivity goes away, you'd have to rely on your ever-helpful logs in investigation why "both" failover devices went down … In fact, looking at logs proactively helps organizations to better realize the value of their existing network, security, and system infrastructure.

It is also critical to stress that some types of organizations have to look at log files and audit tracks due to regulatory pressure of some kind. For example, US HIPAA regulation compels medical organizations to establish audit record and analysis program (even though the enforcement action is notorious lacking). In a more extreme case, PCI DSS has provisions for both log collection and log monitoring and periodic review, highlighting the fact that collection of logs does not stand on its own.

This example below shows that review priorities were based on both risk assessment (DMZ was seen as higher risk) and available skills (thus, application logs were low on the list).

They went from high external risk to inside, and from servers to desktops, and from the tools they know (firewalls and IDSs) to the ones that might matter even, but for which the skill sets were not available.

1. DMZ NIDS
2. DMZ firewall
3. DMZ servers with applications
4. Critical internal servers
5. Other servers
6. Select critical application
7. Other applications

Such approach allows an organization to avoid the overwhelming feeling of how can it ever look at logs if there are so many of them.

Storing for Too Short a Time

The third common mistake is storing logs for too short a time. This makes the security or IT operations team think they have all the logs needed for monitoring and investigation or troubleshooting and then leading to the horrible realization after the incident that all logs are gone due to their shortsighted retention policy. It often happens (especially in the case of insider attacks) that the incident is discovered a long time—sometimes many months—after the crime or abuse has been committed. One might save some money on storage hardware, but lose the tenfold due to regulatory fines.

If low cost is critical, the solution is sometimes in splitting the retention in two parts: shorter-term online storage (that costs more) and long-term offline storage (that is much cheaper). A better three-tier approach is also common and resolves some of the limitations of the previous one. In this case, shorter-term online storage is complemented by a near-line storage where logs are still accessible and searchable. The oldest and the least relevant log records are offloaded to the third tier, such as tape or DVDs, where they can be stored inexpensively, but without any way to selectively access the needed logs.

More specifically, one financial institution was storing logs online for 90 days, then in the near-line searchable storage for two years and then on tape for up to seven years or even more.

Also, it is worth mentioning that a mandatory 7-year log retention requirement is a myth!

It is interesting that it turns out that storing logs for too long can also be a mistake. How can that be? First, let's be reminded that Log Retention equals Log storage + access to stored data + log *destruction*.

So, why *DESTROY LOGS*? Three main factors make storing logs too long a mistake.

First, Privacy regulations, rampant in Europe (but not—yet?—in the states) often limit both data collection and retention. Yes, in some countries keeping logs is illegal and thus needs to be considered when logging policy is planned.

Second, Litigation risk management. Your legal team will definitely remind you that collecting too much information that can be legally discovered in case of a lawsuit is not a good thing. The most known example is that having a log of some activity handy (but not reviewed by the security team!) can be seen as knowing about infringement. Such things can get your organization into legal hot water.

Finally, System resource utilization often drives limiting the amount of stored log data. If you have a set of busy firewalls, keeping logs for several years might be impossible or cost-prohibitive (or, you have to learn how to spell petabyte).

Here is an example of a retention strategy that also teaches an approach to creating one's log retention strategy and avoiding the mistakes.

So, the main model to learn is to use three dimensions for a retention strategy:

1. *Type of log source—firewall, IDS, server, desktop, etc.*
2. *Network location—DMZ, geographic region, branch office, etc.*
3. *Storage tier—online (e.g. a log management system), near line (large hard drive storage of raw logs), offline (tape or CD).*

This means that you pick a type of log source (say, firewall), consider where it is deployed on the network (say, DMZ), and then plan how it would be stored (say, in a quick online storage)—this will give you one number to keep the logs for. In the above example, the DMZ IDS logs are stored online for 90 days,while firewall logs from the same location are stored for 30 days (due to their higher volume). The same logs are then retained in the offline storage (2nd tier) for three years.

The order of picking the devices is also important, as this will define the priority of implementing log capture and retention.

Prioritizing Before Collection

The fourth mistake is related to log record prioritization. While people need a sense of priority to better organize their log analysis efforts, the common mistake nowadays is in prioritizing the log records before collection. In fact, even some "best practice" documents recommend only collecting "the important stuff." But what is important? This is where the above guidance documents fall short by not specifying it in any useful form. While there are some approaches to the problem, all that we are aware of can lead to glaring holes in security posture or even undermine the regulatory compliance efforts.

For example, many people would claim that network intrusion detection and prevention logs are inherently more important than, say, VPN concentrator logs. Well, it might be true in the world where external threats completely dominate the insider abuse (i.e. not in this one). VPN logs, together with server and workstation logs, are what you would most likely need to conduct an internal investigation about the information leak or even a malware infection. Thus, similar claims about the elevated importance of whatever other log type can be similarly disputed, which would lead us to a painful realization that you do need to collect everything (while being mindful of the Morgan loss. We discussed earlier in this chapter).

But can you? Before you answer this, try to answer whether you can make the right call on which log is more important even before seeing it and this problem will stop looking unsolvable. To teach you about avoiding this mistake we will employ the following gross oversimplification.

First, log everything does not mean that a human analyst will review every log record. It means that most if not all log records are available, if needed, for investigators, auditors, etc.

1. Log *everything*.
2. Retain *most everything*.
3. Analyze *enough*.
4. Summarize and report on a *subset*.
5. Monitor *some*.
6. Act on a *few record*, which are actionable.

To put it more simply, it means that information reduction happens AFTER the logs are collected and stored, not before. This will enable you to use the logs for any future situation, whether regulatory or security related.

Ignoring Application Logs

The next mistake is in ignoring the logs from applications, by only focusing on the perimeter and internal network devices and possibly also servers, but not going "higher up the stack" to look at the application logging.

The realm of enterprise applications ranges from SAPs and PeopleSofts of the world to small homegrown applications, which nevertheless handle mission-critical processes for many enterprises. Legacy applications, running on mainframes and midrange systems, are out there as well, often running the core business processes as well. The availability and quality of logs differs wildly across the application, ranging from missing (the case for many homegrown applications) to extremely detailed and voluminous (the case for many mainframe applications). Lack of common logging standards and even of logging guidance for software developers lead to many challenges with application logs.

In fact when applications are deployed in the cloud or if your organization utilizes software as a service (SaaS) cloud model, application logs are the only way to monitor the activities and attacks. Be mindful of the fact that application logs are increasing in importance and they will be a need to include them in your analysis sooner or later.

Despite the challenges, one needs to make sure that the application logs are collected and made available for analysis as well as for longer-term retention. This can be accomplished by configuring your log management software to collect them and by establishing a log review policy, both for the on-incident review and periodic proactive log review.

Only Looking for Known Bad Entries

Even the most advanced and mature organizations fall into the pitfall of the sixth error. It is sneaky and insidious, and can severely reduce the value of a log analysis project. It occurs when organization is only looking at what they know is bad in the logs. Indeed, a vast majority of open source and some commercial tools are set up to filter and look for bad log lines, attack signatures, critical events, etc. For example, "swatch" is a classic free log analysis tool that is powerful, but only at one thing: looking for defined bad things in log files. Moreover, when people talk about log analysis they usually mean sifting through logs looking for things of note.

However, to fully realize the value of log data one has to take it to the next level to log mining: actually discovering things of interest in log files without having any preconceived notion of "what we need to find." It sounds obvious—how can we be sure that we know of all the possible malicious behavior in advance— but it disregarded so often. Sometimes, it is suggested that it is simpler to just list all the known good things and then look for the rest. It sounds like a solution, but such task is not only onerous, but also thankless: it is usually even harder to list all the good things than it is to list all the bad things that might happen on a system or network.

So many different things occur, malfunction or misbehave, that weeding out attack traces just by listing all the possibilities is not effective. A more intelligent approach is needed! Some of the data mining (also called "knowledge discovery in databases" or KDD) and visualization methods actually work on log data with great success—we discussed them elsewhere in the book. They allow organizations to look for real anomalies in log data, beyond "known bad" and "known good."

SUMMARY

We have taken the liberty to define some of the universal truths in the area of logging. It is useful to keep them in mind while planning and operating your projects related to logs as well as while purchasing, building, and using the tools.

Also, avoiding the common mistakes will take your log management program to a next level and enhance the value of the existing security and logging infrastructures.

REFERENCE

Marcus Ranum Logging Laws are from http://ranum.com/security/computer_security/archives/logging-notes.pdf (retrieved May 2012).

Tools for Log Analysis and Collection

INFORMATION IN THIS CHAPTER:

- Outsource, Build, or Buy
- Basic Tools for Log Analysis
- Utilities for Centralizing Log Information
- Log Analysis Tools—Beyond the Basics
- Commercial Vendors

INTRODUCTION

The market place for log management and log analysis tools has grown significantly over the years. Many toolset choices, such as grep and awk, are built into many of the current servers and network devices in use in environments today. We will review open source solutions and a number of good commercial tools to help you centralize, manage, and report on logs inside your environment. The tools range from basic flat file searching, centralized collection of logs, and all the way to more robust tools that incorporate compliance-specific reporting and real-time alerting. The tool that is right for you will depend on the number of systems being monitored and your organization's compliance needs. This chapter is not intended to be all encompassing, but will review a number of log management and log analysis tools widely available today and provide details on the tools and features most applicable to daily log management in your organization.

OUTSOURCE, BUILD, OR BUY

In many businesses, security, and log management is not a core competency and is a cost of doing business rather than a source of revenue. There have been a number of high profile security incidents over the years that have reinforced the

243

cost aspects of poor security. In the latest 2012 Verizon Breach Report, reviewed over 855 incidents were reviewed with the results determining that over 174 million records were compromised in these attacks (Verizon Corporation, 2012). Incidents like these have made many organizations take notice of the potentially high cost and possible lost business involved in not choosing the right system or not having enough talented resources monitoring the systems that are in place.

Many of the recent incidents, such as the recent Global Payments data breach, were at businesses that need to conform with some of the most stringent compliance guidelines like the Payment Card Industry Data Security Standard (PCI DSS). Log management and review is key part of PCI DSS. Though we don't know what role in having the right log management and log analysis system played in each of these events, we can assume that being able to quickly review, correlate, and analyze logs was critical in identifying affected systems and customers so the companies could close gaps in their security and continue to operate their business.

Log management and log analysis systems should be evaluated like any critical IT system in your environment with a critical eye towards decisions to buy, build, or outsource the solution. In many cases, a combination of buy and build, buy and outsource, etc., may provide better overall benefits than a single approach will in meeting your organization's needs. As we discuss the various tools through this chapter, you should consider a number of pros and cons in the buy, build, or outsource decision.

Building a Solution

Many organizations choose to build a solution for log management due to the availability of open source log management solutions and a desire to customize and tune solutions specific to their environment and needs. In many cases, this approach allows an organization to start small with existing resources and limited costs. A number of advantages and risks are associated with this approach:

Advantages:

- You are likely to get a system and solution that exactly what you want for your environment (Chuvakin, 2008).
- You can do things that cannot be found in commercial or open source solutions since in many cases you can modify and update the code to the system.
- You can choose and design the platform, tools, and processes for your system.
- There are limited to no upfront costs in acquiring the system.
- It's fun!

Risks:

- You own the system and will need to allocate resources and time to system maintenance and any updates necessary to continue to meet changes to compliance standards.
- No third-party support. You are the support staff!
- Will you be able to hire, retain, and train staff to continue to maintain the system if any of the key personnel that built the system leave the company?
- Will the system be able to handle the volume of logs from all the systems in the organization and will it continue to scale as the organization grows?

Buy

Many organizations may find the possibility of building a log management system too time consuming and may not have the resources to devote to building and maintaining these systems if systems development is not a core competency of the organization. Larger organizations also need support agreements with vendors to guarantee uptime and legal requirements. Support agreements and legal requirements frequently cannot be met with home-grown solutions based on open source products. Due to these and many other factors, many organizations look to purchase log management systems. The following should be considered when purchasing a log management system.

Advantages:

- "Cash and carry"—pay and you get a solution to your log management and analysis needs (Chuvakin, 2008).
- Purchased solutions support a wide variety of log sources and formats.
- Support agreements typically include service line agreements for uptime and response time for issues.
- Product updates and improvements including updates to meet changes to compliance standards.
- Potential to purchase services and onsite help to help get the system installed and train your internal staff.

Risks:

- Beyond the initial system cost, you will get a system now and will need to hire or train staff to install and use it now. Your organization should consider the impact on current business priorities and budget constraints outside of the initial system cost and the ongoing personnel retention and education costs.
- Does your organization have anyone on staff that has the skills to learn, use, and get value out of the purchased system?

- Gaps in the system that do not have support for installed applications in your environment or processes specific to your compliance needs.
- Vendor maturity, longevity, and risks to the organization being able to change vendors in the future.

Outsource

Many organizations find outsourcing a better alternative in areas where they do not have the talent or resources to build or operate and maintain solutions they purchase. Just like the buy option, outsourcing allows organizations to meet uptime, support, and legal requirements for the systems operating in their environment. The following are items that should be considered when outsourcing:

Advantages:

- Somebody else will worry about the daily tasks and compliance needs for log management in your organization. This frees resources to focus on other items core to the business (Chuvakin, 2008).
- Outsourcing limits the infrastructure footprint and the outsourcing vendor hosts' the infrastructure installed in the organization.
- Less staff needed to devote to log management and the daily activities of reviewing logs and other compliance requirements.

Risks:

- Someone else is worrying about your problems and may not have the same background in your environment or your compliance needs.
- There may be gaps in the system that do not have support for installed applications in your environment or processes specific to your compliance needs.
- The organization loses control of their data. This puts the data at risk for loss if hosted outside the organization and may make it difficult to switch log management providers in the future. We will discuss this in further detail related to cloud vendors in Chapter 21.
- The volume of data from your organization may pose challenges for the vendor and may impact your system SLAs when transporting the data outside the organization.
- Access to log data may be limited based on vendor provided APIs and online data retention times.

Questions for You, Your Organization, and Vendors

As we review tools and solutions in the chapter, consider the following questions and how each tool helps you in your environment answer these questions.

These questions are relevant regardless if your organization chooses to build, buy, or outsource your log management and analysis solution (Chuvakin, 2008).

1. Are you collecting and aggregating 100% of all the log data from all data sources on the network?
2. Are the logs transported and stored securely?
3. Are there packaged reports that suit your needs? Can you create the needed reports to organize collected log data quickly?
4. Can you set alerts on anything in the logs?
5. Are you looking at log data on a daily basis and is there intelligence in the system to aggregate or reduce the time burden of these activities? Can you prove that you are and do you have the tools to perform this function and are able to report on who reviewed the logs and when?
6. Can you perform fast, targeted searches for specific data?
7. Can you contextualize log data and correlate it across the organization for forensics and other operational tasks?
8. Can you readily prove that security, change management, and access control policies are in use and up to date?
9. Can you securely share log data with other applications and users?

BASIC TOOLS FOR LOG ANALYSIS

There are a number of simple yet powerful tools available to do log analysis built into Linux/Unix operating systems, available for download for free over the Internet, or are part of existing office productivity suites already purchased by many organizations. We will review a number of these here and provide examples on using tools to perform log analysis.

Grep

Grep is a command line utility found on most Linux and Unix operating systems today that will search input files based on a pattern or regular expression. The IEEE and The Open Group (2004).

Many of the log files and examples throughout this book note that many systems log directly to human-readable text-based files. These files can be

GREP AND ITS POPULARITY

Grep
The utility has also been ported to many other operating systems including Windows with popular ports of this utility available as grep for Windows by GNU (http://gnuwin32.sourceforge. net/packages/grep.htm) and as part of Cygwin (http://www.cygwin.com/).

easily searched with grep to find useful information for daily log reviews and forensics. Grep, like many of the search tools presented in this chapter, is heavily reliant on the user knowing a search term or what they are looking for (see Table 15.1).

Table 15.1 Common Items to Search for in Reviewing Logs

What to look for on Linux/Unix	
Successful user login	"Accepted password," "Accepted publickey," "session opened"
Failed user login	"authentication failure," "new user," "delete user"
User log off	"session closed"
User account change or deletion	"password changed," "new user," "delete user"
Sudo actions	"sudo: ... COMMAND=...," "FAILED su"
Service failure (Chuvakin, 2011)	"failed" or "failure"

What to look for on Windows	
Event IDs are listed below for Windows 2000/XP. For Vista/7 security event IDs, add 4096 to the event ID	
Most of the events below are in the Security log, but many are only logged on the domain controller	
User logon/logoff events	Successful logon 528,540; failed logon 529–537, 539; logoff 538, 551
User account changes	Created 624; enabled 626; changed 642; disabled 629; deleted 630
Password changes	To self: 628; to others: 627
Service started or stopped	7035, 7036
Object access denied (if auditing enabled)	560, 567

What to look for on Network Devices	
Look at both inbound and outbound activities	
Examples below show log excerpts from Cisco ASA logs; other devices have similar functionality.	
Traffic allowed on firewall	"Built ... connection," "access-list ... -permitted"
Traffic blocked on firewall	"access-list ... denied," "deny inbound," "Deny ... by"
Bytes transferred (large files?)	"Teardown TCP connection ... duration ... bytes ..."
Bandwidth and protocol usage	"limit ... exceeded," "CPU utilization"
Detected attack activity	"attack from"
User account changes	"user added," "user deleted," "user priv level changed"
Administrator access	"AAA user ...," "User ... locked out," "login failed"

Table 15.1 Common Items to Search for in Reviewing Logs (*continued*)

What to look for on Web servers	
Excessive access attempts to non-existent files	
Code (SQL, HTML) seen as part of the URL	
Access to extensions you have not implemented	
Web service stopped/started/failed messages	
Access to "risky" pages that accept user input	
Error code 200 on files that are not yours	
Failed user authentication	Error code 401, 403
Invalid request	Error code 400
Internal server error	Error code 500

Using Grep for Log Analysis

Let's take an example of an Apache access_log. In many of the web server logs in your organization, you will find 403 errors if you have protected content on your website that is being accessed without proper authorization. Let's use grep to isolate these errors and look at what is going on more closely.

```
user$ grep -i -e "paybills.aspx?customer_acct=.* HTTP/1.1.* 403" /var/
    log/httpd/access_log
192.168.0.6 - - [10/Jul/2011:00:00:00 +0200] "GET /paybills.
    aspx?customer_acct=111111111 HTTP/1.1" 403 -
192.168.0.6 - - [10/Jul/2011:00:00:00 +0200] "GET /paybills.
    aspx?customer_acct=111111112 HTTP/1.1" 403 -
192.168.0.6 - - [10/Jul/2011:00:00:00 +0200] "GET /paybills.
    aspx?customer_acct=111111113 HTTP/1.1" 403 -
```

Similar to some of the examples in Chapter 9, we used a regular expression to isolate instances where we are getting 403 errors against our paybills.aspx page. Looking at the result now, it appears that someone at address 192.168.0.6 is doing something malicious by incrementing a customer account number by one and trying to guess the valid accounts we have in the system!

GREP AND REGULAR EXPRESSIONS

Grep and Regular Expressions
For additional details on all the options for grep and regular expressions, go to the GNU site at: http://www.gnu.org/software/grep/manual/grep.html

Awk

Awk is another powerful tool that is available in Linux/Unix platforms that can be used as a log analysis tool to extract and isolate information from log files.

As with grep, there are many ports of this utility to use on other operating systems. We will primarily focus on the "print" command of awk to help us piece together what our malicious attacker is doing or has done from our previous example.

The print command of awk is a powerful option that allows you to use an expression and display the output of this function. In our case, we would

> Learn more about the powerful options available in awk at:
> http://www.gnu.org/software/gawk/manual/gawk.html

like to capture specific fields from our log file. The print command of awk by default considers a space character as the delimiter separating the fields on a line of text and we can reference a specific field using the "$[num]" command in the field expression. Table 15.2 lists the fields in our log file and their specific numeric field identifier.

Now that we know more about how to parse fields from our log file, let's combine our knowledge of using grep and awk. Suppose we want to see only the URLs that were accessed by our attacker at 192.168.0.6 and what pages returned an error, status code 403, and what pages were accessed successfully, status code 200. In the example below, we will use grep to only return log entries from client 192.168.0.6 and then pass this information on to the awk

Table 15.2 Awk Field Identifiers for Our Access_Log

The example data in this table is from the Apache Web server using the common log file format:

192.168.0.6 - - [10/Jul/2011:00:00:00 +0200] "GET /paybills.aspx? customer_acct=111111111 HTTP/1.1" 403 -

AWK Field ID	Access Log Field	Example Data
$1	IP Address	192.168.0.6
$2	Identifier[a]	–
$3	User ID	–
$4	Date and time of entry	[10/Jul/2011:00:00:00
$5	Timezone	+200]
$6	Type of request	"GET
$7	URL and parameters	/paybills.aspx?customer_ acct=111111111
$8	Protocol	HTTP/1.1"
$9	HTTP status code	403
$10	Size of data returned	–

[a]Note: A dash in the log file indicates this value is not available or not present.

command using the Unix "|" to extract the URL, field 7, and the status code, field 9.

```
user$ grep '192.168.0.6' /var/log/httpd/access_log | awk '
   {print $9,$7}'
403 /paybills.aspx?customer_acct=111111111
403 /paybills.aspx?customer_acct=111111112
403 /paybills.aspx?customer_acct=111111113
200 /paybills.aspx?customer_acct=111111114
200 /change_password.aspx?customer_acct=111111114&pwd=1234
```

Utilizing awk and grep together, we get a clearer picture of a possible attack on our Web server and an account that may have been compromised. From the example, it looks like the attacker at 192.168.0.6 was able to brute force guess the account numbers 111111114 as a valid account and changed the password on this client account!

Microsoft Log Parser

A lot of the previous tools in this chapter are tools built into the Linux/Unix operating system with a number of ports to other operating systems like Windows. Many organizations utilize Windows on a daily basis, and Windows has its own specific logs and needs.

A free utility available from Microsoft is the Log Parser utility. The most recent update of this utility can be downloaded from the Microsoft Download Center at http://www.microsoft.com/en-us/download/details. aspx?id=24659. As Microsoft states, "Log parser is a powerful, versatile tool that provides universal query access to text-based data such as log files, XML files, and CSV files, as well as key data sources on the Windows operating system such as the Event Log, the Registry, the file system, and Active Directory."

One of the more useful features of Log Parser is the ability to query the Windows Event log using SQL-like statements. The following example illustrates using the tool to generate a report on event 5159 from the Windows Security Event log.

The Log Parser utility supports many different output formats. In this example, a generated comma-separated values (CSV) format file was chosen. CSV format files can be loaded by a variety of applications. The following below shows the search results from Log Parser in Microsoft Excel where we can filter the results and perform log analysis.

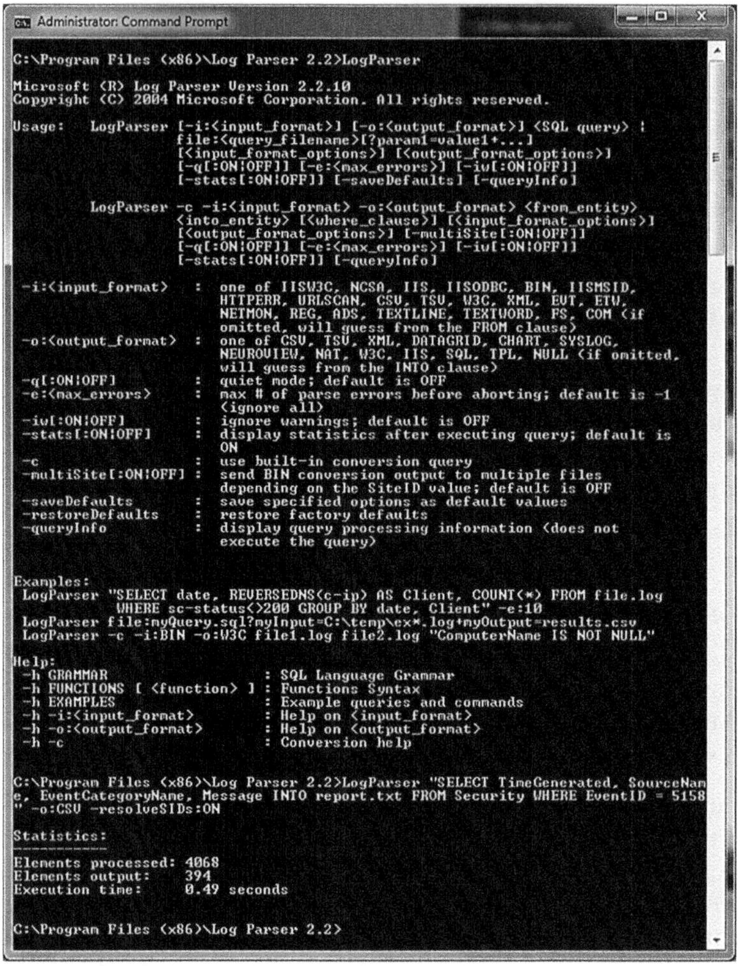

```
Administrator: Command Prompt

C:\Program Files (x86)\Log Parser 2.2>LogParser

Microsoft (R) Log Parser Version 2.2.10
Copyright (C) 2004 Microsoft Corporation. All rights reserved.

Usage:   LogParser [-i:<input_format>] [-o:<output_format>] <SQL query> |
                   file:<query_filename>[?param1=value1+...]
                   [<input_format_options>] [<output_format_options>]
                   [-q[:ON|OFF]] [-e:<max_errors>] [-iw[:ON|OFF]]
                   [-stats[:ON|OFF]] [-saveDefaults] [-queryInfo]

         LogParser -c -i:<input_format> -o:<output_format> <from_entity>
                   <into_entity> [<where_clause>] [<input_format_options>]
                   [<output_format_options>] [-multiSite[:ON|OFF]]
                   [-q[:ON|OFF]] [-e:<max_errors>] [-iw[:ON|OFF]]
                   [-stats[:ON|OFF]] [-queryInfo]

 -i:<input_format>   :  one of IISW3C, NCSA, IIS, IISODBC, BIN, IISMSID,
                        HTTPERR, URLSCAN, CSV, TSV, W3C, XML, EVT, ETW,
                        NETMON, REG, ADS, TEXTLINE, TEXTWORD, FS, COM (if
                        omitted, will guess from the FROM clause)
 -o:<output_format>  :  one of CSV, TSV, XML, DATAGRID, CHART, SYSLOG,
                        NEUROVIEW, NAT, W3C, IIS, SQL, TPL, NULL (if omitted,
                        will guess from the INTO clause)
 -q[:ON|OFF]         :  quiet mode; default is OFF
 -e:<max_errors>     :  max # of parse errors before aborting; default is -1
                        (ignore all)
 -iw[:ON|OFF]        :  ignore warnings; default is OFF
 -stats[:ON|OFF]     :  display statistics after executing query; default is
                        ON
 -c                  :  use built-in conversion query
 -multiSite[:ON|OFF] :  send BIN conversion output to multiple files
                        depending on the SiteID value; default is OFF
 -saveDefaults       :  save specified options as default values
 -restoreDefaults    :  restore factory defaults
 -queryInfo          :  display query processing information (does not
                        execute the query)


Examples:
 LogParser "SELECT date, REVERSEDNS(c-ip) AS Client, COUNT(*) FROM file.log
            WHERE sc-status<>200 GROUP BY date, Client" -e:10
 LogParser file:myQuery.sql?myInput=C:\temp\ex*.log+myOutput=results.csv
 LogParser -c -i:BIN -o:W3C file1.log file2.log "ComputerName IS NOT NULL"

Help:
 -h GRAMMAR                  : SQL Language Grammar
 -h FUNCTIONS [ <function> ] : Functions Syntax
 -h EXAMPLES                 : Example queries and commands
 -h -i:<input_format>        : Help on <input_format>
 -h -o:<output_format>       : Help on <output_format>
 -h -c                       : Conversion help


C:\Program Files (x86)\Log Parser 2.2>LogParser "SELECT TimeGenerated, SourceNam
e, EventCategoryName, Message INTO report.txt FROM Security WHERE EventID = 5158
" -o:CSV -resolveSIDs:ON

Statistics:
-----------
Elements processed: 4068
Elements output:    394
Execution time:     0.49 seconds


C:\Program Files (x86)\Log Parser 2.2>
```

FIGURE 15.1 Microsoft Log Parser

Figure 15.1 shows an example using Microsoft Log Parser to generate a text report.

Other Basic Tools to Consider

We have covered some powerful tools for doing manual log analysis and combined these tools to give you more detailed analysis in reviewing logs. There are many others as well and below are a few others to consider adding to your tool chest:

tail

This utility can be useful in reviewing the end of the log file or actions currently occurring at the end of the log (http://www.gnu.org/software/coreutils/manual/coreutils.html).

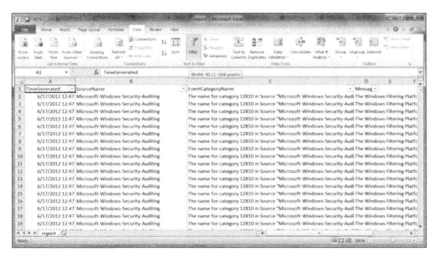

FIGURE 15.2 Search results from Microsoft Excel

Figure 15.2 shows search results from Microsoft Excel.

head

This utility is the opposite of tail and can be useful in retrieving the top portion of a large log file to make it more manageable to review with other utilities (http://www.gnu.org/software/coreutils/manual/coreutils.html).

Sed

Sed is a parsing utility like awk and is useful in doing search and replacements in text to make the log clearer to read or to format the log output for better consumption by other utilities (http://www.gnu.org/software/sed/manual/sed.html).

Logwatch

Logwatch is a useful utility to parse and review your logs offline. Logwatch has a pluggable interface that allows you to customize it to your needs. The utility can be downloaded at http://sourceforge.net/projects/logwatch/.

Lire

Lire is a suite of applications that allows you to generate custom reports from log files. In this respect it is similar to the Microsoft Log Analyzer where you can filter and generate a report off a log file. Lire supports a variety of log files from mostly non-Windows appliances and software. This could be a good complement for Microsoft Log Analyzer for your non-Windows systems. For more information, review the tool's Website at http://www.logreport.org/lire.html.

The Role of the Basic Tools in Log Analysis

In the preceding sections, we showed some great ways to use basic tools that are either freely available or are part systems and packages that you may already be utilizing and managing in your environment. They demonstrated how you can use these utilities to search and refine log data to isolate an attack. However, these tools are best fitted for small organizations and for manual log analysis and review. You should consider some of the limitations of these tools listed below and how they will fit into an environment, the compliance needs of the organization, and the time and resource requirements needed. In many cases, these tools may only best be used for forensics as your log size and environment grows.

Factors to consider:

- You need to know what you are looking for—in the examples, we knew exactly the text we were looking for and used grep and awk and other tools to slice the data based on very specific text. If you are looking for trends or statistical anomalies, these tools may not fit the bill.
- Very long run times on large files—if your organization has terabytes of log information, the time needed to find specific strings may seem like an eternity. These utilities typically search the entire file for what you are looking for.
- Limited ability to correlate across logs—if your log files are dispersed across multiple devices and multiple log files, it will be difficult to sync the different logs from the firewall, Web server, and client workstation. This will make it difficult to get a clear picture of how an attack occurred across the entire network path of an attack.

UTILITIES FOR CENTRALIZING LOG INFORMATION

Throughout the previous chapters we discussed the need to centralize logging information in an organization to allow you to correlate across logs throughout your environment and to facilitate many of the collection and analysis compliance requirements of PCI DSS, HIPAA, and SOX. There are a number of freely available tools to help you centralize logging information in your environment. We will look at syslog, syslog-ng, rsyslog, and Snare and how these tools facilitate centralizing logs.

Syslog

Syslog is the closest thing we have today to a ubiquitous logging solution across all platforms. There is built-in support for syslog logging in network devices, Unix/Linux systems, as well as many programming language library extensions to facilitate an application developers' ability to add syslog logging to applications.

There are two major components of syslog. There is the syslog client that exists on the system that is generating the logs and can be configured to send its logs locally or to a centralized syslog server. Last, there is the syslog daemon, or server-side process, that receives logs from other syslog clients configured to send it data.

As powerful as syslog is in many of the key areas we discussed throughout this book in centralizing log information, the following feature gaps exist in syslog that may be required for your environment.

Guaranteed Delivery of Messages

On many of the stock implementations of syslog, syslog communicates and relays log messages via UDP on port 514. On busy networks User Datagram Protocol (UDP) traffic may drop messages to allow more high priority traffic to be delivered, most notably Transmission Control Protocol (TCP) traffic. So there is no guarantee that every log message from hosts will be recorded on the centralized syslog server.

> See "Unreliable Delivery" in RFC-5426 (http://tools.ietf.org/html/rfc5426) for more details.

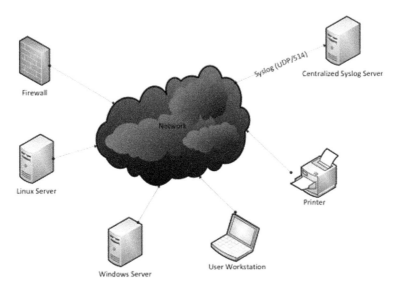

FIGURE 15.3 High-level Depiction of Centralizing Syslog Logs

Figure 15.3 shows a high-level depiction of centralizing syslog logs.

Secure Transport of Log Messages

Though proposed in RFC-5425 (http://tools.ietf.org/html/rfc5425), few syslog implementations encrypt log messages from being snooped or altered across a network. This is important for many of the logging guidelines laid out in this book and is becoming more important to organizations as they increase the number of remote sites and utilize virtualized hosts in the cloud.

Maintaining Log Source Information

In some syslog environments, a relay server is used to collect logs from a remote site or network segment and forward the logs on to the central syslog server. In many stock implementations of syslog, the source information on where the log record was originally generated is lost as part of the relay process. This can make it next to impossible to determine where a log message came from.

Rsyslog

Rsyslog is another open source option and is also freely available in many Linux distributions. There are a few feature differences between syslog-ng (see Chapter 5) and rsyslog, but on the whole, rsyslog and syslog-ng are fairly compatible in feature set. A few key benefits to organizations in choosing rsyslog vs. syslog-ng are as follows:

- Rsyslog is the default logger for Redhat and Fedora Linux systems. Rsyslog will be a more natural choice for organizations with a large Redhat install base.
- Rsyslog has recently added support for the Hadoop (HDFS). Organizations transitioning to Hadoop to enhance their log mining and security intelligence will be able to integrate rsyslog using this feature with limited need to write custom scripts to load data into Hadoop.

Snare

Windows systems in your environment log a significant amount of valuable information into the Windows Event log. Unfortunately, this Event log is a propriety Windows technology with no native support for syslog style messaging. Syslog-ng and rsyslog have options available for purchase to retrieve Event log information from Windows systems. However, another free alternative is Snare.

The Snare (http://www.intersectalliance.com/projects/index.html) Windows agent allows Windows events to be sent via syslog. Snare has agent and server collection

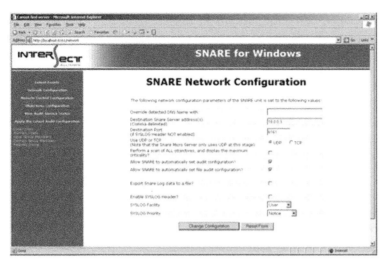

FIGURE 15.4 Snare Network Configuration Screen

Figure 15.4 shows the Snare network configuration screen.

options. However, the free Snare server option is limited only to log collection. If you are on a budget, there are a number of free options that offer both collection and analysis which we will cover later in this chapter.

To utilize the Snare Windows agent to send Event logs via syslog, you will need to do some minor tweaking after the installation of the agent. After installation, go to the network configuration and do the following:

- Set the destination port to the default syslog port of 514.
- Enable the SYSLOG Header.

LOG ANALYSIS TOOLS—BEYOND THE BASICS

We have already covered the basic tools for log analysis. This section covers tools that will give you in-depth analysis of your log information. Some of the tools covered here will allow you to generate alerts on events in real time, generate summary reports that will help you with compliance, and generally give you features that reduce the amount of time needed to do your daily log reviews and perform log forensics when events occur.

OSSEC

OSSEC (www.ossec.net) is a great open source tool for log retention and analysis. The toolset includes agents for many of platforms that exist in many organizations, has support to receive logs from existing syslog feeds, includes support for an agentless option that can check file integrity on many of the platforms where you cannot install the OSSEC agent, and can even be installed on VMWare host systems to monitor your virtualization infrastructure. The tool greatly reduces the manual process of log analysis with many pre-installed rules to help you get started on real-time alerting and a Web-based user interface for further alert and log review. OSSEC is a very lightweight process with only a Unix/Linux option for the centralized management server. We will highlight many of the features of OSSEC relevant to log analysis in this section. There are many great Websites and books dedicated to OSSEC for readers wanting more detailed information on the management and setup of the toolset.

OSSEC has an active user and developer community and has regular updates to provide new features and bug fixes. In 2009, Trend Micro acquired OSSEC and has continued to keep the tool open and free. The relationship could be beneficial to organizations that already have a relationship with Trend Micro. Trend Micro offers commercial support for OSSEC.

OSSEC Settings to Retain All Log Information

There are a number of tweaks and tips you should make to the default OSSEC configuration to conform to your organization's log retention policy. By default, OSSEC only records the log entries that generate an alert. In log retention, we typically want to retain all log information. We can adjust this by updating the OSSEC configuration at /var/ossec/etc/ossec.conf. Simply set the log all option to yes and we will retain all logs.

FIGURE 15.5 OSSEC Setup Setting to Retain All Logs

Figure 15.5 shows the OSSEC setup setting to retain all logs.

OSSEC will use directories in the /var partition on your system to retain the logs by default. You should allocate a significant portion of the systems disk space to this partition or change the default location for logs to make sure you have adequate space for logs.

OSSEC Real-Time Alerting

One of the powerful tools available in OSSEC for log analysis is the built-in rules and the ability to write your own rules. Rules give you the ability to generate real-time alerts based on log events received. By default, all the rules are stored in the rules folder on the server. There are many built-in rules that come with OSSEC to generate alerts on events from firewalls, Windows, Linux/Unix, applications like McAfee and VMWare, and common attacks and rootkits. Documentation on the built in rules is available at http://www.ossec.net/doc/rules/rules/index.html.

The rule syntax is written in an XML format. A rule can generate an alert based on a single event, an atomic (simple) rule, or based on the number of times an event is seen, a composite (correlation) rule. The following shows an example of a built-in atomic rule:

```
<rule id="18100" level="0">
   <category>windows</category>
   <description>Group of windows rules.</description>
</rule>
...
<rule id="18105" level="4">
   <if_sid>18100</if_sid>
   <status>^AUDIT_FAILURE|^failure</status>
   <description>Windows audit failure event.</description>
</rule>
```

In this rule, it is simply looking for an "AUDIT_FAILURE" or "failure" message in the event. A composite rule allows us to tune this further so we can focus on events that may require more immediate attention.

```
<var name="MS_FREQ">6</var>
...
<rule id="18153" level="10" frequency="$MS_FREQ" timeframe="240">
   <if_matched_sid>18105</if_matched_sid>
   <description>Multiple Windows audit failure events.</description>
</rule>
```

In this build-in composite rule, we build off of the atomic failure rule 18105 and create this composite rule that will fire if we see six failures in 4 min (240 s).

We can also build our own rules that may be more relevant for our organization. Perhaps for your environment you want to be alerted if there are 10 login failures that happen after business hours say 5 pm till 9 am. We can write our own composite rule as follows:

```
<rule id="100999" level="10" frequency="10" timeframe="300">
    <if_matched_sid>18105</if_matched_sid>
    <time>5 pm - 9 am</time>
    <description>Windows Logon Failure occurred 10 times after business
    hours</description>
</rule>
```

The rules engine can help your team meet the log review requirements of many of the compliance frameworks. The combination of atomic and composite rules will also help reduce the time requirements of doing a manual review with the basic toolset we discussed and also allow you to tune the alerting to reduce false positives.

OSSEC Log Retention Policy and Storage Options

By default, OSSEC will store your log information at /var/ossec/logs/alerts. OSSEC stores logs in a directory structure based on the year and the month when the log event was generated. The following would be a typical log retention structure in an OSSEC installation:

```
/var/ossec/logs/alerts/2011
/var/ossec/logs/alerts/2011/Jan
/var/ossec/logs/alerts/2011/Feb
/var/ossec/logs/alerts/2011/Mar
...
```

This directory structure makes it fairly easy for us to write a script to clean up our old logs that are older than our log retention period. A simple "rm –f /var/ossec/logs/alerts/2011/Jan" will remove all our logs from January 2011.

Many organizations may want to write their own custom reports or be able to extend the search and forensics capabilities of OSSEC. If you don't have a programmer on staff or you don't want to modify and maintain customized OSSEC source code, another option would be to send OSSEC alerts to a database so you can write SQL queries to get exactly the report or information you need. OSSEC currently supports MySQL and PostgreSQL databases for its alerts. More information on sending your alerts to a database can be found at http://www.ossec.net/doc/manual/output/database-output.html.

OSSIM

OSSIM is more than just log management and retention. OSSIM falls into a group of products considered to be a Secure Information and Event Management (SIEM) system. OSSIM provides what it calls the "5 essential security capabilities"—asset discovery, vulnerability assessment, threat detection, behavioral monitoring, and security intelligence. The following open source tools are utilized internally to provide these capabilities.

- Arpwatch is used for MAC address anomaly detection.
- P0f is used for passive OS detection and OS change analysis.
- Pads is used for service anomaly detection.
- Nessus is used for vulnerability assessment and for cross-correlation (intrusion detection system (IDS) vs. Vulnerability Scanner).
- Snort is used as an intrusion detection system (IDS), and also used for cross correlation with Nessus.
- Tcptrack is used for session data information that can garner useful information for attack correlation.
- Ntop builds an impressive network information database for aberrant behavior anomaly detection.
- Nagios used to monitor host and service availability information based on a host asset database.
- Osiris as a host-based intrusion detection system (HIDS).
- Snare a log collector for windows systems.
- OSSEC a host-based IDS.
- OSSIM also includes its own tools including a generic correlation engine with logical directive support and logs integration with plugins.

As you will note, OSSIM includes two of the tools we already discussed: OSSEC and Snare. OSSIM includes a fairly impressive set of charts and data views that are in their infancy or not part of OSSEC. AlienVault provides both a free and commercial offering. Organizations should consider reviewing OSSIM if they are looking for a full security information management system as opposed to just a log management and retention system. More information is available at http://www.alienvault.com/.

Other Analysis Tools to Consider

We have covered a lot of great tools in this section, and of course there are many others. Here are a few honorable mentions to consider adding to your tool chest.

Logsurfer

Unlike a lot of the tools mentioned in this section, Logsurfer is a useful utility for reviewing logs in real time. Another benefit of Logsurfer is it attempts to group messages that would be considered as events into a single logical event. For example, consider the following FTP sequence of events.

```
somehost tcpd-ftpd[14311]: connect from host.some.where
somehost ftpd[14311]: connection from *@host.some.where [42.42.42.42]
somehost ftpd[14311]: USER anonymous
somehost ftpd[14311]: PASS password
somehost ftpd[14311]: failed login from host.some.where [42.42.42.42],
    anonynous
somehost ftpd[14311]: SYST
somehost ftpd[14311]: PORT
somehost ftpd[14311]: cmd failure - not logged in
somehost ftpd[14311]: LIST
somehost ftpd[14311]: QUIT
somehost ftpd[14311]: FTP session closed
```

Seeing only a single one of these messages may create a false positive security event. However, if we look at the content of the messages as a whole, we can see someone attempted an anonymous login and then logged out. Analysis of the log message would be something like this instead:

```
somehost ftpd[14311]: cmd failure - not logged in
```

The utility can be downloaded from http://www.crypt.gen.nz/logsurfer/

LogHound
LogHound is more of a research tool. LogHound attempts to find frequent line patterns in mining log files utilizing a breadth-first algorithm. More details on the utility and research papers are available on the tool's Website at http://ristov.users.sourceforge.net/loghound/.

Log2Timeline
Log2Timeline is useful in doing forensics analysis. The tool extracts time-line information from some non-traditional sources such as the recycle bin, Firefox history, proxy server data, etc. This can be useful when there is a concern that data or logs have been altered or updated. The tool is available at http://log2timeline.net/.

COMMERCIAL VENDORS

There are a number of superb log analysis and log retention solutions available from leaders in the security space. The offerings range from solutions you can outright purchase and run yourself to manage log management offerings that

---

DISCLAIMER AND COMMERCIAL OFFERINGS

Disclaimer

DISCLAIMER: This book does not explicitly advocate or recommend the commercial offerings in this section. As with any purchase in your environment, we recommend a full review of any commercial offering to determine if it meets your organization's needs. As always, ask a lot of questions and try a proof of concept with a vendor before purchasing the solution that is right for you.

---

allow you to outsource daily log management to a third-party provider. We will review a number of offerings here, but this definitely does not cover the entire set of solutions available. Good resources for further research are available from Gartner (www.gartner.com) and Security Scoreboard (http://www.securityscoreboard.com/).

Splunk

Splunk (www.splunk.com) is a commercial offering that provides many of the same great features we discussed about OSSEC. Splunk will allow you to centralize your logs for forensics and correlation as well as generate real-time alerts based on the types of events that need further investigation or action. A key difference with Splunk is the wide variety of log sources it supports, real-time dashboards to review activity, customizable reporting and dashboards, and vendor-supported APIs to help integrate Splunk into your security infrastructure.

Free vs. Enterprise

One benefit with Splunk is they have a free and Enterprise offering. You can start using Splunk by opening a free account on their Website and downloading the software. There are a number of key limitations with the free offering though.

- A maximum of 500 MB per day of logs in the free offering. Though this sounds like a lot, most medium to large organizations will quickly hit this limit or just a few really busy Web servers can blow past this limit in no time.
- Real-time monitoring and alerting is only available in the Enterprise version of splunk. However, they do let you try the Enterprise edition for 60 days to evaluate this option.
- Role-based authentication is only available in the Enterprise edition.

Log Source Support

Splunk supports a wide variety of data inputs. Splunk supports many input sources we have already discussed in this section such as standard syslog, syslog over TCP, and of course syslog with TLS/SSL encryption. On top of this, Splunk has "forwarders" that can retrieve information from files and directories, retrieve Windows events and registry information, and support for retrieving many Web server logs. There are plenty of "recipes" as splunk call them for things like Web logs, J2EE logs, Windows performance metrics, etc. On inputs that are less common, Splunk lets you define the details as a recipe for Splunk to process and index the data.

Dashboards and Views

Splunk has capabilities to allow users to create their own views of their data as a dashboard or view. These are completely customizable and key differentiator for some organizations compared to the other tools we discussed. Organizations that have a lot of custom reporting needs or need different views of the data for different stakeholders in an organization will find this greatly reduces the time of getting reports from some of the more manual toolsets we have covered.

NetIQ Sentinel

NetIQ Sentinel (https://www.netiq.com/products/sentinel/), like OSSIM we discussed earlier, is another product that is more than log management and analysis and falls into the category of being a SIEM. Sentinel includes anomaly detection and identity management information as additional sources of data that can be useful in handling incident response and conducting forensics on events. If you need more than just log management, the Enterprise Version of NetIQ Sentinel can provide a full security information management tool for your organization.

Free vs. Enterprise

This product was acquired from Novell in 2010 and there is a free version of the product that is limited to only log management with a maximum of 25 events per second. An account can be created at http://www.novell.com/promo/slm/slm25.html. Any load above this will of course require you to purchase the Sentinel product. The product has strong search and reporting capabilities.

IBM q1Labs

QRadar (http://q1labs.com/products.aspx) is the log management solution available from IBM. IBM acquired q1Labs and their product lines in 2011. There used to be a free version available, but since the acquisition, this appears to no longer be available. Like many of the other products we have discussed, QRadar has broad log source support and a wide variety of search and reporting functionality. QRadar can be acquired with some of the additional product lines including a full SIEM offering for organizations needing a complete security information management tool. One of the key differentiators for QRadar is its reporting tailored for many of the current compliance frameworks with reports to support auditing of:

- Payment Card Industry Data Security Standard (PCI DSS)
- North American Electric Reliability Corporation (NERC)
- Health Insurance Portability and Accountability Act (HIPAA)
- Sarbanes-Oxley (SOX), and Federal Information Security Management Act (FISMA)

Loggly

Loggly (http://loggly.com/) is a cloud log provider with your log data being stored offsite in the cloud. We will cover more details about this in Chapter 22 and factors to consider when storing your data in the cloud. The product supports many of the data sources we have already covered as well as publishing data via a programmatic REST API and posting data via HTTP and HTTPS. The product is relatively new and you should review the reporting capabilities from their analytics engine to determine if the product will meet your compliance needs. A key difference with Loggly will be the limited need to install any additional hardware in your environment to retain your logs and having someone else maintain and upgrade your logging system. Review Chapter 22 and the company's Website to see if this is the right solution for your organization. This chapter also has examples of how to use Loggly's Web interface to send and retrieve logs.

SUMMARY

This chapter provided an introduction to some of the most widely used tools to perform log collection and analysis. Both open source and commercial systems were presented. Also, general guidance was given on how to choose a tool.

REFERENCES

AlienVault. OSSIM the open source SIEM. <http://www.alienvault.com/>.

Chuvakin, A. (2008). How would you do it? Selecting a log management approach. <http://www.slideshare.net/anton_chuvakin/choosing-your-log-management-approach-buy-build-or-out-source>.

Chuvakin, A. (2011). Official page for critical log review checklist. <<http://chuvakin.blogspot.com/2010/03/simple-log-review-checklist-released.html >.

GNU.org. GNU Grep 2.13. <http://www.gnu.org/software/grep/manual/grep.html>.

Ossec.net. Rules/decoders documentation. <http://www.ossec.net/doc/rules/rules/index.html>.

Rsyslog.com. Rsyslog home. <http://www.rsyslog.com/>.

Syslog.org. Syslog.org home. <http://www.syslog.org/>.

The IEEE and The Open Group (2004). The open group base specifications issue 6. <http://pubs.opengroup.org/onlinepubs/009695399/utilities/grep.html>.

Verizon Corporation (2012). 2012 Data breach investigations report. Retrieved July 8, 2012, from Verizon Business: <http://www.verizonbusiness.com/resources/reports/rp_data-breach-investigations-report-2012_en_xg.pdf>.

Log Management Procedures: Log Review, Response, and Escalation

INFORMATION IN THIS CHAPTER:

- Assumptions, Requirements, and Precautions
- Common Roles and Responsibilities
- PCI and Log data
- Logging Policy
- Review, Response, and Escalation Procedures and Workflows Validation of Log Review
- Logbook—Evidence of Exception of Investigations
- PCI Compliance Evidence Package
- Management Reporting
- Periodic Operational Tasks Additional Information

INTRODUCTION

You are now fluent in topics like log management, log analysis, correlation, filtering, and so on, what is the next step? The goal of logging and log management is, in essence, to provide you with situational awareness (SA) about the goings-on in your environment, so you can review, respond to and, if need be, escalate when something happens in or on your network. SA is achieved, in part, by enabling log data collection, analysis, and retention. These topics have been covered over the course of this book. This chapter, however, will provide coverage of log data review, response, and escalation.

More than likely your organization falls into one of several of the following reasons for implementing logging:

1. You do it because you want to protect your company's assets (intellectual property, financial data, etc.).

> ## WARNING
>
> ### PCI Compliance Non-Guarantee
> The authors cannot guarantee PCI compliance or passing PCI validation based on implementing the procedures and workflows in this chapter. The material is presented for educational purposes only.

2. You are in an industry (banking, healthcare, credit card processing, etc.) which requires regulatory compliance to ensure you are doing your level best to mitigate against outside and inside threats, data loss, and so on.

3. You just eat, sleep, and breathe all things logging.

Now, number 2 is interesting. Not only do many regulations stipulate what you need to do from a process and procedure standpoint, they also require you to be able to prove that you are actually following and maintaining your policies and procedures. This can mean anything from providing up-to-date documentation on who has access to what systems on your network to producing reports which backup your documentation (login and logout records for example).

The approach used in this chapter is to present repeatable and extensible workflows to provide you with the insight and understanding to allow you to implement these processes as needed. In order to reinforce and drive these points home, examples will be provided using the Payment Card Industry (PCI) Data Security Standard (DSS).

From this point forward, PCI DSS concepts will be used for the remainder of the chapter.

ASSUMPTIONS, REQUIREMENTS, AND PRECAUTIONS

These critical items are essential for success of logging, log management, and log review. It is assumed that the following requirements are satisfied before the log review, response, and escalation procedures are put into practice.

> ## NOTE
>
> ### PCI DSS in a Nutshell
> PCI DSS is a set of technical and operational requirements meant to protect credit cardholder data from misuse. Merchants, processors, issuers, and service providers all have a stake in PCI. The ultimate goal is global adoption of these requirements. A complete treatment of PCI is beyond the scope of this chapter (Requirements and Security Assessment Procedures, 2010).

Requirements

A set of requirements needs to be in place before the operational procedures described in this chapter can be used effectively:

1. Logging policy (see Logging Policy section later in this chapter) is created to codify PCI DSS log-related requirements as well as other regulatory and operational logging requirements.
2. Logging is enabled on the in-scope systems.
3. Interruption or termination of logging is in itself logged and monitored.
4. Event mandated in PCI DSS documentation is logged.
5. Generated logs satisfy PCI DSS logging requirements.
6. Time is synchronized across the in-scope systems and with the reliable time server (NTP, etc.).
7. Time zones of all logging systems are known and recorded and can be reviewed in conjunction with logs.

Items 2 through 7 can be applied to almost every environment, while item 1 seems fairly specific. But it should be noted that item 1 (logging policy) is a best practice and should be followed regardless.

Precautions

These additional precautions need to be taken in order to make logs useful for PCI DSS compliance, other regulations as well as security, forensics, and operational requirement:

- *Key precaution:* The person whose actions are logged on a particular system cannot be the sole party responsible for log review on this system.
- *Key precaution:* PCI DSS mandates log security measures, all access to logs should be logged and monitored to identify attempts to terminate or otherwise affect the presence and quality of logging.

The main idea behind these precautions is to ensure the integrity of the system. Basically, no one person should have enough control such that he or she is able to cover their tracks or those of others.

COMMON ROLES AND RESPONSIBILITIES

Table 16.1 summarizes common roles that are mentioned in this chapter and are involved in review, escalate, and response process.

These roles and responsibilities are covered throughout the chapter. It should be pointed out that you may or may not have all the roles defined for your organization. It might be the case that your organization is small and a single individual fulfills multiple roles.

Table 16.1 Summary of Common Roles and Responsibilities

Role	Responsibility	Example Involvement
Application Administrator	Administers the application	Configured application logging settings, may perform daily log review
System or Network Administrator	Administers the underlying operating system or network	Configured logging settings, may perform daily log review
Application Business Owner	Business manager who is responsible for the application	Approves the changes to application configuration required for logging and log review
Security Administrator	Administers security controls on one or more systems or applications	Configured security and logging settings, performs daily log review
Security Analyst	Deals with operational security processes	Accesses security systems and analyzes logs and other data
Security Director or Manager	Oversees security policy, process, and operation	Owns log review procedures, updates the procedures
Incident Responder	Gets involved in security incident response	Deals with security incidents, reviews logs during the response process

WARNING

Wearing Multiple Hats can Cause Conflicts of Interest Issues
It is often not a good idea for the same person to wear the same hat when it comes to the log data review, response, and escalation. It can be viewed as a conflict of interest and should be avoided if at all possible.

PCI AND LOG DATA

This section covers the basics of PCI DSS logging and what is required by PCI DSS. Requirements and Security Assessment Procedures, (2010). provides the full details on the PCI DSS regulations, including sections, requirements, and other items referenced in this chapter.

Now, logging and monitoring are not constrained to Requirement 10, but, in fact, pervade all 12 of the PCI DSS requirement; the key areas where logging and monitoring are mandated in PCI DSS are Requirement 10 and sections of Requirement 11.

Key Requirement 10

We will go through it line by line and then go into details, examples, and implementation guidance.

10.1

Specifically, Requirement 10.1 covers "establish[ing] a process for linking all access to system components (especially access done with administrative privileges such as root) to each individual user" (Requirements and Security Assessment Procedures, 2010). This is an interesting requirement indeed; it doesn't just mandate for logs to be there or for a logging process to be set, but instead mentions that logs must be tied to individual persons (not computers or "devices" where they are produced). It is this requirement that often creates problems for PCI implementers, since many think of logs as "records of people actions," while in reality they will only have the "records of computer actions." Mapping the latter to actual users often presents an additional challenge. By the way, PCI DSS Requirement 8.1 which mandates that an organization "assigns all users a unique ID before allowing them to access system components or cardholder data" (Requirements and Security Assessment Procedures, 2010) helps to make the logs more useful here.

10.2

Next, Section 10.2 defines a minimum list of system events to be logged (or, to allow "the events to be reconstructed"). Such requirements are motivated by the need to assess and monitor user actions as well as other events that can affect credit card data (such as system failures).

Following is the list from the requirements (events that must be logged) from PCI DSS (v. 2.0; Requirements, and Security Assessment Procedures, 2010):

10.2.1 All individual user accesses to cardholder data.
10.2.2 All actions taken by any individual with root or administrative privileges.

10.2.3 Access to all audit trails.
10.2.4 Invalid logical access attempts.
10.2 5 Use of identification and authentication mechanisms.
10.2.6 Initialization of the audit logs.
10.2.7 Creation and deletion of system-level objects.

As can be seen, this covers data access, privileged user actions, log access and initialization, failed and invalid access attempts, authentication and authorization decisions, and system object changes. It is important to note that such a list has its roots in IT governance "best practices," which prescribe monitoring access, authentication, authorization change management, system availability, and suspicious activity.

10.3

Moreover, PCI DSS Requirement 10 goes into an even deeper level of detail and covers specific data fields or values that need to be logged for each event. They provide a healthy minimum requirement, which is commonly exceeded by logging mechanisms in various IT platforms.

Such fields are:

10.3.1 User identification.
10.3.2 Type of event.
10.3.3 Date and time.
10.3.4 Success or failure indication.
10.3.5 Origination of event.
10.3.6 Identity or name of affected data, system component, or resource.

As can be seen, this minimum list contains all of the basic attributes needed for incident analysis and for answering the questions: when, who, where, what, and where from. For example, if trying to discover who modified a credit card database to copy all of the transactions with all the details into a hidden file (a typical insider privilege abuse), knowing all of the above records is very useful.

10.4

The next requirement, 10.4, addresses a commonly overlooked but critical requirement: a need to have accurate and consistent time in all of the logs (William and Chuvakin, 2012). It seems fairly straightforward that time and security event monitoring would go hand in hand as well. System time is frequently found to be arbitrary in a home or small office network. It's whatever time your server was set at, or if you designed your network for some level of reliance, you're systems are configured to obtain time synchronization from a reliable source, like the Network Time Protocol (NTP) servers.

10.5

Next, one needs to address all of the confidentiality, integrity, and availability (CIA) of logs. Section 10.5.1 of PCI DSS covers the confidentiality: "Limit viewing of audit trails to those with a job-related need" (Requirements and Security Assessment Procedures, 2010). This means that only those who need to see the logs to accomplish their jobs should be able to. One of the obvious reasons is that authentication-related logs will always contain usernames. While not truly secret, username information provides 50% of the information needed for password guessing (password being the other 50%). Moreover, due to users mistyping their credentials, it is not uncommon for passwords themselves to show up in logs. Poorly written Web applications might result in a password being logged together with the Web Uniform Resource Locator (URL) in Web server logs.

Next comes "integrity." As per Section 10.5.2 of PCI DSS, one needs to "protect audit trail files from unauthorized modifications" (Requirements and Security Assessment Procedures, 2010). This one is obvious, since if logs can be modified by unauthorized parties (or by anybody) they stop being an objective assessment trail of system and user activities.

However, one needs to preserve the logs not only from malicious users, but also from system failures and consequences of system configuration errors. This touches upon both the "availability" and "integrity" of log data. Specifically, Section 10.5.3 of PCI DSS covers that one needs to "promptly back-up audit trail files to a centralized log server or media that is difficult to alter" (Requirements and Security Assessment Procedures, 2010). Indeed, centralizing logs to a server or a set of servers that can be used for log analysis is essential for both log protection as well as increasing log usefulness. Backing up logs to CDs or DVDs (or tapes, for that matter) is another consequence of this requirement. One should always keep in mind that logs on tape are not easily accessible and not searchable in case of an incident.

Many pieces of network infrastructure such as routers and switches are designed to log to an external server and only preserve a minimum (or none) of logs on the device itself. Thus, for those systems, centralizing logs is most critical. Requirement 10.5.4 of PCI DSS states the need to "copy logs for wireless networks onto a log server on the internal LAN."

To further decrease the risk of log alteration as well as to enable proof that such alteration didn't take place, Requirement 10.5.5 calls for the "use file integrity monitoring and change detection software on logs to ensure that existing log data cannot be changed without generating alerts" (Requirements and Security Assessment Procedures, 2010). At the same time, adding new log data to a log file should not generate an alert since log files tend to grow and not shrink on their own (unless logs are rotated or archived to external storage). File integrity monitoring systems use cryptographic hashing algorithms to compare files to a known good copy. The issue with logs is that log files tend to grow due to new record addition, thus undermining the missing of integrity checking. To resolve this contradiction, one should note that integrity monitoring can only assure the integrity of logs that are not being actively written to by the logging components.

10.6

The next requirement is truly one of the most important as well as one of the most often overlooked. Many PCI implementers simply forget that PCI Requirement 10 does not just call for "having logs," but also for "having the logs AND looking at them." Specifically, Section 10.6 states that the PCI organization must, as per PCI DSS, "review logs for all system components at least daily. Log reviews must include those servers that perform security functions like IDSes and AAA servers (e.g. RADIUS)" (Requirements and Security Assessment Procedures, 2010). The rest of this chapter covers the detailed log review procedures and practices.

Thus, the requirement covers the scope of log sources that need to be "reviewed daily" and not just configured to log, and have logs preserved or centralized. Given that a large IT environment might produce gigabytes of logs per day, it is humanly impossible to read all of the logs. That is why a note is added to this requirement of PCI DSS that states that "Log harvesting, parsing, and alerting tools may be used to achieve compliance with Requirement 10.6" (Requirements and Security Assessment Procedures, 2010).

10.7

The final requirement (10.7) deals with another hugely important logging question—log retention. It states: "retain audit trail history for at least one year, with a minimum of three months online availability" (Requirements and Security Assessment Procedures, 2010). Unlike countless other requirements, this deals with the complicated log retention question directly. Thus, if you are not able to go back 1 year and look at the logs, you are in violation. Moreover, PCI DSS in its updated version v1.1 got more prescriptive when a one year requirement was added explicitly.

So, let us summarize what we learned so far on logging in PCI:

- PCI Requirement 10 calls for logging specific events with a predefined level of details from all in-scope systems.
- PCI calls for tying the actual users to all logged actions.
- All clocks and time on the in-scope systems should be synchronized.
- The CIA of all collected logs should be protected.
- Logs should be regularly reviewed; specific logs should be reviewed at least daily.
- All in-scope logs should be retained for at least 1 year.

Now we are ready to dig deeper to discover those logs and monitoring "live" not only within Requirement 10, but in all other PCI requirements. While many think that logs in PCI are represented only by Requirement 10, reality is more complicated: logs are in fact present, undercover, in all other sections.

Other Requirements Related to Logging

Just about every claim that is made to satisfy the requirements, such as data encryption or anti-virus updates, can make effective use of log files to actually substantiate it.

For example, Requirement 1, "Install and maintain a firewall configuration to protect cardholder data" (Requirements and Security Assessment Procedures, 2010), mentions that organizations must have "a formal process for approving and testing all external network connections and changes to the firewall configuration" (Requirements and Security Assessment Procedures, 2010). However, after such process is established, one needs to validate that firewall configuration changes do happen with authorization and in accordance with documented change management procedures. That is where logging becomes extremely handy, since it shows you what actually happened and not just what was supposed to happen.

The entire Requirement 1.3 contains guidance to firewall configuration, with specific statements about inbound and outbound connectivity. One must use firewall logs to verify this; even a review of configuration would not be sufficient, since only logs show "how it really happened" and not just "how it was configured."

Similarly, Requirement 2 talks about password management "best practices" as well as general security hardening, such as not running unneeded services. Logs can show when such previously disabled services are being started, either by misinformed system administrators or by attackers.

Further, Requirement 3, which deals with data encryption, has direct and unambiguous links to logging. For example, the entire Subsection 3.6, shown below in an abbreviated form, implies having logs to verify that such activity actually take place. Specifically, key generation, distribution, and revocation are logged by most encryption systems and such logs are critical for satisfying this requirement.

Requirement 4, which also deals with encryption, has logging implications for similar reasons.

Requirement 5 refers to anti-virus defenses. Of course, in order to satisfy Section 5.2, which requires that you "Ensure that all anti-virus mechanisms are current, actively running, and capable of generating audit logs" (Requirements and Security Assessment Procedures, 2010), one needs to see such mentioned logs.

So, even the requirement to "use and regularly update anti-virus software" will likely generate requests for log data during the assessment, since the information is present in anti-virus assessment logs. It is also well known that failed anti-virus updates, also reflected in logs, expose the company to malware risks, since anti-virus without the latest signature updates only creates a false sense of security and undermines the compliance effort.

Requirement 6 is in the same league: it calls for the organizations to "Develop and maintain secure systems and applications" (Requirements and Security Assessment Procedures, 2010), which is unthinkable without a strong assessment logging functions and application security monitoring.

Requirement 7, which states that one needs to "Restrict access to cardholder data by business need-to-know" (Requirements and Security Assessment Procedures, 2010), requires logs to validate who actually had access to said data. If the users that should be prevented from seeing the data appear in the log files as accessing the data usefully, remediation is needed.

Assigning a unique ID to each user accessing the system fits with other security "best practices." In PCI it is not just a "best practice;" it is a requirement (Requirement 8 "Assign a unique ID to each person with computer access;" Requirements and Security Assessment Procedures, 2010). Obviously, one needs to "Control addition, deletion, and modification of user IDs, credentials, and other identifier Objects" (Section 8.5.1 of PCI DSS). Most systems log such activities.

In addition, Section 8.5.9, "Change user passwords at least every 90 days" (Requirements and Security Assessment Procedures, 2010), can also be verified by reviewing the logs files from the server in order to assure that all the accounts have their password changed at least every 90 days.

Requirement 9 presents a new realm of security—physical access control. Even Section 9.4 that covers maintaining a visitor logs (likely in the form of a physical logbook) is connected to log management if such a visitor log is electronic. There are separate data retention requirements for such logs: "Use a visitor log to maintain a physical assessment trail of visitor activity. Retain this log for a minimum of three months, unless otherwise restricted by law" (Requirements and Security Assessment Procedures, 2010).

Requirement 11 addresses the need to scan (or "test") the in-scope systems for vulnerabilities However, it also calls for the use of IDS or IPS in Section 11.4: "Use network intrusion detection systems, host-based intrusion detection systems, and intrusion prevention systems to monitor all network traffic and alert personnel to suspected compromises. Keep all intrusion detection and prevention engines up-to-date" (Requirements and Security Assessment Procedures, 2010). Intrusion detection is only useful if logs and alerts are reviewed.

Requirement 12 covers the issues on a higher level—security policy as well as security standards and daily operational procedures (e.g. a procedure for daily log review mandates by Requirement 10 should be reflected here). However, it also has logging implications, since assessment logging should be a part of every security policy. In addition, incident response requirements are also tied to logging: "Establish, document, and distribute security incident response and escalation procedures to ensure timely and effective handling of all situations" (Requirements and Security Assessment Procedures, 2010) is unthinkable to satisfy without effective collection and timely review of log data.

Thus, event logging and security monitoring in PCI DSS program go much beyond Requirement 10. Only through careful data collection and analysis can companies meet the broad requirements of PCI.

The next section addresses the logging requirements in more details, focusing on Requirements 10 and 12.

LOGGING POLICY

In light of the requirements of PCI DSS, a PCI-derived logging policy must at least contain the following:

- Adequate logging, that covers both logged event types (login/logoffs, resource access, firewall accepts/denies, IPS/IDS alerts, etc.) and details.
- Log aggregation and retention (1 year).
- Log protection (ensuring logs are not tampered with).
- Log review.

A logging policy defines what attributes of log data should be captured for later review, escalation, and response. Again, PCI DSS concepts are used throughout this chapter, but this policy is general enough that it can apply to non-PCI activities, applications, and others.

Let's now focus on log review in depth. PCI DSS states that "Review logs for all system components at least daily. Log reviews must include those servers that perform security functions like intrusion-detection system (IDS) and authentication, authorization, and accounting protocol (AAA) servers (for example, RADIUS)" (Requirements and Security Assessment Procedures, 2010). It then adds that "Log harvesting, parsing, and alerting tools may be used to meet compliance with Requirement 10.6" (Requirements and Security Assessment Procedures, 2010). PCI testing and validation procedures for log review mandate that a Qualified Security Assessors (QSA) should "obtain and examine security policies and procedures to verify that they include procedures to review security logs at least daily and that follow-up to exceptions is required" (Requirements and Security Assessment Procedures, 2010). QSA must also assure that

> **NOTE**
>
> *QSA*
>
> A Qualified Security Assessor (QSA) is a person who is qualified (through training, credentialing, etc.) to perform PCI compliance assessments on firms which handle credit card data.

"Through observation and interviews, verify that regular log reviews are performed for all system components" (Requirements and Security Assessment Procedures, 2010).

To this end, the next section, we discuss application log review procedures and workflows that cover:

1. Log review practices, patterns, and tasks.
2. Exception investigation and analysis.
3. Validation of these procedures and management reporting.

The procedures will be provided for using automated log management tools as well as manually when tools are not available or not compatible with log formats produced by the application.

REVIEW, RESPONSE, AND ESCALATION PROCEDURES AND WORKFLOWS

The overall connection between the three types of PCI-mandates procedures is outlined in Figure 16.1.

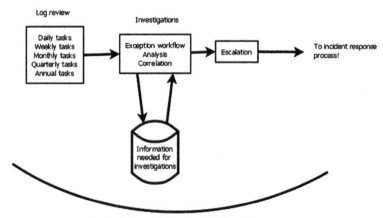

Validated and documented for assuring PCI DSS compliance

FIGURE 16.1 Assuring PCI DSS Compliance

In other words, "Periodic Log Review Practices" are performed every day (or less frequently, if daily review is impossible) and any discovered exceptions or are escalated to "Exception Investigation and Analysis." Both are documented as prescribed in "Validation of Log Review" section of this chapter to create evidence of compliance. We will now provide details on all three types of tasks.

Periodic Log Review Practices and Patterns

This section covers periodic log review procedures for log management. Such review is performed by either application administrator or security administrator (see section Roles and Responsibilities above). Such review can be performed using automated tools (which is explicitly allowed in PCI DSS) or manually, if such automated tools are not available or do not support log types from PCI application.

Let's build the entire end-to-end procedure for both cases and then illustrate it using the examples.

The basic principle of PCI DSS periodic log review (further referred to as "daily log review" even if it might not be performed daily for all the applications) is to accomplish the following:

- Assure that card holder data has not been compromised by the attackers.
- Detect possible risks to cardholder data, as early as possible.
- Satisfy the explicit PCI DSS requirement for log review.

Even given the fact that PCI DSS is the motivation for daily log review, other goals are accomplished by performing daily log review:

- Assure that systems that process cardholder data are operating securely and efficiently.
- Reconcile all possible anomalies observed in logs with other systems, activities (such as application code changes or patch deployments).

In light of the above goals, the daily log review is built around the concept of "baselining" or learning and documenting normal set of messages appearing in logs. See Chapter 10 for a discussion on baselines.

Baselining is then followed by the process of finding "exceptions" from the normal routine and investigating them to assure that no breach of cardholder data has occurred or is imminent.

The process can be visualized in Figure 16.2.

Before PCI daily log review is put into practice, it is critical to become familiar with normal activities logged on each of the applications (Dr Anton Chuvakin Blog, 2011).

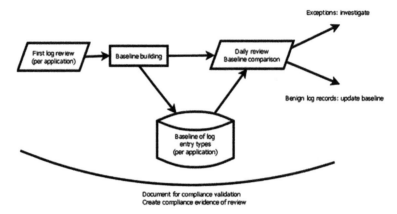

FIGURE 16.2 The Process of Baselining

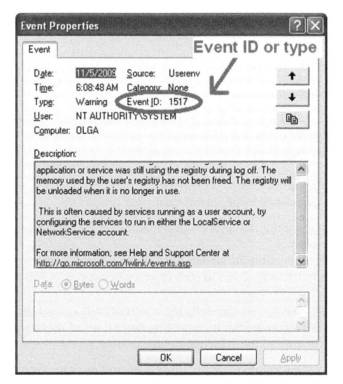

FIGURE 16.3 Windows XP Event ID Example

The main baseline to be built involves log message types. For example, review Figure 16.3.

Figure 16.3 is seen the first time and we confirm that the message does not indicate a critical failure of cardholder data security, we can add it to the expected baseline. Figure 16.4 shows what a Windows 7 event ID example looks like.

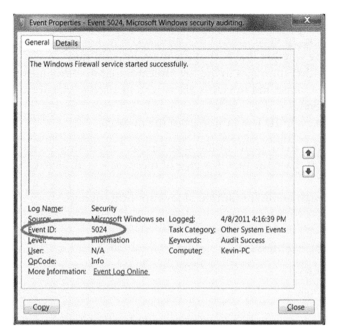

FIGURE 16.4 Windows 7 Event ID Example

It is important to note that explicit event types might not be available for some log types. For example, some Java application logs and some Unix logs don't have explicit log or event types recorded in logs. What is needed is to create an implicit event type (Requirements and Security Assessment Procedures, 2010). The procedure for this case is as follows:

1. Review the log message.
2. Identify which part of the log message identifies what it is about.
3. Determine whether this part of the message is unique.
4. Create an event ID from this part of the message.

Even though log management tools perform the process automatically, it makes sense to go through an example of doing it manually in case manual log review procedure is utilized. For example (Dr Anton Chuvakin Blog, 2011):

Example 1

1. Review the log message

The log message is:

```
[Mon Jan 26 22:55:37 2004] [notice] Digest: generating secret for
   digest authentication.
```

2. Identify which part of the log message identifies what it is about

It is very likely that the key part of the message is "generating secret for digest authentication" or even "generating secret."

3. Determine whether this part of the message is unique

A review of other messages in the log indicates that no other messages contain the same phase and thus this phrase can be used to classify a message as a particular type.

4. Create an event ID from this part of the message

We can create a message ID or message type as "generating_secret." Now we can update our baseline that this type of message was observed today.

Let's go through another example of Java application logs.

Example 2

1. Review the log message.

The log message is:

```
>>>>17 Jul 2008
13:00:57|AFWVGBYMBHWMV|ERROR|MerchantPreferredQuoteStrategy| Error
getting merchant availability, will fall back to XFS
com.factory.service.travel.flying.exception.MerchantSupplierException
    at com.

factory.service.travel.flying.PropertyAvailServiceImpl.
execute(MachineryAvailServiceImpl.java:407)

    at
<truncated>
```

2. Identify which part of the log message identifies what it is about.
It is very likely that the key part of the message is "Error getting merchant availability" or *"Error getting availability"*
3. Determine whether this part of the message is unique.
A review of other messages in the log indicates that no other messages contain the phase "Error getting merchant availability" and thus this phrase can be used to classify a message as a particular type. However, other messages contain the phrase *"Error getting object availability"* and thus it is not recommended to use the *"Error getting availability"* as a message type (Dr Anton Chuvakin Blog, 2011).
4. Create an event ID from this part of the message.
We can create a message ID or message type as "Error_getting_merchant_availability." Now we can update our baseline that this type of message was observed today.

An initial baseline can be quickly built using the following process, presented for two situations: with automated log management tools and without them.

In addition to this "event type," it makes sense to perform a quick assessment of the overlap log entry volume for the past day (past 24 h period). Significant differences in log volume should also be investigated using the procedures define below. In particular, loss of logging (often recognized from a dramatic decrease in log entry volume) needs to be investigated and escalated as a security incident (Dr Anton Chuvakin Blog, 2011).

Building an Initial Baseline Using a Log Management Tool

To build a baseline using a log management tool perform the following:

1. Make sure that relevant logs from a PCI application are aggregated by the log management tools (Chuvakin, n.d.).
2. Confirm that the tool can "understand" (parse, tokenize, etc.) the messages and identify the "event ID" or message type of each log (Chuvakin, n.d.).
3. Select a time period for an initial baseline: "90 days" or "all time" if logs have been collected for less than 90 days (Complete PCI DSS Log Review Procedures Part 8, 2011).
4. Run a report that shows counts for each message type. This report indicates all the log types that are encountered over the 90-day period of system operation (Chuvakin, n.d.).
5. Assuming that no breaches of card data have been discovered, we can accept the above report as a baseline for "routine operation" (Anton Chuvakin, 2011).
6. "An additional step should be performed while creating a baseline: even though we assume that no compromise of card data has taken place, there is a chance that some of the log messages recorded over the 90 day period triggered some kind of action or remediation. Such messages are referred to as "known bad" and should be marked as such" (Complete PCI DSS Log Review Procedures Part 8, 2011).

Let's go through a complete example of the above strategy:

1. Make sure that relevant logs from a PCI application are aggregated by the log management tools.

At this step, we look at the log management tools and verify that logs from PCI applications are aggregated. It can be accomplished by looking at report with all logging devices.

Table 16.2 indicates that aggregation is performed as needed.

2. Confirm that the tool can "understand" (parse, tokenize, etc.) the messages and identify the "event ID" or message type of each log (Anton Chuvakin, 2011).

Table 16.2 Report of All Logging Devices

Device Type	Device Name	Log Messages
Windows 2003	Winserver1	215,762
Windows 2003	Winserver2	215,756
CEMS	CEMS1	53,445
TOPPS	Topps1server	566
TABS	Tabs	3,334,444

Timeframe: January 1, 2009–March 31, 2009 (90 days).

This step is accomplished by comparing the counts of messages in the tool (such as the above report that shows log message counts) to the raw message counts in the original logs.

3. Select a time period for an initial baseline: "90 days" or "all time" if logs have been collected for less than 90 days.

In this example, we are selecting 90 days since logs are available.

4. Run a report that shows counts for each message type. For example, the report might look something like Table 16.3.

This report sample in Table 16.3 indicates all the log types that are encountered over the 90-day period of system operation.

5. Assuming that no breaches of card data have been discovered, we can accept the above report as a baseline for "routine operation."

During the first review it logs, it might be necessary to investigate some of the logged events before we accept them as normal. The next step explains how this is done.

6. An additional step should be performed while creating a baseline: even though we assume that no compromise of card data has taken place, there is a chance that some of the log messages recorded over the 90-day period triggered some kind of action or remediation. Such messages are referred to as "known bad" and should be marked as such (Complete PCI DSS Log Review Procedures Part 8, 2011).

Table 16.3 Report Showing Message Type Counts

Event ID	Event Description	Count	Average Count/Day
1517	Registry failure	212	2.3
562	Login failed	200	2.2
563	Login succeeded	24	0.3
550	User credentials updated	12	0.1

Timeframe: January 1, 2009–March 31, 2009 (90 days).

Table 16.4 90-day Summary Report

Event ID	Event Description	Count	Average Count/Day	Routine or "bad"
1517	Registry failure	212	2.3	
562	Login failed	200	2.2	
563	Login succeeded	24	0.3	
550	User credentials updated	12	0.1	
666	Memory exhausted	1	N/A	Action: restart system

Some of the logs in our 90-day summary are actually indicative of the problems and require an investigation (see Table 16.4).

In this report, we notice the last line, the log record with an event ID = 666 and event name "Memory exhausted" that only occurred once during the 90-day period. Such rarity of the event is at least interesting; the message description ("Memory exhausted") might also indicate a potentially serious issue and thus needs to be investigated as described below in the investigative procedures.

Creating a baseline manually is possible, but more complicated. We explore this in the next section.

Building an Initial Baseline Manually

To build a baseline without using a log management tool has to be done when logs are not compatible with an available tool or the available tool has poor understanding of log data. To do it, perform the following (Complete PCI DSS Log Review Procedures Part 8, 2011):

1. Make sure that relevant logs from a PCI application are saved in one location.
2. Select a time period for an initial baseline: "90 days" or "all time" if logs have been collected for less than 90 days; check the timestamp on the earliest logs to determine that (Complete PCI DSS Log Review Procedures Part 8, 2011).
3. Review log entries starting from the oldest to the newest, attempting to identify their types (Complete PCI DSS Log Review Procedures Part 8, 2011).
4. Manually create a summary of all observed types; if realistic, collect the counts of time each message was seen (not likely in case of high log data volume; Complete PCI DSS Log Review Procedures Part 8, 2011).
5. Assuming that no breaches of card data have been discovered in that time period, we can accept the above report as a baseline for "routine operation" (Complete PCI DSS Log Review Procedures Part 8, 2011).

6. An additional step should be performed while creating a baseline: even though we assume that no compromise of card data has taken place, there is a chance that some of the log messages recorded over the 90-day period triggered some kind of action or remediation. Such messages are referred to as "known bad" and should be marked as such (Complete PCI DSS Log Review Procedures Part 8, 2011).

Guidance for Identifying "Known Bad" Messages

The following are some rough guidelines for marking some messages as "known bad" during the process of creating the baseline. If generated, these messages will be looked at first during the daily review process:

1. Login and other "access granted" log messages occurring at unusual hour. (Technically, this also requires a creation of a baseline for better accuracy. However, logins occurring outside of business hours (for the correct time zone!) are typically at least "interesting.")
2. Credential and access modifications log messages occurring outside of a change window.
3. Any log messages produced by the expired user accounts.
4. Reboot/restart messages outside of maintenance window (if defined).
5. Backup/export of data outside of backup windows (if defined).
6. Log data deletion.
7. Logging termination on system or application.
8. Any change to logging configuration on the system or application.
9. Any log message that has triggered any action in the past: system configuration, investigation, etc.
10. Other logs clearly associated with security policy violations.

As we can see, this list is also very useful for creating "what to monitor in near-real-time?" policy and not just for logging. Over time, this list should be expanded based on the knowledge of local application logs and past investigations.

After we built the initial baselines, we can start the daily log review.

Main Workflow: Daily Log Review

This is the very central piece of the log review—comparing the logs produced over the last day (in case of a daily review) with an accumulated baseline.

Daily workflow follows this model as seen in Figure 16.5.

This summarizes the actions of the log analyst who performs the daily log review. Before we proceed, the issue of frequency of the log review needs to be addressed.

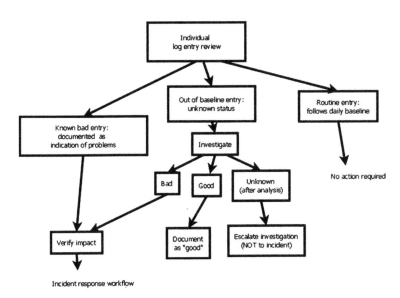

FIGURE 16.5 Daily Workflow

Frequency of Periodic Log Review

PCI DSS Requirement 10.6 explicitly states that "Review logs for all system components at least daily." It is assumed that daily log review procedures will be followed every day (Dr Anton Chuvakin Blog, 2011). Only your QSA may approve less frequent log reviews, based on the same principle that QSA's use for compensating controls. What are some of the reasons when less frequent log reviews may be approved? The list below contains some of the reasons why daily log review may be performed less frequently than every day:

- Application or system does not produce logs every day. If log records are not added every day, then daily log review is unlikely to be needed.
- Log review is performed using a log management system that collects log in batch mode, and batches of logs arrive less frequently than once a day.
- Application does not handle or store credit card data; it is only in-scope since it is directly connected to (Anton Chuvakin, 2011).

Remember that only your QSA's opinion on this is binding and nobody else's!

How does one actually compare today's batch of logs to a baseline? Two methods are possible; both are widely used for log review—the selection can be made based on the available resources and tools used. Figure 16.6 shows this.

Out of the two methods, the first method only considers log types not observed before and can be done manually as well as with tools. Despite its simplicity, it is extremely effective with many types of logs: simply noticing that a new log

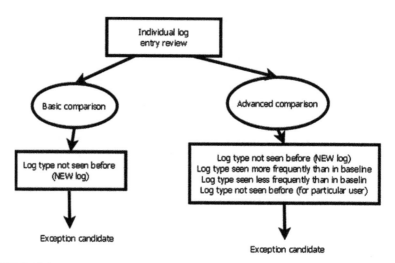

FIGURE 16.6 Exception Candidate Selection

message type is produced is typically very insightful for security, compliance, and operations (Dr Anton Chuvakin Blog, 2011).

For example, if log messages with IDs 1–7 are produced every day in large numbers, but log message with ID 8 is never seen, each occurrence of such log message is reason for an investigation. If it is confirmed that the message is benign and no action is triggered, it can be later added to the baseline.

So, the summary of comparison methods for daily log review is:

- Basic method:
  - Log type not seen before (NEW log message type).
- Advanced methods:
  - Log type not seen before (NEW log message type).
  - Log type seen more frequently than in baseline.
  - Log type seen less frequently than in baseline.
  - Log type not seen before (for particular user).
  - Log type not seen before (for particular application module).
  - Log type not seen before (on the weekend).
  - Log type not seen before (during work day).
  - New user activity noted (any log from a user not seen before on the system).

While following the advanced method, other comparison algorithms can be used by the log management tools as well.

After the message is flagged as an exception, we move to a different stage in our daily workflow—from daily review to investigation and analysis.

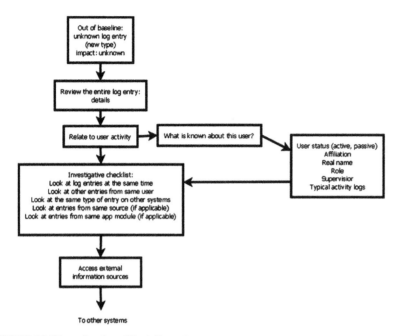

FIGURE 16.7 Investigation of Each Exception

Exception Investigation and Analysis

A message not fitting the profile of a normal is flagged "an exception." It is important to note that an exception is not the same as a security incident, but it might be an early indication that one is taking place.

At this stage we have an individual log message that is outside of routine/normal operation. How do we figure out whether it is significant, determine impact on security and PCI compliance status? (Dr Anton Chuvakin Blog, 2011).

Initial Investigation

Figure 16.7 shows how a high-level investigative process ("Initial Investigation") is used on each "exception" entry (more details are added further in the chapter).

Specifically, this shows a process which makes use of a log investigative checklist, which is explained below in more detail:

1. *Look at log entries at the same time:* This technique involves looking at an increasing range of time periods around the log message that is being investigated. Most log management products can allow you to review logs or to search for all logs within a specific time frame. For example:
   a. First, look at other log messages triggered 1 min before and 1 min after the "suspicious" log.

    b. Second, look at other log messages triggered 10 min before and 10 min after the "suspicious" log.

    c. Third, look at other log messages triggered 1 h before and 1 h after the "suspicious" log.

2. *Look at other entries from same user:* This technique includes looking for other log entries produced by the activities of the same user. It often happens that a particular logged event of a user activity can only be interpreted in the context of other activities of the same user. Most log management products can allow you to "drill down into" or search for a specific user within a specific time frame.

3. *Look at the same type of entry on other systems:* This method covers looking for other log messages of the same type, but on different systems in order to determine its impact. Learning when the same message was products on other system may hold clues to understanding the impact of this log message.

4. *Look at entries from same source (if applicable):* This method involves reviewing all other log messages from the network source address (where relevant).

5. *Look at entries from same app module (if applicable):* This method involves reviewing all other log messages from the same application module or components. While other messages in the same time frame (see item 1. above) may be significant, reviewing all recent logs from the same components typically helps to reveal what is going on.

In some cases, the above checklist will not render the result. Namely, the exception log entry will remain of unknown impact to security and PCI compliance. In this case, we need to acquire information from other systems, such as File Integrity Monitoring (FIM), Patch Management (PM), Change Management (CM), and others (Chuvakin, 2011).

External Information Sources Investigation

This procedure can be expanded to cover other sources of information available at the organization. Figure 16.8 shows the procedure to follow is external sources of information that are to be used during investigation.

The main idea of this procedure is to identify and then query information sources, based on the type of the exception log entry and then to identify its impact and the required actions (if any).

The procedure works to roughly identify the type of a log entry and then to query the relevant information sources. In some cases, the log entry is deemed to be an indication of a serious issue, incident response process is triggered.

However, it sometimes happens that neither the preliminary analysis nor the query of external systems yields the results and the "exception" log entry is

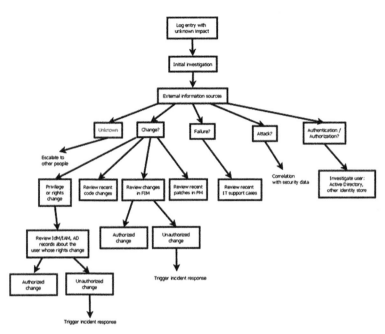

FIGURE 16.8 External Information Usage During Investigation

exceptional. In this case, the collaborative workflow is triggered (Chuvakin Blog, 2011).

Escalation to Other Procedures

This process allows tapping into the knowledge of other people at the organization who might know what this "anomaly" is about. The investigation and escalation process is shown in Figure 16.9.

The main idea of this procedure it to identify and then interview the correct people who might have knowledge about the events taking place on the application then to identify its impact and the required actions (if any).

The very last resource is to query the application vendor; such info request is typically time consuming or even expensive (depends on the support contract available) so it should be used sparingly (Chuvakin, n.d.).

Before we move onto the next section, we need to discuss incident response and escalation. The next section provides more detail on these topics.

Incident Response and Escalation

Many of the workflows presented thus far rely on incident response (IR) and escalation. But what is incident response and escalation? This section provides

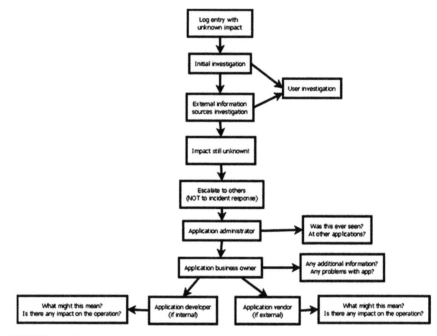

FIGURE 16.9 Escalation to Other Procedures

the needed understand how IR and escalation fit into the overall picture of what has been presented in this chapter. As you will.

Let's first discuss escalation. In log management, and IT in general, an escalation procedure is used to determine when you should escalate the fact that something has occurred.

Figure 16.10 shows the SANS-defined IR processes.

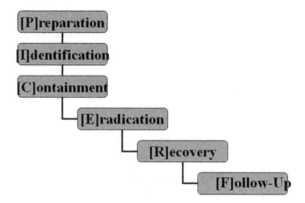

FIGURE 16.10 SANS IR Process

Let's discuss each step in the process.

The *preparation* stage includes tasks that need to be done before the incident: from assembling a team, training people, collecting, and building tools, to deploying additional monitoring and creating processes and incident procedures. This is also the point at which you develop your *escalation* procedure/policy. This policy is all about communicating that something has happened to the proper individual, group, etc. (Anton Chuvakin, 2011).

Identification starts when the signs of an incident are seen. This is not only (and, in fact, not so much) about IDS alerts, but about analyzing all kinds of signals that might reveal an emerging incident. For example, sustained CPU utilization, system reboots and/or configuration changes outside of maintenance windows, and so on, are some signals which may be indicative of something going on which requires further attention.

The *containment* stage is important for documenting what is going on, quarantining the affected systems (or maybe even areas) as well as doing the famous cable pull (i.e. disconnecting or turning off the system). At this stage we also try to assess the scope of the damage by reviewing what other systems might have also been infected, compromised, etc.

Eradication is where we are preparing to return to normal by evaluating the available backups and preparing for either restoration or rebuilding of the systems. Network changes might also be planned.

Recovery is where everything returns to normal. Additional logging and monitoring should be enabled at this stage.

During *follow-Up* you discuss and document lessons learned, reporting the incident to management, as well as planning future improvements in the incident process. This phase is often referred to as a postmortem.

VALIDATION OF LOG REVIEW

The final and critical part of log review is making sure that there is sufficient evidence of the process, its real-world implementation, and diligence in following the process. The good news here is that the same data can be used for management reporting about the logging and log review processes. Let's determine what documentation should be produced as proof of log review.

First, the common misconception is that having the actually logs provides that. That is not really true: "having logs" and "having logs reviewed" are completely different and sometime years of maturing the security and compliance program separates one and the other.

Just to remember, we have several major pieces that we need to prove for PCI DSS compliance validation. Here is the master-list of all compliance proof we will assemble. Unlike other sections, here we will cover proof of logging and not just proof of log review since the latter is so dependent on the former:

■ Presence and adequacy of logging.
■ Presence of log review processes and its implementation.
■ Exception handling process and its implementation.

Now we can organize the proof around those areas and then build processes to collect such proof.

Proof of Logging

The first category is: proof of presence and adequacy of logging. This section is the easiest to prove out of the three.

The following items serve as proof of logging:

1. Documented logging policy, covering both logged events and details logged for each event.
2. System/application configuration files implementing the above policy.
3. Logs produced by the above applications while following the policy.

Proof of Log Review

The second category: proof of log review processes and its implementation. This section is harder to prove compared to the previous one.

The following items serve as proof of log review:

1. Documented logging policy, covering log review.
2. Documented operational procedures, detailing the exact steps taken to review the logs.
3. Records of log review tasks being executed by the appropriate personnel (some log management products create an audit log of reviewed reports and events; such audit trail should cover it—the case of manual review is covered below)—think about this item as "log review log."
4. Also, records of exceptions being investigated (next section) indirectly prove that log review has taken place as well.

Proof of Exception Handling

The third category: proof of exception handling process and its implementation. This section is by far the hardest to prove out of these three.

The following items serve as proof of log exception process:

1. Documented logging policy, covering exceptions and their handling.
2. Documented operational procedures, detailing the exact steps taken to investigate exceptions found during log review.
3. A log of all exceptions investigated with actions taken ("logbook") (Complete PCI DSS Log Review Procedures Part 8, 2011).

The above evidence should provide ample proof that the organization follows PCI DSS guidance with diligence. Let's focus on producing this proof—Table 16.5 has the details.

The critical item from the above list is "a logbook" that is used to record exception follow-up and investigation, thus creating powerful evidence of compliance with PCI DSS requirements. In a more advanced form, the logbook can even grow into an investigative "knowledge base" that contains all past exception analysis cases.

Table 16.5 Proof of Compliance

PCI Compliance Logging Subdomain	Proof of Compliance	How to Obtain Proof?
Proof of presence and adequacy of logging	Documented logging policy	Create policy, if not present
Proof of presence and adequacy of logging	System/application configuration files	After deployment, preserve the configuration files as a master copy
Proof of presence and adequacy of logging	Logs produced by the above applications	Collect sample logs and save as proof of compliance
Proof of log review	Documented logging policy	Create policy, if not present
Proof of log review	Documented operational procedures	Create it based on the workflows and procedures based in this chapter
Proof of log review	Records of log review tasks being executed	Either use the tool or create a "logbook" (format below)
Proof of log review	Records of exceptions being investigated	Create a "logbook" of investigations
Proof of exception handling	Documented logging policy	Create policy, if not present
Proof of exception handling	Documented operational procedures	Create it based on the workflows and procedures based in this chapter
Proof of exception handling	A log of all exceptions investigated	Create a "logbook" of investigations or "knowledge base"

LOGBOOK—EVIDENCE OF EXCEPTION OF INVESTIGATIONS

How to create a logbook? The logbook is used to document everything related to analyzing and investigating the exceptions flagged during daily review. While the same logbook approach is used in the incident handling process (such as SANS Incident Response Workflow), in this document it is utilized as compliance evidence.

The logbook should record all systems involved, all people interviewed, all actions taken as well as their justifications, what outcome resulted, what tools and commands were used (with their results), etc.

The next section details the content of a logbook entry.

Recommended Logbook Format

A logbook entry should contain the following:

1. Date/time/time zone this logbook entry was started.
2. Name and role of the person starting the logbook entry.
3. Reason it is started: log exception (copied from log aggregation tool or from the original log file), make sure that the entire log is copied, especially its time stamp (which is likely to be different from the time of this record) and system from which it came from (what/when/where, etc.).
4. Detailed on why the log is not routine and why this analysis is undertaken.
5. Information about the system that produced the exception log record or the one this log exception is about (Complete PCI DSS Log Review Procedures Part 8, 2011):
   a. Hostname.
   b. OS.
   c. Application name.
   d. IP address(es).
   e. Location.
   f. Ownership (if known).
   g. System criticality (if defined and applicable).
   h. Under patch management, change management, FIM, etc.
6. Information about the user whose activity produced the log (if applicable).
7. Investigation procedure followed, tools used, screenshots, etc.
8. Investigative actions taken.
9. People contacted in the course of the log analysis.

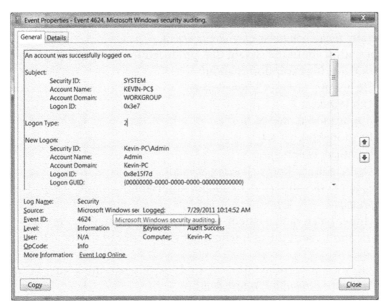

FIGURE 16.11 Windows 7 Event Used for Logbook Example

10. Impact determined during the course of the analysis.
11. Recommendations for actions, mitigations (if needed; Dr Anton Chuvakin Blog, 2011).

Example Logbook Entry

Here is an example following the above pattern, using the log entry in Figure 16.11:

1. Date/time/time zone this logbook entry was started: *June 30, 2011, 4:15 PM EDT.*
2. Name and role of the person starting the logbook entry: Kevin Schmidt.
3. Reason the logbook entry is started: log exception (copied from log aggregation tool or from the original log file), make sure that the entire log is copied, especially its time stamp (which is likely to be different from the time of this record) and system from which it came from (what/when/where, etc.).
Time/date of log: *7/29/2011 10:14:52 AM EDT.*
System: *Kevin-PC.example.com.*
4. Detailed on why the log is not routine and why this analysis is undertaken: *this event ID (Windows event ID 4624, successful account login) from*

this source (Source Microsoft Windows security auditing) was never seen before on any of the systems where logs are reviewed.

5. Information about the system that produced the exception log record or the one this log exception is about:

   a. Hostname: *Kevin-PC.example.com.*

   b. OS: *Windows 7.*

   c. Application name: *N/A.*

   d. IP address(s): *10.1.1.1.*

   e. Location: *Home office.*

   f. Ownership (if known): *Kevin Schmidt.*

   g. System criticality (if defined and applicable): *critical, laptop of the principal.*

   h. Under patch management, change management, FIM, etc.: *no.*

6. Information about the user whose activity produced the log: *N/A, no user activity.*

7. Investigation procedure followed, tools used, screenshots, etc.: *procedure for "Initial Investigation" described above.*

8. Investigative actions taken: following the procedure for "Initial Investigation" described in a section above, it was determined that this log entry is followed by a successful logoff. Specifically, on the same day, less than 1 min later, the log entry in Figure 16.12 appeared.

This entry indicates the successful log off of the action referenced in our exception log entry.

9. People contacted in the course of the log analysis: *none.*

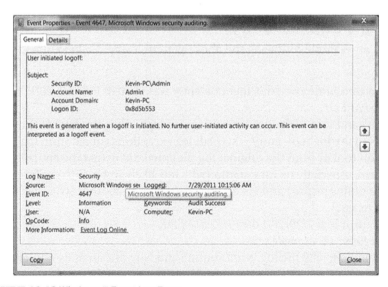

FIGURE 16.12 Windows 7 Event Log Entry

10. Impact determined during the course of the analysis: *impact was deter-mined to be low to non-existent; no functionality was adversely affected, no system was at risk.*
11. Recommendations for actions, mitigations (if needed): *no mitigation needed, added this log entry to baseline to be ignored in the future.*

The logbook of that sort is used as compliance evidence since it establishes log exceptions' follow-up, required in item 10.6.a of PCI DSS testing proce-dure, which states "Obtain and examine security policies and procedures to verify that they include procedures to review security logs at least daily and *that follow-up to exceptions is required.*"

The logbook (whether in electronic or paper form) can be presented to a QSA or other auditor, if requested (Dr Anton Chuvakin Blog, 2011).

PCI COMPLIANCE EVIDENCE PACKAGE

Overall, it is useful to create a "PCI Compliance Evidence Package" to show it to the QSA that will establish three keys of PCI DSS logging requirements:

- Presence and adequacy of logging.
- Log review.
- Exception handling.

While it is possible to prepare the evidence package before the assessment, it is much easier to maintain it on the ongoing basis. For example, keep printed or electronic copies of the following:

1. Logging policy that covers all of the PCI DSS in-scope systems.
2. Logging and log review procedures (this document).
3. List of log sources—all systems and their components (applications) from the in-scope environment.
4. Sampling of configuration files that indicate that logging is configured according to the policy (e.g. /etc/syslog.conf for Unix, screenshots of audit policy for Windows, etc.).
5. Sampling of logs from in-scope systems that indicate that logs are being generated according to the policy and satisfy PCI DSS logging requirements.
6. Exported or printed report from a log management tools that shows that log reviews are taking place.
7. Up-to-date logbook defined above.

This will allow always establishing compliant status and proving ongoing compliance.

MANAGEMENT REPORTING

In addition for compliance evidence, validation activities can be used to report the success of a log management program, processes, and procedures to senior management.

The data accumulated in the above section as proof of PCI DSS compliance can also be used for management reporting. Specifically, the following are useful reports that can be produced:

- Presence and adequacy of logging:
  - No useful management reporting in this section.
- Presence of log review processes and its implementation:
  - Log policy and procedure changes.
  - Application under log review.
  - Log entries reviewed.
- Exception handling process and its implementation:
  - Log exceptions handled by type, analyst name, etc.
  - Exception escalated to incident response.
  - (if relevant) Risk reduced due to timely escalation or incident prevention.
  - Resources saved due to timely escalation or incident prevention.
  - Application performance improvement due to log review.
- Other log management program reporting:
  - Overall compliance readiness (PCI DSS and other).

Finally, let's summarize all the operational tasks the organization should be executing in connection with log review.

PERIODIC OPERATIONAL TASKS

The following section contains a summary of operational tasks related to logging and log review. Some of the tasks are described in detail in previous sections; others are auxiliary tasks needed for successful implementation of PCI DSS log review program.

Daily Tasks

Table 16.6 contains daily tasks, responsible role that performs them as well as what record or evidence is created of their execution.

Weekly Tasks

Table 16.7 contains weekly tasks, responsible role that performs them as well as what record or evidence is created of their execution.

Table 16.6 Daily Tasks

Task	Responsible Role	Evidence
Review all the types of logs produced over the last day as described in the daily log review procedures	Security administrator, security analyst, (if authorized) application administrator	Record of reports being run on a log management tool
(As needed) investigate the anomalous log entries as described in the investigative procedures	Security administrator, security analyst, (if authorized) application administrator	Recorded logbook entries for investigated events
(As needed) take actions as needed to mitigate, remediate, or reconcile the results of the investigations	Security administrator, security analyst, (if authorized) application administrator, other parties	Recorded logbook entries for investigated events and taken actions
Verify that logging is taking place across all in-scope applications	Application administrator	Create a spreadsheet to record such activities for future assessment
(As needed) enabled logging if disabled or stopped	Application administrator	Create a spreadsheet to record such activities for future assessment

Table 16.7 Weekly Tasks

Task	Responsible Party	Evidence
(If approved by a QSA) Review all the types of logs produced on less critical application over the last day as described in the daily log review procedures	Security administrator, security analyst, (if authorized) application administrator	• Record of reports being run on a log management tool • Record of QSA approval for less frequent log reviews and reasons for such approval
(As needed) investigate the anomalous log entries as described in the investigative procedures	Security administrator, security analyst, (if authorized) application administrator	Recorded logbook entries for investigated events
(As needed) take actions as needed to mitigate, remediate, or reconcile the results of the investigations	Security administrator, security analyst, (if authorized) application administrator, other parties	Recorded logbook entries for investigated events and taken actions

Monthly Tasks

Table 16.8 contains daily tasks, responsible role that performs them as well as what record or evidence is created of their execution.

Table 16.8 Monthly Tasks

Task	Responsible Party	Evidence
Prepare a report on investigated log entries	Security analyst, security manager	Prepared report (to be filed)
Report on observed log message types	Security analyst, security manager	Prepared report (to be filed)
Report on observed NEW log message types	Security analyst, security manager	Prepared report (to be filed)
(If approved by a QSA) Review all the types of logs produced on non-critical applications over the last day as described in the daily log review procedures	Security administrator, security analyst, (if authorized) application administrator	• Record of reports being run on a log management tool • Record of QSA approval for less frequent log reviews and reasons for such approval
(As needed) investigate the anomalous log entries as described in the investigative procedures	Security administrator, security analyst, (if authorized) application administrator	Recorded logbook entries for investigated events
(As needed) take actions as needed to mitigate, remediate, or reconcile the results of the investigations	Security administrator, security analyst, (if authorized) application administrator, other parties	Recorded logbook entries for investigated events and taken actions

Quarterly Tasks

Table 16.9 contains daily tasks, who performs them as well as what record or evidence is created of their execution.

Table 16.9 Quarterly Tasks

Task	Responsible Party	Evidence
Verify that all the systems in-scope for PCI are logging and that logs are being reviewed	Security analyst, security manager	
Review daily log review procedures	Security analyst, security manager	
Review log investigation procedures	Security analyst, security manager	
Review collected compliance evidence	Security analyst, security manager	
Review compliance evidence collection procedures	Security analyst, security manager	

Table 16.10 Annual Tasks

Task	Responsible Party	Evidence
Review logging and log review policy	CSO	
Review compliance evidence before the QSA assessment		
Live tests with anomalies	As needed	

Annual Tasks

Table 16.10 contains daily tasks, who performs them as well as what record or evidence is created of their execution.

ADDITIONAL RESOURCES

The following references are useful for PCI DSS log review program and log management in general:

SANS CAG/CSC. "Twenty Critical Security Controls for Effective Cyber Defense: Consensus Audit Guidelines":

http://www.sans.org/critical-security-controls/.

Specifically, the relevant control on audit logs can be found here:

http://www.sans.org/critical-security-controls/control.php?id=6.

NIST 800-92 Logging Guide. "Guide to Computer Security Log Management: Recommendations of the National Institute of Standards and Technology by Karen Kent and Murugiah Souppaya":

http://csrc.nist.gov/publications/nistpubs/800-92/SP800-92.pdf.

NIST 800-66 HIPAA Guide. "An Introductory Resource Guide for Implementing the Health Insurance Portability and Accountability Act (HIPAA) Security Rule":

http://csrc.nist.gov/publications/nistpubs/800-66-Rev1/SP-800-66-Revision1.pdf.

SUMMARY

Log review is the starting point which allows you to enter into the investigation process, as well as provide assurances you are doing what is needed to satisfy your own corporate, regulatory, or other mandates. The key points from this chapter can best be summarized as follows:

1. Make sure you are capturing log data from all your critical systems. You cannot perform log review and response if you are not collecting anything.
2. Develop a logging policy which dictates, among other things, how long you will keep your log data (retention) once it is collected and aggregated.
3. During log review, establish baselines of commonly occurring patterns. This process can be done either manually or with an automated tool. Also, understand how to identify known bad messages.
4. Establish an escalation policy based on your environmental makeup. This will depend on your organization's structure with respect division of responsibility.

REFERENCES

Chuvakin, A. (2011, March 28). Log review for incident response: Part 2. Prism Microsystems. Web June 10, 2011. <http://www.prismmicrosys.com/EventSourceNov2010.php>.

Chuvakin, A. (2011). PCI DSS and logging: What you need to know. N.p. Web October 4, 2011. <http://www.slideshare.net/anton_chuvakin/pci-dss-and-logging-what-you-need-to-kn>.

Chuvakin, A. (2011). http://www.securitywarriorconsulting.com/siemblog/.

Complete PCI DSS Log Review Procedures Part 8. Insert name of site in italics. Web October 4, 2011. <https://www.infosecisland.com/blogview/10796-Complete-PCI-DSS-Log-Review-Procedures-Part-8.html>.

Dr Anton Chuvakin Blog PERSONAL Blog: Complete PCI DSS log. <http://chuvakin.blogspot.com/2010/12/complete-pci-dss-log-review-procedures_07.html>.

Requirements and Security Assessment Procedures (2010, October). *Payment Card Industry (PCI) Data Security Standard*. PCI Security Standards Council. Web July 24, 2011. <https://www.pcisecuritystandards.org/documents/pci_dss_v2.pdf>.

Schmidt, K. J. (2007, April) Introduction to security log analysis. Community Bankers Association of Georgia. Georgia, Callaway Gardens. Presentation.

Williams, Branden R., & Chuvakin, Anton. In Tony Bradley (Ed.), (2007). *PCI compliance: Implementing effective PCI data security standards*. Syngress Publishing.

Attacks Against Logging Systems

INTRODUCTION

A robust log analysis system relies on the integrity of the log data being analyzed. The system has to be resilient to attempts to modify and delete data. On top of this, it also has to allow granular access control to log data. If log data is to be used as evidence in a legal context, the ability to demonstrate the integrity of log data may have an effect on whether or not the data is considered acceptable evidence. This chapter explores possible attacks against the logging system and suggests solutions for mitigating or detecting those attacks.

Why would an attacker target the logging system? Well, first of all, what do we mean by "attacker" in this context? An attacker is someone who is conducting unauthorized activity, regardless of whether they are an "outsider" or an "insider."

A typical case of an outsider is the evil Internet hacker. An insider could be your own system administrator. An attacker may not be directly looking to compromise computers, but cold be someone involved in some malfeasant activity, such as embezzling company funds or selling trade secrets to competitors.

ATTACKS

There are a variety of reasons these attackers might target logs. First of all, the clever attacker usually wants to avoid getting caught. Since log data will provide evidence of his activity, he would want to prevent the information from being found. An even more clever attacker may want to hide her tracks via misdirection, by making the observer think that something else is happening. In addition to hiding tracks, attackers may find information in logs that are useful by themselves, such as transactional data, or information that can assist in attacking other systems, such as passwords or account numbers. Thus there is motivation in not being logged, destroying logs, modifying logs as well as sneaking peeks at logs from various systems for intelligence gathering.

What to Attack?

Attacks against the logging infrastructure can be done at any point in the infrastructure:

- *The source:* The host(s) on which log messages are generated—attacking the system or the logging application itself are both viable choices.
- *In transit:* The network between the sources and the loghost, or between processing and storage.
- *The collector or agent that collects logs:* Where the logs from various sources are collected.
- *The log data store:* The database system on which you store log information (if you use a database for that). Can also apply to any mechanism used for archiving log data—all the way down to utilizing *trained backup tape-eating rats* ☺.
- *At analysis:* The system where analysis is done, and the analysis process itself.
- Finally, one can attack the unavoidable part of any log management—a human analyst looking at data and making decisions.

The attacks themselves can be classified using the "CIA" model of computer threat analysis:

- *Confidentiality:* The ability of the attacker to read log data.
- *Integrity:* The ability of the attacker to alter, corrupt, or insert "constructed" log data.
- *Availability:* The ability of the attacker to delete log data or disable the logging system—or to deny the operation of analytics capability.

For example, a simple attack, often found in rootkits used by remote intruders, is to delete any files found in /var/log. This attack can be mitigated through the use of a secured central loghost—the data is still deleted on the originating host, but a copy is still available at the loghost. An attack of this sort on the loghost itself would be more catastrophic.

Another trivial attack is to flood the network between the source and the log-host, to cause packet loss and prevent the log data from ever reaching the loghost.

This section explores these and other attacks in detail.

Attacks on Confidentiality

Attacks on confidentiality against log data are not about an intruder hiding their tracks, but about gathering intelligence. That intelligence might be information about systems and networks, to be used in another attack, or it might be the collection of information itself which is the attack. Even if the data itself is not obviously sensitive, law or company policy may consider exposure of the data to be a violation.

What can an intruder find in your logs? Here are some useful examples from across the logging realm:

- What applications you are running, and what hosts they are running on. The logs often show the application version, and might information about their configuration. All of this data can be used to find points of vulnerability.
- What you might be looking at in your logs, in order to determine how to avoid being noticed. Or what's not being logged, for the same reason.
- Useful tidbits of information, such as who has privileged access, when people are logged in, etc.
- Accidental exposure of credentials. For example, a user accidentally types their password when prompted for their username, and doesn't realize it until after authentication fails. The mistakenly typed password may be logged as a username in a "failed login" message.
- Locations of data that can be stolen, or transactional records, which might be the actual objective of the attack.

Confidentiality at the Source

The simplest way to get at log data is to get access to the data where they are generated—at the source of the messages. Excessive permissions or indirect access may allow an attacker to read the log data. The simple example is having the log file be world-readable:

```
#ls -l /var/log/messages
-rw-r--r-- 1 root root 327533 Oct 9 15:25 /var/log/messages
```

While it is easier for unprivileged users to diagnose their own problems if they can read the log file, they may be able to read something they shouldn't—such as system administrator typing her password in place of the username—root.

An example of indirect access is having world-read permissions on the device file for the disk partition on which the log file is stored:

```
# ls -l /dev/hd*
brw-r----- 1 root disk 3, 0 Oct 9 04:45 /dev/had
```

In this case, any user in the group "disk" can read the entire disk. On the particular system from which this example was taken, the only user who is a member of that group is "root."

```
# grep disk /etc/group
disk:x:6:root
```

So that's not so bad. But if another user managed to become a member of this group, they could read anything on the disk (not just log files, mind you, but anything! Shadow file, anyone?).

Reading raw disk data might sound difficult, but can be done with standard Unix tools and a little patience. Here is an example:

```
dd if=/dev/hda2 bs=1M | strings | grep '^[A-Z][a-z][a-z] *[0-9][0-9]*
    [0-9][0-9]:[0-9][0-9]:[0-9][0-9] [^ ]'
```

dd is a simple tool used to transfer data between devices. The arguments specify the input device, and the "block size," which in this situation just tells dd how much data to read at a time. The strings command reads binary input and prints anything that looks like a readable string (a series of printable characters). grep matches input against a regular expression, (for more details see Chapter 8). The pattern provided matches the timestamp found at the beginning of syslog messages. The output looks like this:

```
Sep 5 07:29:00 linux syslogd 1.4.1: restart.
Sep 5 07:29:05 linux kernel: klogd 1.4.1, log source = /proc/kmsg
    started.
Sep 5 07:29:05 linux kernel: Inspecting /boot/System.map-2.6.4-52-
    default
Sep 5 07:29:05 linux kernel: Loaded 23439 symbols from /boot/System.
    map-2.6.4-52-default.
```

which is pretty much just how it looks in the log file.

Now this example may take a while on a large disk partition, but an attacker often has all the time in the world. Plus, more sophisticated tools could do this in a shorter amount of time.

This method not entirely accurate, as it will find any data that looks like a log message, included deleted data. In creating this example, our test script surprised us with:

```
Feb 6 22:45:05 glen kernel: HiSax: Driver for Siemens chip set ISDN
    cards
Feb 6 22:45:05 glen kernel: HiSax: Version 2.1
Feb 6 22:45:05 glen kernel: HiSax: Revisions 1.15/1.10/1.10/1.30/1.8
Feb 6 22:45:05 glen kernel: HiSax: Total 1 card defined
Feb 6 22:45:05 glen kernel: HiSax: Card 1 Protocol EDSS1 Id=HiSax (0)
Feb 6 22:45:05 glen kernel: HiSax: AVM driver Rev. 1.6
```

which turned out to be example log messages in a tutorial on configuring ISDN, which was installed with the operating system.

To prevent this type of attack, verify that permissions on the log files and directories restrict access to privileged users. And make sure that all directories above the log directory are writable only by a privileged user. Otherwise, an attacker can rename directories and files and create files that he can read.

If there are users who need access to the logs, create a separate group (e.g. "logs") and provide group read access. Permissions should also be checked on the disk and partition devices (e.g. /dev/hde*). And make sure that any log rotation program set the proper permissions on files.

Aside from direct access to files, if an attacker can modify the syslog configuration file, she could make a second copy of the logs in an alternate location, or forward the logs to another host. Normally the configuration file is not world writeable by default, and you should keep it that way. In fact, there is rarely a reason to have any regular file world writeable. Of course, an attacker with root privileges could still modify the file, but an attacker with root privileges can do just about anything, so at that point you probably have much worse problems to think about than log files.

Some people recommend keeping the configuration file in an alternate location so that it is not so obvious where the logs are. Also, automated rootkits which try and modify the file, using the default location, would fail to do so. A rootkit is a packaged set of intruder tools, which often are designed to automatically erase tracks and install backdoors. Whether or not it is worth the trouble to obfuscate the location of the log files is up to you.

Confidentiality in Transit

If you are forwarding log data to a central loghost, an attacker with access to the network path between the source and the loghost could intercept the data while in transit. This type of attack can be done at either endpoint, with access to the network device on either host, or by "sniffing" (intercepting traffic) on any one of the network segments between the two hosts. Intercepting network traffic is not as hard as it may sound to some. Here is a simple example of sniffing syslog traffic using tcpdump:

```
# tcpdump -s 1600 -w syslog-dump.dmp src host 172.16.90.128 and proto
    UDP and port 514
```

This line collects all User Datagram Protocol UDP packets on port 514 (the syslog port) from the host 172.16.90.128, and writes them to the file syslog-dump.dmp. To view the results, use tcpdump again:

```
# tcpdump -r syslog-dump.dmp source -X -v
```

the result looks like this:

```
12:02:29.402842 anton.syslog > anotherbox.syslog: [udp sum ok] udp 36
    (ttl 128, id 47609, len 64)
0x0000 4500 0040 b9f9 0000 8011 5fdd ac10 5a80  E..@......_...Z.
0x0010 ac10 6e35 0202 0202 002c a5c3 3c31 3839  ..n5.......,..<189
0x0020 3e73 7973 6c6f 673a 206b 6c6f 6764 2073  >syslog:.klogd.s
0x0030 7461 7274 7570 2073 7563 6365 6564 6564  tartup.succeeded
```

Not quite as easy to read as viewing the log file, but readable enough for an attacker. Strings that we cover in this chapter can also help make tcpdump data more readable. Furthermore, the tool plog (discussed in Chapter 6 on covert logging) convert this data back into syslog formatted records.

At this point, someone usually says "we have a switched network, an attacker can't sniff traffic on our network…" Switches can often leak traffic. Some low-end switches are not truly switched on all ports; groups of ports may share the same traffic. And, some switches can be turned into hubs by overflowing their MAC tables.

So don't rely on your network electronics to keep data confidential, it wasn't designed to do it.

There are a variety of methods to mitigate network interception of log data, all based on encryption of log data in transit. The syslog-reliable RFC provides for encryption of the log data stream, provided you are using syslog clients and servers that support the RFC. We discuss the RFC and clients in Chapter 3. syslog-ng allows you to encrypt log data with PGP or crypt or any other method you like (and there's always rot13:)).

That approach is covered in Chapter 5 on syslog-ng. Or, if you are using a TCP-based log transport, traffic can be tunneled over SSL using sslwra, stunnel, or using an SSH tunnel.

Remember, an attacker in control of one of the endpoints (source or loghost) may be able to intercept the log data before it is encrypted, or can intercept the encryption key. Use of a public-key encryption method, such as the PGP example we presented, can mitigate the latter attack by not having the private key stored on either the source or the loghost (the private key only needs to be available where the data is encrypted, not where it is decrypted).

Of course, if you believe you are in good control of the network between the client and the loghost, you may choose not to worry about interception of log traffic. It's a matter of your own judgment and risk analysis.

Confidentiality at the loghost
All of the issues with protecting data confidentiality at the source () apply to the loghost. Additionally, since the loghost should normally be used only for collecting and possibly examining log data, you can restrict the accounts on the loghost to only those users who need access to the log data or to administer the loghost.

For some environments, a stealth loghost may be desirable. A stealth loghost is not visible from network, but hosts on that network can still forward their logs to it. See Chapter 6 for details.

Confidentiality at the Log Store
Databases where logs are stored are another vector for confidentiality attacks. The same issues as for protecting a loghost apply. Additionally, an attacker with a database username and password may be able to connect to the database and query data, or intercept the transactions between the loghost and the database server in transit.

The database server should be considered as critical as the loghost, and protected in the same manner. Connections to the database should be restricted to the loghost and to any systems used for log analysis. The same connections should be encrypted to avoid interception. And access rules for database users should be limited so that only authorized users can query the data.

There are many ways to get logs in a database. All databases support direct network connections, with varying levels of authentication. Another method of getting logs into a database is to "pull" the data from the loghost to the database server using a file transfer mechanism, and then load the data into the database from the local file.

Most databases provide some means of controlling access to the database, both by host and by user. mysql used the same mechanism for both, using the GRANT statement:

```
mysql> GRANT ALL PRIVILEGES ON db.* TO
    someuser@'10.1.2.0/255.255.255.0';
```

This statement allows the user "someuser" to connect to any database from any host on the 10.1.2.0 network, and do anything they want. You probably want to make the privileges even more restrictive, limiting the ability to make changes to just a user on the loghost, and only allow read privileges to others:

```
mysql> GRANT INSERT, UPDATE PRIVILEGES ON logdb TO
logwriter@loghost.example.com;
mysql> GRANT SELECT PRIVILEGES ON logdb TO logreader@analsysis-station.
    example.com;
```

This example allows one user, logwriter, to write to the database, and only from the loghost. Another user, logreader, is only allowed to query the database, but not to make changes, and only from the log analysis station. Note that the logwriter user can't query the data, only insert and change data.

Postgresql has similar access controls, but they are implemented in a different manner. Access controls for hosts and users are put in text file called pg_hba. conf. Implementing the same access controls as in the previous mysql example, we would put the following in pg_hba.conf:

```
hostssl logdb logwriter 192.168.3.2/32 password
hostssl logdb logreader 192.168.3.5/32 password
```

where 192.168.3.2 is the IP address of the loghost, and 192.168.3.5 is the address of the analysis system. Note also that we chose an access method which uses SSL to encrypt the data stream. Then, the SQL GRANT command is used to control what each user can do with the database:

```
admin=> GRANT INSERT, UPDATE logdb TO logwriter;
admin=> GRANT SELECT logdb TO logreader;
```

And Oracle has yet another mechanism for providing similar access.

The advantage of the "pull" method is that the database doesn't have to allow any network connection, eliminating one vector of attack on the database.

As we mentioned, if you don't want to deal with managing database access controls, you can pull the data to the database server and then load it locally.

For example, the "rsync" command, using SSH as a transport, can be used like this:

```
# export RSYNC_RSH = /usr/bin/ssh
# rsync -avz logwriter@loghost.example.com:/var/log/* /var/log/store/
   remotehost1
```

This will copy any files which haven't previously been copied from /var/log on the loghost. You still have to decide whether or not to allow read access for the analysis station, but at least do not have to grant write permissions over the network. Some might consider this "pull" method to be more secure, in that one cannot directly attack the database server over the network.

Confidentiality at Analysis

Analysis systems need access to log data, and therefore are also a point of attack for gaining access to log data, in addition to information on how the logs are being analyzed. As with databases and loghosts, the analysis station should be protected by limiting access to only those who work with the tools, verifying file permissions, and encrypting traffic.

And of course, an attacker could shoulder-surf the security analyst while looking at log data, which is another type of confidentiality attack altogether. And is one to which we don't have a technical solution.

Attacks on Integrity

An attack on log integrity is the ability to corrupt real data by overwriting or inserting false data, or deleting data. An attacker often corrupts data in order to hide evidence of his activity. The most common approach is simply deleting the data in question. A more-clever attacker might delete just the log message that indicates his activity on the system, or simply modify messages so that they appear benign and do not attract attention. An inside attacker might even wish to alter logs in order to "frame" another or to give the appearance that someone else is doing something wrong.

Either type of attacker may want to create a distraction by inserting bogus messages which indicate some other activity is occurring, perhaps which might cause one to overlook the attacker's activity. For example, an attacker might insert bogus error messages to keep the system administrator busy tracking down non-existent issues. Another technique is to show bogus attacks from another host on the same network.

And if log data is to be used for evidentiary purposes, being able to assert the integrity of the log data may have an impact on whether the logs are acceptable as evidence. An attacker who can show that the logs were not safe from corruption can claim that the logs have been forged and aren't evidence of their malfeasance.

Integrity at the Source

Similar to the confidentiality issues that we already explored, improper permissions can allow an attacker to directly modify log data as it is stored.

For example, say a user "anton" on a system is doing something nefarious, and doesn't want the activity to be connected to him. If anton can modify the log files where they are stored, he could replace all instances of "anton" in the logs with "marcus," shifting the blame for the activity onto someone else. This can be easily done like this:

```
% sed 's/anton/marcus/g' < /var/log/logfile > /var/log/logfile.x; /bin/
    mv /var/log/logfile.x /var/log/logfile
```

(and for the pedantic, the syslog daemon would have to be sent a SIGHUP to cause it to start writing to the new log file).

The same approach should be taken to verify permissions on the log data, devices, configuration file, etc. as we talked about in the confidentiality section.

Additionally, having logs forward to a central loghost, while not preventing this attack, creates another set of logs which would have to be modified for the attacker to be effective in hiding his tracks. Multiple sets of logs and multiple sources of log information make it easier to detect an attackers activity, even when some of the log files have been modified. Multiple sources of data are also useful for non-repudiation, when the accused attacker claims "it wasn't me, it was someone else!" "Hackers," when they are caught, often try to make the argument that it was someone else who did the attack. Having logs from multiple sources sometimes goes a long way towards proving the case. Similar attacks—modifying or deleting logs—can also be done on Windows systems and not only on Unix; other platform can be affected as well.

Against the event log, the attack is slightly more difficult as the file is a binary format. One needs a tool to read and write the file, which is just a small matter of programming. And the formats of the files are well enough documented as to make it very simple to write such a tool. By the way, newer Windows variants such as Windows 2008 and Windows 7 make this more difficult.

On Unix systems which support extended attributes, log files can be set to append-only to prevent regular users from overwriting the file. A user with root privileges, of course, can reset this attribute (see comment about intruders having root privileges). But append-only files prevent ordinary users from modifying the data, even with write privileges to the files. And, it even takes root an extra step to make the files writable again, and prevents something or someone from "accidentally" overwriting a file.

Generating bogus log messages is a difficult issue to mitigate. It is rather trivial to do create the messages, for example one can easily use the logger program.

Here is an authentic syslog message from a Linux system:

```
Nov 11 22:41:00 ns1 named[765]: sysquery: findns error (NXDOMAIN) on
    ns2.example.edu?
```

Using `logger`, a standard tool on many Unix and Linux systems, a bogus message is created matching the original:

```
$ logger -t "named[765]" "sysquery: findns error (NXDOMAIN) on ns2.dac.
    net?"
```

The resulting bogus message looks like this:

```
Nov 11 22:45:51 ns1 named[765]: sysquery: findns error (NXDOMAIN) on
    ns2.dac.net?
```

Due to the nature of the syslog mechanism, it is very difficult to protect against this kind of attack. One could remove the logger program from the system, but the attacker can easily bring her own copy.

In fact, it might be possible to create a restricted logger program. This would involve changing the permissions on the logging socket (usually `/dev/log`) to remove world write permissions. Of course there are applications which log data which are not run as root which would not be able to write to the log device. A group for accessing the log device, e.g. log can be created, the log device group ownership changed to log, and those applications that run as daemons under a role account[1] can be added to the log group. We haven't actually tried this, though.

Applications run by regular users would not be able to log however. Possibly a wrapper for logger could be built, which would run setgid logs, and would insert a real process name, and possibly username, into the log message.

Finally, attacks against log timing can be seen as a special, but damaging kind of attacks against integrity.

Integrity in Transit

Standard Unix syslog messages are transported over UDP. There is no authentication of IP addresses in UDP packet headers, so there is no way to know if they are from the actual host they claim to be from. And, the syslog transport is

---

[1] A role account is one created specifically for the purpose of running a specific daemon.

unidirectional; the server does not send any acknowledgment to the client. And since packets received by the server are accepted as coming from the apparent sender, an attacker with access to the network can inject forged syslog messages which appear to be coming from legitimate hosts on the network.

There are many programs for generating arbitrary network packets, most based on libnet. Packit is one example of such a tool. Note that packit itself is not a syslog-generation tool, it is described by its author as a "network auditing tool." Here is an example of generating a fake syslog message using packit:

```
packit -t UDP -d 172.16.110.53 -s 172.16.90.128 -D 514 -S 514 -vvv -p
    '0x 3c 31 38 39 3e 73 79 73 6c 6f 67 3a 20 6b 6c 6f 67 64 20 73 74
    61 72 74 75 70 20 73 75 63 63 65 65 64 65 64'
```

This command creates a UDP packet to be sent to the IP address 172.16.110.53 on port 514, appearing to come from the address 172.16.90.128. with the contents "syslog: klogd startup succeeded." (the numbers you see in the example are the hexadecimal codes for the characters in the message string. This message might be used to make the system administrator think that a system had suddenly rebooted.

An attacker with access to a network segment between the source and destination can intercept and modify IP traffic ("hijack the session") using an ARP-spoofing man-in-the-middle attack. The best defense against all of these network-based attacks is to use a mechanism which verifies message integrity. The syslog-sign protocol provides this mechanism. Another option is using Secure Sockets Layer (SSL) or even Internet Protocol Security (IPSEC).

If those message integrity mechanisms are not feasible on your network, you can mitigate the attacks by implementing appropriate anti-spoofing filters on network borders,[2] and restricting which hosts the loghost will accept messages from.

ARP-spoofing can be prevented by forcing an entry for the loghost on each of the log sources (and vice versa if you want to be thorough). This can be done with the arp command on Unix:

```
# arp -s loghost.example.com AA:BB:CC:DD:EE:FF
```

which creates an arp table entry for loghost.example.com with MAC address aa:bb:cc:dd:ee:ff. You can view the status of your arp cache with:

```
# arp -a" fw.example.com (10.0.0.1) at 00:10:4B:26:46:A0 [ether] on
    eth0 loghost.example.com (10.0.0.127) at AA:BB:CC:DD:EE:FF [ether]
    PERM on eth0
```

---

[2] Which is something you should do anyways. We recommend both ingress and egress filters, so that an attacker on one network segment can't pretend to be on another network segment or from an external host.

The word "PERM" in the second line indicates that the entry has been permanently added to the arp cache and will not be overwritten.

Of course, manually maintaining arp caches can be a nuisance, and cause confusion when moving hosts around. Additionally, when the source and loghost are on different network segments, one has to maintain static entries for gateways instead of the loghost, all of which creates more complication and potential confusion.

There are some who sidestep the issue of network interception and modification by connecting sources to the loghost via serial lines. A bit harder to attack remotely, but can be costly for sites with multiple locations.

Integrity at the Loghost

Integrity attacks on the loghost are basically the same as the attacks at the source, and the same protection techniques apply. The impact of such attacks, however, is greater than the impact on a single source, as the integrity of *all* data collected by the loghost is at stake.

Integrity on the Database

As with attacks on confidentiality on the database, similar rules apply. Limit the ability of database users to write or append to the log data space. Verify that network access protects authentication credentials, and is secure from session hijacking. The best approach is to use a mechanism that verifies data integrity in addition to access rules.

Database brings two key data protection challenges, dealing with "data in motion" and "data at rest." The former refer to data as it arrives into the database, while the latter refers to data stored in the database. Database security is a huge area of knowledge and we will only briefly touch upon some of the challenges related to protecting the databases with log data.

Data in motion is typically protected by encrypting the connection from the application to the database or by using a "push" log collection method, as we mentioned in this chapter.

The main challenge with encrypting connections is that there is no standard mechanism, such as HTTPS for HTTP+SSL. There is now "SQLS" for transferring SQL commands and data over SS, but it is not widely used.

For example, later versions of MySQL database (www.mysql.com) support native SSL encryption. In the Windows realm, Microsoft SQL Server (MSSQL) can also encrypt connections using SSL5 Oracle 8 and 9 requires "Oracle Advanced Security" (OAS) for SSL support.

The only reliable way to protect the data stored in the data is database encryption. At the time of this writing, few databases natively support encryption and third-party software is required.

Integrity at Analysis

Attacks on analysis integrity seek to undermine confidence in the accuracy of the analysis system. Too many false positives and the system is useless. False negatives undermine the confidence that the system is catching everything.

There are three places at which to attack the integrity of the analysis system:

- the data being processed (the input),
- the tools used for analysis (the system), and
- the presentation of the results (the output).

By modifying the input data, the attacker can cause the system to report on false attacks, or not report on actual attacks. The method used by the analysis system for accessing data should have integrity protection mechanisms. If the method is via a database, the same rules the one for storage access apply. If via a file-server, the transport should be secure from session hijacking and data stream corruption.

Targeting the analysis system itself, an attacker could change the analysis tools so that the system behaves differently than expected. The analysis system should have access restricted to only authorized users, and the software used for analysis should be appropriately protected from modification. Consider separate privileges for those users who use the software versus those who can modify it. Revision control or other software should be implemented for tracking changes made to the software (including configuration files), and the integrity of the software verified regularly.

Finally, the system used to present the data can be altered to change or suppress data from being shown to the analyst. This can be done by altering reports created by the system, creating false reports, or hijacking a session when output data is being reviewed.

The security of the output data should be equal to that of the input data, limiting who has write access and who has access to the system.

The presentation system should also be immune to hijacking of sessions. For instance, if using a Web server for reviewing repots, the transport could use SSL with properly signed certificates, along with password controlled access.

Attacks on Availability

Attacks on availability are aimed at preventing legitimate users from access the data or system. As we already mentioned, a common intruder technique is to delete log files upon gaining access to a system. Some availability attacks are very similar to integrity attacks, and use the same vectors for attack. Others take a different approach, such as causing a system to crash in order to prevent access.

Attacks against availability can be considered a type of denial-of-service attack. And in this case "service" can mean human resources as well as computer resources. Staff time is often the most valuable commodity one has, loss of time can be just as devastating as a network being down.

Availability at the Source

The simplest denial of availability is the deletion of log data at the source.

For example, here is the session capture in the compromised Linux honeypot, run by one of the authors as a part of a Honeynet Research Alliance (http://www.honeynet.org/alliance). These are the commands issued by the attacker after gaining root privileges[3]:

```
# killall syslog
# rm ~/.bash_history
# ln -s ~/.bash_history /dev/null
```

Note that his first command was to kill the syslog daemon, indicating that he wanted to stop from possible remote logging (in addition to stopping all local logging). He deletes root's .bash_history file to destroy the record of any commands he has typed, and symlinks it to /dev/null to prevent further recording of any new commands. The intruder then installed a rootkit, which ran the following:

```
# zap /var/log/messages
```

which overwrites with zeros the relevant data in the file /var/log/messages. Zeroing data, as opposed to deleting it, overwrites the data stored on disk, making it impossible to recover. Simply deleting a file leaves data on disk where it may be recovered with the right tools, as shown in Attacks against Confidentiality.[4]

Many hacker tools are written to "sanitize" login records, which mean covertly removing undesirable, implicating records. Common examples of such tools are zap, clear, and cloak. These tools operate in two distinct ways: they either zero out/replace the binary log records (thus stuffing the file with zero records, which is suspicious) or they erase them (thus making the log file shorter, which is also suspicious). Both methods have shortcomings, and both can be detected.

---

[3] For the curious, The example session was the result of an intruder gaining access to the victim system being compromised via an OpenSSL exploit. The attacker then escalated his privileges to "root" by using local exploit against "ptrace".

[4] In a specific investigation of a compromised system led by one of the authors, log files were recovered by using the standard Linux file systems utilities as well as forensics toolkit TCT (The Coroner Toolkit by Dan Farmer and Wietse Venema, see www.fish.com/forensics or www.porcupine.org/forensics). The detailed account of the investigation can be read in chapter 20 of the book "Security Warrior" (O'Reilly, 2004).

FIGURE 17.1 Windows Logs Deletion Failure

Binary formatted files, such as wtmp and pact, are also candidates for erasure. As one of the authors covered in his previous book there are many tools to "sanitize" the binary files, used on Unix and Windows.

Here's what happens if a Windows XP event log is deleted or purged. Let's assume that the attacker has tried deleting the files `AppEvent.Evt`, `SecEvent.Evt`, and `SysEvent.Evt` in `C:\WINDOWS\system32\config` from the standard Windows Explorer shell.

It doesn't work (see Figure 17.1), since the system protects the files that are in use. The EventViewer application can be used to purge the logs (see Figure 17.2).

However, this case, the security log will not be cleaned "cleanly." An event indicating log cleanup will be generated (see Figure 17.3).

The event log can also be deleted by booting into a separate operating system instance (such as a Linux floppy) or using special tools for log clearing. Two examples of slightly dated but still effective tools are WinZapper (http://www.ntsecurity.nu/toolbox/winzapper/) and ClearLogs (http://www.ntsecurity.nu/toolbox/clearlogs/). In addition, the log records can be forced out of the file by abusing the rotation scheme.

The methods for mitigating attacks which involve deletion of data are exactly the same as for integrity attacks.

As shown in our sample, in addition to deleting local log files, the log daemon can be killed, effectively stopping all logging, including forwarding data to a loghost. Currently versions of "standard" syslog are not susceptible to denial-of-service attacks, but some older versions have been.[5]

TCP-based syslog daemons (e.g. syslog-ng) may be vulnerable to SYN flooding attacks. While some, mostly experimental, technology exists to help prevent

---

[5] For example, "Cisco IOS Syslog Denial-of-Service Vulnerability" (http://www.ciac.org/ciac/bulletins/j-023.shtml) can lead to a syslog daemon collapse.

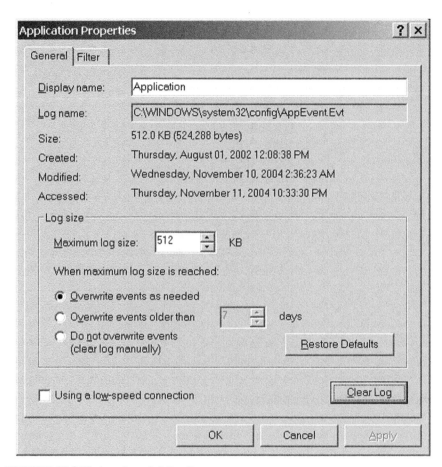

FIGURE 17.2 Windows Logs Deletion Success

such attacks, the simplest approach is to block network access to the log daemon for networks other than the one that it lives on.

Additionally, while it is commonly understood that UDP packets may be dropped on a busy network, we have observed, anecdotally,[6] that such packets may even be dropped on a local network connection (such as "loopback"). An attacker might be able to suppress messages from being recorded by the log daemon by simply flooding the log daemon with bogus traffic. Such an attack can even be conducted on the host itself, by an unprivileged user.

There isn't much in the way of a remedy against local flooding attacks. However, by base lining activity from your systems, and looking for unusual amounts of

---

[6] *Meaning:* We think we have seen it happen, but haven't measured accurately enough to be sure.

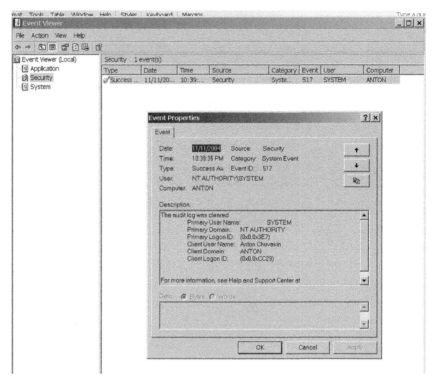

FIGURE 17.3 Windows Logs Deletion Event

log messages, you may be able to detect a flooding attack as it's happening. A similar approach could be used to detect a crashed log server, by looking for a lack of messages from a host.

Another method of suppressing local logging is by filling the disk partition on which the logs are stored. This can be done by flooding the logs, or if the attacker has another method of write access to the partition. Verify that users cannot write to the partition that the logs live on.

An interestingly indirect way of destroying log data is by taking advantage of the log rotation system. Log rotation is used to protect the logging server from overflowing and also for organizing archive log files. Log rotation means simply stashing away the old log file (possibly compressing and/or moving to another location) and switching the logging to a new file. It is done on both Unix and Windows systems.

If an attacker knows that logs are being rotated when they reach a particular size, she may able to destroy evidence of her activity by generating log messages to cause enough rotation to occur to delete the evidence of her activity.

Windows rotates logs based on size, and the default settings are to keep only a small amount, overwriting the old entries when the log file becomes full (see Figure 17.2). It is fairly easy to produce more log records in order to supplant incriminating log messages.

The approaches to mitigating against rotational abuse are just to have enough disk space and a large enough rotation capacity so that you can detect such an abuse before the attacker can fill up the log files.

Availability in Transit

As already mentioned, the standard syslog transport mechanism uses UDP, commonly called an "unreliable" transport. Heavy network traffic can result in UDP packets being dropped between the source and the loghost. An attacker could try to hide his tracks by flooding the network with traffic, causing the traffic he doesn't want you to see to be dropped.

The network does not have to be flooded with log traffic, or even traffic for an actual host on the network. A nifty way for an attacker to stay "under the radar" is to flood the network with completely bogus traffic, either to unused ports on existing hosts, or nonexistent hosts on the network, or on another network. The traffic won't show up as connections on hosts or in any other way that is obvious, short of monitoring utilization statistics on network devices.

One of the simplest ways to flood a network that can easily go unnoticed is by "ping flooding." Many versions of the ping program have an option (usually "-f") which tells the program to put out packets at a rate of at least 100 packets per second, up to the speed that the host being pinged is able to respond. Ping flooding a host on the same network segment as the loghost will probably cause packets to the loghost to be dropped, with no indication on the loghost that there is a problem. In fact, the only indication of anything out of the ordinary would be traffic counters on the router or switch showing dropped packets and a large amount of Internet Control Message Protocol (ICMP) traffic.

Here is an example ping command run against a loghost:

```
# ping -f loghost
```

Notice that only root user on a Unix system can run ping with such option. Here is what happens if a non-root user tries to run it on a Linux system:

```
# ping -f loghost
ping: Operation not permitted
```

Network flooding is difficult to mitigate. How do you differentiate between legitimate traffic and bogus traffic? How can you tell if a burst of network traffic isn't just because business got really good? About the only thing you can do is monitor traffic statistics and look for things that are "unusual" (see Chapter 11).

Availability at the Loghost

Along with flooding the network, the loghost can be flooded, either with false log data, or just bogus traffic. Flooding the loghost with false log traffic can have two effects. First, it can cause legitimate traffic to be dropped either by the network or by the kernel on the loghost. Additionally, the log data can fill up the log file partition, forcing the loghost to stop logging any data. (Sometimes this happens just to do system failure on a host).

Here is an example shell script that can be used to flood the loghost from a client machine that normally forwards the logs to that loghost:

```
i=0
while: do
 i=$i+1
 logger -p "Flooding $i"
done
```

The use of the incrementing variable is to prevent the syslog daemon from aggregating the messages with "last messages repeated X times."

Not flooding fast enough for you? Run several of these in the background at the same time.

This example is useful for flooding the local logs in addition to the remote loghost.

A TCP-based syslog daemon protects you from packet loss, but can be subject to SYN flooding, which can crash the server, or at least cause it to refuse to accept additional connections, just like one can choke all other TCP-based services. The same measures used to protect the loghost from integrity attacks apply here.

In addition, the loghost is subject to the same sorts of denial-of-service attacks as the log source is, and the same protective measures apply.

Finally, databases are subject to similar types of attacks as the loghost—network flooding, SYN floods, exploits to crash the database, and deletion of stored files. The same recommendations as for integrity attacks apply here.

Availability at Analysis

In addition to disabling an analysis system, it can be bogged down by overwhelming it with data to be analyzed. Effective data reduction techniques can help mitigate this.

An interesting, and often overlooked, attack on availability is on the availability of the analyst. An attacker may escape notice simply by executing enough different attacks, or injecting data to make it look like attacks are happening, in order to overwhelm the security analyst, or make her spend time looking at other activity which appears more serious.

And an analysis system which has too many "false alarms" will quickly be considered useless and discarded. The famous examples of such attack were alert flooding tools such as stick, sneeze, and snot, that caused problems for early intrusion detection systems. In addition to straining the system running the intrusion detection software, the alert flooding tools generated so many alerts that the personnel watching the system were left dazed and confused.

Log event collection and analysis need to be organized in a way to minimize an ability of outsiders to inject forged data. Usually, cryptography helps to solve the problem. At the very least, it will solve the data forging problem in transmission from the source to the collection point. For example, replacing UDP-based syslog with reliable syslog tunneled via SSL, SSH, or IPSec will prevent the attackers from injecting data in the collection point.

Source authentication, also supported by some of the mechanisms, will, in addition, prevent an attacker from bringing a fake source of logging online and using it to flood the systems, overwhelming the technological components as well as the analyst.

ATTACK CASE STUDY

In this section, we will describe a fictitious company and how it fared during a server intrusion, followed by an attack on their logging infrastructure.

"Rats R Us" is a global leader in end-to-end rat management for business and consumers. It offers a broad range of products and services for rat management, including rat threat prevention, rat extermination, rat-related incident cleanup as well as raising rats for various purposes, training rats, and creating custom genetically modified rats for commercial clients and government. It offers its services and products direct through its Web site, printed catalogues, and through the network of resellers and partners (combined under "RatOne" partner program).

The company's central office houses several hundred people, including the entire IT staff. The rest of the personnel are spread through regional sales offices and rat spawning facilities. The datacenter is also located in the same building as the central office.

The corporate Web site provides a significant part of the company revenue, so "Rats R Us" has invested in IT security resources. A Demilitarized Zone (DMZ) architecture with two firewalls protects publicly available servers (Web, Email, etc.) and separates them from both internal systems and the Internet. An e-commerce application server, the heart of the web-based rat trading system, is connected to a Web server and is separated with an additional firewall. An intrusion prevention system is sitting behind the external firewall and is supposed to prevent the attacks against the DMZ assets.

One sunny day of May 2009, the intrusion prevention system started generating a huge amount of alerts related to the IRC (Internet Relay Chat) program used on the company network. The IDS was configured not to block such activity automatically when detected as IRC traffic could be legitimate activity. The admin viewing the daily activity reports noticed that 90% of all logged activity was related to IRC communication to multiple IRC servers around the world. He reasoned that one of their systems was compromised and it had to be located in the DMZ, since internal systems did not have a direct link to the Internet. By looking at the IRC messages sources, the admin located one suspect Unix system in the DMZ—a mail server.

Since the machine was obviously compromised, the decision was made to take it offline for investigation and recovery. It was promptly disconnected from a network but kept powered on.[7] When the incident response team looked at the system, they noticed that an unknown process was running with "root" privileges, a pretty good sign of a compromise (see Issues Discovering Compromised Machines for example) So they knew the host was compromised, but did not know how.

The response team tried looking at the logs on the host, and found that they had been erased. The logs files were in place but no content had been recorded for the previous seven days. Old logs were still in place (rotated and compressed by the log rotation script). The old logs provided no insight into the compromise. The server had been configured for remote logging, so the team went to look at the logs on the loghost.

The team was shocked to learn that the syslog server system had no logs for the same time period (seven days) from any of the servers that were supposed to be sending data to it. In fact, they discovered that the syslog daemon was not even running on the loghost. So not only had a host on the DMZ been compromised, but the central loghost had been DoSed, if not compromised.

A network intrusion detection system had been watching the communication between external systems and the DMZ machines, but had not picked up any exploits. The logs on the network IDS (NIDS) contained normal day-to-day noise but no attack activity. Unfortunately, the NIDS was not looking at internal-to-internal communication.

The team tried looking at external connectivity logs on the firewall. They discovered that the company had not configured aggressive logging on their firewall, and were not logging allowed connections, as allowed connections were automatically considered legitimate activity and therefore didn't need to be logged. In fact, the reality was quite the opposite: blocked traffic only showed that the firewall was doing its job—the accepted traffic were the vectors for attack.

So, the next thing the team did was to try and recover the deleted logs. Pulling out their expensive forensic tools, they proceeded to spend hours imaging hard drives and searching for log data. They eventually discovered that the logs had not only been deleted, but had been over-written with zeros.

Not having much evidence to go on, the team hypothesized that the intruder had used a "zero-day" exploit to gain access to the log server. The exploit left telltale traces in the log files, so the intruder had erased the logs to avoid giving away clues as to how the exploit worked. But all they could do was guess, for lack of actual evidence.

The loghost was rebuilt and verified that it was fully patched. Logging levels were increased, and an "intrusion prevention system" deployed on the loghost in the hopes that it might block

---

[7] This decision is always tough on a compromised or infected machine: light off or light on? There are compelling reasons for both approaches.

a new exploit. However, not without much information on how the loghost was compromised, Rats R Us was still probably vulnerable to the same exploit that got them in the first place.

What might the company do to better protect the loghost, or at least preserve log information? They could archive log data to some sort of write-once medium or append-only file, which would not prevent intrusion, but improve the chance of preserving log data up through the time of the intrusion.

The loghost could be configured as a stealth loghost, with login access only from its console, so that remote attack would be difficult, if not impossible.[8] Of course, that makes administration of the loghost a log more difficult, but if the log data is valuable enough, it might be worth it.

If not a stealth loghost, the loghost could be a different OS from the other hosts on the network, in the hopes that heterogeneity will protect against attacks that work on the other hosts.

All of these solutions have their ups and downs. In your environment, do the best that you can. Protect against the obvious things that are usually pretty easy to do, such as check file permissions. Do additional things as you have the resources for, and are merited by the requirements for your site.

SUMMARY

This chapter should have given a good foundation on which to understand what the common attacks are against logging systems. We also provided you with examples on confidentiality, integrity, and other concepts as they apply to log systems.

REFERENCES

For brief intro on SYN flooding, see this old CERT advisory. <http://www.cert.org/advisories/CA-1996-21.html>.

libnet. <http://www.packetfactory.net/libnet/>.

Packit. <http://packit.sourceforge.net>.

Peikari, Cyrus, and Anton Chuvakin. *Security Warrior.* Beijing: O'Reilly & Associates, 2004. Print.

<http://www.eurocompton.net/stick/projects8.html>, <http://www.securiteam.com/tools/5DP0T0AB5G.html>, <http://www.securityfocus.com/tools/113> (see this article "Issues Discovering Compromised Machines" at <http://www.securityfocus.com/infocus/1808> for reference for compromise detection hints).

---

[8] It's pretty darned hard to remotely compromise a host that doesn't transmit packets on the network, but we know better than to use the term "impossible." Did someone say "Titanic?"

Logging for Programmers

INTRODUCTION

Are you a programmer? Have you ever had the support staff come to your desk and ask why your application isn't working right? It is often the case that programmers either don't provide enough information in log messages or provide too much information. The trick is to understand how to balance providing enough information in your logs with security and performance considerations. Additionally, the log messages your software generates might be collected by log collection and analysis tools. This means the parse-ability of your logs is also a consideration which needs to be understood and considered. The concepts presented in this chapter can be applied to any language and environment and can be considered best practices.

ROLES AND RESPONSIBILITIES

Before we dive into the details on logging techniques of programmers, it is important to understand the common roles and responsibilities as they are related to software development and programing. The roles presented in this section are the more common ones; your organization's actual roles may differ. Table 18.1 outlines the common roles and responsibilities.

Separation of duties is a security principle that is needed to provide protection to the production environment. However, it is important to note that in some cases,

Table 18.1 Summary of Internal Roles and Responsibilities (Chuvakin, 2011)

Role	Responsibility
Business/Product Owner	The individual or group who has responsibility for a product, feature set, application, etc.
Security Team	Develop logging standard for internally developed software; Involve business owners in the process
IT/Development Managers	Enforce logging standard as a "must have" feature
IT Support Team	Support production applications; Read log files when applications are misbehaving, etc.
Software Architects	"Get" the value of logging and understand audit vs. debug logging
Software developers/Programmers	Follow the logging standard by using libraries, APIs, and logging features

the software developer is also the architect, who is also the IT support person. This typically happens in smaller organizations. This is not ideal, but it does happen. It's not ideal because when a person wears several different hats, the lines become blurred and judgment and good process can go the way of the dodo bird.

Another reason that separation of duties is critical surrounds regulatory compliance. Various regulatory bodies dictate that software developers cannot have write access to production systems. In some cases, developers cannot have any access to production systems. So how would a developer help troubleshoot a problem in production? There are several avenues for this:

1. The developer shoulder-surfs with the production support staff and provides guidance to the operator.
2. Screen control (like Cisco's Web-ex, Microsoft's Office Communicator, etc.) can be used where the developer is given temporary view and control of the production system, from the perspective of the support staff member's terminal.
3. A security exception can be granted. This is typically allowed if it is documented properly. The gist is that the developer is given temporary access to the system for a short period of time, e.g. 30 min, 1 h, etc.

Make sure you understand what your development staff can and can't do in the context of regulatory compliance. See Chapter 19 for more information.

You may have noticed that these roles are internally facing and do not reflect roles, outside of your organization. Table 18.2 summarizes the common roles and responsibilities found outside of an organization, typically found in commercial and open source organizations.

Table 18.2 Summary of External Roles and Responsibilities Chuvakin (2011)

Role	Responsibility
Commercial software vendors	Develop and then adopt log standards
Open source community	Create logging APIs, libraries, etc. and then use them to gain popularity and adoption
Log analysis vendors	Encourage logging standardization and utilize the standards for consuming the data and representing it inside the products

LOGGING FOR PROGRAMMERS

This section assumes you are a novice to program logging. If you are already somewhat versed in the concepts surrounding logging, you can safely skip this section.

Now, let's briefly look at common reasons why programmers should take care when it comes to logging.

- Programmers are the ultimate source of log messages. It is up to you to ensure your programs are generating great logs that have value and are useful. Well-formed and timely log messages can aid in debugging, more diagnostics gathering, and aid the programmer in understanding what the program is actually doing.
- When the proper information is provided in a log message, it can aid in detecting malicious behavior.

These are just a few of the compelling reasons to care about logging. We are now beginning to get a picture of why logging for programmers is so critical. But as a programmer, what are the mechanics behind logging? Let's look at the high-level steps in the process.

1. The programmer writes the application, decides what to log messages to add to the code.
2. The list of what to log should be reviewed, at the very least, with the IT support staff in order to get their input. A second reason to involve them is so you will be able to understand their requirements from a monitoring standpoint. They may have special requirements that you are not aware of.
3. The programmer writes code that actually makes function or method calls which facilitate the act of logging. The devil is in the details:

    a. Typically there is a configuration file which drives where the logs are written. This includes, local disk, remote disk (network file system (NFS), etc.) Syslog, and so on.

    b. Log rotation schemes are also considered (more on this in a subsequent section).

4. The logs are then used for debugging, analysis, and so on.

That's the process at a high level. But what sort of things should be logged? We explore this in the next section.

What Should Be Logged?

Before discussing this topic, it will be good to understand what makes a log useful. A log message should tell what happened and why it happened. Recall from Chapter 2 the concept of the five W's of Logging. Let's go over them again real quick.

- Who was involved?
- What happened?
- Where did it happen?
- When did it happen?
- Why did it happen?
- How did it happen?

What do you notice, besides the fact that there are actually six items, and the sixth one starts with an "H"? When these are applied to logging, it is easy to see that the five W's have all the components necessary to help understand what happened and why. Generalizing things a bit, with an eye toward the five W's, a useful log should include *state* and *context*. State would be any sort of program information contained in variables, return values, stack information, and so on. Context is the supporting information which helps to describe why the log message is being written in the first place.

Table 18.3 provides basic guidelines for the types of log messages that should be logged.

Table 18.3 is a good rule-of-thumb reference list. This is a good base set of types to always make sure you are logging. Your specific needs will vary from what is listed above, but knowing the basic log types is half the battle.

WARNING

Logging State Information

There are some security ramifications with respect to logging certain information in log files. See the Security Considerations section later in the chapter for more information on this topic.

Table 18.3 Basic Guidelines of Log Types

What Should be Logged	Description
AAA (Authentication, Authorization, Access)	Successful and failed authentication or authorization decisions; System access, data access, and application component access; and Remote access, including from one application component to another in a distributed environment
Change Events	System or application changes (especially privilege changes); Data changes (including creation and destruction); and Application and component installation and changes
"Badness"/Threats	Invalid inputs and other likely application abuses; and Other security issues known to affect the application
Resource Issues	Exhausted resources, exceeded capacities, and so on; Connectivity issues and problems; and Reached limits
Mixed Availability Issues	Startups and shutdowns of systems, applications, and application modules or components; Faults and errors, especially errors affecting the application's availability; and Backup successes and failures that affect availability

Logging APIs for Programmers

It is beyond the scope of this chapter to provide deep details on any one logging API. Instead, a list of commonly used APIs is outlined in Table 18.4.

Let's take a brief example. Logback is a popular logging API for Java. You can control its logging behavior with configuration files, which is the actual idea. The following is a sample Logback configuration file Logback Manual:

```
<configuration>
   <appender name="STDOUT" class="ch.qos.logback.core.
    ConsoleAppender">
     <!-- encoders are assigned the type ch.qos.logback.classic.
          encoder.PatternLayoutEncoder by default -->
   <encoder>
     <pattern>
     %d{HH:mm:ss.SSS} [%thread]%-5level%logger{36} -%msg%n
</pattern>
     </encoder>
   </appender>
   <root level="debug">
     <appender-ref ref="STDOUT" />
   </root>
</configuration>
```

Table 18.4 Summary of Common Logging Libraries by Language

Language	Library
Java	Log4j (http://logging.apache.org/log4j/)
	Logback (http://logback.qos.ch/)
Perl	Log4Perl (http://mschilli.github.com/log4perl/)
C/C++	Log4C (http://log4c.sourceforge.net/)
Unix / Shell	Logger (man logger)

This sample will log to standard out (STDOUT) and is the simplest of examples. The format of a log message generated from an application using the library, with the above configuration, will look like the following:

```
17:44:58.828 [main] INFO chapters.configuration.MyApp2 - Entering
    application.
```

This line in the configuration drives the formatting:

```
%d{HH:mm:ss.SSS} [%thread]%-5level%logger{36} -%msg%n
```

Let's take a look at each parameter in turn:

- `%d{HH:mm:ss.SSS}`:%d outputs the date of the logged event. The left-and-right curly braces tell Logback accept ISO 8601 date formatting.
- `[%thread]`: The left-and-right brackets are literal strings, meaning they will be seen in the log message. %thread will print the thread name (if set) or the method from which the logging message was called.
- `%-5level`: Emit the logging level and left justify it with a minimum width of 5 and no maximum width.
- `%logger{36}`: This parameter prints the logger, up to 36 characters. The logger in this case is the application itself.
- `%msg%n`: %msg is the raw log message that is supplied to the logging call (by the programmer). %n is the platform-dependent line separator character or characters.

The configuration is very readable, which is a key advantage to using an API like Logback. Another nice feature of Logback is you can configure it to notice when changes are made to the configuration file. This is useful because you don't have to stop and restart the application. First, the API detects the change, then loads the changes into the file, and starts using and alteration automatically within the running application. This feature is accomplished with the use of the scan parameter in the configuration block:

```
<configuration scan="true">
…
</configuration>
```

The default scan period is 1 min. This can come in very handy when you want to change the format of your log messages. All you have to do is edit the file, make the change, and save it. The Logback infrastructure takes care of the rest. You have just made a change "on the fly" without needing to recompile the code or restart your application.

For full detail on Logback, please see Logback Manual for more detail.

Log Rotation

It is worth discussing log rotation for a moment. While it is typically not the responsibility of the programmer to worry about log rotation, it is good if you have an understanding of what it is. First off, there are two basic types of log rotation mechanisms:

1. Log rotation scripts are used to manage when logs are rotated and archived off to some external storage location.
2. The application itself handles log rotation duties, which can either be handled by custom-written application code or by using built-in features of a third-party logging library.

However, what *is* log rotation? Log file rotation is a scheme whereby an active log file is moved to an archive copy, and a new, empty file is created for an application to begin writing to. This technique is valuable when multiple copies of a log file are kept around for short-term analysis and/or offsite archival and storage. From the application's standpoint, it doesn't know that log rotation has occurred.

There are several log rotation schemes, which can be employed:

- time based: A log file is rotated based on some time period, e.g. hourly, daily, weekly, etc.
- size based: A log file is rotated when it reaches some predefined sized, e.g. 10 MB, 100 MB, etc.
- size and Time based: This scheme combines both time-and size-based schemes. The log file is archived based on time but each log file is also capped at some predefined size.

Let's briefly look at a Logback configuration for time—and size-based rotation:

```
<configuration>
    <appender name="ROLLING" class="ch.qos.logback.core.rolling.
    RollingFileAppender">
```

```
<file>mylog.txt</file>
<rollingPolicy class="ch.qos.logback.core.rolling.
  TimeBasedRollingPolicy">
   <!-- rollover daily -->
   <fileNamePattern>mylog-%d{yyyy-MM-dd}.%i.txt</fileNamePattern>
   <timeBasedFileNamingAndTriggeringPolicy
         class="ch.qos.logback.core.rolling.
            SizeAndTimeBasedFNATP">
      <!-- or whenever the file size reaches 100MB -->
      <maxFileSize>100MB</maxFileSize>
   </timeBasedFileNamingAndTriggeringPolicy>
</rollingPolicy>
<encoder>
   <pattern>%msg%n</pattern>
</encoder>
</appender>

<root level="DEBUG">
   <appender-ref ref="ROLLING" />
</root>
</configuration>
```

This sample configuration file will rotate the log file each day OR when it reaches 100 MB. This can be a useful technique for applications, which log a high volume of messages. Instead of a log file growing to 1 GB before it's rotated, you can have manageable (and easily searchable!) chunks of log data.

Bad Log Messages

A chapter on logging for programmers would not be complete, unless we talk about the bad habits of log messaging. First let's look at some bad log messages Chuvakin, 2010. First we will look at a message that contains a time stamp missing the year:

```
Aug 11 09:11:19 xx null pif ?exit! 0
```

It is also missing time zone information as well as anything meaningful.

Next up we have a message which not only omits the time stamp all together, but it also doesn't include the actual username of the person transitioning to a privilege level:

```
Message 202 User transitioning priv level
```

The use of magic or secret numbers (in this case 202) is very bad. If there is no documentation on what the number means, it shouldn't have been included in the log entry in the first place.

Finally, this little gem is all too common in the world of logging:

```
userenv[error] 1040 XYZCORP\wsupx No description available
```

It is scary how honest the programmer was: she decided to just give up and tell us that there is no description available.

Table 18.5 outlines some common bad habits which you should avoid like the plague.

Log Message Formatting

The best log messages lend themselves to manual and/or automated analysis. A log message is made up of components that when taken in total allow for greater meaning to be derived. The following list provides a starting point for what to include in a useful log entry:

- The *username* helps answer "who" for those events relevant to user or administrator activities. In addition, it's helpful to include the name of the identity provider or security realm that vouched for the username, if that information is available.
- The *object* helps answer "what" by indicating the affected system component or the object (such as a user account, data resource, or file).
- The *status* also helps answer "what" by explaining whether the action aimed at the object succeeded or failed. (Other types of status are possible, such as "deferred.")
- The *system, application,* or *component* helps answer "where" and must provide relevant application context, such as the initiator and target systems, applications, or components.
- The *source* helps answer "from where" for messages related to network connectivity or distributed application operation. Source can be in the form of an Internet Protocol (IP) address or hostname. Related components that should be used, depending on your application, are *destination, source port,* and *destination port.*
- The *time stamp* and *time zone* help answer "when." The time zone is essential for distributed applications. In addition to the time stamp and time zone, some high-volume systems use a transaction ID.
- The *reason* helps answer "why," so that log analysis doesn't require much digging for a hidden reason. Remember, the log's customers are the security and audit personnel.
- The *action* helps answer "how" by providing the nature of the event.

Table 18.5 Summary of Logging Bad Habits

Bad Habit	Explanation
Missing time stamp and time zone	Without this information, it makes it hard to know when the log actually occurred, which can hurt investigative procedures, data searching, and so on
Magic or Secret Numbers	Magic or secret numbers appear quite often in log messages. The problem is that many times there is no documentation to back up the number. This not only can lead to misinformation on the log reviewer part, but also to frustration
Vague or no Description	Log entries need to be clear, concise and comprehendible. Vague or missing descriptions not only make it difficult for humans and automated tools to decipher a message, it can waste valuable time when investigating systems outages or potential security issues
No source / Destination IP/ Hostnames and ports	Not all applications are connection-oriented. But for systems that are client-server, source and destination IP and port information needs to be included in the log entry
No unique message identifier	It is important that each log message have a unique identifier. This id is generally an integer value that is monotonically increasing. Having a way to uniquely describe a message has value for searching and other applications on the log message. Many programing languages have predefined routines to generate universal unique identifiers (UUIDs). Having said this, unique message identifiers are typically generated by the system or tool which parses log messages
No unique message type identifier	This differs from a unique id in that this is typically an alphanumeric value which identifies the message as belong to a type or class of messages. One approach to solve this is to concatenate together common parts of a log message

- A *priority* helps indicate the event's importance. However, a uniform scale for rating events by importance is impossible because different organizations will have different priorities. (For example, different companies might have different policies regarding information availability versus confidentiality.)
- A unique *session id* can help with grouping together related messages across multiple threads and processes.

- *Process id* (pid) and *thread id* (tid) are both useful to log in order to be able to correlate a running application with its log records. This is largely useful if your application is writing to a log file that other applications are sharing.
- *Activity measurement* is a component which not all applications will need to log. For example, you would use this if your application acts on behalf of a person or other applications to transfer data from one place to another. This component, when logged, could be used by analysis systems to detect when some attempts to transfer a larger-than-expected batch of data.

Alright, based on this guidance, what might a useful log message look like? Let's consider this hypothetical message:

```
2010/12/31 10:00:01AM GMT+7 priority=3, system=mainserver,
module=authentication, source=127.0.0.1, user=kjschmidt(idp:solar),
action=login, object=database, status=failed, reason="password
   incorrect"
```

We see that this message has many of the components we just discussed. Name/value pairs are used for each component. This common technique uses the equal character to create a name to value mapping. A comma is then used as a delimiter to mark the separation between name/value pairs. Also, you should see there is no ambiguity with respect to how to parse the message. You would first split on the comma which will get you a list of the name/value pairs. You then split on the equal character for each name/value pair which gives you both the name and its value.

To bring things full circle we should inspect the log message against our Five W's to see if it stands up to scrutiny. Let's do that now:

- Who was involved: *kjschmidt*
- What happened: *failed authentication*
- Where did it happen: *database*
- When did it happen: *2010/12/31 10:00:01AM GMT+7*

NOTE

Delimiters

While a comma is commonly used as a delimiter, care needs to be taken. If you anticipate any of the values for your name/value pairs containing commas, it might be wise to choose a different delimiter character. For example, if you have something like `reason="1, 2, 3,"` the commas between the numbers might cause issues with the parsing mechanism.

> **NOTE**
>
> *Unique Message Type Identifier*
> Recall from Table 21.5 that one of the bad habits is "No unique message identifier." If we use the hypothetical log message presented in this section, one way "object-action-status" to give an identifier of "database-login-failed." The goal is to create a unique message identifier that can be used to uniquely identify what happened in this log message. Keep in mind that other log message may have the same unique message identifier, but have differing parameters (like username, system, etc.).

- Why did it happen: *Password incorrect*
- How did it happen: *The user entered a bad password*

As you can see, the format allowed use to easily answer the Five W's questions very easily. This really exemplifies the end goal: clarity in understanding what happened so resolution can take place in a timely manner.

SECURITY CONSIDERATIONS

There are certain things which should never, ever be logged with a log message. Any data that can be used to identify people, financial records, birthdates, and other items like this should not be logged. Basically anything that is personally identifiable information (PII) is off limits. This includes:

- Passwords (database, user, etc.)
- Social Security Numbers
- Birthdates
- Phone Numbers
- Full Names
- Credit Card Numbers
- Driver's License Numbers
- Genetic Information
- Insurance Information
- Any sort of identifying number
- Biometric Information

You get the picture. Some programmers try to be cute and format log messages which look something like this:

```
...Database login failure for user=Bob, password=XXXXXX
```

Why would you log the password parameter just to X it out? This is a waste of time and space. Just resist the temptation to write log messages in this manner.

PERFORMANCE CONSIDERATIONS

By now you should have been asking yourself about how all this logging is going to affect performance of your application. Consider this pseudo-code example that reads records from a database and processes them:

```
While(resultSet) {
    Log("Getting record..\n");
    Record = getRecord();
    Log("About to process record\n");
    processRecord(Record);
    Log("Done processing record\n");
}
```

If we are only processing a few hundred records each time there is a result set from the database, this is no big deal. But what about thousands, tens of thousands or even hundreds of thousands records per result set? What if we are getting this volume of record data every minute? Each time we call the Log() method, it will, effectively, open the log file and write the log message. Now, this doesn't account for if the operating system is buffering the output or not. But let's assume each time we call Log(), it writes directly to the log file. This means that for each record, we write three log messages. This is a lot if you spread it out of hundreds of thousands of records. Instead of logging each operation your program is executing, it is a better idea to have a logging level scheme in place.

Most logging APIs allow you to specify a logging level along with the actual log message itself. Log levels generally include INFO, DEBUG, WARN, ERROR, and FATAL. The meaning of each log level is pretty self-explanatory. These same APIs also typically allow you to turn on and turn off which log levels to log to the log file; this is done at the configuration level. Table 18.6 is a sample log level scheme.

The idea is to understand your threshold for what levels you want to log by default and which ones will get "turned on" when a problem arises. For example, if an application is not operating properly, the following set of steps might be followed:

1. Enable DEBUG logging level in configuration file.
2. Allow application to write debug-level log messages for a period of time.
3. Disable DEBUG logging level in configuration file.

This allows you to collect the log messages you need while balancing the need to make sure your application is operating optimally.

Table 18.6 Sample Log Level Scheme

Log Level	Description	Log by default?
INFO	INFO is used to log normal processing messages and status of an application	No
DEBUG	This level is used to identify log messages that can aid developers with debugging	No
WARN	The WARN level is used to draw attention to possibly harmful log messages	Yes
ERROR	An ERROR is a condition that is abnormal to the operation of application, but it doesn't necessarily cause the application to fail	Yes
FATAL	The FATAL level is for severe situations that will cause the application to halt	Yes

Another thing to be aware of is that the large the log message is, the more disk space it will take up. Today, however, disk space is pretty cheap. It is possible to have a vast amount of disk space available for you to periodically archive off application log files.

SUMMARY

We can summarize this chapter with the following set of rules-of-thumb:

1. Make sure your applications are generating clear, concise, and parse-able log messages.
2. Understand log rotation.
3. Understand what NOT to put in a log message.
4. Understand the basic performance considerations and how to deal with them.

REFERENCES

Chuvakin, A. (2011). Application logging good bad ugly ... beautiful? *Upload & Share PowerPoint Presentations and Documents*.Web, August 5. <http://www.slideshare.net/anton_chuvakin/application-logging-good-bad-ugly-beautiful-presentation>.

Chuvakin, A. (2010). How to do application logging right. *Building Security In*. Web. <http://arctec-group.net/pdf/howtoapplogging.pdf>.

Logback Manual. Web, August 5, 2011. <http://logback.qos.ch/manual/>.

Logs and Compliance

INFORMATION IN THIS CHAPTER:

- PCI DSS
- ISO2700x Series
- HIPAA
- FISMA

INTRODUCTION

Logs, while often underappreciated by IT managers, can provide useful information for security management. However, getting that data takes time and energy—both of which are often in short supply inside IT organizations. It can seem daunting at first, given the sheer volume and subjective nature of the data. Adding to their strategic value, logs are increasingly more than just a source of data for system administrators. Logging—and tracking such activity through log management software or other tools—is a primary means of IT accountability because most user and system actions can be recorded in logs. There are many other means of accountability inside an organization, but logs are the one mechanism that pervades all of IT, stretching even beyond the bounds of technology. If your IT operation is not accountable, that means your business is not accountable.

If your organization doesn't take logs seriously, it should raise flags about just how attentive you are when it comes to IT accountability. This is why logging is a perfect compliance technology, now mandated by a raft of regulations and laws, including PCI DSS, FISMA, HIPAA, and best practice frameworks such as ISO2700 and COBIT.

As already mentioned, all IT users, whether they are malicious or good corporate citizens, leave behind traces of their activity in various logs. These digital fingerprints are generated by a number of IT components, such as user-owned desktops, servers and firewalls, routers, databases, and business applications. Such records accumulate over time, creating mountains of different types of log data.

Overall regulations require some or all of the following related to log data:

- Typical logging, log management, and security monitoring requirements in the above regulations include:

  - Have adequate logging. Regulations vary significantly regarding the meaning of adequate. Some mandates stop after stipulating that an organization have audit logging.
  - Collect logs centrally. Some regulations prescribe collection of logs and centralized storage and analysis.
  - Review log data. The most onerous part of many regulations is a mandate for log review. PCI DSS, for example, calls for daily review of logs from in-scope systems. Clearly, this does not mean that every single log entry needs to be read by a person.
  - Retain logs for a period of time. Regulations prescribe various retention periods for logs, from months to years. Some stop at saying that an organization must have a log retention policy without specifying the exact number.
  - Monitor security. Some regulations prescribe reviews of network and Web alerts, and that an incident response process be deployed when required. Additional tasks may include protection of log data, time synchronization, etc. (source: http://searchcompliance.techtarget.com/tip/Log-management-and-compliance-Whats-the-real-story).

It's a common misconception that such regulations mandate only that you possess the log data.

Let's review a few popular regulations and how they relate to logging, log analysis, and log management.

PCI DSS

This section covers the basics of PCI DSS logging and what is required by PCI DSS.

Overall, logging and monitoring are not constrained to Requirement 10, but, in fact, pervades all 12 of the PCI DSS requirement; the key areas where logging and monitoring are mandated in PCI DSS are Requirement 10 and sections of Requirements 11 and 12.

Key Requirement 10

Specifically, Requirement 10.1 covers "establish[ing] a process for linking all access to system components (especially access done with administrative privileges such as root) to each individual user." This is an interesting requirement indeed; it doesn't just mandate for logs to be there or for a logging process to be set, but instead mentions that logs must be tied to individual persons (not computers or "devices" where they are produced). It is this requirement that often creates problems for PCI implementers, since many think of logs as "records of people actions," while in reality they will only have the "records of computer actions." Mapping the latter to actual users often presents an additional challenge. By the way, PCI DSS requirement 8.1 which mandates that an organization "assigns all users a unique ID before allowing them to access system components or cardholder data" helps to make the logs more useful here (source: http://chuvakin.blogspot.com/2010/11/complete-pci-dss-log-review-procedures_30.html).

Next, Section 10.2 defines a minimum list of system events to be logged (or, to allow "the events to be reconstructed"). Such requirements are motivated by the need to assess and monitor user actions as well as other events that can affect credit card data (such as system failures) (source: http://chuvakin.blogspot.com/2010/11/complete-pci-dss-log-review-procedures_30.html).

Following is the list from the requirements (events that must be logged) from PCI DSS (v. 2.0):

> 10.2.1 All individual user accesses to cardholder data.
> 10.2.2 All actions taken by any individual with root or administrative privileges.
> 10.2.3 Access to all audit trails.
> 10.2.4 Invalid logical access attempts.
> 10.2.5 Use of identification and authentication mechanisms.
> 10.2.6 Initialization of the audit logs.
> 10.2.7 Creation and deletion of system-level objects.

As can be seen, this covers data access, privileged user actions, log access and initialization, failed and invalid access attempts, authentication and authorization decisions, and system object changes. It is important to note that such a list has its roots in IT governance "best practices," which prescribe monitoring access, authentication, authorization change management, system availability, and suspicious activity.

Moreover, PCI DSS Requirement 10 goes into an even deeper level of detail and covers specific data fields or values that need to be logged for each event.

They provide a healthy minimum requirement, which is commonly exceeded by logging mechanisms in various IT platforms.

Such fields are:

> 10.3.1 User identification.
> 10.3.2 Type of event.
> 10.3.3 Date and time.
> 10.3.4 Success or failure indication.
> 10.3.5 Origination of event.
> 10.3.6 Identity or name of affected data, system component, or resource.(Source: PCI DSS from www.pcisecuritystandards.org.)

As can be seen, this minimum list contains all of the basic attributes needed for incident analysis and for answering the questions: when, who, where, what, and where from. For example, if trying to discover who modified a credit card database to copy all of the transactions with all the details into a hidden file (a typical insider privilege abuse), knowing all of the above records is very useful.

The next requirement, 10.4, addresses a commonly overlooked but critical requirement: a need to have accurate and consistent time in all of the logs. It seems fairly straightforward that time and security event monitoring would go hand in hand as well. System time is frequently found to be arbitrary in a home or small office network. It's whatever time your server was set at, or if you designed your network for some level of reliance, your systems are configured to obtain time synchronization from a reliable source, like the Network Time Protocol (NTP) servers.

Next, one needs to address all of the confidentiality, integrity, and availability (CIA) of logs. Section 10.5.1 of PCI DSS covers the confidentiality: "Limit viewing of audit trails to those with a job-related need." This means that only those who need to see the logs to accomplish their jobs should be able to. One of the obvious reasons is that authentication-related logs will always contain usernames. While not truly secret, username information provides 50% of the information needed for password guessing (password being the other 50%). Moreover, due to users mistyping their credentials, it is not uncommon for passwords themselves to show up in logs. Poorly written Web applications might result in a password being logged together with the Web Uniform Resource Locator (URL) in Web server logs.

Next comes "integrity." As per section 10.5.2 of PCI DSS, one needs to "protect audit trail files from unauthorized modifications." This one is obvious, since if logs can be modified by unauthorized parties (or by anybody) they stop being an objective assessment trail of system and user activities.

However, one needs to preserve the logs not only from malicious users, but also from system failures and consequences of system configuration errors. This touches upon both the "availability" and "integrity" of log data. Specifically, Section 10.5.3 of PCI DSS covers that one needs to "promptly back up audit trail files to a centralized log server or media that is difficult to alter." Indeed, centralizing logs to a server or a set of servers that can be used for log analysis is essential for both log protection as well as increasing log usefulness. Backing up logs to CDs or DVDs (or tapes, for that matter) is another consequence of this requirement. One should always keep in mind that logs on tape are not easily accessible and not searchable in case of an incident.

Many pieces of network infrastructure such as routers and switches are designed to log to an external server and only preserve a minimum (or none) of logs on the device itself. Thus, for those systems, centralizing logs is most critical. Requirement 10.5.4 of PCI DSS states the need to "copy logs for wireless networks onto a log server on the internal LAN."

To further decrease the risk of log alteration as well as to enable proof that such alteration didn't take place, Requirement 10.5.5 calls for the "use file integrity monitoring and change detection software on logs to ensure that existing log data cannot be changed without generating alerts." At the same time, adding new log data to a log file should not generate an alert since log files tend to grow and not shrink on their own (unless logs are rotated or archived to external storage). File integrity monitoring systems use cryptographic hashing algorithms to compare files to a known good copy. The issue with logs is that log files tend to grow due to new record addition, thus undermining the missing of integrity checking. To resolve this contradiction, one should note that integrity monitoring can only assure the integrity of logs that are not being actively written to by the logging components.

The next requirement is truly one of the most important as well as one of the most often overlooked. Many PCI implementers simply forget that PCI Requirement 10 does not just call for "having logs," but also for "having the logs AND looking at them." Specifically, Section 10.6 states that the PCI organization must, as per PCI DSS, "review logs for all system components at least daily. Log reviews must include those servers that perform security functions like IDSes and AAA servers (e.g. RADIUS)." The rest of this document covers the detailed log review procedures and practices.

Thus the requirement covers the scope of log sources that need to be "reviewed daily" and not just configured to log, and have logs preserved or centralized. Given that a large IT environment might produce gigabytes of logs per day, it is humanly impossible to read all of the logs. That is why a note is added to this requirement of PCI DSS that states that "Log harvesting, parsing, and alerting tools may be used to achieve compliance with Requirement 10.6."

The final requirement (10.7) deals with another hugely important logging question—log retention. It says: "retain audit trail history for at least 1 year, with a minimum of 3 months online availability." Unlike countless other requirements, this deals with the complicated log retention question directly. Thus, if you are not able to go back one year and look at the logs, you are in violation. Moreover, PCI DSS in its updated version v1.1 got more prescriptive when a one-year requirement was added explicitly.

So, let us summarize what we learned so far on logging in PCI:

- PCI Requirement 10 calls for logging-specific events with a pre-defined level of details from all in-scope systems.
- PCI calls for tying the actual users to all logged actions.
- All clocks and time on the in-scope systems should be synchronized.
- The CIA of all collected logs should be protected.
- Logs should be regularly reviewed; specific logs should be reviewed at least daily.
- All in-scope logs should be retained for at least 1 year.

Now we are ready to dig deeper to discover that logs and monitoring "live" not only within Requirement 10, but in all other PCI requirements. While many think that logs in PCI are represented only by Requirement 10, reality is more complicated: logs are in fact present, undercover, in all other sections (source: http://chuvakin.blogspot.com/2010/12/complete-pci-dss-log-review-procedures.html) .

Just about every claim that is made to satisfy the requirements, such as data encryption or anti-virus updates, can make effective use of log files to actually substantiate it.

For example, Requirement 1, "Install and maintain a firewall configuration to protect cardholder data" mentions that organizations must have "a formal process for approving and testing all external network connections and changes to the firewall configuration." However, after such process is established, one needs to validate that firewall configuration changes do happen with authorization and in accordance with documented change management procedures. That is where logging becomes extremely handy, since it shows you what actually happened and not just what was supposed to happen.

The entire Requirement 1.3 contains guidance to firewall configuration, with specific statements about inbound and outbound connectivity. One must use firewall logs to verify this; even a review of configuration would not be sufficient, since only logs show "how it really happened" and not just "how it was configured."

Similarly, Requirement 2 talks about password management "best practices" as well as general security hardening, such as not running unneeded services.

Logs can show when such previously disabled services are being started, either by misinformed system administrators or by attackers.

Further, Requirement 3, which deals with data encryption, has direct and unambiguous links to logging. For example, the entire subsection 3.6, shown below in an abbreviated form, implies having logs to verify that such activity actually take place. Specifically, key generation, distribution, and revocation are logged by most encryption systems and such logs are critical for satisfying this requirement.

Requirement 4, which also deals with encryption, has logging implications for similar reasons.

Requirement 5 refers to anti-virus defenses. Of course, in order to satisfy Section 5.2, which requires that you "Ensure that all anti-virus mechanisms are current, actively running, and capable of generating audit logs," one needs to see such mentioned logs.

So, even the requirement to "use and regularly update anti-virus software" will likely generate requests for log data during the assessment, since the information is present in anti-virus assessment logs. It is also well known that failed anti-virus updates, also reflected in logs, expose the company to malware risks, since anti-virus without the latest signature updates only creates a false sense of security and undermines the compliance effort.

Requirement 6 is in the same league: it calls for the organizations to "Develop and maintain secure systems and applications," which is unthinkable without a strong assessment logging functions and application security monitoring.

Requirement 7, which states that one needs to "Restrict access to cardholder data by business need-to-know," requires logs to validate who actually had access to said data. If the users that should be prevented from seeing the data appear in the log files as accessing the data usefully, remediation is needed.

Assigning a unique ID to each user accessing the system fits with other security "best practices." In PCI it is not just a "best practice," it is a requirement (Requirement 8 "Assign a unique ID to each person with computer access"). Obviously, one needs to "Control addition, deletion, and modification of user IDs, credentials, and other identifier Objects" (Section 8.5.1 of PCI DSS) Most systems log such activities.

In addition, Section 8.5.9, "Change user passwords at least every 90 days," can also be verified by reviewing the logs files from the server in order to assure that all the accounts have their password changed at least every 90 days.

Requirement 9 presents a new realm of security—physical access control. Even Section 9.4 that covers maintaining visitor logs (likely in the form of a physical logbook) is connected to log management if such a visitor log is electronic. There are separate data retention requirements for such logs: "Use a visitor log to maintain a physical assessment trail of visitor activity. Retain this log for a minimum of three months, unless otherwise restricted by law."

Requirement 11 addresses the need to scan (or "test") the in-scope systems for vulnerabilities. However, it also calls for the use of IDS or IPS in Section 11.4: "Use network intrusion detection systems, host-based intrusion detection systems, and intrusion prevention systems to monitor all network traffic and alert personnel to suspected compromises. Keep all intrusion detection and prevention engines up to date." Intrusion detection is only useful if logs and alerts are reviewed.

Requirement 12 covers the issues on a higher level—security policy as well as security standards and daily operational procedures (e.g. a procedure for daily log review mandates by Requirement 10 should be reflected here). However, it also has logging implications, since assessment logging should be a part of every security policy. In addition, incident response requirements are also tied to logging: "Establish, document, and distribute security incident response and escalation procedures to ensure timely and effective handling of all situations" is unthinkable to satisfy without effective collection and timely review of log data.

Thus, event logging and security monitoring in PCI DSS program go much beyond Requirement 10. Only through careful data collection and analysis can companies meet the broad requirements of PCI.

ISO2700X SERIES

ISO27001 belongs to the ISO27000 family of standards. It is an Information Security Management System (ISMS) standard published by International Organization for Standardization (ISO). Its full name is ISO/IEC 27001:2005 "Information technology—Security techniques—Information security management systems—Requirements." The specification can be found at http://www.27000.org and in other places (sadly, for a fee).

Let's focus on specific ISO controls related to logging and monitoring. These are concentrated in section "A.10.10 Monitoring" which has the following objective: "to detect unauthorized information processing activities." This follows the security mission of ISO27001 framework and also places emphasis on detection—rather than investigation—of security issues.

ISO Section A.10.10.1 Audit Logging states that "Audit logs recording user activities, exceptions, and information security events shall be produced and kept for an agreed period to assist in future investigations and access control monitoring." This prescribes having logs and also retaining them for a pre-defined period of time—your log retention policy. It also briefly highlights what types of events need to be recorded in logs, and follows a traditional set of compliance relevant log categories as mentioned in the Introduction section.

Broadening the above definition and including additional requirements from Section A.10.10.4 Administrator and Operator Logs ("System administrator and system operator activities shall be logged") and Section A.10.10.5 Fault Logging ("Faults shall be logged, analyzed, and appropriate action taken"), we can summarize the types of events that need to be logged across all systems in an ISO environment in Table 19.1.

All of these may provide useful initial evidence for security incidents such as data theft.

On Windows, the above will cover a broad range of events from logins to policy changes to application updates as well as user operations with data. On network devices, it will include security and availability issues.

Table 19.1 Types of Events Which Need to be Logged in an ISO Environment

Logged Message Category	Purpose Within ISO27000 Logging and Monitoring
Authentication, authorization, and access events, such as successful and failed authentication decisions (logins), system access, data access, and application component access; and especially remote access	Tracking and investigating access to systems by authorized users as well as attackers and malicious insiders
Changes such as system or application changes (especially privilege changes), data changes (including creation and destruction), and even application and component installations and updates	Monitoring for changes that can expose system to attacks as well as for changes made by attackers and malicious insiders
Availability issues such as startups and shutdowns of systems, applications, and application modules or components and also faults and errors, especially errors affecting the application's availability and data security	Monitoring for operational issues as well as security related failures and loss of system availability for business
Fourth type is resource issues covering the range of exhausted resources, exceeded capacities, and network connectivity availability issues, various reached limits. All of these may provide useful initial evidence for security incidents such as data theft	Detecting resource issues due to security and operational reasons
Known threats such as invalid inputs and other likely application abuses, exploits and known attacks	Detecting and blocking attacks, as well as investigating their consequences

Special attention is paid to privileged user monitoring such as "system administrator and system operator activities." These are in fact some of the most important logs you would create under an ISO program as they serve as the key vehicle of accountability for all-powerful IT administrators. However, to be useful for such purpose, logs have to be removed from the control of such administrators via a log management solution.

The above sections also contain additional requirements for log retention and investigation. Unlike PCI DSS that prescribes a clear 1 year log retention, ISO only touches upon log retention and requires a separate policy to define the log retention period. In fact, retaining security relevant logs for 1 year presents a common industry practice. It is recommended that organizations implement such log retention across the entire environment, and over both physical and virtual components.

Also note the "action to be taken" requirement in Section 10.10.5. This hints at not just collecting logs but also defining policies and procedures for monitoring, investigation, and exception follow-up.

ISO27002 provides additional details useful when implementing the ISO series in practice. For example, addition guidance for 10.10.1 "Audit logging" states that "use of privileges" and "use of system utilities and applications" must be logged.

Specifically, the next Section A.10.10.2 Monitoring System Use mandates that *"procedures for monitoring use of information processing facilities shall be established and the results of the monitoring activities reviewed regularly."* This calls for a logging policy and operational procedures for monitoring. ISO does hint at an ongoing review of such policies and procedures as well. For example, such operational procedures must cover periodic or real-time log review workflows for systems and applications in scope for the ISO project. Such review is performed by either application administrator or security administrator using automated tools or manually (even though the latter is unlikely for larger environments due to a volume of logs being collected and retained).

The ISO27002 suggests that "the level of monitoring required for individual facilities should be determined by a risk assessment" which allows for a sensible foundation for security monitoring activities, without either gaps or excessive controls. It is interesting that "I/O device attachment/detachment" is specifically called out as a monitoring goal.

Overall this key controls calls for the creation of a logging policy that defines logging, log collection and retention, as well as review and analysis—and likely real-time alerting as well.

ISO27001 does cover the subject of securing logs from unauthorized modification and observation. Section A.10.10.3 Protection of Log Information states that *"Logging facilities and log information shall be protected against tampering and unauthorized access."* Note the dual focus of log protection: access control (preserves log confidentiality) and integrity protection (preserved log integrity). Most modern log management and SIEM systems will offer stringent role-based access controls to limit law operations to authorized parties on a "need-to-know" basis. On top of this, systems also employ integrity checking using cryptographic mechanisms to detect any possible log changes. As a last resort, logs can be written to "write-once" media such as DVD or network backup archives. Without explicitly mentioning this, this control implies that malicious insiders should not be able to use logs to further their nefarious goals—log security measures should work against both outside attackers and malicious (as well as careless) insiders.

In addition, the organization must monitor for "storage capacity of the log file media being exceeded, resulting in either the failure to record events or overwriting of past recorded events" (as per ISO27002). Such accidental loss of log data should not be tolerated.

Finally, ISO Section A.10.10.6 Clock synchronization states *"the clocks of all relevant information processing systems within an organization or security domain shall be synchronized with an agreed accurate time source."*

Just like in PCI DSS, log timing is important for security monitoring, forensics, and troubleshooting. It is a best practice to make sure that all collected and analyzed logs have correct timestamps, and relevant time zone information is preserved. Using NTP or other reliable timing mechanisms for logs need to be used in order to preserve the accurate sequence of events as well as their absolute timings.

HIPAA

The Health Insurance Portability and Accountability Act of 1996 (HIPAA) outlines relevant security and privacy standards for health information—both electronic and physical. The main mission of the law is "to improve portability and continuity of health insurance coverage in the group and individual markets, to combat waste, fraud, and abuse in health insurance and health care delivery" (HIPAA Act of 1996). The copy of the act can be obtained at the HHS Website (http://www.hhs.gov/ocr/privacy/hipaa/).

In particular, Title II of the law, "Preventing Health Care Fraud and Abuse; Administrative Simplification; Medical Liability Reform," contains Security Rule (Section 2.3) that covers Electronic Protected Health Information (EPHI) and Privacy Rule (Section 2.1) that covers all Protected Health Information (PHI).

A recent enhancement to HIPAA is called Health Information Technology for Economic and Clinical Health Act or HITECH Act. The act seeks to "promote the adoption and meaningful use of health information technology" and "addresses the privacy and security concerns associated with the electronic transmission of health information, in part, through several provisions that strengthen the civil and criminal enforcement of the HIPAA rules" (HITECH Act of 2009).

Unlike PCI DSS, HIPAA itself does not descend to the level of security controls and technologies to implement. This requires the organizations affected by HIPAA—also known as "covered entities"—to try to follow the spirit of the regulation as opposed to its letter. What is also interesting to note is that insurance companies and many hospitals that accept payment cards are subject to both HIPAA and PCI DSS. Understandably, the scope of their applicability across the organization might be different since payment processing systems should not store patient health information and vice versa. Still, considering the same technical and administrative controls for both regulations is prudent and will save money in both the short term and long term.

The following HIPAA requirements are broadly applicable to logging, log review, and security monitoring:

- Section 164.308(a)(5)(ii)(C) "Log-in Monitoring" calls for monitoring the systems touching patient information for login and access. The requirement applies to "login attempts" which implies both failed and successful logins.
- Section 164.312(b) "Audit Controls" broadly covers audit logging and other audit trails on systems that deal with sensitive health information. Review of such audit logs seem to be implied by this requirement.
- Section 164.308(a)(1)(ii)(D) "Information System Activity Review" prescribes review of various records of IT activities such as logs, systems utilization reports, incident reports, and other indications of security relevant activities.
- Other requirements in HIPAA might potentially affect logging as well (source: http://www.prismmicrosys.com/EventSourceNewsletters-June10.php).

The above reveals that, compared to PCI DSS, logging and monitoring requirements inside HIPAA itself do not really help companies to answer key questions needed to deploy and operationalize logging and log management—from both technical and policy/procedure point of view.

In particular, the following questions are left unanswered:

- What information should be logged by "audit controls"? What activities and events? What details for each activity or event?
- Should the log records be centrally collected?

- For how long should the records be retained?
- What particular "activities" should be reviewed? How often?
- How should security monitoring and "log-in monitoring" be performed?
- How should audit records be protected?

In light of this, it is often noticed that HIPAA log collection and review seems to be a perpetual stumbling point for organizations of all sizes. Log requirements can be difficult for some companies, such as organizations with complex systems in place, or small shops that lack the time, money, and expertise. And vague guidance does not help the organization to get motivated to do logging and log review. On top of this, logging and log review complexity rises dramatically when custom applications—not simply Windows servers or Cisco firewalls—are in scope. Despite the movement away from legacy and custom applications, a lot of medical data still sits inside homegrown applications where logging can be a nightmare to configure.

In addition to the above questions, another issue is unclear: do these controls apply to the actual application that handles sensitive health data or do they apply to the underlying platform as well (source: http://www.prismmicrosys.com/EventSourceNewsletters-June10.php).

Fortunately, some additional details for HIPAA Security Rule implementation are covered in NIST Publication 800-66 "An Introductory Resource Guide for Implementing the Health Insurance Portability and Accountability Act (HIPAA) Security Rule" (see http://csrc.nist.gov/publications/nistpubs/800-66-Rev1/SP-800-66-Revision1.pdf).

NIST SP 800-66 guide details log management requirements for the securing of electronic protected health information—based on HIPAA security rule.

Section 4.1 of NIST 800-66 describes the need for regular review of information system activity, such as audit logs, information and system access reports, and security incident tracking reports. The section asks questions ("How often will reviews take place?" and "Where will audit information reside (e.g. separate server)?") rather than providing answers.

Section 4.15 attempts to provide additional guidance on "audit controls." While striving to provide the methodology and questions that implementers need to be asking such as "What activities will be monitored (e.g. creation, reading, updating, and/or deleting of files or records containing EPHI)?" and "What should the audit record include (e.g. user ID, event type/date/time)?", the document does not really address key implementation concern—in other words, it does not tell covered entities what they must do to be compliant.

Also, Section 4.22 specifies that documentation of actions and activities need to be retained for at least 6 years—and leaves the discussion of whether security activity records such as logs are considered "documentation" to implementers.

A recommended strategy suggests that the company starts from information security activity review policy and processes. Using the guiding questions from NIST 800-66, one can formulate what such policy should cover: requirement applicability, recorded activities, and recorded details, review procedures, exception monitoring process, etc.

Quoting from NIST 800-66:

- "Who is responsible for the overall process and results?
- How often will reviews take place?
- How often will review results be analyzed?
- What is the organization's sanction policy for employee violations?
- Where will audit information reside (e.g. separate server)?"

Next, the organization has to actually implement the above process for both logging and log review. This would make sure that log records are created on covered systems and have sufficient details (logging). By the way, such details can be borrowed from the corresponding PCI DSS guidance. Also, it will create the procedures to "regularly review records of information system activity, such as audit logs, access reports, and security incident tracking reports" (log review). While daily log reviews are not required, if they are performed for PCI DSS, they can be expanded to cover HIPAA systems as well.

On this, NIST 800-66 advices:

- "Develop Appropriate Standard Operating Procedures.
- Determine the types of audit trail data and monitoring procedures that will be needed to derive exception reports.
- How will exception reports or logs be reviewed?
- Where will monitoring reports be filed and maintained?"

Only then is the organization ready to proceed to the next step and initiate logging and then start ongoing log reviews.

Even though HIPAA does not provide detailed step-by-step guidance on logging and log management, it gives companies an opportunity to follow the spirit of the regulation and not simply the letter. Understandably, a few organizations might be waiting for fines and enforcement activity to be started before taking any action. Such shortsighted approach to logging simply plays for the "bad guys" side—allowing cyber-criminals to steal the most sensitive data all of us will ever have...

Furthermore, HIPAA itself does not descend to the level of security controls and technologies to implement. This requires the organizations affected by

HIPAA—also known as "covered entities"—to try to follow the spirit of the regulation as opposed to its letter. What is also interesting to note is that insurance companies and many hospitals that accept payment cards are subject to both HIPAA and PCI DSS. Understandably, the scope of their applicability across the organization might be different since payment processing systems should not store patient health information and vice versa. Still, considering the same technical and administrative controls for both regulations is prudent in both the short term and long term.

While platform level logging is useful for protecting sensitive health information, and it is a fact that a majority of health information is stored in databases and processed by healthcare-specific applications, such applications are either procured from specialty vendors or developed internally—via outsourced developers.

HIPAA of audit controls, mentioned in Section 164.312(b), apply to application logging as much or more than to platform logging. This means that custom applications need to be engineered to have adequate logging. Existing application logging needs to be assessed having adequate logging—it should be noted that many legacy applications will often not record sufficient details for events and might even skip logging events altogether. Thus, before embarking on this project, it makes sense to determine which applications within your organization contain Protected Health Information (PHI) and what their existing levels and methods of logging are.

Let's define some of the guidance for what to log to satisfy the spirit and letter of HIPAA Security Requirement as well as NIST 800-66 HIPAA clarifications.

From high level, best audit logs tell you exactly what happened—when, where, and how—as well as who was involved. Such logs are suitable for manual, semi-automated, and automated analysis. Ideally, they can be analyzed without having the application that produced them at hand—and definitely without having the application developer on call. In case of healthcare applications, such developer might not be available at all and the security team will have to proceed on their own. From the log management point of view, the logs can be centralized for analysis and retention. Finally, they should not slow the system down and can be proven reliable, if used as forensic evidence (source: http://www.prismmicrosys.com/EventSourceNewsletters-July10.php).

Two primary things need to be defined:

- First, there are types of activities or events that always need to be recorded. For example, authentication decisions, health information access, and system changes should always appear in logs.
- Second, for each type of a recorded event there are particulate details that are mandatory for its interpretation, whether by a human or by an automated system. For example, every log should have a reliable timestamp and every log related to user activity should contain the username of that user.

It should also be noted that certain details should never be logged. The example is obvious: application or system passwords should never appear in logs (this, sadly, still happens for Web applications sometimes). Just as obviously, the health information itself should be kept out of logs.

What events should we log? What is the overall theme for selecting which events to log?

Clearly, we need to know who, when, and why accesses any of health information. We also need to know who adds, changes, or deletes it. But this is not all—we also need to note who tries but fails to read, change, or delete information. If we are unable to record access to each piece of data, we need to carefully record all access to the application itself.

Next, we need to know who performs other actions on systems that process health information as such activities might affect future access to healthcare data. For example, we need to record if somebody turns logging off or adds a new component to the system which might enable unfettered access to data. In addition, we need to record other critical events caring on health information systems as such events might present circumstantial evidence for unauthorized access.

The following list presents a structured view of the above criteria:

- *Authentication, Authorization, Access:*
    - Authentication/authorization decisions, successful and failed (see "status" below)—and especially privileged authentication.
    - Recording user logoffs is also important for knowing when user no longer had access to the application.
    - Switching from one user account to another.
    - System access, data access, application component access.
    - Network access to the application, including remote access from one application component to another in a distribute environment.

- *Changes:*
    - System/application changes (especially privilege changes).
    - Data change (creation and destruction are changes too).
    - Application and component installation and updates as well as removals.
    - Sensitive data changes, additions, and deletions.

- *Availability Issues:*
    - Startups and shutdowns of systems, applications and application modules/components.
    - Faults and errors, especially those errors that affect the availability of the application.
    - Backups' successes and failures (affect availability).

- *"Badness"/Threats:*

  - Invalid inputs other likely application abuses.
  - Malicious software detection events.
  - Attempts—successful and failed—to disrupt or disable security controls or logging.
  - Logging termination events and possible attempts to modify or delete the logs.
  - Other security issues that are known to affect the application.

While creating a comprehensive "what to log" list for every healthcare application in existence is probably impossible, the above list should give you a useful starting point for your relevant applications. It can be converted into your application logging policy without much extra work.

What details should we log? Next, what data should you log for each event, and at what level of detail should you log it? The overall theme we use here is the following:

- Who was involved?
- What happened?
- Where did it happen?
- When did it happen?
- Why did it happen?
- How did it happen?

We also mentioned above that being able to easily centralize logs is essential for distributed log analysis either across multiple systems or across multiple application components of a distributed application. While syslog has been the king of log centralization due to its easy UDP delivery, modern cross-platform application frameworks like a call for publish/subscribe model for log delivery, similar to the ones used in modern Windows versions. In this case security monitoring tool can request a subscription for a particular type of a logged event—and receive all relevant logs in near real time, if needed.

In addition to that very basic conclusion—you must log access to sensitive healthcare data—we have to remind our readers that the importance of logging will only grow—along with growing application complexity. In particular, the need to analyze application behavior and movement of sensitive information across distributed and cloud-based application calls for us to finally get application logging under control.

Software architects and implementers need to "get" logging—there is NO other way since infrastructure logging from network devices and operating systems won't do it for detecting and investigating application level threats to ePHI. Security team—ultimately responsible for log review—will need to guide developers towards useful and effective logging that can be used for both monitoring and investigative activities.

Certainly, logging standards such as MITRE CEE (cee.mitre.org) will help—but it might take a few years before they are developed and their adoption increases. Pending a global standard, an organization should quickly build and then use its own application logging standard for applications. HIPAA compliance presents a great motivation to creating and adopting such logging standards (source: http://www.prismmicrosys.com/EventSourceNewsletters-July10.php).

FISMA

The Federal Information Security Management Act of 2002 (FISMA) "requires each federal agency to develop, document, and implement an agency-wide program to provide information security for the information and information systems that support the operations and assets of the agency, including those provided or managed by another agency, contractor, or other source."

While some criticize FISMA for being "all documentation and no action," the law emphasizes the need for each Federal agency to develop, document, and implement an organization-wide program to secure the information systems that support its operations and assets.

The law itself does not prescribe any logging, log management, or security monitoring since it stays on a high level of policy, planning, and risk to federal systems. In accordance with the law, detailed guidance has been developed by NIST to cover the specifics of FISMA compliance. For example, the following umbrella page http://csrc.nist.gov/groups/SMA/fisma/overview.html covers how to plan a FISMA project at a federal agency. In addition to NIST, OMB was tasked with collecting agency reports on compliance—FISMA periodic validation regime.

The main source for detailed guidance is NIST Special Publication 800-53 "Recommended Security Controls for Federal Information Systems," now in revision 3 (http://csrc.nist.gov/publications/nistpubs/800-53-Rev3/sp800-53-rev3-final_updated-errata_05-01-2010.pdf). Among other things, the document describes log management controls including the generation, review, protection, and retention of audit records, and steps to take in the event of audit failure (source: http://www.prismmicrosys.com/EventSourceNewsletters-Aug10.php).

Let's review the guidance in detail.

NIST 800-53 Logging Guidance

The section "AUDIT AND ACCOUNTABILITY POLICY AND PROCEDURES" (AU controls) focuses on AU-1 "AUDIT AND ACCOUNTABILITY POLICY AND PROCEDURES" that covers "Formal, documented procedures to facilitate the implementation of the audit and accountability policy and associated audit and accountability controls." This is indeed the right way to approach audit logging by starting from the logging policy and procedures for log collection and review. While audit controls in FISMA go beyond logging, the above guidance is very true for log management.

AU-2 "AUDITABLE EVENTS" refers to NIST 800-92, covered in the next part of the series. As expected, risk assessment as well as logging needs for other organizational units needs to be considered for creating a list of auditable events. Events that are only audited under "special circumstances," such as after an incident, are also defined here.

Logically, after the list of events to audit is established, AU-3 "CONTENT OF AUDIT RECORDS" clarifies the level of details recorded for each event. Examples such as "timestamps, source and destination addresses, user/process identifiers, event descriptions, success/fail indications, filenames involved, and access control or flow control rules invoked" which should be in every good log records are provided. Refer to CEE standard work (http://cee.mitre.org) for further discussion of high-quality logging.

AU-4 "AUDIT STORAGE CAPACITY" and actually AU-11 "AUDIT RECORD RETENTION" cover the subject critical for many organizations—log retention. Unlike PCI DSS, NIST guidance only offers tips for selecting the right attention and not a simple answer (like, 1 year in PCI).

AU-5 "RESPONSE TO AUDIT PROCESSING FAILURES" mandates an important but commonly overlooked aspect of logging and log analysis—you have to act when logging fails. Examples that require action include "software/hardware errors, failures in the audit capturing mechanisms, and audit storage capacity being reached or exceeded" as well as other issues affecting logging.

AU-6 "AUDIT REVIEW, ANALYSIS, AND REPORTING" is about what happens with collected log data. Specifically it prescribes that organization "reviews and analyzes information system audit records for indications of inappropriate or unusual activity" at "organization-defined frequency." Again, NIST/FISMA guidance stays away from giving a simple answer (like daily log reviews in PCI DSS).

AU-7 "AUDIT REDUCTION AND REPORT GENERATION" deals with reporting and summarization, the most common way to review log data.

AU-8 "TIME STAMPS" and AU-9 "PROTECTION OF AUDIT INFORMATION" as well as AU-10 "NON-REPUDIATION" address log reliability for investigative and monitoring purposes. Logs must be accurately timed and stored in a manner preventing changes. One mentioned choice is "hardware-enforced, write-once media." The use of cryptography is another mentioned method.

AU-12 "AUDIT GENERATION" essentially makes sure that the organization "generates audit records for the list of audited events defined in AU-2 with the content as defined in AU-3."

Next, logging guidance ends and security monitoring part begins: AU-13 "MONITORING FOR INFORMATION DISCLOSURE" focuses on information theft ("exfiltration" of sensitive data) and AU-14 "SESSION AUDIT" covers recording and analysis of user activity ("session data"). We often say that logging is largely futile without exception handling and response procedures.

Overall, here is what is likely needed for a successful FISMA-driven log management implementation. The way to address the requirement can vary across the type of an organization, as it is the case for all log management projects (source: http://www.prismmicrosys.com/EventSourceNewsletters-Aug10.php).

What do you actually need to do? The following distills FISMA/NIST guidance into actionable items that can be implemented and maintained, for as long as FISMA compliance is desired or mandated:

- Logging policy comes first. But it means nothing without operational procedures which are developed base and policy and then put into practice (AU-1).
- This will likely require configuration changes to multiple types of systems; updates to configuration standards prescribed elsewhere in the document are in order.
- Based on the policy, define which event will be logged (AU-2) and what details will be generated and recorded for each event (AU-3). Start the logging as per AU-12.
- Consider logging all outbound connectivity to detect exfiltration of data (as per AU-13) and make sure that user access sessions are recorded (AU-14).
- Define log storage methods and retention times (AU-4 and AU-11) and retain the generated logs.
- Protect logs from changes, keep time accurate to preserve the evidentiary power of logs (AU-8–10).
- Also according to policy, implement log review procedures and report generation (AU-6, AU-7). Distributing reports to parties that should see the information (also as per policy created in item 1).

At this point, your organization should be prepared for FISMA compliance on both policy level and technical level. It is now up to you to maintain that awareness for as long as needed. A dangerous mistake that some organization make is to stay on the policy and procedure level and never configure actual systems for logging. Remember—documents don't stop malicious hackers, policies don't help investigate incidents when log data is missing and talking about "alignment of compliance strategy" does not make you secure—or even compliant…

FISMA itself does not prescribe any logging, log management, or security monitoring since it stays on a high level of policy, planning, and risk to federal systems. In accordance with the law, detailed guidance has been developed by NIST to cover the specifics of FISMA compliance. The main source for detailed guidance is NIST Special Publication 800-53 "Recommended Security Controls for Federal Information Systems," now in revision 3, that we covered in the previous issue. Among other things, the document describes log management controls including the generation, review, protection, and retention of audit records, and steps to take in the event of audit failure. On top of this, NIST has created a dedicated "Guide to Computer Security Log Management." The guide states "Implementing the following recommendations should assist in facilitating more efficient and effective log management for Federal departments and agencies." (Source: http://www.prismmicrosys.com/EventSourceNewsletters-Aug10.php). A lot of additional guidance has been built for FISMA. SANS Institute, in particular, has created "Twenty Critical Security Controls for Effective Cyber Defense: Consensus Audit Guidelines" by SANS (**http://www.sans.org/critical-security-controls/**). One of the top controls, "Critical Control 6: Maintenance, Monitoring, and Analysis of Audit Logs," is about logging and log management. It maps to NIST 800-53 AU and other controls—in particular "AC-17 (1), AC-19, AU-2 (4), AU-3 (1, 2), AU-4, AU-5, AU-6 (a, 1, 5), AU-8, AU-9 (1, 2), AU-12 (2), SI-4 (8)" that we also covered previously. Unlike end to end coverage of logging in NIST 800-92 which can be overwhelming for casual reader, SANS document contains "quick wins" that agencies can follow immediately to ramp up their FISMA efforts.

How can you use NIST 800-92 document in your organization? First, let's become familiar with what is inside the 80 page document. The guide starts with an introduction to computer security log management and follows with three main sections:

- Log management infrastructure.
- Log management planning.
- Log management operational processes.

Indeed, this is the right way to think about any log management project since organizations usually have challenges with planning, logging architecture building, and then with ongoing operation—that has to be maintained for as long as the organization exists.

The guide defines log management as "the process for generating, transmitting, storing, analyzing, and disposing of computer security log data." By the way, keep in mind that security log management must cover both "Logs from Security Applications" (e.g. IPS alerts) and "Security Logs from Applications" (e.g. user authentication decisions from a business application). Focusing on just one is a mistake.

In the area of log management infrastructure, the guide defines three tiers of log management architecture:

- Log generation.
- Log analysis and storage.
- Log monitoring.

Following this order is simply log common sense; but many organizations, unfortunately, sometimes start from purchasing an expensive tool without thinking about their logging policy and they use for logs. Thinking of the needs (what you want to get from logs?) and logs (what logs can help me get there?) before thinking about boxes and software will save your organization many headaches.

Log management project planning starts from focusing on a key item—organization roles. Log management is inherently "horizontal" and touches many areas of an organization. NIST suggests that system and network administrators, security administrators, incident respondents, CSOs, auditors, and—yes!—even internal application developers be invited to the party. This will help the organization choose and implement the right answer to their log management question (source: http://www.prismmicrosys.com/EventSource-Newsletters-Aug10.php).

Next—the real work starts: creation of a logging policy. It is a common theme that security starts from a policy; this strongly applies to logging. According to the guide, such policies need to cover:

- *Log generation:* What events are logged, with what level of detail.
- *Log transmission:* How logs are collected and centralized across the entire environment.
- *Log storage and disposal:* How and where the logs are retained and then disposed of.
- *Log analysis:* How are the logged events interpreted and what actions are taken as a result.

What does this mean in practical terms? It means that configuring tools need to happen only after the policy that covers what will be done is created. Goals first, infrastructure choices second! In case of privacy and other regulations on top of FISMA, the legal department should also have their say, however unpalatable it may be to the security team.

After defining policy and building the systems to implement the policy, as well as configuring the log sources, the hard work of building lasting ongoing program begins. The core of such a program is about performing periodic analysis of log data and taking appropriate responses to identified exceptions. Obviously, no external guide can define what is most important to your organization—but hopefully using this book, NIST, and other guidance, you already have some idea about what logs you would care the most about (source: http://www.prismmicrosys.com/EventSourceNewsletters-Sep10.php).

On a less frequent basis, the agency will perform tasks related to long-term management of log data. It is a surprisingly hard problem, if your log data volume goes into terabytes of data or more. NIST 800-92 suggests first choosing "a log format for the data to be archived"—original, parsed, etc. It also contains guidance on storing log data securely and with integrity verification, just like in PCI DSS.

First, it gives a solid foundation to build a log management program—a lot of other mandates focus on tools, but this contains hugely useful program management tips, all the way down to how to avoid log analyst burnout from looking at too many logs.

Second, you can use the guide to learn about commonly overlooked aspects of log management: log protection, storage management, etc. For example, it contains a few useful tips on how to prioritize log records for review.

Third, it provides you with a way to justify your decisions in the area of log management—even if you don't work for a government agency.

At the same time, the guide is mostly about process, and less about bits and bytes. It won't tell you which tool is the best for you.

In fact, even though NIST 800-92 is not binding guidance outside of federal government, commercial organizations can profit from it as well. For example, one retail organization built its log management program based on 800-92 even though complying with PCI DSS was their primary goal. They used the NIST guide for tool selection, as a source of template policies and even to assure ongoing operational success for their log management project.

Other technical log management guidance for agencies subject to FISMA is published by SANS in the form of their "Twenty Critical Security Controls for Effective Cyber Defense" or CSC20. If you are looking for quick actionable tips (called "QuickWins" in the document), that is the resource for you. For example:

- "Validate audit log settings for each hardware device and the software installed on it, ensuring that logs include a date, timestamp, source addresses, destination addresses, and various other useful elements of each packet and/or transaction. Systems should record logs in a standardized format such as syslog entries or those outlined by the Common Event Expression (CEE) initiative."

- "System administrators and security personnel should devise profiles of common events from given systems, so that they can tune detection to focus on unusual activity…"
- "All remote access to an internal network, whether through VPN, dial-up, or other mechanism, should be logged verbosely."

It is recommended to use all of NIST 800-53, NIST 800-92, and SANS CSC20 to optimize your logging for FISMA compliance project.

To conclude, NIST 800-92 and SANS CSC20 teach us to do the following, whether for FISMA compliance alone, for multi-regulation programs, or simply improve security and operations:

- Find the critical systems where logging is essential.
- Enable logging—and make sure that logs satisfy the "good log" criteria mentioned in the standards.
- Involve different teams in logging initiatives—logging cuts horizontally across the agency.
- Look at your logs! You'd be happy you started now and not tomorrow.
- Automate log management, where possible, and have solid repeatable process in all areas.(Source: http://www.prismmicrosys.com/EventSource-Newsletters-Sep10.php.)

On top of this, NIST 800-92 brings log management to the attention of people who thought "Logs? Let them rot." Its process guidance is more widely represented than technical guidance which makes it very useful for IT management and not just for "in the trenches" people, who might already know that there is gold in the logs…

SUMMARY

To conclude, logging and regulatory compliance are closely linked and will likely remain so for the future. Despite log challenges, logging is a primary means of IT accountability since most user and system actions can be recorded in logs. That's exactly why logging is a perfect compliance technology, mandated by many regulations and laws.

Planning Your Own Log Analysis System

INTRODUCTION

Now that we have come close to the end of the book, it's time to put some practical guidance on paper. In this chapter, we take you through a checklist of sorts which can be used when planning or considering a log analysis system deployment. If you are paying for a commercial system, most of what is presented here will typically be handled by the vendor you chose. However, you must stay involved in the project every step of the way. Ultimately, it is you who need to have your needs met by the vendor. Not the other way around. If you find yourself needing to deploy an open source solution, of which there are many, this chapter will serve you well. It should be noted that, depending on where you are in the process, parts of or all of the sections covered can apply to you. For example, if you have already settled on software, but have no clue about hardware allocation, then you can safely ignore the Software Selection section. Whichever path you are on, you can use the guidance provided here in many situations.

PLANNING

The very first thing you need to do, outside of deciding on a product or service, is to understand what your exact need is for such a product. The sort of things you should be considering include:

- Use cases: Can you define exact scenarios which show how a system like this will be used? For example, here is a sample use case: "As a user of the system, I would like to be able to run a report which shows me the login failures for my Windows servers over the last 24 h."
- Drivers: What is "driving" you to embark on such a project? Is it for fun, necessity, government regulation or, what? If you can answer this an assign a priority to your driver (e.g. if it's for fun, this would be low), this can help you see clearly about how you want to allocate your time, money, and resources.
- Problems Solved: Will deploying a log analysis system help solve other problems? For example, due to the type of information you will be collecting, a log analysis system could help you with server or network monitoring.
- Security and Compliance: Does such a product help you prove compliance to auditors, regulators, and so on?

Alright, now that this is out of the way, you need to begin planning. If you have your own project management team, then this is probably the sort of project you would want them to help you manage and track. If not you can still do it yourself. You will just be doing double duty.

Roles and Responsibilities

One of the first things you need to establish is the roles and responsibilities. One reason is because it can help you identify who you might need to include during the planning and implementation phase of the project. But a second reason is because the exercise helps you understand who in your organization might be users of a log analysis system. For example, programmers are users of a logging system since the applications they write will need to create log messages for diagnostic and troubleshooting purposes.

Table 20.1 provides a summary of common roles and responsibilities.

Resources

Resourcing has to do with understanding your organization's need with respect to logging and what impact it will make on your environment. Here are some general questions you can ask yourself during the planning phase.

1. What existing staff do you have who can perform log analysis and monitoring?
2. What existing staff do you have who can perform administration of a log analysis system?
3. Will you operate 24 × 7, in a lights out mode, or hybrid?

Table 20.1 Summary of Roles and Responsibilities

Role	Responsibility
Log analysis system administrator	It is likely this role falls to you. As this person, you are responsible for the maintenance and upkeep of the system. This will include installing software updates, configuring log collectors, and other tasks. Another task is working with other constituents in your organization to understand their needs and requirements as they pertain to the analysis system. In other words, how do you help others derive value from the system.
Business / Product owner	The individual or group who has responsibility for a product, feature set, application, etc. This group will typically have their own requirements with respect to logging, but they may not know or need to know that there is a log analysis system. It might fall to you to help tease out their requirements.
Security team	The security team is typically responsible for configuring logging on security devices and ensuring the security posture of an organization.
IT / Development managers	Enforce logging standard as a "must have" feature, which impacts the organization as a whole.
IT support team / Administrators / Network operators	This team supports production applications; They might have a use case to read and analyze log files when applications are misbehaving, etc.
Software developers / Programmers	Follow logging standards by using libraries, APIs, and logging features. The log analysis system can also be useful to developers when they need to track down application issues and so forth.
Incident response team	The incident response team can be considered a customer of the log analysis system. They will use the collected logs during incident response and escalations.
Internal / External auditors	Depending on what sort of business you are in, you may have to deal with auditors. Auditors often need for you to verify that you are collecting certain types of logs in order to be in compliance with various regulations.

4. Do you have a need to build out a security operations center (SOC) or will you have a virtual SOC? A virtual SOC is a team who is not sitting and watching screens 24 × 7, but rather use alerting to drive response, workflow, etc.

5. What is your plan for incident response?

6. What kind of budget do you have for building a log analysis system?

7. What kind of budget do you have for running and maintaining the system over time (hardware upgrades, network upgrades, people upgrades, etc.)?

The answers to these questions will help you better understand the resourcing needs of the project and ultimate implementation. For example, if you plan to have a 24 × 7 operations center, you will need to consider things like the following:

- Will you need to hire new staff or use internal staff?
- Do you have real estate in your office to host a 24 × 7 operations center?
- Do you have the power capacity to handle a 24 × 7 center?
- Do you have budget to purchase the hardware and software necessary to run an operation such as this?
- What will your incident response and escalation procedures be?
- What sort of reporting will you be responsible for producing (like for executives, etc.)?

You kind of get the picture, right? The list could go on for pages.

A final few things to consider are the hard and soft costs associated with deploying a log analysis system. Hard costs typically deal with capital expenditure. Hardware on which to run the system, infrastructure upgrades to support the system, operating system costs, etc. The soft costs tend center around the time required to deploy, maintain, monitor, etc., such as system. While it might not seem like these sort of activities have cost, in fact they do.

It is apparent that when undertaking a venture such as planning for the implementation of a log analysis system, you have a lot to think about.

Goals

It is critical to set goals before, during, and after the project. Goals help you know that you are making progress. Some of your goals might actually be milestones which mark major deliverables for the project. A sample set of goals and milestones for planning a log analysis system follows.

- Goal 1—Pre-planning
- Goal 2—Stakeholder Identification
- Goal 3—Requirements Gathering
- Milestone 1—Project plan creation
- Goal 4—Log analysis tool evaluation
- Goal 5—Log analysis tool selection
- Goal 6—Hardware requirements gathering
- Milestone 2—Procurement of hardware and software
- Goal 7—Deployment of software
- Goal 8—Build out of operations center
- Goal 9—Staff up the operations center
- Goal 10—Define incident response and escalation procedures
- Milestone 3—System goes live

Selecting Systems and Devices for Logging

A log analysis system is no good if you don't have devices logging to it. A critical aspect of the planning process is to establish a repeatable process for evaluating and selecting systems and devices for logging. Assigning a criticality to a device is one way to do this. For example, your firewalls will have higher criticality than workstations. An example process for selecting sources of log data might look like this:

1. Criticality: You need to understand how critical a log data source is to your environment. Is it you business's primary Web server? Is it a critical R&D server with company secrets? Systems which can threaten your very existence if they are compromised should be at the top of the list. It is also the case that different log sources will have different criticalities to your business. For example, your DNS server might have lower criticality than your credit processing server.
2. Validation: Once you have identified a data source, it is likely another group owns the system (sometimes such a group might come to you). You need to get the stakeholders together and verify that the source is indeed a critical asset which needs to be brought into the log analysis system.
3. Incident Response: Finally, you will need to establish a workflow around how incident handling and response is carried out when a given log data source is compromised. Who is the person you need to call when something happens? Does the system have a hot standby that you can fail over to while investigation is happening on the compromised primary?

SOFTWARE SELECTION

When choosing your log analysis system, there are various considerations depending on if it's open source, commercial or a managed service. This section briefly outlines the top items you should consider when looking at a log analysis solution.

Open Source

There are various open source options for log analysis. Some of these have been enumerated in Chapter 15. This section will provide with some of the more important things to consider when looking at such tools.

1. Update Frequency: How often is the project contributed to by the community and/or core development team? If you haven't seen activity in a few months or more, it might be a clue that it's a dead project.
2. Cost: Some say open source means "free." This isn't always the case. There are several ways open source can cost you. You will generally

expend more effort acquiring, learning, and deploying an open source solution.

3. License: It is often times good to pay attention to the opens source license under which the application is released. The license used can restrict how you deploy the software and even dictate how you integrate your of custom-built software with the tool.

4. Support: Many-open source tools offer support contracts you can purchase with e-mail support and other features. Some tools even provide a "free" version of the tool (sometimes called community editions) in addition to a pay-for version which is more enhanced version of the tool. The enhanced version usually comes with some level or support.

5. Features: Make sure you fully understand what the tool can and cannot do. This is when you really need to understand your requirements. If you define your requirements first, you will be better equipped to evaluate log analysis tools.

6. Documentation: This is pretty obvious. If the application comes with a single README text file for its documentation, then it might not be a good "purchase."

7. Community: This can sometimes be a critical feature. You will want to see if the open source tool has some sort of community support behind it. This typically manifests itself in the form of a message board. This is a great place where you get help and support for the application.

8. Extensibility: If you envision extending your log analysis system (maybe with custom scripts, programs, etc.) then you might want to see how extensible the platform is. Does it have an API or some other integration point? And if the platform supports this, who ultimately supports this when things break?

9. Features: Some of the features to think about and explore include:

   a. Supported log acquisition methods (Syslog, raw file, Checkpoint's OPSEC API, etc.)
   b. Ease of maintenance and upkeep (For example, how easy is it to add support for a new device source?)
   c. Correlation (Does it support rules-based, statistical, etc.)
   d. Reporting (What sort of reports come out of the box and how easy is it to create new reports?)

Commercial

For many different market segments in the software world, the word commercial is often associated with enterprise grade solutions. This is often the case, but in the world of logging and log analysis, the devil is in the details with commercial solutions. Let's look at a few things you need to be aware of when considering a commercial log analysis system.

1. **Cost**: This is fairly obvious. The cost of a commercial log analysis system can vary depending on things like how large your network is, how much data you plan to retain, and so on.
2. **Support Model**: Proper support for a commercial solution is key to making sure you get the most of the platform. You need to understand all aspects of the support model and understand how it aligns with your business requirements for things like uptime, turnaround time, etc.
3. **Professional Services**: Most commercial vendors offer some kind of professional services for helping with installation and setup. This usually costs extra, i.e. it's not a freebee.
4. **Features**: The items outlined in the section on open source are identical for commercial.
5. **Extensibility**: Similar to the open source version of this, you should get a feel for how extensible the product is.

Managed Security Services Provider (MSSP)

MSSPs offer an alternative to build it / deploy it yourself log analysis. While looking toward an MSSP isn't exactly in line with the nature of this chapter, it is worth mentioning as a viable alternative. The main appeal is that an organization doesn't need to worry about hiring and training staff, deploying and maintaining software and hardware, and other mundane things. A distinct advantage of an MSSP, especially to top-tier ones, is they have highly trained and certified analysts on staff. This can be a huge win for a customer who doesn't have the same expertise on staff. Some of the things to think about when looking at an MSSP are as follows:

1. **Features**: The features to explore for an MSSP differ from that of an on-site log analysis system. Much of the other features mentioned before are maintained by the MSSP. Features you should be more concerned about include how useful the customer portal is. The portal is the primary interface you will use to search for log messages, run reports, respond to incidents and tickets and so on.
2. **Analysis and Incident Response**: One thing to look at is how the MSSP conducts analysis and incident response. This can be critical to your business and you must make sure the MSSP is in alignment with you.
3. **Professional Services**: Professional services provided by the MSSP can be useful, especially if you require on-site incident response due to breaches. Usually these services tend to be offered at additional cost above and beyond your normal service fees.

4. Data Retention: Make sure you understand how long your log data is retained. You might have to meet certain regulatory guidelines related to retention. You might likely need at least one year, possibly longer.
5. Cloud Logging: Chapter 21 provides detailed coverage on the topic of cloud logging. The basic gist is that the provider provides an environment in their data center in which you can forward your logs to them. This approach requires no special hardware to be on premise. This can be ideal for some organizations, but for others it might not be. Various compliance and regulations might prohibit some organizations from operating in such a manner.
6. Service Level Agreement: MSSPs offer Service Level Agreements (SLA). An SLA, in the context of MSSPs, dictates minimums and maximums for analysis, incident response, and escalation. These are typically baked into the contract you sign.
7. Using Data to Protect Data: Because MSSPs monitor the security for a great number of customers, when a threat or intrusion is detected at one, protections are created and applied to all customers. This is a powerful tool where all customers benefit.

POLICY DEFINITION

Policy definition deals with creating a set of procedures you follow as part of a routine. This section will briefly describe the more common and necessary policies which need to be considered when planning a log analysis system. It is also critical to periodically and regularly review your policies to make sure they are in alignment with your organization's needs, requirements, etc.

Logging Policy

The most immediate concern is to define a logging policy for your organization. A set of logging policies include:

- Adequate logging which covers both logged event types (login/logoff's, resource access, firewall accepts/denies, IPS/IDS alerts, etc.) and details.
- Log aggregation and retention (1 year, etc.).
- Log protection (ensuring logs are not tampered with).
- Log review.

A logging policy defines what attributes of log data should be captured for later review, escalation, and response. A logging policy also extends to applications as well. For example, if you have custom-built applications, it is necessary you work with the stakeholders of the application to define what sort of things should be logged and made available to the logging system.

Log File Rotation

Log file rotation is another policy which needs to be defined. As the log files you are monitoring grow, disk on the local system is filling up. When disks fill up, applications tend to stop working properly. Worse yet, you will potentially miss critical log data you might need. So develop a log file rotation policy across your organization which adheres to the following:

- Time based: Rotate log files based on time boundaries, i.e. minutes, hours, etc.
- Maximize usefulness: The key here is to make the system useful to those who use it. It's a balancing act to keep rotated logs around just long enough to be useful while not impacting the system as a whole.
- Move to long-term storage soonest: The idea here is to keep rotated logs around on the source system just long enough for them to be useful for review. Depending on how busy the system is, this could be on the order of hours.

Log Data Collection

Data collection is the most import part of a log analysis system. Without it you are not going to accomplish much with your log analysis system. As such you should understand what devices in environment should be configured to generate log data. For example, just because your laser print can generate log data, doesn't mean you want to capture it. A policy for log data collection needs to be tailored to your environment. For example, it might be the case that you only need to acquire log messages from your external firewalls and IDS/IPS systems. Or you might need to collect log records from every firewall, IPS, server, and desktop in your network. Regardless, you should make sure you continually review this policy every three to six months to make sure the needs of your organization are in alignment with your data collection policies.

Retention/Storage

Log retention is often a requirement of many regulations. Recall from Chapter 4 that log retention is actually comprised of three things: log storage, accessibility, and log destruction. Never use a syslog server as a log retention system. This is a major no-no. Also, something to be aware of is how to size the storage you need for retention. There is a simple way to figure this out:

$$\text{log records per second(in bytes)} * 86400$$

The calculation will tell you how much storage (in bytes) you will need per day. The hard part is knowing how much log records per second are being generated across your environment. This will likely require some early discovery and playing once your analysis system is up and running. You can usually run your system in a provisioning/tuning mode where you acquire log data from log sources, but you don't take any action on the data. This gives you time to make sure your devices are configured properly, as well as the system itself. It is during this phase when you can develop a sense of the log data load for your environment. A general rule of thumb is to add 25% to your log retention capacity needs to help with planning for unforeseen events.

Keep in mind you are not necessarily relegated to going with some huge honking box with huge disk packs attached to it. Depending on the log analysis solution you go with, it might support a distributed storage model. In such a model the system of deployed nodes which receive log data also act as retention points. Just keep this in mind when you are evaluating log analysis systems.

Response

Chapter 16 provided lots of detail on incident response and escalation. We mention it here to draw attention to the fact that it's an important consideration in the policy scheme of things. See Chapter 19 for a more detailed treatment of the topic.

ARCHITECTURE

The deployment of your log analysis systems will greatly depend on the size of your network and also from where in the network you want to collect logs. We discuss four basic deployment models. They are:

1. Basic
2. Log server and log collector
3. Log server and log collector with long-term storage
4. Distributed

Basic

The basic deployment model is the simplest you can use. It consists of a single log server which has several devices sending logs to it. Figure 20.1 depicts this situation.

In this model, you would typically log into the log server to conduct log review. This is not the most ideal situation, but in some instances it is the best you can do.

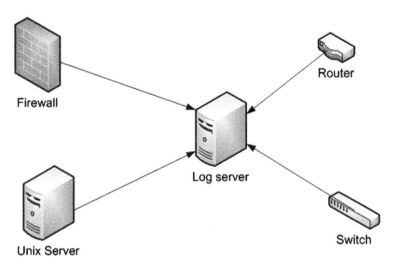

FIGURE 20.1 Basic Log Server Deployment

Log Server and Log Collector

A more common deployment model is one where you distribute log collectors in strategic points in your network. These systems collect logs from devices where they are located. It could be that the log collector is in particular part of your network (maybe an ingress point) and you want to make sure you capture your firewall logs. This log collector will forward logs to a central log server. Figure 20.2 shows such a deployment.

Here we have the log collector sending logs to a log server. Note also that the log server itself can act as a log collector (note the Windows server farm). Depending on the log analysis system you choose, the ins and outs of how you configure a deployment like this will be vendor specific. The log server acts as

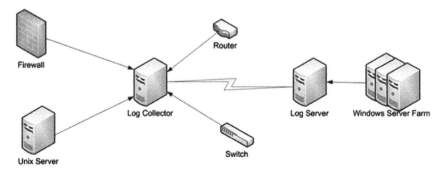

FIGURE 20.2 Log Server and Log Collector Deployment

the central place for reviewing logs, analyzing logs, etc. The log collectors can be thought of as a temporary backup of your logs, but you should never rely on this.

Log Server and Log Collector with Long-Term Storage

In this model we have simply added long-term storage. Figure 20.3 shows this.

The log server is writing to some sort of long-term storage. Again, configuration of this will be vendor specific.

Distributed

The distributed model is really something we have already discussed. You use log collectors distributed throughout your environment for log collecting purposes. These log collectors roll up a log server or in some cases several log servers. In a hierarchical model, you could have multiple log servers rolling up to a central log server which provides a higher-level view of your environment. It is also the case that automated analysis can be performed at the log server level. This allows for a distributed analysis scheme which can reduce the need to have a single server act in this capacity. This reduces load on the server and mitigates a single point of failure.

SCALING

Scaling is an important part of managing a log analysis system. Here are some general tips you can use to help aid this endeavor.

1. Know your environment. In order to scale, you need to have a grasp on what devices are coming on and off your network. Make sure you have weekly meetings with stakeholders to review plans to roll out new gear

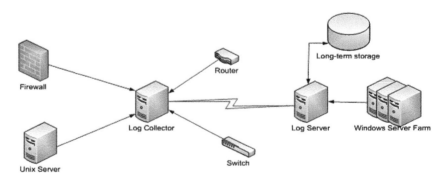

FIGURE 20.3 Basic Log Server Deployment with Long-Term Storage

and equipment. Making sure you get the proper devices logging to the analysis system is critical to maximizing the usefulness of the deployment.

2. Ensure you know what log data on your network takes priority. For example, firewall logs probably take precedence over logs from printers.

3. Understand when your environment is getting saturated. If you notice, during log review, that your log data is hours old, you might have a problem. If you have a distributed deployment, you should investigate the log collector and / or log server to see why they are getting behind. Does the box have high CPU load? Is it having I/O issues? These sorts of things can be signs that your data volume has increased. This can be indications of malicious behavior or just the fact that you need to possibly introduce a new log collector and divert log data to this new server.

SUMMARY

This chapter provided you with a solid set of guidance when you find yourself needing to plan and roll out a log analysis system. We covered planning, policy definition, software selection, deployment, and scaling. These are essential piece parts to understanding the how's and why's of selecting and deploying a log analysis system. For additional resources, you should consult the references listed at the end of this chapter.

Cloud Logging

INFORMATION IN THIS CHAPTER:

- Cloud Computing
- Cloud Logging
- Regulatory, Compliance, and Security Issues
- Big Data in the Cloud
- SIEM in the Cloud
- Pros and Cons of Cloud Logging
- Cloud Logging Provider Inventory
- Additional Resources

INTRODUCTION

This chapter will describe the basic concepts surrounding cloud computing, cloud security, and ultimately cloud logging (this chapter focuses on logging to the cloud). The goal of this chapter is not to make you an expert in these topics, but rather give you the basic knowledge and understanding required to make educated decisions with respect to logging in the cloud. Why is this important? You might find yourself needing to consider using a cloud-based provider for logging, security, Security Information and Event Management (SIEM), or other software applications and systems. The more you know about the ins-and-outs of cloud concepts, the better off you will be to make the right decision when selecting a provider.

CLOUD COMPUTING

What is cloud computing? Cloud computing has been the subject of many commentaries over the last few years. As such there are no shortages of descriptions of what cloud computing is. At its essence cloud computing is a term used to characterize how a user interacts with a set of computer resources (CPU, memory, disk, etc.). To the end user, it appears, he or she is using a single computer system. However, in reality there might be many different, often virtualized, components. A parallel concept that is often used to explain cloud computing is that of the power company. We all have electrical outlets in our home. These outlets can be thought of as simple interfaces. When we want to use a toaster, television, computer, etc., we simply plug it into the wall socket. We don't really care how the power is created. All we know and care about is that it works. A key feature of cloud computing is *elasticity*. Elasticity is the ability to scale out (when more resources are needed) and to scale in when the resources are no longer needed.

For the remainder of the chapter, the terms *provider* and *consumer* will be used. It is critical that we briefly describe each. A provider is someone who provides cloud services. This can be a third-party entity or an internal group within a company. The term *cloud logging provider* will sometimes be used as well. This more concretely describes the type of provider we are discussing in this chapter. A consumer is someone who consumes cloud services. The distinction will become clear soon.

Service Delivery Models

To further clarify cloud computing, it helps to understand the service delivery models. Service delivery models refer to how a particular computing resource is delivered to an end user. In the next several sections, we will discuss the SPI, which stands for Software as a Service, Platform as a Service, and Infrastructure as a Service. We'll discuss these now.

Software as a Service (SaaS)

SaaS is the term used to describe software which resides on a provider's infrastructure. The consumer uses a thin client or Web browsers to interact with and use the software. From the consumer's point of view, they are interacting with a single computer system. They are also not responsible for things like software and hardware maintenance, up keep, and so on. It should be noted that a SaaS provider might be an external third-party provider like Salesforce.com or an internal provider inside of the consumer's own organization. Cloud logging providers fall into this delivery model, i.e. an organization who accepts logs in order to analyze them for other organizations.

Platform as a Service (PaaS)

With PaaS, a consumer can deploy custom-built application or tools to a provider's cloud. As with SaaS, the consumer doesn't have control over the underlying hardware or network (in some cases, the consumer might have access to firewall configuration), but, unlike SaaS, the consumer has control over the deployed application and any associated configuration. Cloud logging providers don't allow consumers to install their own applications.

Infrastructure as a Service (IaaS)

The final service delivery model deals with infrastructure. IaaS allows a consumer to provision computing resources such as CPU, memory, disk, network, and other related resources. The consumer typically controls the operating system, deployed applications, and amount of storage. They do not control the underlying infrastructure.

Storage as a Service

As its name implies, Storage as a Service deals with storage in the cloud. A consumer signs an agreement with a provider to rent space on the provider's network. The pricing is typically based on per gigabyte stored and some data transfer rate. The most common use case for this is an offsite backup and retrieval service. Small- to medium-sized consumers can greatly benefit from a service like this since the IT, hardware, software, and network management are all undertaken by the provider.

Cloud Deployment Models

Now that we have discussed the delivery models for cloud, the next thing to understand is the manner in which services are deployed. "A cloud computing system may be deployed privately or hosted on the premises of a cloud customer, may be shared among a limited number of trusted partners, may be hosted by a third-party, or may be a publically accessible service, i.e. a public cloud" (Web, 2011b). You might be asking yourself why you should care about the different deployment models. The reason it is important, from a cloud logging standpoint, is because you will need to understand your options when evaluating these providers. For example, it might be the case a provider has built their offering on top of one of the many cloud computing providers. Alternatively, it might be the case that the logging provider has built their own private cloud.

Two key concepts to understanding the deployment models are that of *on-premise* versus *off-premise*. On-premise means the infrastructure resides on the consumer's premise, i.e. in their data center. Off-premise, as you might guess, means that the cloud resides off the consumer's premise, i.e. in the cloud provider's data center. The following sections describe the common deployment types.

Public Cloud

As its name implies, the infrastructure is made available to the public. It is typical that an industry group or company owns the cloud and sells cloud services in various forms. The cloud's infrastructure is operated for an organization and might be managed by that organization or by the cloud provider. The infrastructure can reside both on- and off-premise.

Private Cloud

Again, as the name implies, the cloud is private and intended for use by a single organization. The management of the cloud is performed by the organization or the cloud provider. Private clouds can be both on- and off-premise.

Community Cloud

Organizations which have shared concerns can utilize a community cloud. Shared concerns can be "mission, security requirements, policy, or compliance considerations" (Cloud Security Alliance, 2009). The management of the cloud is performed by the community or the cloud provider. Community clouds can be both on- and off-premise.

Hybrid Cloud

A hybrid cloud allows for two or more cloud types (public, private, etc.) to be tied together in a way, which allows portability. For example, a cloud logging provider might allow for a consumer to create their own private cloud so that the provider's application stack can be co-located. This has the advantage of providing a means for the consumer to deal with issues around disaster recovery, centralization, compliance issues, etc.

Characteristics of a Cloud Infrastructure

The next topic we need to cover for cloud computing are the characteristics of a cloud infrastructure. The idea here is to expose the ways that cloud infrastructures differ from traditional computing environments.

- *On-demand self-service*: The consumer can provision aspects of the service (CPU, storage, network, etc.) without the need to interact with the cloud provider. This is typically accomplished with the use of user interfaces and/or APIs.
- *Broad network access*: It is critical that the cloud infrastructure be accessible via variety of network-capable devices, e.g. SmartPhones, PCs, laptops, tablets, and so on.
- *Resource pooling*: The provider uses an infrastructure which allows for the pooling of physical computing resources to service many consumers. This implies a multi-tenant model. The most common technology used to accomplish this is a virtual machine(s). The advantage here is that it allows consumers who do not know or care about how their resources are being managed.

- *Rapid elasticity:* This was already discussed. The basic idea is that resources can quickly be increased or decreased depending on the consumer's needs. The manner in which this is accomplished is either manually or automatically.
- *Measured service:* Cloud providers typically meter and measure the services they provide (CPU, memory, storage, etc.). The time unit or measurement is typically based on the hour. You only pay for what you use. Cloud logging providers typically charge based on the amount of log data you are allowed to send to the cloud, as well as how long you want to retain your log.
- *Multi-tenancy:* Due to the multi-tenant nature of the cloud, there is a need "for policy-driven enforcement, segmentation, isolation, governance, service levels, and chargeback/billing models for different consumer constituencies" (Cloud Security Alliance, 2009).

More details on these topics can be found in Cloud Security Alliance (December 2009) and Web (2011a, 2011b).

Standards? We Don't Need No Stinking Standards!

The final word for this section is on standards. As Cloud Security Alliance (December 2009) points out, "it is also important to note the emergence of many efforts centered around the development of both open and proprietary APIs which seek to enable things such as management, security, and interoperability for cloud." Why is it important to have open APIs for cloud providers? Think about the case where you are using cloud provider XYZ and they increase their usage costs or the Quality of Service (QoS) is going downhill or you decide to bring the functionality back in house. With open standards and APIs, you will be able to migrate from one provider to the next and take your data, metadata, configurations, etc. with you. Some of the standardization efforts already underway include:

- Open Cloud Computing Interface Working Group.
- Amazon EC2 API.
- VMware's vCloud API.
- Rackspace API.
- GoGrid's API.

NOTE

Cloud Computing Providers

It doesn't make sense to provide a detailed list of cloud computing providers, since as soon as this book is printed the content will be out of date. The more common providers today are Dell, Rackspace, and Amazon. We suggest performing some Internet searches to find the current players in the space.

Open APIs can help ensure portability between cloud providers. However, ultimately when providers know that you, as a consumer, can easily migrate to other providers at will, this will force the industry to make sure they are living up to best practices, cause innovation to happen and treat the consumers properly.

CLOUD LOGGING

We have finally made it to the topic of this chapter. While the chapter is about cloud logging, we had to provide lots of supporting information about cloud computing. This is because cloud logging is simply an application of cloud computing. In other words, it is cloud computing which enables cloud logging to exist. In fact, a new deployment model has emerged: Logging as a Service (LaaS). LaaS refers to providers who provide logging services in a cloud setting. That is, providers who take in log data to analyze it on behalf of others. This section will hopefully give you an introduction to what cloud logging is. It will by no means make you an expert. Instead, you will come away with an appreciation of what it is and how it might benefit you and your organization.

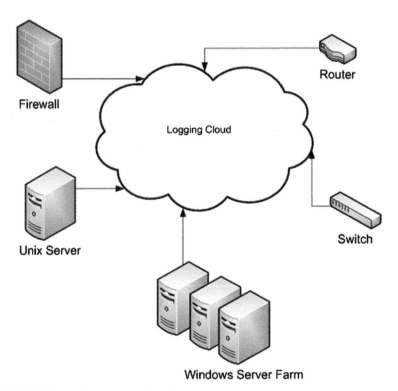

FIGURE 21.1 Logical Layout of a Cloud Logging.

Figure 21.1 shows a high-level depiction of cloud logging.

What we have here is a series of devices logging to a cloud. But what is in the cloud? As a consumer, you don't care. The provider gives you an IP address or hostname at which to point your Syslog configuration and away you go. But, as always, it is more complicated than this, at least for the cloud logging provider. For example, the other end of that IP address might be a load balancer that handles incoming connections. The balancer will hand off the request to one of many machines which will take the data, normalize it (not always), index it, and store it for later retrieval.

The cloud logging space is fairly new and as such the sophistication and features found with the providers are spread out. The following list represents a bare minimum set of features and capabilities shared by cloud logging entities:

- *Log acquisition methods*: For getting data into the cloud, most cloud logging providers support Syslog (TCP/UDP and secure/TLS) and a proprietary API (typically RESTful over HTTP/HTTPS). Syslog covers 95%+ devices in the world. An API allows you to build cloud logging into your applications.
- *Deployment model*: Some cloud logging providers have built their offering on top of cloud computing providers, while others have built their own clouds. It might even be the case that the provider supports a hybrid model.
- *Log retention*: Long-term storage of your log data is something all providers support, but where they differ is what they charge you to store it. Typically, you control the time-period (days, weeks, months) you wish to keep your data. Some providers only allow up to six months of log data to be retained.
- *Core features*: The basic core features of a logging cloud service include log data acquisition, log data indexing (for fast searching, etc.), long-term storage, and a user interface (typically Web-based) to search and review your data. Beyond these, things like correlation, custom alerting, and custom reporting are extras (some providers don't even support these yet).
- *Billing:* Most cloud logging vendors support a pay-as-you-go model. You don't enter into a contract and only pay for the log data you send to them and wish to retain. Also, most providers have "try before you buy" plans which essentially allow you to send through a small number of log messages per day for free in order to try the service and see if you like it.
- *Disaster recovery (DR):* Some cloud logging providers spell out in their terms of service that they are not responsible for loss of data. As it stands now, the cloud logging industry needs to address this in order to make themselves viable to larger consumers.

This space is growing and expanding at a phenomenal rate. Providers are popping up all the time, each boasting the latest in whiz-bang features. However, many providers focus only on operations and not the security and compliance side of things. If you come across provider, you want to use, don't be afraid to ask them questions about the service. This is the best way to get to know what they offer. Here are some basic questions to ask:

1. Is there a director of security or CSO on staff to help set the security posture?
2. What security controls are in place to safeguard my data?
3. What is their overall security posture?
4. How is my data segregated from other people's data?
5. What is the deployment model?
6. What is the billing plan?
7. What are the DR and business continuity plans?
8. What are their SLAs with respect to uptime and availability of

   a. log acquisition service;
   b. log retention service;
   c. user interface;
   d. reporting system.

9. What does the roadmap look like for the next four quarters?
10. What alerting options do they support (email, SMS, etc.)?
11. Do they offer correlation? If so what forms, i.e. statistical and/or rule-based?
12. Similar to number 8 above, what is their maintenance schedule, i.e. do they perform maintenance every Tuesday at 3 am? What is the availability of the service while maintenance is on-going?

A Quick Example: Loggly

Let's briefly look at an example which shows how to get log data into a cloud logging provider. The example is from the logging provider Loggly (www.loggly.com). They have a Web-based API for getting data into their cloud. As you will also see, this is the mechanism you use to search for log data. The first example shows how to use Loggly's API input type:

```
# curl -d "this is a test" https://logs.loggly.com/inputs/dccac609-
  d626-4d49-a826-088efc415c77
{"response":"ok"}
#
```

We are using the `curl` command to simplify things. The URL we use takes the form of the following:

```
httpps://logs.loggly.com/inputs/ [SHA-2 key]
```

The SHA-2 key is generated for each API input you create in the Loggly Web UI. It is used to uniquely identify this API. In the example, we send the log message "this is a test" to the cloud. We get a response of ok. This is a very nice feature because the response is easily parse-able and you can automate the sending of logs to the cloud. If we want to search the cloud we can do so with the following command:

```
# curl -u username:password 'http://foo.loggly.com/api/search?q=test'
{
    "data": [
        {
            "timestamp": "2011-08-24T13:55:12.227Z",
            "isjson": false,
            "ip": "206.55.100.193",
            "inputname": "api",
            "inputid": "1735",
            "text": "{\"this is a test\":\"\"}"
        }
    ],
    "numFound": 1,
    "context": {
        "rows": "100",
        "from": "",
        "until": "NOW",
        "start": 0,
        "query": "test",
        "order": "desc"
    }
}
#
```

This example shows several points. First, the URL for searching and retrieval is different from that of sending data. It takes this form:

```
https://[domain].loggly.com/api/search?q="value to search for"
```

The domain is the domain for your organization. You set this when you first create your account. Our domain is foo. The query parameter is "q" and adheres to standard URI query string format. We searched for "test" which returned a JSON response showing our exact log message, "this is a test". JSON is the default return format, but using the format URL parameter, you specify xml or text return formatting.

Finally, if your search doesn't return anything, here is what the result looks like:

```
# curl -u username:password 'http://foo.loggly.com/api/search?q=foo'
{
    "data": [],
    "numFound": 0,
    "context": {
        "rows": "100",
        "from": "",
        "until": "NOW",
        "start": 0,
        "query": "foo",
        "order": "desc"
    }
}
#
```

Cloud logging providers should support custom APIs like this. Why is having an API like this useful? Here are some reasons:

1. You can send log data from virtually any system or application you control, which may not support Syslog.
2. You can build your own alerting system. By periodically querying the cloud, you can write scripts to look for various things that you care about and, subsequently, send an email, SMS message, etc. A nice side effect is that you can even interface with your internal ticketing system (if you have one).
3. It allows for checks-and-balances. For example, you can meter the amount of data you send to the provider, and you can cross-check billing numbers. You can even detect when data you send to the cloud doesn't make it and resend it if it fails, i.e. you get a bad error response from the provider.

The Cloud Logging Provider Inventory section later in the chapter provides some detail on cloud logging providers and should serve as a good starting point for more research and exploration.

REGULATORY, COMPLIANCE, AND SECURITY ISSUES

By now you are probably thinking that this cloud thing is sounding pretty sweet. And it is. But it should also be obvious that, given how cloud logging providers deploy their software and services, there are regulatory, compliance and security issues that need to be addressed. It is true. Many of the legislative and regulatory requirements were written without an eye toward cloud computing. As such you, as the cloud consumer, need to understand you are responsible for the following (Cloud Security Alliance, 2009):

- Regulatory applicability for the use of a given cloud service. Also, don't forget about cross-border issues like having European Union data in the United States and so on.
- Division of compliance responsibilities between cloud provider and cloud customer.
- Cloud provider's ability to produce evidence needed for compliance.
- Cloud customer's role in bridging the gap between cloud provider and auditor/assessor.

Be sure you work with your internal audit team (if you have one) to coordinate the transition to a cloud provider.

Turning to IT security, the security posture of a cloud provider is really no different from that of regular organizations. Of course they have extra issues to deal with, given the use of virtualized hardware, data separation concerns, identity management, and so on. Let's look at some base best practices cloud providers should adhere to:

- The risk of insider breach (form inside the provider) of your data is a possibility.
- Cloud providers should use background checks as part of the hiring process.
- Cloud providers should employ security policies, controls, etc. which match the most stringent of any customer.
- Contractual agreements or terms of service should outline the specifics of security policies, backup and recovery, business continuity, etc.
- Cloud providers should provide, upon request, documentation outlining the provider's IT security posture.

From a compliance and security standpoint, it's easy to understand the implications of using a public cloud provider. Where it becomes interesting is with a hybrid deployment model. Consider Figure 21.2.

The hybrid cloud spans both the private cloud (on-premise to the consumer and includes two servers) and the public cloud (off-premise to the consumer and includes three servers). The lines become blurred because in this deployment, the consumer is using cloud resources both at the provider's site and on their own site. There are many things to consider like:

1. Who is responsible for securing the link between to two sites?
2. Who is responsible for securing the on-premise gear?

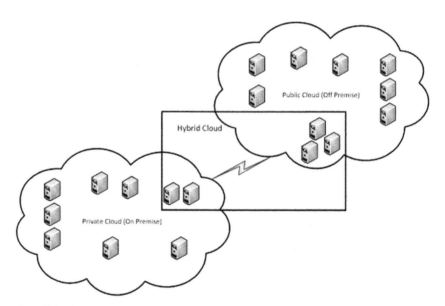

FIGURE 21.2 High-level Hybrid Deployment

3. Who is responsible for securing the off-premise gear?
4. If a breach occurs on the consumer's side from the cloud provider's side, how is incident response and escalation handled?
5. Per any regulatory and legislative mandates for your organization, can you participate in a hybrid deployment?

There is definitely a lot to think about with any decision to move to the cloud. But by approaching cloud computing from a position of understanding what your responsibilities and needs are, you will be able to more clearly make the transition. More detail on regulatory, compliance, and IT security issues with cloud computing can be found in Cloud Security Alliance (2009) and Web (2011b).

BIG DATA IN THE CLOUD

We have a big problem. There is a lot of data across the IT enterprise. It's literally everywhere. As Stephen Marsland stated in his book, "if data had mass, the earth would be a black hole" (Marsland, 2009). This is what has led to the NoSQL and big data movements (see Chapter 4 for a Hadoop example using Amazon's EC2). These movements, and the communities that have sprung up around them, are trying to solve the problem of how you take in, manage, and analyze large volumes of data.

But what is a large volume of data? Let's look at a real-life company. The company (name withheld to protect the innocent!) in question has over 5000 servers, 2000 routers and switches, approximately 600 security devices (Firewalls, IDS, IPS, VPN, content service switches, Anti-Virus), and 50,000 plus desktop firewalls and host anti-virus (desktops and laptops). This is a substantial network to say the least. Across the enterprise, they see about 100,000 log messages a second from all systems. Let's assume an average log message size of 300 bytes. How many log messages per hour do you think this equates to? How much does this equate to over a day? What about a year? To see this, let's do some quick log math:

$$100,000 \text{ log messages/s} \times 300 \text{ bytes/log message} \sim 28.6 \text{ MB}$$
$$\times 3600 \text{ s} \sim 100.6 \text{ GB/h}$$
$$\times 24 \text{ h} \sim 2.35 \text{ TB/day}$$
$$\times 365 \text{ days} \sim 860.5 \text{ TB/year}$$
$$\times 3 \text{ years} \sim 2.52 \text{ PB}$$

This is a lot of data to say the least. Many people will question whether it makes sense to collect this much data. As you have seen throughout this book, we have advocated an approach to logging whereby you continually evaluate what you are collecting. Via this process you don't log anything you never plan to look at, don't care about, or is of little value, and so on. These are generally good principles, but some people want or need to collect as much of their log data as possible. Traditional relational databases (RDBMS) are just made to deal with continually increasing high volumes of data along with stringent query and analysis requirements, i.e. data-intensive applications. This is where NoSQL comes into the picture.

What is NoSQL? It's "Next Generation Databases mostly addressing some of the points: being non-relational, distributed, open-source, and horizontally scalable. The original intention has been modern Web-scale databases. The movement began early 2009 and is growing rapidly. Often more characteristics apply as: schema-free, easy replication support, simple API, eventually consistent /BASE (not ACID), a huge data amount, and more. So the misleading term *"nosql"* (the community now translates it mostly with "not only sql") should be seen as an alias to something like the definition above" (NOSQL Databases, 2011).

The idea is simple: via the use of an architecture which is highly distributed, you achieve greater throughput by breaking up the data in small chunks (on the order of 64 megabytes) and distributing the chunks out to clusters of commodity machines. These machines then crunch on the data and return results. Compare this to the traditional RDBMS technique of scaling up a machine, i.e. a machine with more CPU, RAM, and multiple input/output (I/O) channels.

For example, a machine with two I/O channels which have a throughput of 100 megabytes a second will take 3 hours to read over 2 terabytes. Why is this? Over time, transfer rates have increased, but disk drive seek rates have not increased proportionally. Because of this fact, among others, many people (including cloud logging providers) use systems and software which implement NoSQL concepts in order to provide fast searching, indexing, and other features.

A Quick Example: Hadoop

Hadoop is a leading MapReduce implementation. MapReduce is a technique whereby during a *Map* step, a master node in the takes input and breaks it up into smaller chunks. It then distributes the smaller chunks to worker nodes. Each worker node gets an answer and returns it to the master node. During the *Reduce* step, the master node takes all the answers returned and combines them in a way, which returns an answer to a client. Figure 21.3 shows the logical layout of Hadoop.

What we have here is a Hadoop cloud of commodity machines. These machines run jobs on behalf of the clients (client can be end users, applications, and so on). The clients in-turn are expecting answers to questions. The reason the

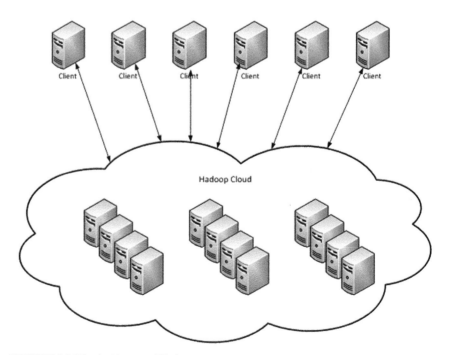

FIGURE 21.3 Logical Layout of Hadoop

Map/Reduce approach works so well is because the data, and subsequent analysis that needs to be done on the data, allows for batch processing. The Hadoop cloud in Figure 21.3 is a distributed system which allows for data to be chunked and executed upon in parallel. Another technique at the core of Hadoop and MapReduce is that of *data locality*. Data locality deals with executing the Map step against data on the file system on which it lives. This allows administrators of Hadoop clusters to configure which servers are closest to the data with respect job execution. This can cut down on network bandwidth and response times.

A complete treatment of big data, NoSQL, Hadoop, MapReduce, and other related technologies is beyond the scope of this section. Please refer to NOSQL Databases (2011) for more information.

SIEM IN THE CLOUD

This chapter would not be complete without a discussion of SIEM in the cloud. Traditionally, SIEM systems are shrink wrapped. This means you buy a license for the software and depending on the complexity of the software, you spend money on consultants who in-turn spend long periods of time installing and configuring the SIEM. SIEM software companies have realized that companies are unwilling to spend hundreds of thousands of dollars (or more) on SIEM deployments. In fact many of these software companies are scrambling to retro-fit their software to be cloud deployable.

This is where Managed Security Service Providers (MSSPs) have really shined over the years (in fact MSSPs were doing cloud logging way before cloud logging was a phrase). MSSPs are companies which take on the burden of managing network security for another organization. The different models are typically monitoring only, management only or monitoring and management.

Figure 21.4 shows the logical layout for a SIEM cloud.

What is the first thing you notice? It looks very similar to the cloud logging figure we saw in the Cloud Logging section. The main difference is that the SIEM cloud tends to be a little more on the mature side with respect to feature sets. The other obvious difference is that of an application stack in the cloud. This is used to show that SIEM cloud has a robust set of features all accessible via an API or set of APIs. This is key not only to providing services to internal customers and systems (Operations, Security Operations Center (SOC), Network Operations Center (NOC), billing, HR, etc.), but also for external customers. For example, customers will often want to export tickets from the provider to their internal systems. Most providers implement some sort of Web-based API (RESTful, SOAP, etc.). This makes it easy for the customer to write custom application code to obtain their tickets.

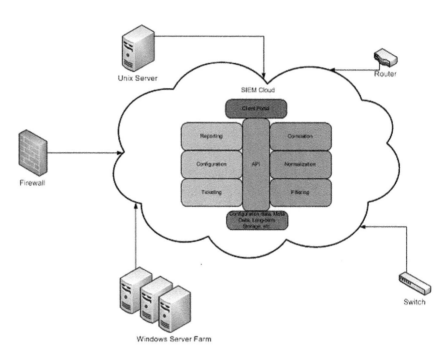

FIGURE 21.4 Logical Layout of SIEM Cloud

PROS AND CONS OF CLOUD LOGGING

Let's discuss some of the pros and cons related to logging to a cloud. This is not an exhaustive list, but it does outline some of the common pros and cons encountered with cloud logging. Of course, depending on your own requirements, you will likely need to perform some analysis to understand if migrating to a log provider makes sense for you. Table 21.1 reviews the pros and cons.

CLOUD LOGGING PROVIDER INVENTORY

Now we will provide you with some information on some logging providers. Table 21.2 provides an inventory of some cloud logging providers.

ADDITIONAL RESOURCES

If you only visit two Web sites in your search for information about all things cloud, you should visit these:

- NIST Cloud Computing: http://www.nist.gov/itl/cloud/.
- Cloud Security Alliance (CSA): https://cloudsecurityalliance.org.

Table 21.1 Pros and Cons of Cloud Logging

Pro	Con	Mitigation against Con
Management: Someone else manages the hardware, software, etc.		
Pay-as-you-go Model: Pay for what you use.		
You control what to send, when to send it, etc.		
API Support: Many logging providers have robust APIs which allow you transmit log data to the cloud via means other than Syslog. You typically also use this API to search the cloud for data, etc.	*API Support*	This can be both a pro and a con. If the API itself is not secure (authentication and privacy) and you have regulatory and/or compliance issues to deal with, this might be a sticky point
Off-premise storage: The storage burden is handled by the vendor. The best part is, typically, you can choose how long and/or how much data you want to keep	*Off-premise storage*	Yes, this is also a con. Depending on the security controls, trust matrix, and other security-related criteria employed by the provider, it may not be feasible to store your log data in the cloud. Find out if the provider utilizes a hybrid deployment model which allows for portions of their stack to reside in your data center
	Security: Security is a concern due to the nature of the "graceful loss of control" that comes with migrating to the cloud	Understand your provider's overall security posture

Table 21.2 Inventory of Cloud Logging Vendors

Vendor	Web site	Information
Dell SecureWorks	www.secureworks.com	Dell SecureWorks is a Managed Security Services Provider (MSSP) who offers a full log retention and management service
Loggly	www.loggly.com	Loggly is a full LaaS provider. They offer a searching console in the browser, a try-before-you-buy option
SplunkStorm	www.splunkstorm.com/	SplunkStorm is a LaaS offering from Splunk. It is currently in beta, but they are planning to offer pay-as-you-go billing and other features

Table 21.2 Inventory of Cloud Logging Vendors (*continued*)

Vendor	Web site	Information
Sumo Logic	www.sumologic.com	SUMO LOGIC is a LaaS and aims to provide consumers with real-time forensic and log management capabilities
Log Entries	www.logentries.com	The goal of Log Entries is to provide those managing, building, and testing large enterprise systems with tools which allow for root cause analysis of IT issues
Papertrail	www.papertrailapp.com	Papertrail is a hosted log management service for servers, applications, and cloud services

These are two great sites with lots of information and resources. And, of course, Internet searches will return more results than you can shake a log at.

SUMMARY

We covered a lot of material in this chapter. The main points you need to take away are:

- *Cloud service delivery models:* The three basic types are SaaS, IaaS, and PaaS
- *Cloud deployment models:* The four basic types are Public, Private, Community, and Hybrid
- *Cloud logging:* It's a young field which is growing every day. Be sure you understand what it is you and your organization require before you embark on logging all your log data to the cloud. Be sure to ask lots of questions of whatever perspective provider you are interested in using.
- *SIEM in the cloud:* MSSPs have supported this model for years. Traditional Shrink-wrapped SIEM vendors are starting to realize the value in this model and are scrambling to build cloud capabilities and offerings into their products.
- *Security concerns:* Be sure you understand how the provider approaches IT security. Also, make sure you understand your responsibility when it comes to legislative and regulatory compliance when operating in a cloud environment.

REFERENCES

Cloud Security Alliance (2009). Security guidance for critical areas of focus in cloud computing V2.1. Web, August 17, 2011. <https://cloudsecurityalliance.org/guidance/csaguide.v2.1.pdf>.

Logging challenges and logging in the cloud – PodCast. Loggly Blog. Loggly, December 2010. Web August 13, 2011. <http://loggly.com/blog/2010/12/logging-challenges-and-logging-in-the-cloud-podcast/>.

Marsland, S. (2009). *Machine learning: An algorithmic perspective*. Boca Raton: Chapman & Hall/CRC. (print)

NOSQL Databases. Web, August 28, 2011. <http://nosql-database.org/>.

Storage as a Service (SaaS). Web, January 02, 2012. <http://searchstorage.techtarget.com/definition/Storage-as-a-Service-SaaS>.

Web (August 20, 2011a). <http://collaborate.nist.gov/twiki-cloud-computing/pub/CloudComputing/StandardsRoadmap/NIST_SP_500-291_Jul5A.pdf>.

Web (August 20, 2011b). <http://csrc.nist.gov/publications/drafts/800-146/Draft-NIST-SP800-146.pdf>.

10 things to think about with cloud computing and forensics. Web, January 02, 2012. <http://www.cloudave.com/670/10-things-to-think-about-with-cloud-computing-and-forensics/>.

Log Standards and Future Trends

INFORMATION IN THIS CHAPTER:

- Extrapolations of Today to the Future
- Log Future and Standards
- Desired Future

INTRODUCTION

Richard Feynman, a noted physicist in the 20th century, once won a lot of prediction bets by simply predicting that the future will look exactly as the present. Admittedly, in our ever-changing IT environments that seems like a recipe for failure. However, many things do stay the same, and in the area of logging and log analysis that is more true than in other domains.

More than enough of problems that IT administrators and organizations in general dealt with in late 1980–early 1990s—which is more than two decades ago—are still with us in a nearly untouched form. This is also true, by the way, with many information security problems as well—is sometimes said that no information security problem has actually been solved for good. For example, password failures were reported as a security problem nearly 50 years ago (and, essentially, may even go way back before the computer age), yet companies still failed in a spectacular way with the same issue today. Over the years that authors have been in the industry, logs are constantly called "untapped riches"—likely from the 1990s until now—and it is up to the IT community to make sure they would not be called that in the future.

Organizations ability to collect various IT records, including logs, has definitely improved in the last decade or two. However, companies still struggle with this domain, despite access to service providers and expensive tools, as well as much expanded knowledge base about this domain. Logs have moved from the domain of IT by compliance, logs now has to move again to high level of intelligence.

Let's start our discussion about the future with a quick discussion of what they can extrapolate from today. Note that this chapter is not only the future of logs but also the future of people who look at logs and make conclusions than take actions.

EXTRAPOLATIONS OF TODAY TO THE FUTURE

As a form of a very quick historical overview, we can mention that syslog was born as a part of Eric Allman sendmail project in the early 1980s. Admittedly, the history of logging and log analysis has started before that, but this date marks a 30 year span of evolution (1982–2012).

Over the course of that time frame, the volume of logged data has increased dramatically. In addition, not only the quantity but also the quality of log data has increased. New log sources, and even conceptually new IT environments such as mobile computing, cloud computing and virtualization have emerged and became mainstream. In fact, even a PC was born in the same timeframe, and logging predates this important advance, which now seems commonplace mundane and even obsolete.

It appears that the analysis methods to make sense of log data as well as the quality and usefulness of the information, communicated in the form of log files, have not increased nearly enough. Instead of looking at syslog from UNIX systems and Event Logs from Windows (a 1990s invention), people now have to look at the much wider set of logs, ranging from barely comprehensible text to highly structured XML (that sadly, often uses megabytes of data to communicate the meaning that a 50 byte syslog message will hold just fine).

More Log Data

Our first extrapolation is simply more log data. This splits into multiple dimensions, each more dangerous than the other.

Definitely, and sheer volume of logged data will be increasing in the next 5–7 years and likely more. More computing resources are brought online and more of them are capable of producing logs. Regulatory pressure motivates organization to also increase the volume of logging from which system and application.

In addition to a simple volume increase, there will be a increase in the number of systems producing logs. Dealing with one or two systems is always easy. Dealing with thousands gets to be pretty challenging. However, it is expected that the upcoming "Internet of things" where a lot of different systems are brought online as well as growth in mobile and cloud computing, will result in dramatic increases of both volume and the number of logging instances.

In addition to increased number of systems that produce logs, existing systems are expected to produce more log data or produce more detailed, and thus more voluminous, log data piles. For example, where a system used to login failed access attempts a few years ago will now log successful attempts as well as other activities. It would not surprise the authors if the same system will log all access to sensitive files in a year or so. While in a few years, it is expected that many more activities would create an audit trail which needs to be analyzed, retained, and acted upon in some cases.

There is also a trend towards auditing more access and more activity through logs; for example, few of the file server, storage, or database vendors cared much about logging, but now they do (well, some do and some start to). What used to be just about access to data is now evolving into auditable access to data.

Regulatory as well as investigative pressure leads organizations to save logs for longer, thus increasing the volume of retained data. Even having the same number of log sources, producing the same volume of logged data—a very unlikely assumption—will lead to increased log volumes being stored and collected, due to increased retention periods. It was quite uncommon to see organizations preserve the logs for more than three months a few years ago—now a year is much more common. In many cases, such longer retention periods are not driven by regulations and external mandates but by the need to investigate entrenched threats inside the organization, insider activities, state-sponsored threats, and other advanced malicious activities.

Increased volume of data leads to challenges with analysis and comprehension. It might not be obvious to some of the readers but many of the tasks that are trivial on 10 MB of log data and easy on 1 GB of log data, become grand scheme of challenges when the data hits petabyte ranges. Admittedly, few organizations today have to analyze even 1 PB of log data, but they are a known to exist and their numbers are growing. And with that type of volume, even simply copying the data, much less passing it through an analysis engine, becomes an engineering and architectural challenge.

The log the same line, a massive increase of log volume will come applications: where a system is used to analyze and infrastructure logs, the shift the application logging in addition to infrastructure logging will happen. For some of the cloud scenarios, discussed in Chapter 24, application logging is the only logging that the organization can have. From enterprise traditional applications, the cloud applications, to mobile applications—increase of produced the log data is expected across the board.

Moreover, IT logging will likely be accompanied by OT—operational technology—and by CT—communication technology—logging as well. From mobile phone provider equipment to elevator and building control systems, the world of log data will be expanded beyond IT with a corresponding increase in the volume and diversity of data.

Today few people even know that some of the mobile applications can also be made to produce audit trails of activities. As enterprise use of various mobile technologies expands, the need to analyze logs from such devices will come into the picture in the coming years. First used for operational purposes, such logs will also likely to be used for security purposes as well as prescribed by various regulations.

Always made some people conclude that the arrival of the "big data" age is here. In reality, many organizations struggle with essentially "small data." If the tools your organizations have had trouble analyzing 10 GB of data, it makes no sense to even look up the word "petabyte" in a dictionary... Existing tools are barely manage to help people understand what happens in their environments, before any discussion of big data happens. Deal with small data first and build your own knowledge base—then start thinking about big data. Many organizations will be puzzled by an individual log line, a single record, and thus are unprepared to deal with trillions of such messages.

More Motivations

Our second extrapolation is more motivations for taking logs seriously. Analysts estimate that a large percentage of log analysis and log management tools (including commercial SIEM tools) are deployed for regulatory compliance. However, the language regarding log management prescriptions is vague, which can lead to confusion. Still, compliance is motivated a large set of advances in log management and log analysis in recent years and it is expected to continue being a force for further improvements. We discuss logging and compliance in other chapters.

The prediction here is that more mandates, control frameworks, laws and other external guidance will compel organizations to expand what they do with log data. Getting the value of the data takes time and energy—both of which are often in short supply inside IT organizations. It can seem daunting at first, given the sheer volume and subjective nature of the data. Despite such challenges, logging is a primary means of IT accountability since most user and system actions can be recorded in logs. That's exactly why logging is a perfect compliance technology, mandated by many regulations and laws—and it continued to be that for the foreseeable future.

Additional motivation for taking logs seriously will come from environments where the organization has less control, and thus has to compensate with more visibility. I'm looking at you, Cloud! It is expected that the needs to monitor the assets deployed outside of direct control would require more monitoring and more visibility features, often relying on logs.

More Analysis

Our third extrapolation is more controversial (even though it shouldn't be)—more analysis methods and more ways to get value out of log data. Many predict that we are now at the critical junction for many data analysis technologies, including log data analysis for security. Some of the industry observers noted that in the past a simple Netflix movie selection action triggers more algorithm brainpower on the backend than is available in all log analysis products combined. In many regards, we are reaching the limits of current analysis methods.

It is expected that new analysis methods will emerge as well as existing methods—from rule-based correlation to statistical analysis to data mining—will be used more widely to analyze log data. Such algorithms has to satisfy requirement such as analysis of distributed logs (such as coming components of cloud applications), analysis of data of any scale, any user, any system, any log—and for multiple purposes.

In addition, other types of data such as context data are likely to be analyzed widely in the future together with log data. A full range of tools from small to enterprise need to emerge to help people make sense of the data of various kinds.

This prediction is less of an extrapolation but it is also look at some new capabilities and your possibilities that opened by the new analytics age.

In addition to extrapolations listed above there would be absolutely new challenges that stem from the changing tide of information technology today. While one can consider an application, deployed inside the public cloud provider environment, to be somewhat of a remote application, in reality cloud computing brings some new technologies as well as new operational practices that affect how logs are produced and utilized.

In general, a recent media noise about "big data" (and especially "big data" ANALYSIS, not just handling of petabytes of it) is directly relevant of log data. Several companies have been launched to use Hadoop and other big data-associated technologies to collect and analyze log data. It is done, in some cases, in the cloud for many customers, while on-premise for others.

LOG FUTURE AND STANDARDS

Given such possibilities for increased challenges what are some of the good things that the future of logging and log analysis might bring. The primary factor is log standardization. Emergence of log standards such as Common Event Expression (CEE)[1] will have a chance to dramatically change how the future will look like.

But first, why now? More than 30 years have passed by without IT logging standardization. But what about syslog, an old workhorse of logging?

Syslog, encoded as a "standard" in RFC3164, is really a "nonstandard standard." Even its RFC document is full of "Since the beginning, life has relied upon the transmission of messages. For the self-aware organic unit, these messages can relay many different things" which reminds us that syslog was created in Bekreley, CA, possibly a pot smoking capital of the United States. Further, "Since each process, application and operating system was written somewhat independently, there is little uniformity to the content of syslog messages. For this reason, no assumption is made upon the formatting or contents of the messages." The last sentence firmly states that it is the standard of nothing, but the way to move log from place A to place B, using the UDP protocol. Marcus Ranum once called syslog "the worst logging architecture known to man—and also the most used."[2]

Today, Common Event Expression (CEE) work has resulted in a draft specification being created. The standard has the chance of putting an end to fuzzy, ambiguous, and unstructured log data. Instead, it would replace it with logs that are human readable and machine readable, effective and efficient, concise and unambiguous. This draft standard seeks to influence all aspects of the logging ecosystem (see Figure 22.1).

Specifically, it would define how logs are produced, transferred, analyzed, and so on. At the time of this writing, the following specifications are published:

CEE Architecture Overview Specification, Version 1.0α

The CEE Overview provides a high-level overview of CEE along with details on the overall architecture and introduces each of the CEE components including the CEE Profile, CEE Log Syntax, and the CEE Log Transport. The CEE Overview is the first in a collection of documents and specifications, whose combination provides the necessary pieces to create the complete CEE event log standard:

---

[1] http://cee.mitre.org/.
[2] http://www.scribd.com/doc/94205026/16/Syslog-RFC-3164.

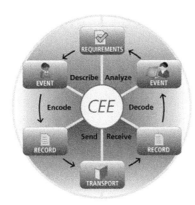

FIGURE 22.1 CEE Influences the Whole Ecosystem, http://cee.mitre.org/docs/overview.html

■ CEE Profiles Specification, Version 1.0α

The CEE Profile allows for the improved interpretation and analysis of event data by allowing users to define how events are structured and what data they provide. The Profile consists of three components that provide a standardize field dictionary, event taxonomy, and base requirements for CEE-compatible events:

■ CEE Log Syntax (CLS) Specification, Version 1.0α

The CLS Specification describes the requirements for encoding and decoding for a Common Event Expression (CEE) Event, and provides encoding declarations for XML and JSON event records:

■ CEE Log Transport (CLT) Specification, Version 1.0α

The CEE Log Transport (CLT) provides the technical support necessary for a secure and reliable log infrastructure. The CLT Specification defines a listing of requirements conformant log transports must meet. In addition, the CLT defines transport mappings, which define a standard methodology for transmitting encoded CEE Event Records over certain protocols."[3]

CEE also defines a taxonomy that will unify what to log messages mean and allow developers to unambiguously define which specific events have transpired and is being recorded in logs. The taxonomy will be included in event profile specification. The key idea for taxonomy is defining each event using the fields: Object (what it happened with?), Action (what happened?), and

---

[3] http://cee.mitre.org/about/documents.html.

Status (what was the result?) (O-A-S). An early version of a taxonomy can be found at http://cee.mitre.org/repository/schemas/v10alpha/taxonomy.xsd.

It includes the following values for Object:

- System
- File
- User
- Directory
- Connection

Values for Action include:

- Open
- Close
- Delete.
- Update

Finally, Status includes:

- Success
- Failure
- Deferred

The most useful way to think of this taxonomy approach is to think of every log is a complete sentence: what happened, what happened with, what was the result?

As a result, the standard can accommodate all of the required domain standardization. See Figure 22.2. What needs to be logged, how to log it, what details to log, how to transport the record from generation to analysis.

Even today, a developer can choose to use CEE formats and create logs that look like this:

Let's look at a CEE XML example:[4]

```
<?xml version="1.0" encoding="UTF-8"?>
<CEE>
  <Event>
    <crit>123</crit>
    <id>abc</id>
    <p_app>application</p_app>
    <p_proc>auth</p_proc>
    <p_proc_id>123</p_proc_id>
```

---

[4] http://cee.mitre.org/docs/cls.html.

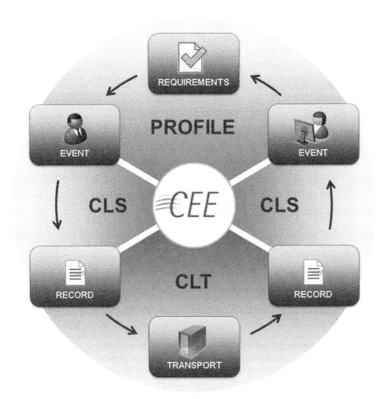

FIGURE 22.2 Domain Standardization, http://cee.mitre.org/docs/overview.html

```
        <p_sys>system.example.com</p_sys>
        <pri>10</pri>
        <time>2011-12-20T12:38:05.123456-05:00</time>
        <Type>
            <action>login</action>
            <domain>app</domain>
            <object>account</object>
            <service>web</service>
            <status>success</status>
        </Type>
    </Event>
</CEE>
```

Next we see a CEE JSON example, which can be used for syslog transport.[4]

```
{"Event":{"crit":123,"id":"abc","p_app":"application","p_
proc":"auth","p_proc_id":123,"p_sys":"system.example.
```

```
com","pri":10,"time":"2011-12-20T12:38:05.123456-05:00",
"Type":{"action":"login","domain":"app","object":"account",
"service":"web","status":"success"}},"Module":[{"Augment":{
"p_proc":"my_process","p_proc_id":123,"p_sys":"syslog-relay.
example.com","time":"2011-12-20T17:41:12Z"}},{"Augment":{"p_
proc":"my_process","p_proc_id":123,"p_sys":"syslog-relay.example.
com","time":"2011-12-20T17:41:12Z"}}]}
```

These logs can be easily consumed by any current log analysis system, effortlessly integrated into commercial SIEM tools and (in case of JSON) trivially understood by human analysts. The JSON/text logs, in particular, are just as easy to create as other name=value pair formats and are much more useful than traditional free-form logs.

Such logs can be stored in relational databases or in modern Hadoop-based or other NoSQL storage facilities.

Adoption Trends

Given the miserable track record of past attempts to standardize logging, CEE adoption is no assured matter. How can adoption happen? What can log producers, log consumers, government, and regulators do?

Strategically, adoption can happen to multiple mechanisms:

- MITRE is close to US government procurement contracts that can be used to push adoption, just as happened with vulnerability formats such as C, and vulnerabilities and exposures (CVE) a few years ago.
- Smaller software vendors can use CEE in place of their nascent formats and achieve standard compliance when CEE is finished.
- Open source logging tools can facilitate conversion from native UNIX logs and other syslog logs into structured CEE (in JSON format).

As of today, open source logging tools such as rsyslog (covered in Chapter 15) and syslog-ng (covered in Chapter 5) built their support for CEE. Several commercial SIEM vendors also use CEE formats and ideas internally in their tools, making them easily usable in environments where some logs are produced in this format natively. Operating system vendors are looking in the converters from their formats to CEE.

DESIRED FUTURE

Apart from making predictions, let's try to define how the desired future will look like. Here are some of things that he would like to see in the world of logging in the next few years:

- Log standard is widely adopted by log producers. Application and equipment makers, as well as cloud platform makers, old produce logs in a standard format. Ambiguity of log data and the need to treat logs as broken English is gone—hopefully forever.
- Application developers implement useful logs right away when the application is written, using log standards and standard libraries and APIs. The resulting data is not only standards-based—but also comprehensive, not excessively voluminous, and useful for most operational, security and regulatory needs.
- In general we have more transparent, visible, and accountability- enabled systems, whether mobile cloud virtual of traditional. As Dan Geer once said "The problem is, these technologies [access control—A.C.] do not scale and if you try to have ever finer control over the avalanche of new data items appearing by the second, you will be contributing to the complexity that is the bane of security. What does scale is Accountability. In a free country, you don't have to ask permission for much of anything, but that freedom is buttressed by the certain knowledge that if you sufficiently screw things then up you will have to pay."[5]
- Tools that help make sense of the logs must become smarter, as well as easier-to-use at the same time. The tools can consume data, whether standard compliant or legacy, and produce useful recommendations and conclusions based on the data with minimal human tuning and interactions. However, those humans that want to interact with the tools can absolutely do so and receive even greater results.
- More companies move up on log maturity curve and more organizations become more enlightened in regard to analyzing and making sense of log data. Such enlightenment does not come cheap—but improved tools and improved logs, described above, makes their experience bearable.
- Finally, people—within and outside the domain of IT—use logs more across purposes, backed up by tools, improved log data as well as improved, mature practices and processes that center on obtaining useful insights for business and technology, protecting systems and compliant with regulations.

SUMMARY

How can organizations prepare for that future? Use the principle highlighted one of the notable science-fiction writers: the future is here, it's just unevenly distributed.

---

[5] http://geer.tinho.net/geer.housetestimony.070423.txt.

For example, you can choose to wait until the log standards of mainstream and supported by every software manufacturer (decades). We can use the material from the emerging standards to create your own organization wide standard that will be derived and inspired by the future global standard. This would allow you to gain some of the value and produce more useful logs that would tell you more information about what happened and the systems and networks, as well as in the cloud.

Instead of waiting for smarter tools to arrive and become common, you can write your own tool that is smarter in some aspects useful for you.

Instead of being afraid of a large log volume, start analyzing the data you have so that you gain expertise given the small log data (which in this day and age means gigabytes of data) so that you're ready for the future of 10x–1000x log volumes.

In essence, prepare for the future don't fear it. And it will bring things useful for you and your organization in regard to logging and log analysis.

Index

Note: Page numbers followed by "f" and "t" indicate figures and tables respectively

Printed and bound by CPI Group (UK) Ltd, Croydon, CR0 4YY
03/10/2024
01040340-0011